THE DUKE OF HAVANA

STEVE FAINARU and
RAY SÁNCHEZ

VILLARD NEW YORK

THE
DUKE OF
HAVANA

Baseball,

Cuba, and the Search

for the American

Dream

Library of Congress Cataloging-in-Publication Data

Fainaru, Steve.
    The Duke of Havana : baseball, Cuba, and the
search for the American dream/Steve Fainaru and
Ray Sánchez.
        p. cm.
            ISBN 978-0-812-99256-4
    1. Baseball—Political aspects—Cuba.
2. Baseball players—Cuba—History—20th
century.   3. Cubans—United States—History—
20th century.   4. Hernández, Orlando.
5. Cuba—Relations—United States.   6. United
States—Relations—Cuba.   I. Sánchez, Ray.
II. Title.

GV863.25.A2 F35 2001
796.357'097291—dc21   00-047322

Villard Books website address: www.villard.com

Book design by Barbara M. Bachman

146484122

To Willie

Inside every Cuban there's a ballplayer

waiting to get out.

—ORLANDO "EL DUQUE" HERNÁNDEZ

"Cuba produces two things: ballplayers and whores."
"Hey, that's offensive. My mother still lives over there."
"Oh, really? What position does she play?"

—MIAMI JOKE

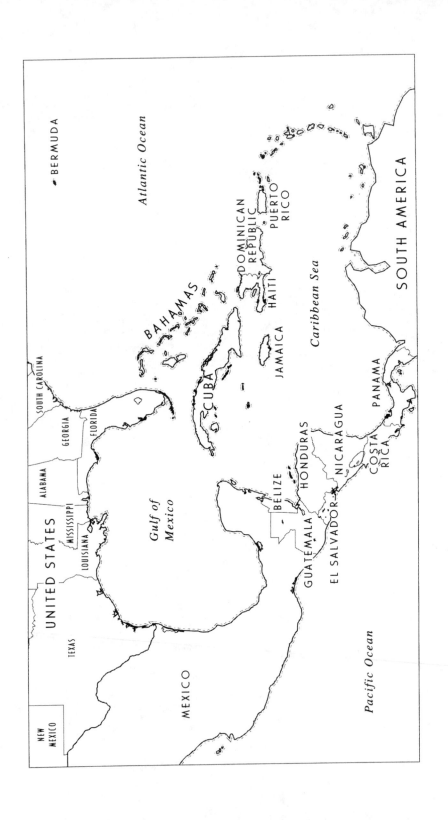

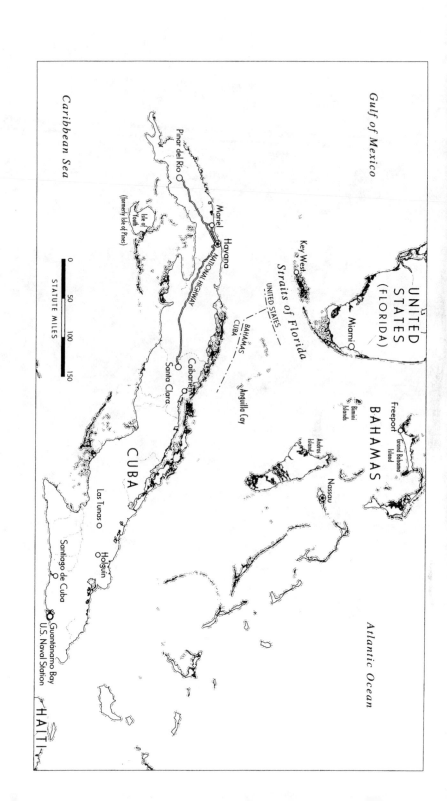

CONTENTS

THIS BOOK GREW OUT OF SEVERAL ARTICLES WRITTEN FOR *THE Boston Globe* and *Newsday* on the Cuban government's decision, on October 28, 1996, to ban pitcher Orlando "El Duque" Hernández from revolutionary baseball. From the very beginning, both of us viewed this event not only as a fascinating sports story but also as a window into the surreal state of affairs in Cuba following the collapse of the Soviet Union and the end of the Cold War.

When we started writing these stories, El Duque was living in a cinder-block shack a few blocks from the José Martí International Airport in Havana. The government's ban was total: The pitcher was forbidden to set foot on any official government field—essentially, every ballpark in the country. As we got to know El Duque, a couple of things were striking. One was that he was by far the most resilient, relentlessly optimistic man we had ever met. Another was that the punishment did not fit the crime, for there was no real crime, at least as far as we could discern.

Over time, the saga of El Duque evolved into what certainly was the most dramatic story that either of us covered during our respective tours of Latin America. As foreign correspondents for our newspapers, we wrote hundreds of articles about drug trafficking, epic corruption, guerrilla uprisings, hostage takings, hurricanes, earthquakes, illegal immigration, border wars, free trade, and, in Mexico, a democratic revolution. And yet, to both of us, the one story that best captured what was happening in the region involved a baseball player, a pitcher. With a mixture of admiration and horror, we watched as El Duque stood up to his antiquated government—a government resisting the tide of history—which proceeded to torture him, not physically but by stripping him of his very essence.

As we watched the story unfold, we came to see it as a parable of the Castro government's futile efforts to stave off its own obsolescence. Others may not see it this way, which of course is fine. At its core, the following story is about a baseball player chasing his major-league dreams. It doesn't have to be any more meaningful than that.

A quick word about narration. This book is a collaborative effort, reported by Steve Fainaru and Ray Sánchez, and written by Fainaru. For reasons of narrative flow, it is written in the first person. The word "I" refers to Fainaru, at the time the Mexico City bureau chief for *The Boston Globe*. Sánchez, his friend and counterpart for *Newsday*, is identified as "Sánchez." The material in these pages comes primarily from our own observations and experiences and from more than one hundred interviews conducted in the United States, Cuba, Costa Rica, Venezuela, and Canada.

This is a true story, although even now it seems hard to believe.

Steve Fainaru
Ray Sánchez
New York City
October 2000

BEFORE THE ESCAPE

IT WAS THE WINTER THAT FIDEL LEGALIZED CHRISTMAS. ONE would think that such a monumental decision, the reversal of a twenty-eight-year ban on the celebration of Jesus' birth, would merit banner headlines: WELCOME BACK, SANTA, perhaps, or COMANDANTE TO PROLETARIAT: ¡FELIZ NAVIDAD! But the news caused barely a stir. The announcement was buried inside *Granma*, the slim Communist party daily. On the streets of Havana little changed. A few bold citizens strung lights around their windows. At the state-run dollar stores there was a minor run on plastic trees. One of the most striking changes was the return of Midnight Mass. One thousand people crammed into the restored cathedral in Old Havana to hear the controversial archbishop Jaime Ortega usher in the holiday. "We have *always* celebrated Christmas," Ortega told the crowd. "Sometimes we have made great sacrifices to celebrate."

Fidel had brought back Christmas as a gesture to Pope John Paul II, who was to visit the following month. The brittle, peripatetic pope had preached to every other Spanish-speaking country in Latin America, but decades of repression against all religion, particularly Catholicism, had kept him away from Cuba. The trip was shrouded in the richest political symbolism. Two decades earlier, the pope's exhortations of solidarity during a visit to his native Poland had helped trigger the collapse of communism in Eastern Europe. The international media was hyping the Cuba excursion in similar terms, casting the pope as an aging Cold Warrior trekking into one of the last surviving outposts of the Evil Empire. On T-shirts, on posters, on newscasts throughout the world, John Paul and Fidel were paired off like venerable, aging heavyweights: the frail, still wily pontiff, slayer of communism, versus the indomitable Fidel, fallen Catholic, survivor of nine American presidents, a CIA-sponsored invasion, a nuclear showdown and an untold number of exploding cigars.

The papal visit offered a field day for the seers of Fidel's inevitable demise. The drumbeat had started with the collapse of the Soviet Union, and had continued, year after year, without cessation. In 1992, Andres Oppenheimer, the veteran *Miami Herald* reporter, had published *Castro's Final Hour*—a catchy title for an illuminating book, but unfortunate as predictions go. Since then Fidel had survived some 50,000 final hours and, at seventy-one, seemed as robust and cantankerous as ever. During one particularly hot stretch in late summer, yet another rumor of his death bounced around the hemisphere—from Havana to Mexico City, from Mexico City to Miami, from Miami to Washington—until the Cuban Foreign Ministry was finally forced to deny it. For several days, life in Cuba seemed to imitate art, more specifically *The Autumn of the Patriarch*, the Gabriel García Márquez novel about the protracted final days of a Latin American despot: "[T]he more certain the rumors of his death seemed, he would appear even more alive and authoritarian at the least expected moment to impose other unforeseen directions to our destiny." Sure enough, Fidel finally resurfaced at a ceremony to kick off the school year and delivered a forty-five-minute speech in the driving rain. His olive military uniform was drenched. Beads of rain collected and fell from his beard. Speaking into the antiquated microphone, he looked like he might electrocute himself. "Whoever falls may fall!" he roared over the limp, miserable crowd. "Whoever dies may die! And some of us, they try to kill off on a regular basis."

In truth, there had been a lot of fodder for the latest round of speculation that the revolution—if not Fidel himself—was in trouble. Uprisings can begin anywhere—in a Boston harbor, in a Gdańsk shipyard—so you never really know. For months Havana had been plagued by a series of mysterious bombings at tourist sites, including one that blew out the upper tier of the Bodeguita del Medio, a bar-restaurant on the Hemingway Drank Here! circuit. The bombings were small; the only death was an Italian tourist whose throat had been slashed by a shard of metal as he nursed a drink at the Copacabana hotel. But many Cubans had been shaken. The economy was a shambles, and there was growing tension between those with access to U.S. dollars, or *fula*, the greenback's street name, and the poor unfortunates who still queued up for eggs and milk with their tattered government ration booklets. The papal visit had turned into a huge gamble for Fidel. The pope would attract some 2,000 foreign journalists to the island. And although he could be counted on to denounce the U.S. trade embargo against Cuba, he was also unquestionably a force against communism. Already his picture had begun to appear alongside the ubiquitous portraits of the revolutionary icons: Che Guevara, Camilo Cienfuegos, and now, suddenly, "the Pope—Messenger of Truth and Hope." Elizardo Sánchez, Cuba's leading dissident, said the Catholic church was fast becoming a refuge for permissible opposition, "a uniform that people put on to criticize the government." In the city of Santa Clara, where Che's bones, recently unearthed in Bolivia, had been entombed, nine members of a group calling itself the Party for Human Rights had been arrested after gathering for a "prayer fast" beneath the portraits of John Paul and the Virgin Mary. Real or not, a scent of change had begun to waft over Cuba, and the government had become absorbed with the task of making the papal visit a symbol of endurance and renewal, not one of rigor mortis setting in.

ALL IN ALL, it was a brilliant cover for Orlando "El Duque" Hernández, fallen hero of the revolution. Under normal circumstances El Duque, a deeply spiritual man, would have been looking forward to the historic papal visit. His mother, María Julia Pedroso, kissed her living room floor when the pope finally touched down. But El Duque wasn't praying for the pope that winter. He was praying to get the hell out.

After the last of several unsuccessful attempts to escape the island, agents from the Interior Ministry had taken him into custody, interrogated him for a day, and then warned that he would be followed so closely that Havana would seem as if it were the size of "a penny." In desperation he had turned to a *palero*, one of the priests who communicate with the spirit world in Santería, a fusion of Catholicism and Yoruba, an African faith often compared with voodoo. The priest had officially baptized El Duque by carving lines into his right shoulder in a bloody communion with Changó, a Santería deity. El Duque, later safely out of the country, would pull back his sleeve and recall the ceremony as the turning point of his life, the moment when he was liberated from a system that had built him up, then torn him down with a vengeance.

For although Fidel had reinstated Santa Claus, he had not found it in himself to reinstate the most successful pitcher in the history of the revolution. El Duque drifted in a surreal state of existence and nonexistence that winter—at least as far as the government was concerned. On the one hand, he was one of the most famous people on the island, for a decade an unhittable whirling showman for Havana's Industriales, the Yankees of Cuban baseball. His 129–47 career record represented the highest winning percentage (.733) of any pitcher since the revolution; no one else was even close. He had appeared in a total of 246 games, a career that spanned ten seasons and 1,514⅓ innings from the mid-eighties to the mid-nineties. People called his name as he walked down the street. On the other hand, he had recently been erased by his own government and cast into the forced anonymity of the officially spurned. On October 28, 1996, the Cuban Sports Ministry had summoned him and two other star players, Germán Mesa, a wispy shortstop known as El Mago (the Magician), and catcher Alberto Hernández (no relation) to the baseball commissioner's office inside Estadio Latinoamericano, the historic old stadium in the Havana neighborhood of El Cerro. Separately, the players had been marched into a basement room surrounded by concrete walls. Mesa went first, and when he came out he dragged his finger across his throat. The players had been banned from baseball for life for consorting with a Cuban American sports agent who had urged them to defect. The decision, it was made clear, had been approved by the Council of Ministers and thus, it was presumed, Fidel himself. "You have to understand," said a sympathetic sports official as I later tried to sort it all out, "it's as if they're dead, as if they no longer exist."

Two years later, when El Duque was pitching for the real Yankees, his story was recalled as a clipped summary of implausible events. The summary alone was remarkable, more than adequate to carry any newspaper or magazine article: Fourteen months after his banishment, El Duque escaped from Cuba in a thirty-foot boat along with his catcher, his girlfriend, his cousin, his best friend and three acquaintances. The group disembarked on the Bahamian island of Anguilla Cay after the boat—at least according to its passengers—began to take on water and, ultimately, sank. The group survived for four days on conch, Spam, sugar and the little water they had brought with them. They were rescued finally by a passing U.S. Coast Guard cutter, which delivered them to Bahamian immigration authorities. After spending New Year's Eve inside a Nassau detention center, the group gained political asylum in San José, Costa Rica, where El Duque participated in a tryout before sixty major-league scouts, then signed a $6.6 million, four-year contract with the Yankees. By October, he was facing down the Cleveland Indians in Game 4 of the American League Championship Series, the most important victory in the Yankees' 125-win season, perhaps the greatest in the club's storied history.

Contrary to popular belief, that summary is basically accurate, give or take a few key details. But it does little to describe how Orlando "El Duque" Hernández Pedroso became one of the most compelling figures to emerge from contemporary Cuba, or how his saga perfectly captured the utter absurdity of the never-ending hostilities between the U.S. government and Fidel Castro. Perhaps only enemy nations who share baseball as a national pastime could turn a stylish right-handed pitcher into a symbol of the best and the worst of two societies. El Duque, or at least his dramatic ordeal, was the product of his strange times. The Cold War had ended, and Cuba was suddenly adrift in the world, surviving on a discredited ideology, an embarrassing relationship with the almighty dollar and the hurricane force of a seventy-one-year-old man's personality. Capitalism, alas, had prevailed, and even Moscow was in its thuggish grip. The American economy had entered the longest peacetime expansion in its history, and there was no longer any such thing as an embarrassment of riches—not for venture capitalists, not for twenty-five-year-old Internet tycoons, and certainly not for professional second basemen or middle relievers. In Cuba, with the fall of the Soviet Union, an economic and spiritual torpor had settled over the island, a kind of extended mourning for a distant uncle who had provided over the years, but, in the end, died penniless, leaving nothing to his heirs, not even a note. As the rest of the world was reaching out, booting up and interconnecting across borders, Cuba was actually going back in time. In some large cities, horse-drawn carriages were more prevalent than automobiles. Meanwhile, just ninety miles away, in the *Cubaneo* of exile Florida, anything seemed possible. To faintly understand these crosscutting forces, consider that based on his $8.75 monthly salary in Cuba, it would have taken El Duque one million years to earn the equivalent of the $105 million contract that pitcher Kevin Brown signed with the Los Angeles Dodgers in 1998. El Duque and Brown held the same job.

EL DUQUE CAME to the affair as a true child of the revolution. He was born on October 11, 1965,* less than seven years after Fidel took power. Unlike his parents, he had lived his entire life under communism. He was well schooled and extremely bright, a beneficiary of one of the great literacy campaigns of the twentieth century, which transformed a society in which 40 percent of adults could neither read nor write into one whose literacy rate now rivals that

---

*This date appears on El Duque's passport, Havana divorce agreement and the back of his Cuban baseball card, for which he provided the information to CubaDeportes, the marketing arm of the Cuban Sports Ministry.

of the United States. Although he was black, he never had to experience the segregation of prerevolution Cuban baseball, when players of color—including the greats like Martín Dihigo and Orestes "Minnie" Miñoso, as well as El Duque's own father—were excluded from the popular Amateur League. In his style, his penetrating intelligence, his fearlessness and optimism, he seemed to represent the best that Castro had to offer. On his uniform he wore number 26, one of the revolution's most powerful symbols, representing the date, July 26, 1953, when Fidel launched his famous attack on the Moncada barracks in Santiago, effectively launching the Cuban revolution. El Duque later wore the same number with the Yankees. The number held no political significance to him— he had inherited it from his father—but for a time he was so articulate in defending the principles of the revolution that he became known around international baseball circles as a true believer. The scouts and agents who circled the rare and valuable Cuban ballplayers never really believed he would defect. Gordon Blakeley, the Yankees' director of international scouting, followed El Duque for years, from Barcelona to Buenos Aires, salivating and penning a half dozen reports that merely disappeared in his files. "I know the prettiest word in the world is *money*," El Duque once said while sitting in the living room of his three-bedroom house near the Havana airport. "But I believe that words like *loyalty* and *patriotism* are very beautiful as well."

El Duque could have been a model had he grown up in the States. He was tall, about six-foot-two, weighed 190 pounds and had the flexibility of Gumby, a result of early-morning yoga exercises he continued even after he was banned. He had the kind of presence that takes over a room and the voice to match, a low roar that seemed to emanate from somewhere around his spikes. He had a slick, bald head, which he shaved not to imitate Michael Jordan or Charles Barkley but because his hair had started falling out in clumps after applying some cheap Soviet hair tonic. El Duque's favorite expression, a kind of signature greeting, was ¡Todo bien! (All is well!), and he employed it constantly as both a question and an answer: "¿Todo bien? Sí, ¡todo bien! ¡Todo bien!" The expression had originated with his charismatic older brother, Arnaldo, a ballplayer and a barber who had died suddenly at thirty. El Duque looked like a major-leaguer long before he ever was one, particularly when he wore his blue Yankee pullover, a gift from a friend in the States. After he was banned, he wore the jersey to the only games in which he was allowed to participate, those in a neighborhood league that convened each weekend in front of several sorry-looking cows at Vladimir Ilyich Lenin Park. El Duque was manager and third baseman; he was forbidden to pitch for the same reason that Roger

Clemens would be forbidden to pitch if he came out for the thirty-five-and-over league in the Bronx.

El Duque couldn't stop himself from competing. He argued with the umpires and chewed out his ragtag ball club, but it was obvious to everyone that *todo* was definitely not *bien*. His wife, Norma Manzo, had left him in his disgrace, and he was living with his new girlfriend, Noris Bosch, in a cramped one-room cinder-block extension of her parents' house. He spent most of his time hanging out with his best friend, Osmany Lorenzo, who owned a house that abutted the parking lot of the Havana airport's international terminal. Lorenzo had no real job; he had been fired as an airport bartender for playing cassette tapes of a Miami comedian who made his living cracking jokes about Fidel. But the dismissal had freed up Lorenzo for his true calling: the shadowy life of the black-marketeer. He was one of a new breed of Cubans who knew how to exploit the recent legalization of the dollar and, with his contacts at the airport, he was especially well situated. All day people came and went through his back door, hauling cases of Hatuey Beer, toilet paper, even jet fuel that could be used in some of the old Soviet-made Muscovys that chugged around the capital. Lorenzo's primary role in this lucrative enterprise was to advise the couriers—"Hey, *chico*, put it over there."

In some ways, the harsh punishment against El Duque was odd, because Fidel knew better than anyone the pressures building inside the country, particularly for ballplayers whose skills were worth millions in another world. "If you have to compete against six million dollars versus three thousand Cuban pesos you cannot win," he admitted to a group of visiting American newspaper editors one evening inside the Palace of the Revolution. Because of the cancellation of the Soviet Union's annual $6 billion subsidy to Cuba—the result, of course, of the cancellation of the Soviet Union—the Cuban economy had contracted by 35 percent between 1989 and 1994. In effect, it had imploded. The ensuing depression corroded every aspect of Cuban life, including, inevitably, the powerhouse sports system of which baseball was king. Soon, bats and balls were scarce. Games were canceled because of power outages. Fans watching the nightly televised games would see relief pitchers exchange spikes with the pitchers they had replaced, right there on the mound. One typical night, Sánchez and I bought tickets from a scalper for a weeknight game between Sancti Spíritus and Metropolitanos, the other Havana club. We were taken beneath the stands and were being led to our box seats by way of the home dugout when we were approached suddenly by a player, in uniform, hanging out near the clubhouse.

"Hey!" the player shouted, motioning for us to stop.

We froze, fearing that we had been busted.

"You guys want to buy a ball?" the player asked. "They're two dollars apiece."

While Cuba's economic crisis was deepening, and fewer and fewer people were attending the games—about 300 turned out at the 55,000-seat stadium the night of the ball-selling incident—Major League Baseball, despite its poverty-pleading owners, was expanding into cities such as Miami and Tampa and Phoenix. The demand for new players accelerated the globalization of the sport. Baseball was no different from Gillette or Nike in this respect; it was the age of free trade, and the game was on the lookout for new, relatively cheap labor. Teams began to send scouts into remote places where the game had been mostly a rumor. They searched for players in such far-flung countries as South Korea and Australia. Cuba, meanwhile, which had been playing baseball since the 1860s, which before the revolution had produced Dolf Luque, Camilo Pascual, Tony Pérez, Luis Tiant and Bert Campaneris (and José Canseco and Rafael Palmeiro, who left as babies), remained untapped, an island ninety miles from Florida, teeming with impoverished, disgruntled, bored young prospects. Cuba was a forbidden gold mine, the last great frontier. The trade embargo prohibited teams from doing business there. (Theoretically, the Canadian clubs—the Toronto Blue Jays and the Montreal Expos—could have cut their own deals, but the Commissioner's Office sent out directives making the island off-limits to everyone.) So the only way to sign up a Cuban was to get him to leave his country. A few players figured this out for themselves. But for most, a middleman was needed to orchestrate the often harrowing defections, then work through the migratory hassles that inevitably followed.

THE ENTREPRENEUR who stepped forward to introduce supply to demand happened to be named, implausibly enough, Joe Cubas. And he brought much more than his name to the role. In many ways Cubas was the perfect man for the job. He walked like a Cuban and talked like a Cuban even though he had never set foot on the island. A squat, angry-looking man, he seemed ready to explode with raw ambition and an inbred hatred of Fidel, passed on to him by his mother, Berta, whose family had lost everything to the revolution. Cubas's fervor and political savvy helped him recruit the support of the heavyweights in the Miami exile community: the politicians and the businessmen who for nearly four decades had shaped U.S. policy toward Cuba. When Cubas needed a visa or a plane, he could enlist the help of the Cuban American National Foundation, the powerful lobbying group, or Brothers to the Rescue, the volunteer aviators whose unarmed planes were attacked and shot down by Cuban MiGs in 1996. Cubas was the classic "man of action" out of Joan Didion's *Miami*. He wasn't afraid to break a law or grease a palm to get things done. But Cubas's singular talent was that he was a bullshit artist without peer. He was able to get people to do extraordinary things for him, often for free. He extracted money and favors from a wide range of relatives and acquaintances who seldom saw either returned.

For years, Cubas trailed Cuba's national baseball team around the world. He wooed the ballplayers in Tennessee hotel rooms, in Tokyo shopping malls, in hundreds of dark corridors, promising the holy trinity of American-style capitalism: baseball, apple pie and Chevrolet. Technically, Cubas was an agent, but he was like no agent that professional sports had ever seen. He was part Jerry Maguire, part Oliver North. The Cuban players who saw him lurking around every corner began to refer to him as El Gordo (the Fat Man). He was the kind of agent who held conversations over encrypted phone lines, with smugglers who traveled with code names like "Santa Claus." His operatives seemed to have walked straight off the set of *Scarface*. René Guim, who worked as Cubas's publicist, recalled asking one of the agent's burly cousins, a former West Palm Beach bouncer named Iggy Fong, whether it was true that he carried a gun. The two were standing inside Victor's Café, a famous exile haunt, but Fong enthusiastically pulled a nine-millimeter pistol out of his fanny pack. "I want you to meet Cheech," he said to Guim. Then he hiked up a pant leg to reveal a .38-caliber revolver holstered to his ankle. "And this is Chong."

Cubas would have been the logical man to help El Duque defect that winter, but circumstances had gotten in the way. In 1995, Cubas had engineered the escape of El Duque's younger half brother—another pitcher, named Liván Hernández—while the Cuban national team was training in Monterrey, Mexico. Shortly before midnight, Liván had gathered up his belongings, sneaked out of his dorm room and stumbled through his tears into Cubas's waiting rental car. With Cubas negotiating, Liván, who had earned the equivalent of five dollars a month in Cuba, signed a $4.5 million contract to pitch for the Florida Marlins. But after taking his commission Cubas disappeared, leaving Liván to fend for himself in his strange new world. Liván, alone, nearly ate himself out of baseball, as they say, having discovered one of the ubiquitous manifestations of American capitalism: the Burger King drive-through window. He defected again—to another agent. And he alleged publicly that Cubas had tried to charge him a 25 percent commission, some 20 percent above the industry norm. The breakup left both men extremely bitter, so much so that Cubas told one of his associates, Ramón Batista, that he wanted nothing to do with El Duque, who was likely "to fuck me the way his brother did."

El Duque pinned most of his hopes on his great-uncle Ocilio Cruz, a private investigator who worked out of an office down the street from *The Miami Herald*. To his family and friends, Cruz was known as Tío (Spanish for *uncle*). He was among the tens of thousands of Cubans who had come to Miami during the 1980 Mariel boatlift. A large, bald man with an easy smile who could be both intimidating and disarming, he had risen to become a bodyguard for Jorge Mas Canosa, the late, much-feared chieftain of the exile community. Tío was especially sensitive to his grandnephew's plight. A former first baseman himself, after the revolution he had spent fifteen years playing baseball in a prison on the Isle of Youth, off Cuba's southern coast. He had been sent there because of his membership in an anti-Castro terrorist cell that had organized itself around the Havana bus terminal, where he had worked as a security guard.

Using his sources in the Miami underworld, a melting pot of smugglers and spies, Tío set out to liberate El Duque from Castro's grip. He used an anonymous courier to deliver $4,000—a small fortune in Cuba—to El Duque, who then entrusted the task of hiring an escape vessel to his best friend, Osmany Lorenzo, shadow master of the Cuban economy. Osmany located the perfect candidate: a fisherman from Caibarién, a small city on Cuba's northern coast that had become a mecca for rafters setting out for the United States. In exchange for a guarantee that he could bring himself and his wife to America, Lorenzo agreed to use his thirty-foot fishing boat to smuggle El Duque and his entourage out of the country.

It was December 1997. The plan was to leave Havana under the cover of Cuba's first legal Christmas since 1969. Because it was a holiday, the streets would be empty. There was less likelihood that El Duque would be followed. The group planned to spend the day in normal activities, doing nothing that would attract attention, then gather after midnight near an on-ramp to the National Highway for the five-hour journey to Caibarién. On Christmas Eve, El Duque went to see his mother. He spent several hours with her but never told her about his plans. On Christmas Day, he and Noris attended the wedding reception of a friend, the Italian photographer Ernesto Bazan. El Duque betrayed nothing. Tom Miller, an American who wrote *Trading with the Enemy,* an account of his travels through Cuba, happened to be at the reception. When he introduced himself to El Duque, the pitcher wrote down his Havana address and invited Miller to visit him some time.

The afternoon wore on. White-coated waiters filtered through the reception, bearing trays filled with *mojitos* and Cuba Libres. By the time night fell over Havana, nearly everyone was drunk. El Duque, a moderate drinker, lingered in the background, sipping juice and talking to friends. He wore a Nike cap, a white vest thrown over an aqua T-shirt, a gold crucifix dangling from his neck. He chain-smoked Marlboros, devoured a plate of pork chops and rice and beans, and then cleaned the plates of everyone around him. Someone turned on some music, and he and Noris got up to dance. Noris was an expert; she belonged to a modern-dance troupe in Havana and had once been on television. Together they made a stunning pair: the finest pitcher in modern Cuban history, the beloved El Duque, and his slender, dark-haired *novia*. The song was by the masters of Cuban *son*, Los Van Van, and the familiar lyrics washed over the crowd:

> *¡Ay dios, ampárame! [O God, protect me!]*
> *¡Ampárame!*
> *¡Ampárame!*
> *¡Ampárame!*

PART ONE

CHAPTER ONE

TODO BIEN

THE DAY HE DROPPED DEAD, ARNALDO HERNÁNDEZ HAD NEVER been more alive. He had begun his morning early, clearing a flower bed for his girlfriend, Arelis Ruiz, and burning the weeds and the dead leaves in a mini bonfire in front of their house in rural Havana. Then he headed out. It was April 22, 1994, an ordinary day, another day to get by. Arnaldo had been working two jobs. On most days he clipped hair for five pesos a head at the local barbershop or occasionally on his front porch. On nights and weekends, he manned the front door of the Círculo Social, a community center and disco, tossing out the bad drunks and letting in his friends for free. He also played first base for San Miguel, a provincial league team on the other side of the capital. With relentless good cheer, he shuttled between these various responsibilities, shouting out *"¡Todo bien!"* from the seat of his Chinese-made bicycle, a beater that he often loaded up with his girlfriend, his glove and his beloved white poodle, Duque. He seemed more than able to balance it all. He was thirty years old, six-foot-four, well over two hundred pounds. "He had so much energy," said Arelis. "Sometimes he'd make these trips all day without eating."

Arnaldo and his younger brother, Orlando, had grown up inseparable. The boys were less than two years apart in age, and they had slept in the same bed until they were in their teens. The bed had finally collapsed one evening under the collective bulk of their expanding, man-child bodies. "Then we moved to the floor," recalled Orlando. Together the boys had acquired an obsession with baseball—the obsession, of course, of the entire nation, but also "the family business," as their uncle "Miñosito," a slick infielder in his own right, had put it.

Arnaldo had been huge, "an animal," according to his uncle, a pitcher with a terrifying fastball and a burning ambition to follow in the footsteps of his colorful father, Arnaldo Hernández Montero, the original "El Duque." Orlando was smaller, craftier, more creative on the mound, blessed even as a youth with what one of his coaches called a *perra curva,* a bitch of a curve. The boys often slept with their gloves on, so as to make it that much easier to hit the field in the morning. "We slept with tremendous dignity," Orlando said years later. "Every day, when we went to bed, when we got up, we were thinking about baseball."

Later on, though, the brothers drifted apart, divided not so much by bad blood as by the economic earthquake that was splitting apart the country. Nineteen ninety-four was the worst year of a bleak period in Cuban history known as "the Special Period in Time of Peace." The name was an attempt by Fidel to recapture the early romance of the revolution, the adventure and the blind sacrifice, but to most Cubans it signified only pitch-darkness and want. The Soviet Union had collapsed, and with it had gone the economic assistance that for decades had propped up Cuba's economy. Havana, a cradle of good times regardless of political ideology, was suddenly a desperate, crumbling city. During the day, the streets were overrun by hundreds of thousands of bicycles, substitutes for motorized vehicles in a society that lacked fuel. At dusk, the lights often flickered out, plunging the capital into darkness until morning. For many Cubans, the era was defined by these sweltering, silent evenings. In the darkness, parents waved pieces of cardboard over their children as they slept. "That was all you could do to keep the mosquitoes away," said Roberto Martinez, a longtime friend of the Hernández family. "It was a black time. As a Cuban, it touched every part of your life."

Some had it a little easier, though, and Orlando Hernández was among them. As a star pitcher for the Havana Industriales and Team Cuba, the powerhouse national baseball team, he was a *niño lindo* of the revolution, one of Fidel's favorite sons. As his career advanced, the Cuban Sports Ministry had given him a series of bigger apartments and, finally, in the early nineties, a blue three-bedroom house in Calixto Suárez, a neighborhood tucked behind Terminal 2 of the José Martí International Airport. El Duque lived with his wife, Norma, and their two young daughters, Yahumara and Steffi, and the pitcher's growing cache of trophies and medals, which he kept in a glass case in the living room. El Duque was not immune to the nation's problems, the blackouts and the scarcity. But the government gave him and other top athletes full run of the *diplomercados,* the state-run dollar stores that were kept well stocked with meat and poultry, soap and cooking oil—in short, everything that was disappearing from the shelves of bodegas all across the country.

His brother Arnaldo lived in a different world, the one occupied by most Cubans of the era. Arnaldo's baseball career had never really taken off, a bitter disappointment that his relatives attributed to a horrific injury he suffered in his teens. He and Arelis were living out the Special Period in a tiny house that her brother had abandoned when he moved to Russia with his wife, a former Soviet engineer. The house was a squat concrete box in the sticks of rural Havana. It sat at the end of a dirt road that often dissolved in the afternoon rains. Arnaldo and Arelis sometimes talked about getting married, like Orlando and Norma, but it was simply impossible; the reception alone would be too expensive. "Anybody can go and just sign the papers, but you have to have a big fiesta, you have to have good memories," Arelis said years later. "I decided that if it was going to be garbage, I'd rather not get married."

At times it seemed as if the couple were surviving on Arnaldo's buoyant personality alone. El Duque's older brother used his boundless energy, his contagious exuberance, to support his family. He worked constantly, and when he wasn't working he hustled. When he and Arelis ran out of cooking oil, a constant occurrence, Arnaldo would ride his bike down to the local bakery, where his friends would slip him some pork fat, sometimes in exchange for a haircut. "If we needed rice or anything else, he would just go out and get them because he got along with everybody," said Arelis. At night, the couple would light candles and read. Outside, all was black and silent except for the sounds of a few livestock and the clucking of chickens. There was rarely any electricity, and thus no fans, so when it was time to sleep, Arnaldo and Arelis would set their mattress at the threshold of the front door and sleep facing the thick night air.

Despite all the hardships, Arnaldo, by all accounts, was happy; seemingly he was *always* happy. He loved working as a bouncer at the Círculo Social, the disco, because it allowed him to mingle with his friends. He stood sentry at the front door, a towering figure with a coffee-colored complexion, his father's complexion, lighter than his brother's, taking tickets and flirting with women and greeting people with his signature "*¡Todo bien!*" Even though Orlando had long surpassed him as a ballplayer, he still lived for the game. On weekends he set out on his bike with Duque—the poodle, not his brother. "With one jump, the dog would land on the bicycle, like a person," said Arelis. "It was up and down, it went everywhere. The dog really was like a person. He ate what we ate." Even in his late twenties Arnaldo would head down to the field every weekend and play all-day pickup games for money—60 pesos here, 120 pesos there—each team pooling its meager resources. Afterward he would bathe and pedal off to work or stay home and write poems by candlelight. Growing up, Arnaldo had struggled as a student; Orlando had shone. But later, Arnaldo discovered the joys of reading and writing. He devoured mysteries and crime novels. He wrote poems about his girlfriend, about baseball, about his chickens and his poodle. "Then one day the dog got sick; it got some kind of bacteria and died," said Arelis. "Arnaldo cried and cried. He buried the dog near the patio. He wrote a poem and dedicated it to the dog. He placed it over him, and then he buried the poem along with the dog."

Right before he died, Arelis said, Arnaldo had been writing poems lamenting the distance between him and his brother. It was not bitterness, just a tug of regret that the relationship was not what it had been. Growing up, Orlando had followed his brother everywhere. The boys' father had left when they were little, and Arnaldo, in many ways, had been the man of the house. Now their roles had changed. Orlando was a national figure, a hero of the revolution, the next "El Duque." He brought back exotic trinkets from his travels abroad: necklaces, T-shirts, an aluminum bat that Arnaldo loved so much he insisted on keeping it next to his bed. ("Do you know how obsessed you have to be to sleep with a bat?" said his mother, María Julia, shaking her head years later.) But there had been a series of small mix-ups—and, of course, the widening economic gap in their lives. The brothers lived within a few miles of each other, but the distance seemed increasingly great.

It was dusk when I spoke to Arelis Ruiz, a light-skinned woman with dark hair whose face glowed when she reminisced about her late boyfriend. We sat in the cramped living room of the house where she and Arnaldo had lived. At one point, Arelis excused herself to pick up her ten-month-old daughter, scurrying over the plywood base of her makeshift playpen. Arelis set the baby down in front of a black-and-white television, tuned it to cartoons, apologized, then, quietly, began to sob. When she used to come home, she said, she would often find Arnaldo surrounded by children, like the Pied Piper of the neighborhood. The children ran after him as he pedaled through the streets on his bike. She and Arnaldo had wanted to have children of their own, but they had been waiting until they could afford them, for the time when the Special Period would finally come to an end. She said she wished she could pull out Arnaldo's old poems and read a few to me. But a few years after Arnaldo died, a new boyfriend had come upon the poems in a closet. In a jealous fit, the boyfriend had carried the poems into the front yard, hundreds stacked in a cardboard box, and used them to make his own little bonfire.

"YOU CANNOT TELL the story of Orlando 'El Duque' Hernández without telling the story of his brother, Arnaldo," advised a close friend of El Duque's, known universally as Lache, as we sat on his front porch in Havana one afternoon. It is in that spirit that we begin this story.

Arnaldo had been named after his father, Arnaldo Hernández Montero, the original El Duque. The father had been a talented right-handed pitcher, and from the beginning he envisioned creating a legacy of hurlers. In Latin America, a child commonly inherits both parents' last names. And so the first pitcher born to Arnaldo "El Duque" Hernández and his wife, María Julia Pedroso, was called Arnaldo Hernández Pedroso—aka El Duque.

Arnaldo—the father—liked the name so much that he decided to make it a trend. He wanted to name his second-born son Arnoldo, changing just one letter to distinguish between the two boys. This second boy, just like his father and his older brother, would also grow up a pitcher and would also be known as El Duque.

Several years later, however, the father's aggressive strategy for legacy building began to collapse. Legend has it that the younger boy, Arnoldo, turned out to be independent and headstrong and, among other things, he rebelled against his own name. "¡Yo soy Orlando!" ("I am Orlando!), he would snap, rejecting what was, after all, essentially the same name as his older brother's.

"It's true," the boys' father, the original El Duque, told me some thirty years later. "Orlando's real name was Arnoldo. I had wanted to make it a trilogy, but he didn't like it. So we called him Orlando."

Arnaldo and Orlando were four and two, respectively, when their father left to play baseball and create pitchers on other parts of the island. They grew up with María Julia and her extended family. The family was packed into adjoining row houses next to the church in Wajay (pronounced "Wah-high"), a rural suburb in southwest Havana. There was María Julia and the boys (including another son, Gerardo, from María Julia's second marriage); María Julia's parents; a cousin; and a diminutive uncle, Miñosito (Little Miñoso), so named because of his resemblance to Orestes "Minnie" Miñoso, the spark plug of the Chicago White Sox of the 1950s. The houses were white and looked vaguely Spanish; three small rooms led from one to the next, from the front of the house to the back. Concrete walls separated the rooms. Conditions in Cuba are better than they used to be, but a recent tour of the El Duque family home had to be conducted by candlelight because the electricity—emitted by naked lightbulbs strung from the crumbling ceiling—had gone out.

Arnaldo and Orlando slept together in the middle room with their grandparents Juan Antonio Pedroso and Antolina Cruz. Before the 1959 revolution, Juan Antonio had owned a country store, Taller Pedroso, from which he repaired bicycles, shined shoes and delivered the newspaper and the town mail.

He was a permanent fixture on the southwest Havana run, from Wajay to La Lisa, dropping off papers with the local vendors and, along the way, picking up shoes that he would shine and return the next day. He earned a decent living and cut a dashing figure in his small town. His neighbors, most of them white, called him "Charoli," or patent leather, something brilliantly black. (The nickname was meant as a term of endearment and was taken as one.) Juan Antonio was also insistently apolitical. To him the Cuban revolution was a distant adventure, with little relevance to his own life. That changed one afternoon in 1967 when the government launched its latest crackdown against private enterprise. The first wave of expropriations, in the early sixties, had hit the big companies: Bacardi, IT&T, United Fruit, the American banks. This second one was aimed at small businesses like Taller Pedroso.

"They intervened us," recalled Antolina Cruz, whose husband had died the previous fall after fifty-seven years of marriage. "There were two people from the government, two big guys, and they had these big ledgers. First they forced my husband to sign the books. Then they took his adding machine. They just picked it up and carted it off. He couldn't touch a thing. They let him take a few things with him, you know, personal items, and then they sealed the place up with a big piece of paper with the word INTERVENIDO. They told us that if we broke the seal we'd all go to jail."

Orlando was two at the time, but he figured out later what had happened: "My grandfather lost everything to the revolution."

Juan Antonio moved the business into his house, but it wasn't the same. A government accountant came by to regulate his already meager earnings. Arnaldo and Orlando competed for space with the broken-down bikes and the shoes. The family subsisted mostly on their *libretas,* ration booklets handed out by the revolutionary government. Each family received a monthly allotment of staples: six pounds of rice, six pounds of beans, three bars of soap, five pounds of sugar, two packs of cigarettes, twelve beers and so on. The idea, of course, was to create a utopian society, one that eliminated the extreme poverty that had killed thousands before the revolution, while the mobsters and the American businessmen had lived like sultans. But the result was a kind of uniform squalor. The Hernández brothers never starved, but they never had much, either. "I had one pair of pants that I called 'the Weeklies,' " recalled Orlando. "Why did I call them 'the Weeklies'? Because I wore the same pants every day. I had another pair of pants that I called 'the Big Saturdays.' I wore them every Saturday to go to a party. I had the same shirt. Sometimes I had two shirts."

With their father gone, Arnaldo and Orlando were drawn closer together. In early memories of the two boys, they are forever intertwined. Mario Cobo, who lived around the block, thought of them as a kind of fraternal battery—one would pitch, the other would catch, and then they would switch. When the brothers weren't playing ball, they romped in the orchards surrounding Wajay. "We were always buying fruit; stealing fruit is more like it," recalled Orlando. "The dogs would come after us, and we'd be running with the mangoes that we stole from the *guajiros* [peasants] on the farms. Then we'd take a swim in the lake. We'd go down there with our haul of mangoes. No one ever caught us. We were just a couple of rambunctious country boys." By all accounts, El Duque worshiped Arnaldo. Years later, it was still difficult for him to talk about his brother. Several times, Sánchez and I tried to engage him on the subject.

"Next question," he'd respond, staring into space.

One afternoon in Havana, Antolina Cruz, the boys' grandmother, sat in her Havana home, her son Miñosito at her side. Above her bed was an old black-and-white portrait of Arnaldo. Antola, as she's known to her family, was once a teacher's aide, and when I asked her about the similarities and differences between the two brothers, she responded: "Orlando always had better penmanship than Arnaldo."

"But Arnaldo was much better looking than Orlando," said Miñosito.

"Arnaldo went to school on Twenty-sixth of July Street with the poorer students," said Antola. "The ones who were left behind. They used to call me from that school all the time, my God. And how he loved the girls."

"He had a thousand women," said Miñosito.

"Oh, he was something else."

"And he was taller than Orlando."

"Seven feet tall!" said Antola.

"No way was he seven feet tall," said Miñosito.

"*Muchacho*, of course he was seven feet tall. Look, when Arnaldo died we couldn't find a big enough casket for him. We were worried that they were going to try to cut his feet off to make him fit in the box. María Julia knew something about the business, and she warned them that they better not do it. When she went to see him before the wake, it was okay. He was still whole. They had made a bigger casket for him."

"That casket was huge," said Miñosito.

"Arnaldo and Orlando were always very close," said Antola. "Arnaldo was always giving his brother advice. He was always warning him, 'You have to do this, you have to do that.'"

"Arnaldo used to fight with Orlando when Orlando didn't follow what he said," said Miñosito.

"He wanted to dominate him," said Antola.

"He *did* dominate him," said Miñosito.

Orlando imitated his brother's speech, his mannerisms and his dreams. Back then, Major League Baseball was like Oz in Cuba, distant and unattainable, scarcely even real. The government had blacked out the World Series since the early sixties, along with all other news about professional baseball in the States. The boys could dream as far as they could see, and that was Industriales, Team Cuba. Arnaldo, with his size and strength, may have held the most promise. "He was going to be the best," said his father, who later had two other sons pitch in the major leagues.

Arnaldo's relatives believe his promising baseball career was derailed one afternoon in one of the groves surrounding Wajay. Arnaldo and Orlando had disappeared that day with a rusted machete to hack tamarind fruit together. At some point, the two boys apparently were playing, and Orlando, according to Miñosito, took a wild swing with the machete. The tool clipped Arnaldo's right wrist. By the time Miñosito arrived on the scene, there was blood everywhere. "This bone, right here, was hanging loose," said Miñosito, pointing to the hook-shaped hamate bone that protrudes from the wrist.

Arnaldo's fastball was never the same. "He didn't have the same velocity that he had before," said Miñosito. For years after the accident, Arnaldo tried to make it back as a pitcher. To Rolando Núñez, one of the boys' first coaches, it was clear that he was desperate to duplicate the success of his father, to become the next El Duque. But he couldn't. His velocity was gone. It wasn't until later that he finally became a first baseman. Arnaldo had always been a better hitter than Orlando, and the switch was enough to vault him into the National Series, Cuba's equivalent of the major leagues. By then, Orlando was a star with Industriales. Arnaldo had always wanted to play with his brother, but he played instead with Metropolitanos, a kind of entry-level team in the capital. He was twenty-eight years old. He lasted one season. He batted .224 with two home runs and six RBIs in ninety-four at-bats. And then, after that one season, he returned to the sandlots and the provincial league and the haircuts in the Special Period in Time of Peace.

WHEN ARNALDO RODE UP on his bicycle that fateful, ordinary afternoon, his grandmother Antola was sitting on the porch. Arelis was in the house, making dinner. Arnaldo had come from baseball practice and was still in his uniform. He went to inspect the garden. He and Arelis were thinking about planting peppers. He checked the chicken coop, then went into the house to wash up. When he came out of the bathroom, dinner was waiting on the table: shredded beef, fried pork fat, rice and a glass of tamarind juice. Arnaldo walked straight past it and went back out on the porch. "Ay, Grandmother, I have an unbelievable headache," he told Antola. "It feels like my head is going to explode."

"What about dinner?" said Arelis. She thought food might help.

Arnaldo didn't respond. He walked back inside and stood for several moments with his head in his hands. Then he fell to his knees and pounded his head twice against a small wooden table. "I can't take this anymore, Arelis," he said. "I can't. Get me an aspirin or something." Arelis walked into the kitchen and came back with the aspirin. She carefully sliced the tablet in two and gave half to Arnaldo, who bolted it down with the juice. Aspirin was especially hard to come by in the Special Period, and Arelis didn't want to waste an entire tablet on a headache.

Arelis pulled out a mattress and laid it across the living room floor. Arnaldo was scheduled to work at the disco that night. As he lay down, he told his girlfriend: "Wake me up in a while. Let's see if the aspirin takes care of it." Arelis went back outside to sit with Arnaldo's grandmother. "After about fifteen minutes, I could hear him snoring really loudly," she said. "But it wasn't like snoring, it was louder. It wasn't natural." The noise was so loud that Arelis went inside to see what was wrong.

Arelis walked into the living room to find the mattress covered in blood. Arnaldo was unconscious, foaming at the mouth. Arelis nearly collapsed beside him. She tried to pull him up, begged him to get up, but he wouldn't move. Antola rushed into the living room and gasped at the sight of her strapping grandson, stricken on the floor. Neither woman knew what to do. There was no phone, no way to call for help. Arelis ran outside. It was late now, about 7:30, and she ran along the desolate dirt road, searching for help in the gathering darkness. She searched for a car, but even those neighbors who had cars lacked the fuel to make them run. The search went on and on. Arelis later thought that it was exactly like a nightmare, unfolding in hazy slow motion, her loudest screams met with oblivious silence. Finally, after about half an hour, she was able to flag down a Soviet-made jeep driven by a thin fifteen-year-old boy.

Arelis directed the boy to the house. Antola was standing on the porch, screaming, "Arnaldo's dying on me! He's dying on me! I know he's dying!" While Arelis was away, Antola had wiped Arnaldo's forehead with rubbing alcohol. He didn't respond. "He was so pale, so pale," Antola said. She and Arelis returned to the living room. Arnaldo's condition hadn't changed: He was spread across the floor, breathing blood and foam onto the mattress. The three of them—Arelis, the skinny teenager and Arnaldo's seventy-four-year-old grandmother—half-carried, half-dragged Arnaldo to the jeep. "He was unconscious," said Arelis. "He was so heavy; I don't know how we got him in there. He didn't fit. He was so tall." They were finally able to prop Arnaldo up in the front seat. Arelis climbed in the back, and the boy started the engine. But he had been driving only a short time when the engine stalled. "We spent another ten minutes trying to get it started," Arelis recalled. Finally, the boy wheeled the jeep down the dirt road. After several hundred yards, the vehicle reached the pavement, turned left and headed toward Wajay.

They drove in total darkness, their path guided only by the vehicle's faint headlights. Arelis screamed for Arnaldo to wake up. She thought he stirred slightly. Then, just outside of town, near the entrance to Wajay, the jeep suddenly died again. This time the boy couldn't get the vehicle started. They were stranded in the dark. The teenager and Arelis leaped out and tried to push-start the jeep without success. They tried to flag down help. "No one would stop," said Arelis. "I don't know why. It was getting late, and maybe they were afraid of getting robbed." Several cars passed before a man pulled up in a white Lada sedan, a Russian-made compact about the size of a Toyota. The man recognized Arnaldo. He leaped out and helped Arelis and the boy lift Arnaldo out of the jeep and carry him across the road, into the backseat of the Lada.

By the time they finally pulled up at the medical clinic, Arnaldo was dead. Arelis and Arnaldo lived just a few miles outside of town. But a full hour had passed since Arnaldo had been stricken. He was pronounced dead at the clinic. The cause was a cerebral hemorrhage brought on by an aneurysm. Arnaldo was thirty years old.

All over Wajay, people would debate whether Arnaldo Hernández could have been saved. He appears to have had the classic symptoms of an aneurysm, which can strike undetected at any time. But others wondered whether he was also, in his own way, a victim of the Special Period in Time of Peace. They wondered whether a telephone or gasoline or electricity or an ambulance might have saved him. It was not lost on anyone that the circumstances of Arnaldo's death mirrored in many ways those of their own lives, their everyday struggles, their own deep fears and frustrations with the never-ending economic crisis, a crisis brought on by the demise of a faraway country, by Cuba's unique and incomprehensible isolation in the world. "If they get him to a doctor, he survives, that's what I believe," said Miñosito. "Sadly, this is how things are in this country."

Around eleven P.M., Roberto "Pelusa" Martínez, one of El Duque's best friends, woke up to someone rapping gently on his bedroom window. When he opened it, he saw his friend standing in the dark, crying.

"Pelusa, Arnaldo's dead. He's dead!" said El Duque.

"Your father? Your father's dead?" said Pelusa, bolting upright.

"No, Arnaldo, my brother, my brother," Orlando cried.

Pelusa took Orlando home, stayed with him and helped the family prepare for the burial. María Julia had decided to hold the wake in the house across from the old Catholic church, the house where the boys had grown up. She decided to bury her son in a red, white and blue Team Cuba warm-up suit that Orlando had given Arnaldo as a present.

The funeral drew much of the Cuban baseball establishment. The entire Industriales and Metropolitanos teams were there, along with dozens of players from the National Series and the provincial league. There were families from Wajay, people who had had their hair cut by Arnaldo, and children, dozens of children. A black hearse carrying Arnaldo and his specially built casket led the long procession up to the municipal cemetery on the outskirts of town. The mourners crowded into the small cemetery and gathered around the gray concrete tomb in which Arnaldo would be buried.

The tomb rested aboveground, beneath an engraved headstone that read:

ARNALDO A

HNDEZ PEDROSO

YOUR FAMILY

DOES NOT FORGET YOU

23 3 64

22 4 94

¡TODO BIEN!

Not long after the funeral began, it started to pour. Years later, no one would forget the rain. It came down in sheets, creating puddles around the tomb and the dull grass of the old cemetery. The mourners, many without umbrellas, stood there, drenched, trying to figure out how one of the strongest, most vibrant men in town was suddenly dead. It was inconceivable. Then the mourners scattered into the rain. Later, some of them would recall that Arnaldo Hernández, the original El Duque, had been unable to attend the funeral. The Hernández brothers' father had been living at the time on the Isle of Youth, off Cuba's southern coast. He later said he had been delayed because of the weather. When he finally arrived, people in Wajay recalled seeing him outside the local bodegas, chasing his sorrow with a bottle.

CHAPTER TWO

EL DUQUE

As Arnaldo "El Duque" Hernández tells the story, Fidel Castro, Cuba's number one fan, presented the idea to the Central Committee of the Communist party. This was years before El Duque's third son, Liván, had fallen to his knees and shouted, "I love you, Miami!" (in English, no less) after winning the 1997 World Series, and before his second son, Orlando, had gone on *60 Minutes* and referred to Fidel as "the Devil." El Duque said he heard the story from a high-ranking member of the National Assembly. "Let's find an is-land to give to El Duque," the Maximum Leader had proposed. "And some women, too. We'll get him twenty big *mulatas*, two cases of beer and a bottle of rum, and he can create pitching for the future." The original El Duque loved that story, even if it may have been told to him in jest. "It's true," he told me. "I make pitchers."

No one was particularly surprised that El Duque had arrived late for Ar-naldo's funeral. Ever since the breakup with María Julia, he had been a sporadic presence in his sons' lives. Arnaldo "El Duque" Hernández was many things. He was a bon vivant and a rake, the life of the party wherever he happened to land. In his time, he had been a serious baseball talent. As some have described him, he was a poor man's Martín Dihigo, El Inmortal, one of two Cubans to make the American Baseball Hall of Fame (Tony Pérez is the other). Like Dihigo, El Duque had played every position at one time or another; primarily he pitched. And although he stood no taller than five-foot-nine, and was much slighter than his sons, he was utterly fearless. His pitching philosophy was relatively simple: "Fastball to the head, other pitches to the zone."

But El Duque had not been the most responsible of men. He had fathered six children—four boys and two girls—with four different women in four different cities. He lived the life of a transient, skipping town every few months or so, often without warning. At any given time his own family (or families) had no idea where he was. His arrivals were equally unpredictable. He would show up without so much as a phone call, often bearing little more than a suitcase and a smile as big as the Hotel Habana Libre. Then he would stay for months. It was difficult to stay angry with him for very long, though; he was a kind of rogue innocent. "There are some people who just want to be too alive," Miñosito explained one day. He said that the day his sister María Julia broke up with El Duque was one of the happiest of his life. "But he's not a bad guy," he added. "He's just a little unstable. He's one of those guys who doesn't want to confront the situations of real life."

He is also not a particularly easy man to locate. At the time that this book was being prepared, there were rumored sightings of El Duque in the Marianao district of Havana, in the central city of Santa Clara, on the Isle of Youth and in the agricultural city of Las Tunas on the other side of the island. Calls were placed to each location, phone numbers were exchanged, but no one seemed to have seen him. "You'd have about as much chance of tracking down Fidel," one family friend advised me. After several unsuccessful leads, a call was placed to his son Orlando, who was training with the Yankees in Tampa. He laughed. "Go look for him in the mountains!" he roared. He hadn't the slightest clue where his father was. A decision was finally made to follow the consensus opinion, which was that El Duque was probably in Las Tunas, where he kept a home.

The plane, a Soviet-made Ilyushin that resembled a blimp with wings, touched down in Las Tunas in the middle of a blinding afternoon. The doors swung open, and blast-furnace heat rushed into the cabin. It was like landing on the sun. At the front of the airport, a squat terminal planted in the middle of a field, horse-drawn carriages and bicycle taxis were lined up ten deep. There were a few automobile taxis, and it was one of those that led the search for El Duque. The first stop, logically, was the baseball stadium, but the Las Tunas nine was away that afternoon. Someone suggested checking the local branch of the Sports Ministry. Raúl, our helpful driver, pulled up and walked inside. He came out with a friendly local official. "My son will know where he lives," the man said, climbing into the car. Five minutes later we pulled up at his son's house. He, too, got in. By the time the taxi turned down a gravel lane and eased beside the modest two-story house, we were a full-blown delegation.

A striking teenage boy, about five-foot-ten, met us at the front door. The sports official took charge.

"Is Duque home?"

The boy invited us to wait in a small living room and then disappeared into the back. There was a portrait of Jesus on one wall, and someone had placed a Barbie on top of a sixteen-inch color television. There was nothing to suggest that the father of two major-league pitchers lived here. In particular, there were no photos of Orlando or Liván. Someone asked the sports official if the strapping youngster at the door was another of El Duque's sons. He said he was, but he didn't play baseball. His two brothers had already defected, he explained, and the government had decided that it wasn't about to groom another traitor for the major leagues. He said the kid was playing field hockey, instead.

It was then that Arnaldo "El Duque" Hernández emerged, blinking and smiling and puffing on an unfiltered Aroma cigarette, the harshest brand in Cuba. He was wearing a weathered T-shirt, white cutoff shorts and flip-flops. I introduced myself and extended my hand. Instead of shaking it, El Duque embraced me like a long-lost relative. He was elated to see everyone else as well: the sports official, his son, Raúl the cabdriver. All of us were greeted like family. Then El Duque turned to the boy.

"Did you meet Marlon?" he asked. I said that indeed I had, adding that he looked like an athlete. El Duque then dispelled the notion that the Cuban government could prevent his fourth son from becoming a major-league ballplayer.

"This one," El Duque said proudly, "this one is for the Cleveland Indians."

EL DUQUE WAS a product of one of the most vibrant, colorful eras in the history of baseball. Before the revolution, baseball in Cuba, particularly in Havana, was played with an intensity found only in New York before the Dodgers and Giants moved west. The range of the sport may have been unrivaled. The Cuban Amateur League remained segregated right up until the revolution in 1959. But the professional league was integrated years before Jackie Robinson broke in with the Dodgers in 1947. The Cuban League featured up-and-coming (and down-and-outing) major-leaguers, Negro League legends like Satchel Paige and Cool Papa Bell, and Cuban stalwarts like Orestes Miñoso and Camilo Pascual. Havana even supported a Reds farm team, the Triple-A Sugar Kings, who played in the Florida International League.

"Baseball was central to life," recalled Doug Logan, whose grandfather owned the Almendares, Havana's most popular professional team. After leaving Cuba, Logan became, among other things, a rock concert promoter and, later, the commissioner of Major League Soccer. He has spent considerable time around the Rolling Stones and the World Cup finals. But he said he has found nothing to match the spectacle of Cuban baseball back then. "It was how people identified themselves," he said. "My experiences at the ballpark became a kind of measuring stick for what an exciting event was supposed to look like for the rest of my life."

The island was filled with news about the major leagues. To this day, older Cuban fans hoard boxes filled with baseball cards of Vic Raschi and Al Kaline and Marv Throneberry. The World Series was televised every year, many of the regular season games were broadcast on the radio, and news of the American game was disseminated through a half dozen daily newspapers. Then, after the season ended, at the height of tourist season, the major-leaguers would descend on the island to participate in the four-team Cuban winter league. Cuba has never seemed so close as it did then. Roberto González Echevarría writes in *The Pride of Havana*, his epic history of Cuban baseball, that Almendares pitcher Max Lanier, better known for his career with the St. Louis Cardinals, used to shuttle between Havana and Miami to pick up groceries for his family. Lanier made the thirty-minute flight so often—sometimes on the same day— that he earned the nickname El Piloto (the Pilot).

The sport was as colorful as the culture in which it thrived. This was back when the mob ran Havana and there were numbers runners on every street corner. To Major League Baseball, gamblers are the lowest life-form, a scourge upon the earth, Joe Jackson and Pete Rose being the most well-known examples. In 1947, commissioner A. B. "Happy" Chandler tried to apply this standard to Cuba. He suspended Leo Durocher for accusing Yankee president Larry MacPhail of consorting with gamblers before an exhibition game in Havana. But Durocher might as well have accused MacPhail of consorting with palm trees. In prerevolutionary Cuba, gambling was *encouraged* at the ballpark. The bookies were like hot-dog vendors. "They roamed the aisles," said Logan. "And you could bet on almost anything. You could get odds on three runs being scored in the next inning. They wore the big zoot-suit pants, and they always had the big key chains and the traditional two-toned shoes." How pervasive was it? As Lanier ran off the field after beating the Havana Reds in the famous 1947 Cuban League finals, the bettors mobbed him, stuffing dollars into his uniform as if he were a stripper exiting the runway. By the time he reached the clubhouse he was $1,500 richer.

Gambling to a large extent drove the game, and it tended to create a take-no-prisoners atmosphere. Players changed teams as often as they changed their shirts, sometimes not of their own volition. Agapito Mayor, a pitcher who went by the unfortunate nickname Triple Feo (Thrice Ugly), was actually kidnapped early in his career. Mayor was supposedly an amateur, but he was making $300 a month pitching for Hershey when a police car pulled up at the ballpark one afternoon. Two men got out and pointed pistols at the pitcher.

"Get in the car!" the men shouted.

"*Señores*, I'm just a peasant playing baseball," pleaded Mayor.

"Get in the car!"

"I said to myself, 'Now I'm really fucked,' " said Mayor, a slight, distinguished-looking man, recounting the incident in the dining room of his Tampa home. The two men handcuffed Mayor in his uniform and drove him to Havana, finally pulling up at a social club called Fortuna. He was led into an office, where behind a table sat the club's "athletic director" and the secretary of amateur baseball. " 'Listen, Mayor,' they told me, 'you're not playing for Hershey anymore, you're playing for Fortuna.' I said, 'But they already paid me three hundred dollars.' They said, 'No, no, just take the three hundred back to Hershey and come back here.' I told them, 'But Hershey is also paying my brother.' They said, 'Don't worry, your brother can play tomorrow with Marianao.' I said, 'Well, okay.' "

Mayor later signed on to play for Almendares with Adolfo "Dolf" Luque, known as "the Havana Perfecto" and "the Pride of Havana" (after the cigars). In many ways, Luque defined the freewheeling Cuban game. He was five-foot-seven and mean, a noted headhunter at a time when the beanball wasn't the cause of a near riot. He won 194 games with the Reds, Dodgers and Giants between 1918 and 1935. He was white, but coming out of Cuba he endured the racial taunting of the era. In 1923, Luque led the National League with 27 wins and a 1.93 ERA. His curveball was a backbreaker. But the most famous story of his career involves a racial slur. While pitching for the Reds one afternoon, Luque tore off the mound and launched himself into the New York Giants' dugout after someone called him a "Cuban nigger." No one is certain who was responsible for the epithet, but Luque ended up punching outfielder Casey Stengel in the face.

When Luque came back to Cuba to manage after his career, he was packing more than just a surly disposition. Luque carried a .38-caliber revolver, and not just for show. On one occasion, he went to pull pitcher Ted "Double Duty" Radcliffe, a Negro League star. An argument ensued between the pitcher and the manager, and it spilled into the clubhouse. Rodolfo Fernández, who had relieved Radcliffe, walked in to see Luque, still in uniform, pointing his gun at his starting pitcher. "If I hadn't been there, there could have been a death,"

Fernández told Sánchez during an interview in his apartment in upper Manhattan. "He fired a shot at the man! I grabbed Luque by the arm and he just missed him. The bullet went right through his baggy pants." The next day, Fernández ran into Radcliffe near the stadium. "He was going to pick up his things," said Fernández. Incredibly, Luque tried to convince the pitcher to stay—without success.

Tommy Lasorda also played for Luque and called him "the worst human being I have ever known." One night, Luque was trying to persuade a pitcher named Terry McDuffie to work on two days' rest. McDuffie refused and finally announced that he was packing his bags. "Less than a minute later, Luque came back carrying a pistol with a barrel that looked approximately a quarter-mile long," Lasorda wrote in his autobiography, *The Artful Dodger*. Luque put the gun to McDuffie's head. "You're pitching tonight," he announced. McDuffie eagerly concurred: "Gimme the ball," he said. "I'm ready to go."

For all its apparent lawlessness, its rough-and-tumble, Cuba was a dream getaway for the American players. This was long before free agency, a time when many major-leaguers took jobs during the off-season to make ends meet. Cuba was a pleasant place to pick up some extra cash. It was like a working vacation in Las Vegas, only instead of cactus and the prime rib specials, you had the beach and the women and the finest cigars in the world. In 1951, Don Zimmer, then an infielder in the Dodgers' farm system, was sitting at home in Cincinnati with his wife, Jean, when he got a call from Al Campanis, the Dodger scouting director. "It was fifteen degrees above zero with about four feet of snow on the ground," Zimmer recalled. "Campanis says to me, 'You want to go to Havana, Cuba, and play for the rest of the winter?' I say, 'Are you kidding me?' He says, 'How soon can you get there?' I say, '*Tomorrow.*' "

Zimmer, arriving from Ohio via Miami, took over at shortstop the following night for Cienfuegos, which had a working agreement with the Dodgers. He made $500 a month, and another $500 under the table. He recalls less about the games than he does about the lifestyle. Jean brought over the family Ford on the overnight ferry from Miami. The team set up the recently married couple at Club Nautico, a group of luxury apartments on a beach with sand the consistency of powdered sugar. The team played just three times a week, always in the same packed stadium, and, better yet, there was never any travel. "We lived right on the water," said Zimmer, smiling at the memory in the Yankee dugout one afternoon. "When we'd get up in the morning, the salt would be on our car. We had a maid—something that I never really believed in—but for just a dollar a day she would come in and clean for you. It was just a great, great place. I've been to Puerto Rico. I've been to the Dominican Republic. I've been to all the winter leagues. But there was nothing like Cuba. It was a *resort*."

For the Cuban ballplayers, particularly blacks, it was an entirely different story, of course. Luis Tiant, the Red Sox star, grew up in Havana as the son of one of the finest pitchers the island has produced: a lefty also named Luis Tiant. The son went on to win 229 games in the majors, only to have people tell him: "You're good, but your father was better." But the elder Tiant came up before Robinson broke the color barrier. He made so little playing in Cuba— 50 cents a game, at one point, a buck for a doubleheader—he tried to persuade his son to give up the sport. Tiant said his mother saved his career: "She said, 'Hey, leave him alone, if he wants to play, let him play.' "

Tiant's first baseball was a rounded piece of cork with nails hammered into it, the entire sphere then covered with tape. He fashioned his first glove out of a cigarette carton. "One time a friend of mine—he's dead now—one time I hit him in the back with one of those nail balls," said Tiant. "About forty-five minutes before, we had been eating bananas behind his house, and then we went to play. I hit him in the back with that nail ball and he started to puke. That's the way we played when I was growing up." Tiant was so skeptical about his future as a ballplayer that he studied for a year to be a mechanic. He reasoned that he had a lot working against him: "I'm black and I'm Hispanic: I'm fucked both ways." His color prevented him from even setting foot inside Club Nautico, where Zimmer and his wife had spent their Havana winter. But Tiant clung to the dream. "That was your only chance to be somebody," he said. "You don't give a shit how much money you're making, you just want to get out."

The Indians offered Tiant $150 to pitch for Mexico City, which had a working agreement with the Tribe. I noted that $150 wasn't much of a signing bonus. "Bonus? Are you kidding me, what fucking bonus?" railed Tiant. "I had to live on that shit. I used that hundred and fifty dollars to pay for the hotel, for the food, to send money to my mom and dad. If I had something left, I used it to buy a cigar." In 1962, the Indians sent Tiant to pitch for their minor-league team in Charleston, South Carolina. In Cuba, Tiant had lived with segregation, but he was stunned with the racism he encountered in the States. "It was worse," he said. "Most of what you saw in Cuba at that time, it was more of a society thing. You had rich people, and they had their clubs and all that bullshit. But the regular people, we lived together, white and black. I didn't have any problem. When I got here, forget it. It don't make no fucking difference whether you are high class or low class, you go *back*! You go back to where you fucking belong and don't come in here, don't eat here. You can't go to any bar.

You can't go to any club. It makes you feel like you're not human. When the other blacks would come in with the other teams, the fans ate their asses *alive:* It was, 'Nigger, go back to the jungle, go back to Africa, you don't belong here, monkey,' all kinds of shit. And you couldn't do shit about it, either. You go over there to fight, they *kill* your ass."

Not long after he was in the States, Tiant received a message from his father: Don't bother coming home. The Tiants had been among the thousands of working-class poor who had flooded the streets of Havana on January 1, 1959, when Castro came to power. Tiant himself had been there, awaiting Fidel's triumphant arrival. "We were all shouting, 'Castro's coming! Batista's gone!' We were thinking that it was going to get better." But things were changing fast. In 1961, the year that Castro announced his conversion to Marxism-Leninism, the government also declared the end of professional baseball in Cuba. Players would no longer be bartered like merchandise. The entire sports system would be taken over by a National Institute of Sports, Education and Recreation (INDER). The new system would be modeled after one that had turned the Soviet Union into a powerhouse in international "amateur" competition. Children would be screened for their athletic potential, then groomed in special schools for the day when they would demonstrate the superiority of socialism to the rest of the world. Baseball, the national sport, would be no different. The players would not go on to serve the major leagues or entertain Americans. Rather, they would stay in their own country to entertain their own people—admission would be free—and the very best of them would venture forth to demonstrate the fallacy that baseball was the American game.

Tiant never went back. He didn't see his father again until the old man came to Boston for the 1975 World Series. When I met with him, Tiant's distinguished career in baseball was winding down in Savannah, Georgia, of all places, where he was head coach at the Savannah College of Art and Design, a Division 3 school better known for churning out historical preservationists and graphic artists. Tiant, nearly sixty, liked the job. He enjoyed teaching baseball, and the weather allowed him to play golf year-round. But the players, with their cars and their inflated egos and their limited work ethic, bewildered him. "They think everything is coming from the sky," he said. "Nothing comes from the sky." Some even complained about him swearing in the dugout.

One chilly spring morning Tiant sat by an empty ballfield, puffing on a Dominican cigar the size of a small branch. His famous Fu Manchu mustache had turned white, as if covered by frost, and he wore a black-and-yellow baseball cap with the school mascot, an agitated bumblebee. "I'm not really a politics person," he said. "I don't care about all that bullshit. I never really cared too much about politics at all. But I never went back, and I don't even know if I can go back. It's just hard. I lost seventeen years of my life with my father. People don't understand. Only Cubans can understand."

ARNALDO HERNÁNDEZ, the original El Duque, wanted to do the interview at the Hotel Las Tunas, a hulking monument to socialism that looked as if it had been transplanted from Kazakhstan. He brought along Marlon, who turned out to be all of fifteen (El Duque settled on the name Marlon after reading an item about Marlon Brando in *Juventud Rebelde*). We decided to sit by the pool, and moved a white plastic table into the only sliver of shade to be found. It was broiling. As we were settling in, El Duque said: "You are going to find that I am a very complicated man." The bar wasn't open yet, but he persuaded a waitress to bring him a double shot of rum. The drink arrived neat in a clear plastic cup. It was 9:43 A.M.

El Duque opened by saying that he was one of thirty-three children. His father, Virgilio Hernández, was a lieutenant in the Batista army, the head of a military base in the city of Sancti Spíritus. Young Arnaldo was shuttled between the two sides of his family, spending much of his time with his grandmother and his uncles, who owned gaming houses in Remedio, a sugar-mill town in Villa Clara. Arnaldo had at first wanted to be a basketball player, but that changed on October 8, 1956. He was eleven. With dozens of others he came up with a dime to watch Game 5 of the World Series between the Yankees and Dodgers on "the town TV." It turned out to be the day that Don Larsen hurled the only no-hitter in Series history, a perfect game. "You could feel the silence at Yankee Stadium through the television," El Duque said. "Back then, the Yankees had no blacks. They had one *mulato*, a light-skinned right fielder. I said to myself, '*Coño*, I'll have to paint myself white to play for the Yankees.' But that was always my dream. Larsen was my idol, and he inspired me to go forward in baseball. Today I have a *son* playing for the New York Yankees. Can you imagine?"

He motioned to Marlon, who was sipping a Coke. "And Marlon will be even greater," he predicted. "If there is a team bigger than the New York Yankees, and I doubt there is, then Marlon will play on that team."

By the time Arnaldo Hernández was Marlon's age, he was playing shortstop for a beer company, La Cristal, and subsisting, he said, on fifteen Pepsis a day. He then moved to the province of Matanzas to play in the Liga Pedro

Betancourt, an integrated circuit created as a response to the racism of the Ama-teur League. With the major leagues now beginning to integrate, the Liga Pedro Betancourt became a feeder system for clubs on the lookout for nonwhite tal-ent. Tony Pérez played there, as did Tony Taylor, a versatile infielder who amassed 2,007 hits, mostly with the Phillies. El Duque played for Pasta Gravy, a toothpaste company. He was fifteen years old and wore number 26. It was then that he picked up the nickname that, like his number, he would pass on to his sons. Then, as today, nearly every Cuban had a nickname. They ranged from Manuel "Cocaína" García, a pitcher with an uncanny ability to anes-thetize hitters, to the slugger Roberto "El Tarzan" Estalella. As El Duque tells it, one of his first coaches, Chico Fuentes, first tried to call him El Conde (the Count). "I was a *campesino,* and whenever anyone asked for me for anything, I'd say, 'Take it,' " he recalled. " 'Toothpaste? Take it. You need some deodorant? Take it. A piece of ham, eat it.' So one day Chico Fuentes said, 'What a noble young man,' and the first name he gave me was El Conde. But it didn't sound right: El Conde Hernández. So then he decided to call me El Duque. He said, 'You are now El Duque Hernández.' I think it also came from Duke Snider. And from then on my real name disappeared.

"I was a rookie with aspirations to turn pro," said El Duque. His ultimate goal was to play for the Sugar Kings, then vault into the majors. But the Cuban revolution interceded. After Castro came to power, El Duque's father was ar-rested and put on trial for his involvement with Batista. "They gave him ninety-something years," said El Duque. "He died in prison in Cienfuegos in 1973. I visited him every week to take him food." The revolution also began to redefine the national sport. Fidel threw out the first ball at the Sugar Kings opener in 1960, but change was already in the air. The freighter *La Coubre* blew up in the Havana port that March, killing eighty-one, the Soviets had begun to establish diplomatic and economic ties with Castro, and although no one knew it yet, the CIA was formulating plans for the Bay of Pigs the following year. It wasn't until January 14, 1962, that Castro made his famous comment while kicking off the reconfigured Cuban League: "This is a triumph of free baseball over slave baseball." But the International League saw the writing on the wall and moved the Sugar Kings to Jersey City in the middle of a road trip during the 1960 season. El Duque said he was all but oblivious to politics—he was only fourteen, after all, when the revolution occurred—but he found himself a bud-ding young baseball star in the middle of a transformation well beyond his comprehension. It was a transition to socialism that, among other things, could not accommodate his major-league dreams. The door was slamming shut without him even knowing it.

Instead of signing with the Yankees, he was invited to play for the Havana Psychiatric Hospital. Before the revolution, the hospital, which sprawls across several acres of southwest Havana, had been a notorious insane asylum called the Cuban Hospital for the Demented. It suffered some of the worst abuses of the Batista dictatorship. When Castro's rebels threw open the doors, they found thousands of patients roaming the halls in a kind of medieval hell. There were few beds. Some patients were sleeping in their own feces. Others were half starved. Castro put the entire complex under Eduardo B. Ordáz, a decorated *comandante*, a physician-guerrilla who had supervised the construction of field hospitals in the Sierra Maestra. Under Ordáz, the hospital was to become a symbol of the revolution's enlightened health care system. The number of patients was cut in half, and the staff and facilities were dramatically improved. But the hospital still had its sinister side: In the 1980s, political dissidents began to come forward with grim stories of electroshock therapy, involuntary psychotropic drug treatments and confinement alongside the truly, dangerously ill. The dissidents said they had been detained in the hospital's Carbo-Servia ward, where a short, paunchy man known to inmates as El Enfermero (the Nurse) administered a daily cocktail of unspeakable torment.

Amaro Gómez Boix, an opposition journalist, told interviewers that he was detained in the ward after being arrested with ten unpublished manuscripts and a copy of Aleksandr Solzhenitsyn's *The Gulag Archipelago*. Gómez described the therapy meted out by the Nurse, later identified as Heriberto Mederos: "Almost every day, his various assistants call out loudly the names of the unfortunate chosen who will be asked to lie down on the wet cement so that the electrical current will travel better. Mederos then fastens the electrodes and the entire process is performed routinely, which often entails overlooking the placement of a rubber bit in the prisoner's mouth. It is no surprise then that when that first jolt of power zaps the prisoner's body, his teeth grind down on his tongue, turning his mouth into a bloodied foam."

The Miami Herald caught up with Mederos in 1992 working at, of all places, a convalescent home in Hialeah. He was sixty-nine. He recognized many of his accusers and admitted that he had administered the electroshock treatments on the bare floor, often without anesthesia, but—no surprise here—he said he was merely following orders. "In Cuba it's normal not to give anesthesia," he explained. "Besides, when the shock is applied, the person loses control of his bladder and bowels. We didn't have the facilities to do it any better. That's why it was done on the floor."

Ordáz's full name was Eduardo Bernabe Ordáz Ducúnge. He was a flamboyant man who came out of the Sierra wearing a cowboy hat and a beard and kept both for the next forty years. His two great passions were music and base-ball, and he sought to include both in the hospital's rehabilitation program. One of his first moves was to form a symphonic orchestra whose exclusive engagement would be to provide music for the patients. The orchestra, which grew to 115 players, played Wagner and Beethoven, war marches and show tunes. The American journalist David Abel caught one of the twice-weekly performances during the summer of 1998, the fourth decade of the orchestra's surreal run. He found the aging musicians playing the "Spanish Military March" to an audience of four gardeners. "Beneath a specially built portico whose sallow paint has seen brighter days, the half-absent orchestra churns out tinny tunes on old, dented instruments and follows brittle handwritten music sheets," Abel wrote. "Some players doze off during the three-hour performance's frequent intermissions."

The sports component of the rehabilitation program appears to have been more successful—if not for the patients, at least for the players. Ordáz built an outdoor track and a baseball stadium that resembled a well-tended minor-league park. On the outfield fence, where the advertisements for Red Lobster and the local Elks Club would go, he placed a slogan: SPORT IS A FACTOR IN MENTAL REHABILITATION. He recruited some of the best players in the country. El Duque didn't do anything except play ball. It was at the Havana Psychiatric Hospital that he learned to pitch, and where he met his first wife, María Julia, who was working at the hospital as a lab technician. Almost all of María Julia's family had worked at the hospital at one time or another. Her grandfather was a cook in the 1930s. Her mother was a nurse as were several uncles and cousins. Her son Arnaldo would learn how to cut hair there. Her son Gerardo would work as a carpenter. And her son Orlando would work as a rehabilitation therapist for 207 pesos a month after Fidel Castro banned him from baseball for life in 1996.

El Duque and María Julia met on the bus on the way to a ball game. "There was a bus that left from the hospital for the stadium," she said. "I saw this man with a little caramel-colored hat and a gold tooth and I asked who he was. They said, 'That's El Duque. He's come here to play baseball.' He got my attention. We became friends. We fell in love. Before you know it we were married and we had two sons." The marriage didn't last long, though. El Duque played around. He drank. The provincial league serves as a kind of minor-league system for the National Series, and El Duque moved up. By then, Arnaldo and Orlando rarely saw their father. He was everywhere and he was nowhere. But when he played downtown at Estadio Latinoamericano, María Julia invariably would gather up the boys. Her marriage was over, her husband was gone, but she figured that it was still important that they see their father play. So she dragged them down to the bus stop in Wajay—Arnaldo strapped to one hip, Orlando to the other—and waited to make the hour-long journey into downtown Havana to see her ex-husband, the absent father of her two boys, play baseball.

"Marriage is one thing," she told Sánchez and me years later. "Baseball is another."

It was now around noon at the Hotel Las Tunas. El Duque was saying that he played seventeen seasons in the National Series. Cuba's official baseball guide shows that he played nine. It shows that he compiled a 26–24 record with a 2.52 ERA as a pitcher. As a hitter, he batted .238 with 6 homers in 1,087 at-bats. By all accounts, those numbers do not nearly reflect his ability. Pedro Chávez, a postrevolutionary star, hit off El Duque dozens of times. "He had a tremendous curveball," he said. "And if he didn't beat you with his arm he beat you with his bat." The statistics probably do reflect the way El Duque squandered his talent. As he grew older, he hit the bottle more frequently. After his career ended, he drifted around the country, working at times as a pitching coach or an assistant. When he was around his son Orlando, who rarely drank, he would steal off for a nip, and Orlando would chase him down and chastise him. To friends and relatives, it was as if their roles were reversed. "Orlando was taking care of *him*," said Miñosito.

El Duque lit another Aroma, which smelled as if someone had pitched a tire into a burning fireplace. "Don't tell Orlando that I'm smoking," he said.

People were starting to gather around the pool, not guests but dozens of privileged Cubans with dollars sent by their families in the States or earned in the tourist sector or perhaps on the black market. The plastic cups kept coming. El Duque was slurring his words. He argued with the waitresses, hurled insults at the young women in their bathing suits and their makeup. He told me that Marlon was like my nephew now, that I would be his agent in the States when Marlon negotiated his contract with the major leagues. Marlon had gone off to take a swim, and when he got back we helped his father stand up, threw his arms around our shoulders and helped him across the deck of the pool under the bright, blistering sun, through the hotel and into a cab. El Duque wanted to stop at a friend's house along the way, but Marlon talked him out of it. By the time we got him home, the interview was clearly over for the day.

The subject of El Duque came up one day during an interview with Euclides Rojas, Cuba's all-time saves leader. Rojas left the island on a crowded boat in 1994 and drifted at sea for five days before the U.S. Coast Guard rescued him and his family. He once roomed with the younger El Duque and knew the father as well. He said matter-of-factly that there were a lot of men like El Duque in Cuba. "They were successful ballplayers once, but they didn't have the time to get an education and now they have nothing to do," he said. "They have no way of making a living. So they drink and they die."

CHAPTER THREE

SEÑOR PELOTERO
(MR. BASEBALL)

A COUPLE OF YEARS AFTER ARRIVING IN THE UNITED STATES, Orlando "El Duque" Hernández was limbering up with the rest of the Yankees one morning at Legends Field in Tampa. José Cardenal, then the club's first-base coach, was sitting in the dugout in his uniform, nursing a cup of coffee. Cardenal left Cuba after the revolution and went on to a solid, if itinerant, major-league career. He and El Duque had become close, and on this morning he began to heckle the pitcher. "Duque, you ingrate," Cardenal was yelling. "Everything you have you owe to Fidel. Fidel Castro *made* you! You're just another product of the revolution." El Duque chuckled, waved off the coach and went back to his morning exercises.

Cardenal was joking, of course, but back in Cuba it was taken as gospel by many of the Communist-party faithful that El Duque had turned his back on a system that had nurtured him almost since birth. And it wasn't just him. All the defectors had burned their makers, the coaches and trainers who had taught them everything they knew. One day, José Rodríguez, the baseball commissioner of Cuba's junior program, was doing an interview with Sánchez at a tournament in Caracas. The interview amounted to the usual defense of the revolution, Cuba's dominance in sports against all odds, when suddenly a consular officer burst into the conversation to weigh in on the defectors. "The state gave them everything!" he said. "This is the truth, the *absolute* truth. Make sure you write that down."

In the case of El Duque, at least, that truth was far from absolute. It could be argued, in fact, that he succeeded in spite of the dogmatic Cuban system. The story of the rejected athlete coming back to prove his coaches wrong is well embedded in sporting lore. Even Michael Jordan, as has been definitively documented, was cut from the varsity basketball team. But El Duque was rejected by an entire system. He was denied entrance into one of the "sports schools" where athlete-revolutionaries are groomed. Entrance into the system meant at least three hours a day of training under the finest coaches in the country and a balanced diet, no small thing as the economy began to collapse. It also meant a streamlined path to the national teams. It was not that an athlete couldn't make it without going through the sports schools, but the difference was like making it into Harvard from Taft High in the Bronx as opposed to Phillips Andover. "It's incredibly difficult," said Rolando Núñez, one of El Duque's first coaches, "because the path is already laid."

Cuba's revolutionary sports system was modeled after those in the Soviet Union and East Germany. Neither country knew much about baseball, of course, but the Cubans adopted the same organizational structures to mold their athletes. Cuba's sports authorities believed that by age nine a child should be channeled into one sport. If the child was found to be proficient enough, he or she would then practice that sport—and only that sport—at one of the Sports Initiation Schools (EIDEs). The child-athletes, thousands across the country, studied in the morning and trained in the afternoon; many lived in dorms, away from their parents the entire week. Coaches and trainers, including Soviet imports, were always in great abundance. "We do the same things they do in other countries," explained Miguel Borroto, technical director of Cuba's junior baseball team. "But in Cuba we're pushing physical education from the time of preschool. The children are developing their muscles early on. The teachers are professionals, trained in universities, who know how not to traumatize the muscle development of these children. When a child is fourteen, fifteen, he's already developed physically. He has had physical education every day from elementary to high school." The ultimate goal was to create superathletes who would vanquish those from the larger, more developed countries, thus demonstrating the superiority of Cuban socialism. "Our competition is with the rich and the powerful," Fidel has said. The athletes were expected to be nothing less than the embodiment of a new ideal. "Cuba's outstanding athletes are supposed to be examples for others to emulate," wrote Paula J. Pettavino and Geralyn Pye in their book *Sport in Cuba*. "They are expected not only to be a vanguard for the development of full human potential in physical culture, but also to be models of the 'New Man.' "

From the start, athletic achievement was a pillar of the revolution. The state's goals of encouraging mass participation in sports and developing world-class athletes were no different from its campaign to achieve 100 percent literacy or provide free health care for every citizen. "It is impossible to conceive of a revolutionary who is not an athlete as well," Castro has said. (It is worth noting at this point that Fidel, who stands about six-foot-two, was once a fine basketball player at Colegio Belén, a Catholic high school, and possibly a baseball player at the University of Havana. But he was never, as many have suggested, a major-league prospect. The myth of his prowess—his tryout with the Senators, his funky windup and his dancing curve—has been all but demolished by such writers as González Echevarría and S. L. Price. Fidel's main contributions to Cuban baseball have been to preside over the remaking of the sport and the suspensions of some of its top players. In that regard, he is like a Cuban version of Judge Kenesaw Mountain Landis, the game's first dictator.)

EL DUQUE TRIED OUT for the EIDE when he was eleven. He recalled little about the experience except that he was rejected out of hand. "They told me I had no quality," he said. "I don't know why. There was a tryout and I came in first and second in all the tests. I guess it was because of my size. I grew after the age of thirteen. I was pretty short back then."

The rejection did nothing to quell his hunger for the sport, or his self-confidence. His father was long gone, but most everyone else in the family also played at one time or another. His uncle Miñosito was a scrappy infielder with Constructores, one of the teams in the newly configured Cuban league, now known as the National Series. Unlike El Duque's father, Miñosito was around most of the time, and was only too willing to play ball with the boys. "Really my uncle taught me the game," said El Duque. His great-uncle Gonzalo was a second baseman turned umpire. Another great-uncle, Ocilio, was a power-hitting first baseman. El Duque's mother was a huge fan who had once played softball. The game was all around him; playing it was as much a part of life as eating and breathing.

El Duque grew up in Rancho Boyeros, a district of Havana particularly fertile when it comes to producing ballplayers. As long as anyone can remember, there have been such places, odd geographic talent pools where people go around saying, "It must be the water." San Pedro de Macorís, a nondescript seaport in the Dominican Republic, produced Sammy Sosa, Julio Franco, Tony Fernández, Alfredo Griffin, Rafael Santana, Rafael Ramírez and Manny Lee, churning out so many infielders that it became known around the majors as "Shortstop City." Western Hills High, on the west side of Cincinnati, produced

Pete Rose, Clyde Vollmer, Eddie Brinkman and no fewer than four players who went on to become major-league managers: Rose, Don Zimmer, Jim Frey and Russ Nixon. Rancho Boyeros was such a place. Players seemed to spring from the earth. The district, a cluster of towns encircling the Havana airport, produced Pedro Chávez, a two-time batting champion; Agustín Marquetti, who played twenty-two seasons in the National Series; a legendary slugger named Armando Capiró; Juan Padilla, a second baseman on the national team; and no fewer than five players who have defected and signed contracts with major-league clubs.

If you dig deep enough in these places, you often find one coach who has sparked greatness in seemingly untalented players. In Cincinnati, it was a high school coach named Paul Nohr. In Boyeros, for years it was Rolando Núñez, a small, gentle man universally known as Chavito (Little Chávez), a nickname he acquired as the nephew of postrevolutionary star Pedro Chávez. Chavito worshiped his uncle but had nowhere near his ability. He caught for a few years, then turned to his life's work: teaching children to play baseball. This he did most days, heading out in the morning with a glove, a bat and a cheese sandwich stuffed in his pocket. The government was always trying to persuade Chavito to take over baseball instruction at the local EIDE. The move would have meant a promotion, a raise and good standing with the omnipotent party, but it wasn't his style. His preferred domain was Estadio la Catalina, the sunbleached, overgrown field in Santiago de las Vegas, just down the road from Wajay. In Cuba, players are divided into six age groups: seven to eight, nine to ten and so on. Chavito routinely presided over all six, shuffling the teams on and off the field all day long. It was all very chaotic and much different from the EIDE with its coaches, its proper diets and its sports psychologists. But Chavito loved it; he loved developing players who had been passed over by the system. One of his favorite pupils was an eight-year-old boy named Lázaro Vichot, who showed up at one of his tryouts one day even though he was born with only two fingers on each hand. "My mother had told me, 'Don't go, they won't take you the way you are,' " Vichot, now a grown man, told me after demonstrating his wicked curve in front of his house one afternoon. "I went out to the tryout, and when it was my turn Rolando Núñez took one look at me and he just chuckled. He said, 'Is your arm warm?' "

"Chavito's greatness was his ability to teach," said Juan Angulo, another coach from the district. "It seemed like any child he touched from the age of nine turned into a tremendous ballplayer."

Chavito had grown up in Boyeros when American baseball was still legal and thriving. He idolized two players: his uncle Pedro and Mickey Mantle. He absorbed the game with a child's intensity. In 1958, desperate to watch the World Series between the Milwaukee Braves and his beloved Yankees, he held a hot compress under his arm to fake his mother into believing that he had a fever. His mother bought the ruse (with a nod and a wink, no doubt), and Chavito watched at home in the town of Santiago de las Vegas, district of Boyeros, city of Havana, as Mantle and the Bronx Bombers came back against Warren Spahn and Lew Burdette to win it all. It was three months before Fidel Castro came to power. It was inconceivable that life would ever be any different.

By the time Mantle died, on August 13, 1995, the World Series and all news about the major leagues had long been banned in Cuba. Chavito, who had been a baseball coach for some twenty-five years, happened to be in Italy. The government had essentially rented him out, getting him a coaching job with the Italian baseball federation but pocketing 80 percent of his pay. Chavito read the news about his idol in one of the Italian papers and found himself sitting in a sidewalk café, crying away the morning. He then went back to his room and poured out his sorrow in a poem that ran 240 lines over five full pages. The poem, "Decimas a Mickey Mantle," loses some of its rhythm in the translation but none of its sentiment:

> *You transcended borders*
> *And although you didn't notice*
> *You left us with beautiful memories*
> *But do not think because of that*
> *That no one is suffering*
> *Because I want to say to you*
> *That today baseball fans*
> *Wherever they may be*
> *Weep because you're gone*

PEDRO CHÁVEZ POINTED the way to Chavito's house. It was a Saturday afternoon, and Chávez, a major *figura* of recent Cuban lore, was umpiring first base in a pickup game. It was like stumbling upon Willie Stargell at a public park in Pittsburgh. Chávez, at sixty-three, wore old gray sweats and a T-shirt. The game was taking place on a vacant lot that had been converted into a ball field. It was one of those scenes that define Cuba's passion for the sport. Dozens of young men ringed the field holding limp baseball gloves and scuffed-up balls, waiting for their turn to play. Two boys no older than ten were playing pepper. One was using a two-by-four as a bat. The other was pitching rocks culled from the rubble of a crumbling building.

Chavito's house sat behind a low chain-link fence, nearly indistinguishable from others around it. A diminutive man with black hair and a broad, open face, Chavito came to the door wearing a Chicago Bulls T-shirt and red track sweats. He said he had just come back from baseball practice. His living room was sparsely furnished: a thirteen-inch color television, a VCR, a plaque that he had received for his work in Italy and little else.

Chavito mostly wanted to talk about Mantle, but the conversation eventually came around to his most famous pupil: Orlando "El Duque" Hernández. "I can tell you that El Duque is just a case of incredible perseverance," he began. "As a boy, he did not distinguish himself as a ballplayer. It was just his perseverance that won out in the end—his dedication." El Duque was a good player among many good players, Chavito said. He made the provincial league all-star team a few years but never advanced beyond that. He was small. He had a curveball that was occasionally startling, and he threw it with deadly accuracy. But what made him stand out was his resolve, his conditioning, how he never seemed to quit even though the system had already rejected him. "He was in love with the game, it's as simple as that," he said. "He loved the game with everything he had. He trained more than any player I've ever seen. He ran for miles and miles and miles and miles. I really can't take credit for what he's done. He did it by himself. He simply worked harder than anybody else. He's like Nolan Ryan—how he invented his own training program. It wasn't a secret; everyone in Boyeros saw him running. And that developed his legs. It's like when they asked Warren Spahn when he planned to retire, and he said, 'I'll retire when my legs retire.' El Duque knew he needed his legs to pitch."

One of the main differences between Cuba and the United States is that youngsters simply play more. A common lament among American scouts is that young players grow up distracted—distracted by other sports like soccer and basketball, by television, by Nintendo, by the various and sundry diversions of the richest nation in the world. In Cuba (and the Dominican Republic and Venezuela among others), few such diversions exist, and so El Duque was able to find a constant outlet for his passion. There were games all the time—in the street with his brother, at the fields in Wajay and Santiago. Chavito and the other coaches recognized his drive and encouraged him. Chavito, above all, stressed fundamentals. He pounded them into his players. He told his pitchers:

Throw strikes, don't pitch from behind, *think* on the mound, *know* what you want to do, *concentrate*. By the time El Duque was fourteen, he seemed to have absorbed it all and then some. "His tactical thinking by the age of thirteen, fourteen, was incredible," said Juan Angulo. "He was just extremely intelligent. And he was never content. He would pitch and win, and then he would run around the field in Wajay twenty-five times. I'd tell him to take a rest and he would just say, 'No.' Where it all came from, I don't know. There were no other boys like him. The coordination of his pitches, the location, was nearly perfect. He had a tremendous curve and an acceptable fastball. But most of all, a thirteen-, fourteen-year-old who concentrated like Orlando, who had the power to concentrate like this boy, I never saw that in my twenty-five years as a coach."

El Duque had developed enough by the time he was sixteen to be accepted into the Higher Institute of Athletic Perfection (ESPA), a kind of high school for athletes the level above the EIDE. Now he was on track. From there he was drafted into the army—not to fight but to play. The army's various divisions were fielding their own teams in the provincial league. Recruiting was competitive. El Duque never fired a gun, but the army allowed him to train harder than ever. He also ate better. Chavito lost track of his prize pupil for a time, but when El Duque came back from the army his old coach was stunned. "It stopped me cold," said Chavito. "He looked like a different person. He was bigger, and now he really knew how to pitch." El Duque pitched for the Ejército Occidental, the Western Army. Pedro Chávez, who was then managing Industriales, spotted him and brought him to play for the hometown team, "the Blues," as they are often called because of the color of their uniforms.

El Duque made his debut in 1986 against Pinar del Río, a powerhouse from the western side of the island. Even now, the game remains part of Cuban baseball lore. El Duque would pitch ten years in Cuba. He would win two National Series titles and an Olympic gold medal. He would eventually become the most successful pitcher in the history of revolutionary baseball. And yet none of his performances would be recalled as vividly as his dramatic debut. It was the seventh inning when El Duque entered the game. The score was tied and the bases were loaded. Pedro Chávez decided the timing was perfect to bring in the untested rookie, for the next batter was Luis Giraldo Casanova.

Casanova was already a legend, a certain major-leaguer had he grown up outside the hermetic isolation of the era. Six feet tall and solid as a boulder, he hit 312 homers with 1,069 RBIs and had a .322 average over seventeen seasons. Bobby Salamanca, the play-by-play man, called him Señor Pelotero (Mr. Baseball). When Casanova strode to the plate from the on-deck circle, Salamanca would announce: "Here comes Mr. Baseball. After *you*, Your Majesty." The old saying about the pure hitter is "He could get a hit falling out of bed." Casanova's reputation extended further. "Casanova would come to the stadium drunk; he'd be completely lost and he'd still get his two singles and a pair of homers," said René Arocha, a former Industriales hurler who defected in 1991. "One day our catcher saw Casanova coming up to the plate. He was plastered. He was mumbling. The catcher called time-out, walked out to the mound and told our pitcher, Iván Alvarez, 'Look, he's gone, just put it right in there.' He threw a fastball right down the middle and Casanova hit it five hundred feet. Iván came back to the dugout and said, 'Too bad he was drunk. If he was sober I would have hopped on the ball and rode it back to Havana.'

"Oh, man, he played with such ease, Señor Pelotero," said Arocha. "He played in sneakers; he didn't play in spikes. He played left, center, right, first, catcher. Wherever you put him, he had an arm. I don't like to make comparisons, but I've seen video of Roberto Clemente. That reminds me of Casanova: his style, his demeanor, his incredible bat speed. He never hit a homer off me. But he would come up and say, 'Kid, the day I get one off you it's going a *long* way.' "

El Duque peered in for the sign. "The catcher called for a curve two or three times and I said, 'No, no, no,' " recalled El Duque. "I wanted the fastball." He uncorked the first pitch of his career. This was still the age of aluminum in Cuba, and the sound of Señor Pelotero's bat meeting El Duque's fastball, that sickening *ping* that aluminum bats make, ripped through El Latino. Long home runs are like caught fish: they always seem to grow in the retelling. But the consensus is that Casanova's grand slam off El Duque traveled a good 475 feet and was still rising when it carried the left center field wall. It landed deep in the bleachers in front of an immense work of party propaganda.

El Duque was devastated. "I left there so frustrated," he said. "I kept telling myself that I was worthless, that I was shit. I kept saying, 'I can't do it.' " Euclides Rojas, Cuba's all-time saves leader, had been warming up alongside El Duque when Chávez made the call to go with the rookie. "Afterward, El Duque was saying to me, 'I wasn't ready to pitch to him,' " recalled Rojas. "He was saying, 'You were the one who was supposed to be in there.' He kept telling me he wasn't ready."

El Duque was still sulking when he got home. The game had been televised and he feared that his career had been irreparably damaged. "He kept telling me that he was shit, that he was a nobody," said his friend, Mario Cobo, aka Onion. "I said to him, 'Listen, what are you talking about? That's baseball. Who do you think you are?' "

No one took more heat than Pedro Chávez, who had trotted out an untested rookie against a legend. Debate about the move raged all over town; it was the number one topic on the radio, with many fans suggesting that the manager had probably ruined the poor kid. Chávez finally lashed out in an interview: "Just wait," he said, "this guy's going to win so many games you'll be sick of him by the time he's done."

Years later Chávez told me, "I just wanted to test him. You knew he had the talent. But after that he lost all fear. He was afraid of nothing."

Chávez brought in El Duque again the following night with the bases loaded. He nearly gave up another grand slam to the first hitter, but the ball died at the warning track as a sacrifice fly. He struck out the second hitter and began to gather his confidence. He ended up pitching well, then came back and beat Matanzas in relief. By the end of the season, he was pitching well enough to make the Selectiva, a kind of second season featuring all-stars from each province.

Years later, El Duque sat in his backyard in Miami and reminisced about his inauspicious debut. "What a time, what a time," he repeated, over and over, laughing at the memory.

"That moment made me a pitcher," said El Duque. "It taught me to respect *los grandes* [the great ones]. I thought I was tough, valiant. It was the bravado of youth."

"I've had an opportunity to play for the two greatest teams in the world," said El Duque. "When I play for the Yankees, I'm still part of Industriales of the capital. Not only Industriales but all of Cuba."

For good reason, the Industriales were known as the Yankees of Cuban baseball. When the club traveled to the provinces, it was an event not unlike the Yankees venturing into Minneapolis or Kansas City. The players were met with the same mix of awe and resentment. The Industriales were the men from Gotham, the titans from Havana, epicenter of the country. They were larger than life. Lázaro Valle, a converted catcher, threw nearly one hundred miles per hour. Germán Mesa, the slithery shortstop, was like an Olympic gymnast on the field. El Duque, with his cosmopolitan aura, his high-kicking style, his cap curled hard over his eyes, was part of the image. His pitches were mesmerizing, tantalizing, eminently hittable, and yet he never seemed to lose. "He had the prettiest windup in Cuban baseball," said Michel Contreras, the sports editor of *Juventud Rebelde,* one of the Communist-party papers. "He was the only one who wore his cap pulled over his eyes. He was the only one who wore his pant legs short and his socks high. He always covered his face when taking the sign." Cuba isn't the kind of place where you'll hear fans screaming: "Industriales suck!" When the club went out on the road for a particularly big game, it would often be greeted by the rhythmic chanting—singing, almost—of a packed stadium: "*¡Que venga, El Duque, te estamos esperando!*" (Hey, Duque, come and get it, we are waiting for *you!*)

Over time, Duque became recognized as one of the finest pitchers in the country, but it took a while. Just when he was emerging as a true star, his reputation suffered a terrific blow at the 1992 Barcelona Olympics. For Cuba, the stakes could not have been higher: no less than the country's place in the New World Order. The year before, Cuba had spent $100 million to stage the Pan American Games in Havana, fiddling away the summer while Moscow burned (the Games coincided with the failed August putsch against Mikhail Gorbachev). By the time the Olympics came around, the Soviet Union had been pronounced dead, and its disparate parts were competing as an odd consortium known as the Unified Team. In many ways, Barcelona was a celebration of capitalism's triumph. It was the year of the Dream Team, and the image of Michael Jordan, spokesman for the free market, loomed over Catalonia. In place of the Soviets, a new group of Olympic superpowers had emerged: the corporations and the shoe companies who were underwriting the whole thing. Nike rented out the top of an office tower and brought over a team larger than the teams of 129 of the 172 countries represented in the Olympics. Allegiances between shoe and country became blurred. I was covering the Games for the *Globe,* and at one point I asked Dan O'Brien, an American decathlete, if he felt more loyalty to Reebok or the United States of America. O'Brien paused, then offered his Solomonic response: "Dan O'Brien."

With this onslaught of corporatism, there emerged a wave of nostalgia for—who would have guessed it?—the Cold War. There was a yearning for the old-fashioned matchup of Good vs. Evil, Us vs. Them. As it turned out, one of the few venues where you could still find the Cold War was the old ballpark. The Barcelona Games were the first to include baseball as a medal sport. Cuba, having not lost a game in the previous five years of international competition, was the odds-on favorite. Anticipation mounted for the first confrontation with Cuba's archrivals, the country that invented the sport.

Orlando "El Duque" Hernández drew the starting assignment. In the United States, the game would quickly be forgotten. Even the best American players, whose number included Nomar Garciaparra and Charles Johnson, were unknowns at the time. Cuba, on the other hand, approached the game like a reenactment of the Bay of Pigs. There were rumors that Fidel might attend. He didn't, despite heavy preemptive security, but the stadium was filled with Cubans and not a few Spaniards who viewed the contest as an opportunity to repudiate expanding American imperialism. Long before the first pitch, the crowd was chanting: "*¡Cuba sí, Yanquis no! ¡Cuba sí, Yanquis no!*"

In this politically charged atmosphere, El Duque retired exactly one batter. He gave up a three-run homer to Michael Tucker, a Kansas City Royals first-round draft pick, and was still getting pounded when Chad McConnell drilled a single, making it 5–0. At that point, Cuban manager Jorge Fuentes pulled out a cigarette and lit up right in the dugout. Fuentes took a long drag, then, with one out in the first inning, went to his *closer,* Omar Ajete. Ajete threw 96 miles per hour and looked astonishingly like Vida Blue. He shut down the Americans the rest of the night. Cuba came back and won, 9–6, and eventually won the gold medal, but El Duque returned to Havana with his reputation severely damaged.

I was actually at that game, but I didn't remember that El Duque had pitched until the subject came up years later in Havana. It turned out that no one in Cuba had forgotten.

"I know it must sound crazy to you now, but people here really thought he couldn't win the big one after that," said a Cuban official who follows the game closely. Our conversation was taking place over wonton soup in Havana's renovated Chinatown. The Yankees had wrapped up their second straight World Series a few weeks earlier, and El Duque was now the ace of a staff that included Roger Clemens and David Cone. He was the stopper that the Yankees turned to in their most critical situations, when they absolutely, positively needed a win. "A lot of people thought he couldn't handle the pressure; some *still* believe that," the official said, rolling his eyes. "After that, they would send him out against Italy and Holland but never in the most important games."

In some Cuban circles, it is still possible to hear this Duque-as-choker theory. In 1999, during the Pan American Games in Winnipeg, Michel Contreras, the sports editor for *Juventud Rebelde,* tried to make just such a case. Contreras, a bohemian fellow with a tuft of hair protruding from his lower lip, said that El Duque spit the bit in Barcelona and never lived it down. "That was the only time he was handed such an important responsibility and they exploded all over him," he said dismissively. "After that he didn't want to pitch in the big game. He didn't want the ball."

El Duque had to work hard to rebuild his standing. He didn't waste time. The following season, Industriales traveled to Pinar del Río in the middle of the pennant race. The small city sits in the heart of Cuba's tobacco region, about 120 miles west of Havana. Its team, Vegueros (the Tobaccomen), was perennially strong and featured a third baseman, Omar Linares, who boasted the same nickname as Ted Williams ("the Kid") and was held in the same reverence by Cuban fans. Many believed that Linares was the best Cuban player of all time. He had Mike Schmidt power and a cannon for an arm but also hit for average: That year he batted .446, albeit with an aluminum bat over a short season. The Pinar-Industriales rivalry is perhaps the closest thing that Cuba has to the Red Sox and Yankees.

There were 15,000 fans packed into Capitán San Luis Stadium, which resembles a nice Triple-A park. The score was 3–3 in the eighth. The crowd was already buzzing when El Duque, in a rare relief appearance—he was used primarily as a starter after his rookie season—trotted in from the bullpen. He surveyed the entire stadium, settling his gaze finally on the Industriales dugout. Then he pointed to the mound and pounded his fist into his chest, as if to say, "This game is mine!" The crowd exploded. Some fans littered the field with cups and paper plates. Obscenities rained down. El Duque went on to pitch six scoreless innings, handcuffing Linares. Industriales won it in the fourteenth.

El Duque was entering his prime. Cuban baseball statistics, it should be noted, are thoroughly unreliable. Citing a lack of paper, the Sports Ministry didn't publish its annual baseball guide from the beginning of the Special Period in 1990 until 1998. With that caveat in mind, El Duque's record from 1992 to 1996 was an astonishing 41–8 with 7 shutouts and 27 complete games. "He was basically unhittable at that point," said the sports official. After years of tinkering with his unique delivery, he had now perfected it. It was a style he had developed incrementally. After Dwight Gooden's magical 1985 season, when Gooden went 24–4 with a 1.53 ERA and 268 strikeouts, El Duque managed to get his hands on a Mets video from a group of touring Japanese players. Such videos, obviously, were unattainable in Cuba and technically illegal; El Duque and his friends sat around watching Doc Gooden as if he were Sidd Finch, George Plimpton's mythical fireballer. Gooden became his favorite pitcher. He began to incorporate Gooden's leg kick into his own delivery. "He loved him," said Euclides Rojas, El Duque's former teammate. "We all used to call him Gooden. He'd be out there throwing and we'd be yelling, 'Gooden! Gooden!' "

The notion that El Duque might ever meet Dwight Gooden—much less play with him or against him—was a pipe dream back then, a fantasy as faint and remote as walking on the moon. In fact, El Duque, if pressed, would have said he was a Yankees fan. Growing up, it was the team that he had heard about from his uncle Miñosito, from his father, and from Rolando Núñez, all of whom remembered the days when the New York Yankees were held up as heroes on both sides of the Florida Straits. But now, the Yankees were from another world entirely. El Duque was a proud member of Industriales, of the gold-medal national baseball team. "I dreamed of being a Yankee, yes," he would later say. "I was always a fan of the Yankees. But it was a fleeting thing."

CHAPTER FOUR

INDEPENDENCE DAY

O N THE EVENING OF SEPTEMBER 28, 1990, FIDEL CASTRO stepped to the podium at the Karl Marx Theater in Havana. He wore, as usual, an olive-green uniform, symbol of a revolution in progress. The event was the thirtieth anniversary of the Committees for the Defense of the Revolution, neighborhood groups known for planting flowers, repairing sidewalks and, more notoriously, spying on behalf of the government. There were thousands of Committees for the Defense of the Revolution all over Cuba, and the hall was packed to hear Fidel celebrate three decades of revolutionary vigilance.

The speech had come at a pivotal time in human history. The Soviet Union, Cuba's economic and political *patrón,* was on the brink of disintegration. Inside Cuba, there had been little official news of the earthshaking developments sweeping across Eastern Europe. But a steady stream of information on Radio Bemba—the island's sprawling network of unfiltered gossip—had fed the growing concern, if not outright panic. Certainly, something dramatic was taking place. For months, all across Cuba the staples of daily life had been rapidly disappearing: gasoline, meat, cooking oil, electricity. All had been drastically cut back or were simply unavailable.

As the revolution entered its fourth decade, it was impossible to conceive of life without the Soviets. The relationship between the two Communist nations—one immense, the other tiny—went well beyond ideology or shared animosity toward the United States. Cuba's entire economy was based on trade with the Soviet Union and its allies. Every year, good or bad, Cuba exported the bulk of its sugar harvest to Eastern Europe. The Soviets, in turn, supplied Cuba with all the oil it needed. By the late 1980s, fully 86 percent of Cuba's commercial trade occurred with the socialist-bloc nations. And now, suddenly, Cuba's trading partners were not merely suffering, not merely enduring economic downturns or periods of upheaval. They were disappearing from the face of the earth.

"This is a truly historic date," Fidel began. "We commemorate it at a truly historic time. It is good that we meet here, that we do not invest a lot of resources, that we do not spend fuel, that we make our presence felt. . . ."

To read the speech now is to recall the wonder of recent history, a time when governments imploded with the swiftness of dynamited skyscrapers. No one seemed more surprised about these developments than Fidel. "All of a sudden," he said, "the socialist camp has disappeared. It is a euphemism to speak of a socialist camp now. Some of those countries with which we have established very close relations . . . have virtually disappeared. As a result, the country has lost those pillars represented by agreements with many of those countries from the socialist camp.

"The USSR, of all the pillars, was the strongest pillar of our economic and social development," said Fidel. Cubans, of course, knew this, but Fidel then began to explain, in astonishing detail, exactly what the Soviet collapse would mean to Cuba. Years of labor, billions of pesos and rubles, nuclear reactors, hospitals, an immense nickel-production plant—the entire infrastructure of Cuba's economy was rapidly going down the drain. "That is why we should be very familiar with things," he said, "very familiar with how things are."

Fidel tried to dispel the notion that the USSR had turned against its Caribbean brother: "Does the USSR or the government of the USSR want to hurt us like this? No. The USSR does not want to hurt us like this."

But he then warned of the coming darkness. He said the government had prepared a special contingency plan. The plan had been developed in case of war. But now it had been adapted "to face these problems I have mentioned, the problems that have occurred in Eastern Europe, the USSR.

"The concept of the Special Period in Time of Peace has emerged," said Fidel. "We are undoubtedly entering this Special Period in Time of Peace. It is inevitable that we will fall into this Special Period in all its harshness. We will have to undergo this trial. We must be prepared to work with less and less and less and less and almost with nothing."

He tried some gallows humor.

"Our plan includes the domestication of three thousand teams of oxen. Many of these are oxen that have been pardoned. We have told some of them:

'Gentlemen, you are not going to be part of our diet anymore. You are now going to work. You are now going to contribute to a Special Period in Time of Peace.' To avoid unnecessary sacrifices as long as we can, there is a national program to domesticate one hundred thousand bulls in six months.

"The manufacture of bicycles has also become a top priority," he continued. "We have purchased two hundred thousand. We are waiting to purchase an additional five hundred thousand, and we have given instructions to quickly purchase the equipment for five bicycle factories. . . . What do we want to do with these bicycles? We want to hand them out. . . . This is the era of the bicycle! We will not be the only ones. What is happening is terrible. [But] what will befall the Third World is much worse than that."

During this Special Period, Fidel warned, the country would need to be vigilant against cowards, against traitors, against "rats that want to abandon the ship of the revolution.

"We must confront them!" he said. "In difficult times, the worms will try to raise their heads. We must fight them and tell them: 'Worms, back to your holes! Worms, back to your garbage, and shut your mouth!' "

Lest anyone get any ideas, Fidel reminded the nation that there were 7.5 million rank-and-file members of the Committees for the Defense of the Revolution—*7.5 million!*—a spy on every corner. He ended the speech with his historic refrain: "*¡Socialismo o muerte! ¡Patria o muerte! ¡Venceremos!*"

Socialism or death! Fatherland or death! We will win!

The transcript indicates that people laughed at some of the more draconian solutions to the impending Soviet collapse. Oxen? Bicycles? Reality had not yet set in. The next day, *Granma*, the official Communist-party newspaper, published the entire speech, accompanied by a cartoon. The cartoon showed a construction worker, a housewife, a fist-shaking grandmother, a machete-wielding farmer and a Wonder Woman–like member of the Committees for the Defense of the Revolution. The group was chasing a four-legged worm back into the dark hole whence it came.

FOR ALL THE SCARCITY and base desperation created by the Special Period in Time of Peace, its biggest effect was to turn Cuba into a nation of hustlers. Julio Carranza, one of the island's brightest economists, estimated that between 1989 and 1993 the black market grew nearly tenfold. Vices that had been stifled for years by the State Security apparatus suddenly began to flourish in broad daylight. Prostitutes took over Havana's most prosperous thoroughfares, the sea-hugging Malecón and Fifth Avenue, legions of nubile hitchhikers decked out in colorful spandex body suits. Many were teenagers, children really, willing to exchange sex for toiletries or a decent meal.

But it wasn't just the prostitutes; most everyone in Cuba was suddenly on the make. The Special Period acquired its own culture, its own warped vocabulary. Two of the most commonly heard verbs in Cuba were *inventar* (to invent) and *resolver* (to resolve). The words were applied to activities as diverse as scrounging up a chicken for a holiday meal to replacing an automobile part with a coat hanger. There was still the state-controlled economy, with its worthless pesos and its ration booklets and the hopelessly barren shelves of the bodegas. But what mattered most was the informal economy, the black market, where virtually anything was available for U.S. dollars.

In this odd world of scrappers and scam artists, the members of Cuba's national baseball team were among the privileged. The players traveled frequently outside the country and were expert in the art of the deal. Once abroad, they hit the ground selling. To get their hands on precious dollars, the players sold any valuable piece of Cuba they could cart along with them: Cohiba cigars, Havana Club rum, a pill called PPG—the Cuban precursor to Viagra. They then turned around and snapped up everything that was forbidden and unavailable in their own country: VCRs, portable refrigerators, Tampax for their wives and girlfriends. Nothing was off-limits. Euclides Rojas, a reliever, sold the uniform off his back during a tournament in Italy. "It was some Italian guy; he wanted one of the white Cuba uniforms," he said. "We met in the lobby and I told him to come up to my room because we couldn't talk there. He offered me two hundred dollars for my uniform. Keep in mind that the state had given us a total of forty dollars to last the entire trip."

The transaction would be difficult because the Cubans were scheduled to play in the finals the following afternoon.

"Here, take the two hundred and give me the uniform after the game," the Italian proposed.

"Thank you very much, sir," responded Rojas, grabbing the cash.

"So I played that final game in a uniform that wasn't really mine," said Rojas. "We were playing the Americans for the title. That year they had [future major-leaguers] Robin Ventura at third, Dave Silvestri at short, Mickey Morandini at second, and Tino Martinez at first. Andy Benes started the game and we won by a run. I came in in relief. Then after the game I went back to the hotel. The Italian guy was sitting there waiting for me. I told him, 'Here, thanks for lending me your uniform. It's yours.' "

It was all a matter of survival, and so what the players couldn't buy, they stole. "We stole anything and everything, whatever we needed," recalled El Duque. "In the hotels, you know the little bottles of shampoo and conditioner? We took those. We took the towels." El Duque himself walked into a Mexico City shoe store one afternoon and swiped two tiny pairs of patent-leather shoes (one black, one white) for his daughters.

"I stuck them in my waistband, like this," he said years later, rising to re-create the scene in the Chicago Westin coffee shop during a Yankee road trip. "They must have been looking at my face, because my knees were knocking against each other. I don't know how I wasn't caught. It was one of the scariest moments of my life, and you know what I've been through. I still get nervous thinking about it." He never stole again. "I sold cigars and PPG instead," he said. "I still had to take care of the family. You do what you can to *resolver.*"

The ballplayers were not the most inconspicuous of thieves. One year, while playing at a tournament in Amsterdam, the players ventured out en masse to a downtown department store. Some wore their Team Cuba warm-up suits. Others brought along equipment bags, the easier to carry the loot. During the subsequent spree, a right fielder named Luis García pocketed a pair of scissors. He was sauntering out the front door when a security guard asked him to empty his pockets.

The other players, spread out all over the store, saw what was happening and scurried for the exits. When El Duque came upon his teammate, García was on his knees, begging the guard and the store manager to let him go. "He was close to tears," recalled El Duque. "He kept saying, 'I'm sorry, I'm sorry. *Por favor, por favor.*' Then he would look over to some of us. He'd say, 'Help me, guys, help me. Don't leave me. Help me out.' "

So pitiful was the scene that the manager finally sent García off with a warning. "Oh, thank you, *gracias,*" said the player. He then sprinted out the door. When the players got back to their hotel, they discovered that as a group they had actually done quite well. They emptied the haul onto their beds: shirts, underwear, jeans, watches; all that was missing was the ill-fated scissors to remove the price tags. "That was how you tried to survive," said El Duque. "And remember: We were better off than other Cubans. We were the privileged ones."

There was no shortage of irony in the players' desperation. These were the finest amateur baseball players in the world, the icons of Cuban socialism. Baseball is perhaps the cruelest sport, a game in which consistency and endurance are rewarded amid inevitable, unrelenting failure. A team that wins 60 percent of its games (or less) is often a champion. And yet, from 1987 to 1997, an entire decade, Cuba's national baseball team went 152 games without a loss in international competition, a winning streak almost beyond comprehension. Team Cuba was such a source of national pride that nearly all the players had been made automatic members of the Union of Communist Youth or even the Communist party itself. To the government, the national team's dominance was a validation of the Cuban system, of its obvious superiority. "The Cuban system is ideal," Domingo Zabala, the Cuban baseball commissioner, once told me. Professional baseball in the United States was the equivalent of "converting men into merchandise." The Cuban players, he said, played for pride and country, for Fidel, for the revolution.

Perhaps long ago that sentiment prevailed, but no longer. As the Special Period wore on, Team Cuba began to reflect the growing fissures within Cuban society. Certainly, there were revolutionaries, players like Omar Linares and Victor Mesa whose parents had raised them as good party men. Once, I drove out to Pinar del Río to interview Linares at his home. At that point, El Niño was an almost mythical figure in international baseball circles, the Babe Ruth of communism. He defined what had become known among major-league scouts as "the Cuban Mystique." I had seen Linares play five times in three different countries and each time he had homered, low-trajectory blasts that resembled planes taking off. There were reports that the Yankees had offered Linares $1.5 million to defect, that the Toronto Blue Jays had offered him a contract by which he could play only home games to avoid traveling to the United States. But Linares lived modestly by the standards of a legend. His house, provided by the government, was located on Pinar's busiest street and contained three tiny bedrooms, a small living room and a kitchen. Inside the front door were two photos: one of the player's four-year-old daughter, Samira, another of him and Fidel. In one of the bedrooms, Linares kept his trophies and medals; they were lined up next to cheap Che Guevara memorabilia and a dozen bound volumes entitled *The Complete Works of Lenin*.

I asked Linares whether it was true that the Yankees had offered him $1.5 million. He said it was. "Every year the teams offer me more money," he said matter-of-factly. "None of it means anything to me. I know you're curious, but I am not. Money doesn't interest me." Linares said that to defect "would be an act of treason. It will never happen." He said he was content to stay in Cuba, playing baseball, "the nourishment of the people." Later that afternoon, I went to visit his father, Fidel, a former ballplayer who lived in a small concrete house out in the tobacco fields surrounding Pinar. The house's aqua facade was bleached and fading. The small living room was crowded with rusted trophies, cracked, withered photographs and a black rotary phone that the elder Linares described as "decorative." Like his son, Fidel Linares had served several years as a federal deputy. He had lived in the same house for forty-three years. "Everyone who has come from this home has been devoted to the revolution," he told me. "There is no way that this family will ever be broken up over money."

But for all his greatness, many of Omar Linares's peers looked upon him as tragically out of touch or, worse, simply brainwashed. None of the players had been alive during the heady days when Fidel took power. Although they believed in Cuba, in the country itself, and even in some of the successes of the revolution—its free education, its health care system—they were hardly true believers. Many were deeply cynical. Ariel Prieto, a pitcher from the Isle of Youth who later signed with the Oakland A's, recalled the day he received his membership in the Union of Communist Youth. "I was in Havana getting my arm worked on when they suddenly announced: 'Ariel has earned his youth card.' It meant that I was a militant young Communist. I was young, but I was no militant, and I was certainly no Communist. I was just the best player on my team. My mother was driving me crazy. She said, 'You're a militant now, you should be so proud.' I told her, 'Mom, the first chance I get I'm going to wipe my ass with it.' Later they wanted me to become a full-fledged party member, the red Communist party card and all that. I didn't know shit about communism or socialism. And I didn't give a shit, either. All I knew was how to pitch."

But for all their cynicism, their adventures in off-the-books capitalism, none of the immensely talented players had defected in the first three decades of the revolution. There was talk, of course, dreams of playing in the majors, but it never got beyond that. Back when he was a college coach, Al Avila, later the Florida Marlins scouting director, traveled to Nicaragua with a team from St. Thomas University in Miami. The Cubans were there, too. "What I remember most is that they accepted everything we had: shaving cream, blades, equipment, clothes, chocolate, you name it," Avila recalled. "And they were just awesome on the field. It was almost like they didn't want to embarrass us. But then I got to talk to a few of them and I quickly realized, 'Hey, a lot of these guys are wondering what's out there.'"

There were many obstacles, though. The players had families, and there was always the question of how Fidel would react, whether the state would punish friends and relatives to get back at the players. There was also the guilt: Fidel's constant rant about the *gusanos,* the worms, the traitors to the revolution. The players were supposed to be the leaders of the country, model revolutionaries in this Special Period in Time of Peace. And, of course, there was the fear of whether they were even good enough to play in the United States, the great behemoth to the north. There was no precedent. No Cuban player had defected since the revolution had slammed the door on the major leagues. No one had ever made the great leap.

And then, on July 4, 1991, René Arocha missed his plane.

I HAVE NO IDEA how old Arocha was when we spoke over lunch in Jupiter, Florida, one hot afternoon. He said he was fifteen when he started pitching in the National Series in 1980. That would have made him, as he claimed, thirty-four. He looked older, his face tanned and creased, more like a broadcaster than a ballplayer. He had just come from pitching a minor-league intrasquad game with the New York Mets, who were giving him a spring tryout. I stood behind the backstop and watched his pitches flash across the radar gun. His fastball topped out at 91 miles per hour but the Mets' Double-A team hammered him nonetheless.

"Everything in life has its moment," said Arocha, reflecting back. "This was my moment."

Team Cuba had stopped over in Miami after playing a series of exhibition games in Millington, Tennessee. Later, the exhibitions would be canceled and Team Cuba would travel under tight security, seldom announcing their movements in advance. They certainly would never again spend the night in Miami, the unofficial capital of the Cuban exile community. But this was a different time. The notion that one of the great revolutionaries from Team Cuba would defect was the furthest thing from anyone's mind.

Arocha was a hard-throwing right-hander with a long list of grievances against the government. In 1980, the year his career began, his father fled to Miami in the Mariel boatlift. Arocha heard the stunning news that he had been selected to play for Havana's Metropolitanos over the radio. "It was like a child hearing that he was going to pitch in the big leagues," he recalled. "When I got there the players asked me, 'Who the hell are you?' " Exhilarated and terrified, Arocha looked down the bench and spotted one of his new teammates, Rey Vicente Anglada, a second baseman described by Cubans as a cross between Roberto Alomar and Rickey Henderson. Anglada was Arocha's idol. "I thought, This can't be happening," said Arocha. "It was like a dream. He called me *nene* [little boy]. He took me under his wing."

Within two years, Arocha's dream had turned into a nightmare. A vast betting scandal struck the National Series. Authorities dragged Arocha down to Villa Marista, the headquarters for Cuba's notorious secret police. "They kept asking me, 'Why did you lose these ball games? Why did this guy hit a homer?' I kept telling them, 'Look, that's baseball.' " When the interrogation was over, the agent showed Arocha a long list of players—eighteen plus an umpire—who had been arrested for throwing games. Arocha wasn't on the list. Rey Vicente Anglada was at the top.

"It was the downfall of a hero," said Arocha. "In a way, he became like a martyr."

Arocha's disillusionment crested a year later. Still a teenager playing for Team Cuba in the world junior championships, he was called upon to pitch every day. By the middle of the final game, against Venezuela, he could barely lift his arm. "I couldn't go on," he said. "So the team doctor, this doctor from Cuba, great medical superpower of the world, as Fidel likes to call it, this team doctor right there in the dugout—*in the dugout!*—gave me a cortisone injection so I could keep pitching. By the seventh inning, my elbow was like this [holds up hands in the shape of a basketball]. But they didn't take me out. I finished the game, all nine innings. It cost me three years. I couldn't pitch for *three years.*

"Really, what was I going to like about the Cuban system?" said Arocha. His grandfather Lalo Rodríguez spent a year under house arrest for running a neighborhood lottery. His uncle Edel Arocha spent two years in jail for holding dollars. "He went to a *diplotienda* [dollar store] to buy a pair of pants," said Arocha. "He was going to sell the pants for Cuban pesos and use that money to buy more dollars. It cost him two years of his life." Arocha eventually made it back to the National Series, but by then Cuban baseball was in the throes of the Special Period. The playing conditions were out of Dickens. One night at El Latino, a game was postponed because of a power failure, and before long all night games had been canceled to save electricity. The players traveled in ramshackle Soviet-made school buses, numbing themselves with rum. They slept inside the stadiums, in dorm rooms that were like barracks. "Imagine traveling from Havana to Guantánamo on a bus with no air-conditioning," said Arocha, referring to the eastern city some fifteen hours from Havana. "Sometimes the bus would break down at dawn in the middle of nowhere. You waited hours in the heat for another bus. Then you finally get to Guantánamo and there's no running water. Then, after the game, you have thirty players staying in the same room in their sweaty, dirty clothes. A lot of the time we slept in the stands. We dragged our sleeping mats into the stands and laid them on top of the dugout. The mosquitoes were the size of portable radios, but you didn't have any choice."

To maintain the fiction that the players were amateurs, the government paid them for jobs they never performed. "I was a typographer," said Arocha, laughing. "I didn't know anything about typography. I didn't know what typography was! But that's what they called me to justify paying me 186 pesos." Converted to dollars, his monthly salary was $7.45.

"By '91 I'd had enough," said Arocha. "Something just told me to get out. It's all in the moment."

His plan was hardly elaborate. When Team Cuba stopped in Miami after the exhibition series in Millington, Arocha's father, also René, and his aunt Delia met him at the hotel. Arocha hadn't seen his father in eleven years. "We were standing there, catching up, talking, trying to make up for eleven years in a matter of minutes," he said. "We were standing there in the lobby. I said, 'Let's go back to your house.' When we were in the car I just told them right then. I said, 'I'm not going back to Cuba.' "

That night, Arocha got together with his best friends on the team: Euclides Rojas and Lázaro Valle. He asked if they, too, wanted to stay. Rojas wanted to jump right then, but his wife, Marta, was pregnant back in Havana and he didn't want to leave her. Valle had talked constantly about defecting but could never pull the trigger. He broke down crying. The players embraced and headed back to the hotel.

The next morning, with Arocha a no-show for the flight back to Havana, panic broke out around Team Cuba. Team officials launched a search of the Miami airport, believing that the pitcher had somehow gotten lost or couldn't find the gate. "They kept saying that maybe he had been drugged or kidnapped or something," said Rojas. "They didn't want to accept the truth." The officials held the plane for one hour, two hours, scouring the airport with Miami police for a man asleep in bed at his aunt Delia's house. Then a curious thing happened. The players, most of whom either knew or suspected that Arocha had defected, grew defiant. Many had spent the entire night partying and were still half in the bag when they boarded the plane. From the middle of the cabin shouts were suddenly heard: "C'mon, let's get the fuck out of here!" "Let's go, you're not going to find him!" "*Vamos, vamos.* Let's go."

The commotion had settled to a dull roar when Victor Mesa suddenly spoke up. In Cuba, Mesa was an icon. He was known as El Loco for his strange deportment on the field. He frequently yelped from the batter's box for no apparent reason. His home-run trots were like Andrew Lloyd Webber productions. But there was never any question that El Loco was down with the program. His status as team captain had as much to do with the purity of his political ideology as it did with his leadership abilities and his batting average (.318 lifetime as this book was being written). Like Linares, Mesa was a federal deputy, a party man with four photos of Fidel hanging on his living room wall. But times were changing. Earlier, when coaches had come around with the pitiful $2-per-day meal allowance, Mesa had snapped: "Are you kidding? You couldn't wipe your ass with this." Now, as the plane sat on the tarmac in Miami, waiting for a pitcher who had just walked away from his team and his country on the Fourth of July, El Loco was ready to weigh in on the latest developments. "Maybe now you'll treat us with some respect!" he yelled, loud enough for anyone in authority to hear. "You don't treat us like the world champions you say we are. You want to pay us two dollars a day? Fine. Arocha's on his way to the major leagues. Maybe we can *all* play in the major leagues."

WHEN THE PLANE FINALLY landed in Havana, the players, groggy, hungover, still reeling from Arocha's defection, shuffled to the baggage claim. The luggage had been taken off the carousel and was sitting on the floor. One by one, the players grabbed their gear until just one bag was left. It was Arocha's. No one knew what to do. The players stared at the bag, then at each other, then back at the bag. Finally, Rojas walked over, picked up his friend's belongings and carried them off to deliver to Arocha's wife.

The Sports Ministry wasted little time addressing the matter. "I was so drunk from the night before that I didn't even notice that René was gone until we got back to Havana," said Ariel Prieto. "Then the meetings started." That day, the INDER convened an emergency meeting at the headquarters of the Union of Communist Youth in Havana. The speaker was Reynaldo González, a short, heavyset man, vice president of the INDER. He got directly to the point. Arocha was "a traitor," he told the players. He said that they now needed to demonstrate that his defection meant nothing. "You must not fall! You must continue to fight! This will not hurt our revolutionary morale!" Later, there would be many similar meetings, always with the same message. Arocha had been weak. Arocha had betrayed his country. "We must have had five million meetings on Arocha," said Prieto. "We met with everybody: the council of state, the INDER, everybody except Fidel."

In truth, the world of Cuban baseball had been changed forever. For many players, Arocha was Jackie Robinson. He had transformed their very perception of the world. "He was the one who taught us how to think," said El Duque. "We called him a deserter because that was the phrase the state used. But the only thing he did was stand up for his ideas." Arocha had thought that his pitching career was over when he defected. "I wasn't even thinking about baseball," he said. "I just wanted a better life." But in a matter of weeks he had an agent, then a contract with the St. Louis Cardinals. His signing bonus was a joke, $15,000, but a revelation nonetheless, a fortune back in Cuba. After he made it to the major leagues, winning 11 games for the Cardinals in 1993, his legend was cemented. In Havana, players passed around bootleg videos of Arocha like Soviet naval officers sneaking around Murmansk with copies of *The Hunt for Red October.* To them, Arocha was a historic figure, a pioneer. "The Communists say that José Martí was the intellectual author behind Moncada," said Rojas, a reference to the father of Cuban nationalism and his ideological influence over Fidel's famous attack. "To me," Rojas continued, "René Arocha was the intellectual author of Cuban baseball in exile."

There would soon be many imitators, of course. One afternoon in Niagara Falls, a pitcher named Eddie Oropesa kicked off his spikes at Sal Maglie Stadium during the World University Games, scaled a twelve-foot chain-link fence and defected in his socks. He later signed a contract with the Los Angeles Dodgers. One of his teammates, future Mets shortstop Rey Ordóñez, defected the following day.

Euclides Rojas decided to make his move during the summer of 1994. It was a summer when one could have easily concluded that the entire population of Cuba was headed toward the United States. There was little meat that summer. The monthly food rations had dwindled to rice, beans, sugar, and bread. Cuban gunboats rammed a tugboat filled with fleeing refugees. Forty-one people drowned, including many children. Then, one hot afternoon, hundreds of people gathered along the Malecón to protest everything that fell under the heading Special Period in Time of Peace—the scarcity and the oppression and the crushing boredom of a society no longer able to afford diversions. The police came and people fought. Some looted the dollar stores, walking away with forbidden irons and pants, cardboard boxes filled with soap. Finally, in an act not unlike releasing the valve on a pressure cooker, Fidel announced that the coasts of Cuba would be left unguarded. Anyone who wanted to was free to leave.

Rojas was no longer a member of Cuba's national baseball team. After Arocha's defection, he had been interrogated several times. Then he was taken off the team without explanation. Rojas pondered his future and concluded that he didn't have one. The only thing keeping him in Cuba was his mother. For years, she had pleaded with him to stay. Then one afternoon she made the decision for him.

"I don't want to harm you anymore," she said. "There's no future for you here."

Rojas could only nod. He went to break the news to his wife, Marta. He sat her down and explained the situation. He said that he would send for her and their son, Eduardo, after he got settled in Miami.

"No, we're going with you," she responded. "If we die, we die together as a family."

So it was that Euclides Rojas, Cuba's all-time saves leader, crowded into a fifteen-foot boat with his wife, his two-year-old son, and ten desperate others. It was nighttime, and the moon was rising over the Morro Castle in Havana. The four men in the group waded into the black, calm sea and pushed the boat north. Three fifty-five-gallon oil drums were lashed to either side to keep it from tipping. "We had a small motor," said Rojas, "but it died quickly and we had to take turns rowing. We rowed in two-hour shifts." When dawn broke the pitcher and his group found that they were hardly alone. There were people spread out across the horizon, thousands floating on inner tubes, in small boats like their own. People were confused and desperate. "You'd see people going the wrong way and you'd ask them, 'Where are you going?' " said Rojas. "They'd say, 'Miami!' And then someone else would point in another direction and say, 'No, no, it's *that* way.' " Fortunately, the weather was good, but after a few days Rojas's group ran out of water. But there were so many rafters that they were able to swap food for water with other boats, right there in the middle of the Florida Straits. "It got really bad the last night," said Rojas. "My son wouldn't stop crying. He kept thinking he was at the pool. He wanted to get in the water."

On August 21, after five days, a passing U.S. Coast Guard cutter plucked Rojas, his family and the others from the sea. They were twenty-three miles off Key West. They were among 1,058 people rescued by the Coast Guard that day alone. There were so many rafters that summer—an estimated 40,000, of whom several thousand are believed to have drowned—that the U.S. government had to erect a city for them at the U.S. naval base at Guantánamo. The base was one of the ironies of the rafter crisis, a relic of American imperialism that sat on the eastern edge of Cuba, hemmed in by enemy territory, land mines, barbed wire and the sea. To escape Cuba, it turned out, the rafters first had to go back to it. For several months, the desolate base was home to some 32,000 Cubans waiting to be admitted to the United States. Anxiety and boredom permeated the base, and soon the Miami exile community began to pitch in. Entertainers flew out to perform in USO-like shows. There were comedians and singers like Gloria Estefan and Willy Chirino and Celia Cruz. The exiles brought toys and sports equipment. Rojas and a few other rafters, including Alex Sánchez, a young outfielder who later signed with the Tampa Bay Devil Rays, put together a baseball team.

Several sports figures flew in. There was a sports agent who called himself Joe Cubas; the Cuban American slugger José Canseco; the promising shortstop Alex Rodríguez. One afternoon, Rojas was standing in his dirt city—in Cuba but no longer of Cuba—when he saw another celebrity making his way toward the camp. The crowd surged forward. Rojas began to recognize him. It was his best friend, René Arocha, the famous Cuban pitcher with the St. Louis Cardinals. Everyone was invited to come meet him.

PART TWO

CHAPTER FIVE

EL GORDO

H E LIKED TO WORK IN THE SHADOWS, AWAY FROM THE BIG-eared and the curious, so Joe Cubas asked Louie Eljaua (pronounced El-*ha*-wah) to meet him after the game. Eljaua couldn't imagine what could be so important. Cubas was an acquaintance, a minor sports agent from the area, and Eljaua, too, was pretty low on the baseball totem pole. It was the fall of 1994, and Eljaua was working as an area scout for the Florida Marlins, the major-league expansion franchise in Miami. He spent most of his time at games like the one he was watching now, a high school all-star game at Miami-Dade North Community College. He and Cubas were cogs in an expanding global industry whose primary objective was to develop young baseball players. As an agent, Cubas was looking for players to represent. As a scout, Eljaua was looking for players to sign. But Cubas's interest in meeting that night went well beyond those modest parameters.

After the game, the two men walked to the parking lot. The lights had been turned off, and so Eljaua stood in the dark as Cubas, in hushed tones, unveiled his top-secret project. Cubas swore the scout to secrecy: "You cannot tell anyone outside the organization about this. No one else can know." The agent then explained that he had secretly been meeting with the players on Cuba's national baseball team. He said that most had confided to him that they wanted to defect to play in the major leagues. Cubas told Eljaua that he was prepared to help the players defect by any means necessary and take them to a country such as the Dominican Republic or Venezuela, where they would declare themselves free agents and open negotiations with major-league clubs. "It was like something out of a movie, the way he was describing it," Eljaua later recalled. "He went on and on like that in the dark. He wanted me to go to the Florida Marlins with this crazy idea that he had and present it to them.

"I thought he was nuts," said Eljaua. But he was also intrigued. As the son of Cuban immigrants, Eljaua knew the stranglehold that baseball had on the exile community. A Cuban defector playing in Miami for the Florida Marlins? On paper, at least, it was a natural. Eljaua had seen enough of Team Cuba to know that the potential was staggering. In amateur baseball, the Cubans were men among boys. And now here was this agent, Joe Cubas, telling him that he could deliver Omar Linares, the great El Duque, even Omar Ajete, the lefty fireballer of Barcelona. Eljaua thought about whom he could possibly go to. "I was just an area guy," he said. "If I go to Dave Dombrowski, our general manager, or Gary Hughes, who was our scouting director, or even Al Avila, who was in charge of Latin American scouting, they're going to think I'm crazy. I was just trying to do my job and not piss anybody off."

Eljaua finally decided to tell Avila, a fellow Cuban American. Avila's father, Ralph, had helped lead the troops into Havana under machine-gun fire as part of Castro's 26th of July Movement, then, frustrated with what the revolution had become, tried to overthrow Fidel at the Bay of Pigs. He ended up working his way up as a scout with the Los Angeles Dodgers, succeeding Al Campanis as the team's guru in Latin America. Al Avila was almost totally ignorant of his father's past in bloody Cuban politics—"I can't say I have a good history on that," he said—but he knew enough to hate Fidel. He also had become something of an expert on Cuban baseball, one of a handful of men who had scouted Team Cuba for years. "When I went to Al and told him about it he just kind of laughed," said Eljaua. "But he was interested. I told him, 'He's just beginning to contact these people; there's nothing concrete right now.' So we put it on the back burner.

"After that, every time Joe saw me at a game he'd call me off to the side and whisper into my ear," said Eljaua. The following spring, the Marlins were training at their complex in Melbourne, Florida, four hours up the coast from Miami near Cape Canaveral. Cubas called Eljaua and asked for a meeting with the Marlins' top brass: Avila, Dave Dombrowski and Gary Hughes. "Gary has always been the type of guy who's aggressive; this kind of stuff was right up his alley," said Eljaua. "Gary asked me, 'When do you think Joe can meet?' So I called Joe. He was up there the next day." The group sat at a conference table as Cubas spun his tale of international intrigue: his plot to help the players defect, to spirit them to the Dominican Republic, and to open up negotiations with major-league clubs. Someone asked Cubas if he thought the Commissioner's Office would permit such an outrageous scheme. "He said that if Major League Baseball wouldn't go along with it he was going to file a grievance against them, because there was nothing written in the rules that said he couldn't do it," said Eljaua. Cubas told the Marlins that the defections would probably take place when the Cubans traveled to Tokyo in May. "He was really throwing Linares's name around," said Eljaua. "I don't know if that was to attract us more or what. At the time Omar was still at the level where everybody thought he was a major-league third baseman, an all-star-quality guy." Cubas said he wanted the Marlins to accompany him to Japan. "We were going to have the inside track on the whole situation," said Eljaua. "It was kind of exciting."

The Marlins decided to send Avila. But what the team didn't know was that Cubas himself was scraping together enough money to make the trip. The agent was broke, increasingly desperate. His marriage was falling apart. He had been chasing Team Cuba for more than two years and not one player had defected. He and his business partner, Juan Iglesias, had been working out of Cubas's garage, and Iglesias was tired of what had turned into a wild-goose chase. "I had a real negative feeling about the whole thing," Iglesias said. "I didn't think anybody was ever going to defect. We were spending way too much time and way too much money. Joe was getting very close to bankruptcy. I would have to pay the phone bills, the office expenses, everything."

Cubas asked Iglesias for $10,000 to make the trip to Japan. Iglesias refused. "Number one, you're not going to be able to pay me back," he told his partner. "The only reason I would even think about giving you the money is if I thought you were going to get some business out of it. And number two, I don't think anything is going to happen out there." Iglesias pleaded with Cubas not to go: "Joe, you've been all over the world and *not one thing* has happened."

"For some reason Joe thought that Japan was going to be his breakthrough trip," said Iglesias. Undaunted, Cubas borrowed the money from one of his cousins, Juan Ignacio Hernández, a part-time truck driver and full-time schemer with a taste for adventure. Cubas invited his cousin to tag along.

From the moment they arrived, however, it was obvious that the trip would not be the breakthrough that Cubas had envisioned. The agent was out of his element. He knew neither the language nor the customs. He went to the Dominican embassy to inquire about the visas. But no one knew how Japan might react if the players actually defected. The government might hand them back to Cuba, and then where would everyone be? It quickly became clear that no one—not Omar Linares, not Omar Ajete, not anyone—would be defecting in Japan. As Cubas later admitted, there were too many obstacles: "We were on the other side of the world."

The week's lowlight came outside the stadium in Tokyo one afternoon. Cubas was trying to chat up El Duque and the pitcher's younger half brother, Liván Hernández. In the middle of the conversation, El Duque suddenly exploded. "You know, if I went to the United States I'd be just one more nigger!" The pitcher was screaming. Other players boarding the team bus turned to look. "Just one more nigger for them to sic the dogs on!" El Duque then grabbed Liván and headed off toward the bus.

Cubas had no idea what had set El Duque off. He stood there, humiliated and seething. "I didn't know what to say. It left me with a bitter taste in my mouth. I was like, 'This guy is a fucking Communist. Either a Communist or he's been brainwashed.'"

Least pleased were the Florida Marlins, who had traveled to the other end of the earth for a nonevent. Years later, Avila would brush aside any disappointment he may have felt about the trip. But Eljaua said the scout came back fuming. "Al was pretty pissed. He went all the way to Japan and he saw no light at the end of the tunnel. We thought two or maybe three guys were going to defect on that trip."

"Joe likes to make it out like he's this man of intrigue," said Eljaua. "I know him well enough now to know when he's bullshitting me. I respect him in a certain way. He's a friend of mine. But you always take everything he says with a grain of salt and kind of laugh it off after he walks away.

"Make sure you don't put that I said he's full of shit more than once in there," said Eljaua, laughing. "He'll take that personally. He's very touchy about that type of stuff."

LONG BEFORE HE revolutionized the business of sports agentry, as practitioners of the trade like to call it, José Ignacio "Joe" Cubas learned about the business of revolution. He learned, in particular, how there were winners and losers. "I lost half my family in Cuba," he said. "I've got cousins there, family members throughout the island that are still stuck. My family, like every other Cuban family, has suffered the consequences of Fidel Castro over the past forty-one years."

Cubas's father, Pepe, and his mother, Berta, were married in Havana on February 5, 1960. Two days later, the couple flew to Miami on their honeymoon. Not long after that, the newlyweds received a call from relatives in Cuba telling them not to come home. "That was a shock to them, obviously," said

Cubas. "My dad has never been able to go back. My mom went back in 1984 or '85. Her father had already passed away. Her oldest brother was very fragile and she went to see him before he died."

The story of Cubas's family is the story of thousands of prosperous Cubans who migrated to Miami after the revolution, their lives abruptly torn asunder. Berta's father had owned several hundred acres of farmland in Havana province, on which he harvested sugarcane and raised livestock. The family also operated a Havana bus line. Within the first decade of the revolution, according to Cubas (both his parents declined to be interviewed), the Castro government had seized all but a tiny fraction of the family holdings. "In 1968 or '69 there was another clash, and they basically took everything," said Cubas. "They left my grandfather with a small house and a small piece of land. The day after that happened, he had a heart attack and passed away. That's why my family is so bitter to this day."

The trauma of his family splitting apart played out in Cubas's earliest memories. "I remember vividly the day we got the news from Cuba that my grandfather—my father's father—had passed away," he said. "I was six years old. My dad was twenty-five or twenty-six and I remember him sitting on the side of the bed, locked in his room, crying his heart out. It was a shock, the first time I had ever seen my father cry. I don't think I really understood what was going on until I was twelve, thirteen, maybe fourteen years old. Then you could see the exodus of your own family happening before your eyes. One day a woman shows up at your house and it's like, 'This is your aunt, who you've heard me talk about all the time.' Our family grew and grew in the late sixties and early seventies."

The Cuban diaspora is marked by spasms of mass migration—Operation Pedro Pan, Camarioca, Mariel, the great human wave of 1994—and Cubas grew up hearing stories of his relatives cowering in garages with little to eat or drink, waiting to be let out of the country. Several came over on the "freedom flights" that brought 260,000 Cubans to the United States between 1965 and 1973. "I remember a time in the seventies when two sisters and a brother from my mom's side of the family came over with their families," said Cubas. "We had something like twenty members of the family all living in our house at the same time. My mom and dad had been the first ones of the family to arrive in America, and so all the cousins came through my house until they could get out on their own."

Cubas's parents attacked their new lives with the same ferocity that enabled the Cuban exile community to make over Miami. It was a world of strivers, of people literally rebuilding their lives from scratch, reinventing themselves and, in the process, an entire city. Pepe Cubas set up a business delivering *cantinas,* boxed Cuban meals, to families working so hard to establish themselves that they didn't have time to cook. "This was the age of Cubans trying to assimilate and get involved; it was a work-and-produce mentality," said Cubas. "My dad's business was to bring people affordable, good old Cuban meals. It was like, 'You work. We'll cook for you and send you your *cantina.'* " Pepe Cubas did the cooking. Berta kept the books and earned extra money cleaning offices in Hialeah. After school, Cubas would come home, help prepare *cantinas,* then do his homework in the office of his parents' business. It was a lifestyle that he came to respect and loathe. "I hated the business," he said. "I hated to see how many hours my father had to work. My father, until recently, got up every single day at two A.M. The business was three blocks away, and, at one time, Dad was doing about eight hundred *cantinas* a day. He would work until two or three in the afternoon, come home and take a nap, then go back to work around five-thirty for another few hours."

Cubas knew early on that it was not a life he wanted for himself. He married at twenty. He met his wife, María, taking a high school Spanish course that neither of them needed, and his father-in-law, an exile named Reynaldo Carles, brought him into the construction business. "He taught me about the wheeling and dealing, the business life," said Cubas. Cubas searched several years before finding his true calling. He took classes in business administration at Miami-Dade but never completed his degree. He worked part-time in the computer operations department at Florida Power & Light. He helped his father-in-law in the construction business and worked on his own as a contractor before stumbling into the high-powered world of professional sports.

Cubas circulated with other young, ambitious Cuban Americans, the sons of exiles who had inherited their parents' hard-edged politics and drive. Most spoke English and high-octane Cuban Spanish with equal fluidity, shifting back and forth in mid-conversation. Cubas played softball with a short, heavyset entrepreneur named Juan Iglesias who had done well in the sports-memorabilia business. Iglesias's primary asset was his relationship with the Cuban American slugger José Canseco. He arranged shows in which the slugger earned thousands of dollars by signing his name to baseball cards for a few hours. Cubas attended one such show and was hooked immediately. "Joe liked the whole concept of baseball and marketing," recalled Iglesias. "I needed to expand, so we became partners in the marketing business. We did a bunch of different things with José. And then Joe decided he wanted to become an agent. He wanted to become an agent because he noticed that every time we wanted to contact a player for a show an agent was also involved, and the agent was always the head honcho."

As Cubas was soon to discover, there are few prerequisites for becoming a professional baseball agent. The Major League Baseball Players Association, which regulates the industry, will certify most anyone with at least one client on a major-league roster, the minimum requirement. Cubas's baseball experience had ended with his career as a catcher at LaSalle High. The only contracts he had negotiated were with plumbers and roofers. But he had no problem meeting the union's standards. He got his first client through a childhood friend, Rudy Santín (pronounced San-*teen*).

Santín and Cubas had grown up playing ball together at Curtis Park in northwest Miami. The two men and their wives had all attended LaSalle High, a Catholic school dominated by the children of middle-class exiles. In high school, Santín had sometimes pitched ambidextrously—"He's the only guy I've ever seen call a time-out in the middle of a game to switch gloves," said Cubas, who sometimes caught his friend—and after a run through the minor leagues as a left-handed pitcher, he accepted a job with the New York Yankees, first as an area scout, then as the club's director of Latin American scouting.

Santín was able to hook up Cubas with a Yankee prospect, Bobby Muñoz, a promising six-foot-eight pitcher. But the scout had bigger things in store for his childhood friend. Santín had a bold new plan that, if everything fell into place just right, would produce a windfall of prospects for the New York Yankees and a windfall of cash for the aspiring sports agent Joe Cubas. As the Yankee representative in Latin America, Santín had begun to see a lot of Team Cuba. Over time, he had gotten to know several players, and to his astonishment he found that they had more than a passing interest in (1) major-league baseball, and (2) money, not necessarily in that order.

In fact, as the players got to know Santín better, they began to hit him up for cash and talk openly about their dreams of playing in the major leagues. At times, it was difficult to tell which players were serious and which were working an angle. "They used to come up to my room all the time to talk," said Santín. "But a lot of these guys were schemers. Lázaro Valle, for example, was the perfect schemer. He would always look for people to tell that he was defecting. He just needed five hundred dollars to prepare some things he needed to take care of. He was always going to defect on the next trip out."

But other players appeared to be giving the idea serious consideration.

Santín grew bolder and began to openly recruit. One night, during a tournament in Argentina, he made the infamous play for Omar Linares and Antonio Pacheco, a power-hitting second baseman. Santín plied his two recruits with food and beer while giving a crash course in big-league economics. The Yankees had just signed their number one draft pick, a left-handed pitcher named Brien Taylor, for $1.55 million. Santín used that as his benchmark to woo Linares. "It wasn't really an offer," he said. "They way I put it to him was, 'Do you realize that if you went to the States right now you'd be the best amateur player in the country? And the best amateur player in the country just got $1.5 million. You would have to get at least that, or more.' "

For all of Linares's later claims that he never gave the idea a second thought, Santín believed that the vaunted revolutionary was given pause. "He thought about it, both him and Pacheco, definitely," he said. "They were deep in thought about it. You could tell." Santín was ultimately able to make the same pitch to nearly every player on Team Cuba. "If they could, they would *all* play here," he said. "The biggest thing holding them back is their families."

The more Santín saw of the Cubans, the more his frustration grew. Part of it was personal: Santín had been born in Cuba and he hated what the revolution had done to his own family. His father, Rodolfo, had fought on Castro's side, then turned against the revolution in 1960 and fled to the United States. Santín, who was a baby at the time, didn't meet his father until he was nine.

Santín was also offended for aesthetic reasons: Here were some of the finest baseball players in the world, and yet they were prohibited from competing at the highest level of the sport. But most of the scout's frustration was professional. These were players he wanted to sign in the worst way, yet even if they defected and announced that they wanted to play for the New York Yankees, they couldn't, and it had nothing to do with Cuba or communism. The players would have to submit themselves to a more benign form of authoritarianism: the major-league draft.

In truth, Major League Baseball hadn't a clue how to handle the defectors. As they began to trickle out, they were like baseball orphans. After René Arocha defected in 1991, a Miami radio reporter referred him to a Cuban American marketing wiz named Gus Domínguez, who was based in Los Angeles. Domínguez knew almost nothing about negotiating a baseball contract, and so he tried to hand off Arocha to the powerful Beverly Hills Sports Council, which handled José Canseco. The agents of the Beverly Hills Sports Council thought so highly of René Arocha that they refused to represent him.

Domínguez went back to Arocha. "I gotta tell it to you like it is," he said. "They don't have time for you."

"Well, fuck 'em," said the pitcher. "You represent me."

"Look, I know the game, but I've never represented anybody in my life."

"That's okay. We'll learn together."

Domínguez thus became an instant agent. But he found that there wasn't much for him to negotiate. Under Major League rules, players born in the United States and Puerto Rico are subject to the annual draft. Foreign-born players are regarded as free agents; they can negotiate with any team. Arocha was a foreign-born player who had taken up residence in the United States as a political refugee. So which category did he fall into? Not surprisingly, the Commissioner's Office, acting on behalf of the owners, opted for the cheapest route available. It was decided that a special lottery would be held for all teams interested in signing Arocha. The winning team would hold exclusive rights to him.

In a sense, Arocha had been delivered from postrevolutionary Cuba into prerevolutionary baseball. He was essentially powerless. After a series of tryouts, fifteen teams expressed interest in signing him. The names of the teams were then dropped into a hat. The St. Louis Cardinals won. They offered the hard-throwing immigrant $15,000. "They had us like *this*," said Domínguez, grabbing his crotch. "He should have been allowed to be a free agent. We thought he could get close to a million. But we were stuck. We pleaded, we begged, we got on our knees and said, 'Listen, this guy has family back in Cuba that he has to support.'" The club refused to budge. It was take it or leave it.

"Let's take it," said Arocha, who claimed to be twenty-five. "I'm getting old."

The following spring, in an exhibition game in St. Petersburg, Florida, Arocha trotted in from the Cardinal bullpen wearing number 73. He proceeded to blow away six Pirate hitters—Jay Bell, Andy Van Slyke, Kirk Gibson, Barry Bonds, Jeff Richardson and Mike LaValliere—"as easily as birthday candles," wrote Dan LeBatard of *The Miami Herald*. The performance was so remarkable that third baseman Steve Buechele raced out of the Pirate dugout to find a bio of the unknown pitcher. His teammates crowded around to look it over. Van Slyke, informed that the Cardinals had picked up Arocha in a special lottery, responded: "What kind of lottery was that? The Florida lottery or the Missouri lottery?"

Arocha, of course, had been pitching on Mars and was as ignorant of his opponents as they were of him. "Who is Gibson?" he asked.

It was exactly that kind of situation that Rudy Santín wanted to avoid. He was afraid that Omar Linares or El Duque might jump into his car one afternoon, ask for a contract, and Santín would have to turn his player over to the

Commissioner's Office. After Arocha, subsequent Cuban defectors were either placed in the draft or thrown into another lottery. (The one held for Rey Ordóñez produced a bigger, although by no means overwhelming, $125,000 contract.) No way was Santín going to let that happen. There had to be some other way to ensure that the Yankees got the players they so rightfully deserved.

Years later when *60 Minutes* was featuring Joe Cubas as "the Great Liberator," and *George* magazine was naming him as one of the "20 Most Fascinating Men in Politics"—an honor he shared with Bill Clinton and UN secretary general Kofi Annan, among others—no one ever mentioned Rudy Santín. In a way, that was good for both the agent and the scout, who by then shared many dark secrets. It was fine for Cubas to claim that he was the trailblazer who had figured out how the Cuban ballplayers could defect and enrich themselves in the process. But in the beginning, Santín was the mastermind, Cubas his willing errand boy.

"I was the one who thought up the whole idea," said Santín. "And anybody who tells you they had that figured out is just lying. I had been thinking about this for years. One day I was thinking, 'If some of these guys could go to a foreign country, for example, Mexico, and become a Mexican resident, how then would they have to enter the draft?' There was nothing written in the rules that says you couldn't do that, and the Commissioner's Office wouldn't be able to do anything about it."

As a team employee, Santín was prohibited from negotiating with the Cubans; he certainly couldn't help them defect. But there was nothing to prevent Cubas from assisting with the defections. He could take the players to a third country, file for free agency, and then gently nudge the players toward the New York Yankees. It was a classic win-win-win situation. The players would get out of Cuba and, as free agents, receive fair-market value. As their agent, Cubas would get a hefty commission and, of course, the publicity. And Santín and the Yankees, who had money to burn, would get some of the top amateur players in the world. As Santín explained the scheme: "We had it so [the Yankees] would get all the players. It was kind of like a thing between me and Joe. It was agreed that the first group was our thing. And after that Joe would have a responsibility to his clients, a responsibility to all teams to be fair."

SANTÍN AND CUBAS thus set out on their global mission. For Santín, who was traveling on the Yankees' dime, money wasn't an issue. But Cubas was on his own. He financed the trips with occasional contracting jobs and memorabilia gigs, and what he didn't have he borrowed or put on his credit cards. The project was not inexpensive. Wherever Team Cuba went, Cubas followed. He was constantly shelling out walking-around money to the players—$50 here, $100 there—but they didn't seem to be responding. Cubas brought along a player who had defected past his prime, Rafael Rodríguez, thinking that would help win the players' trust. Instead, it merely spooked them; no one wanted to be seen with a known defector. "Joe didn't really hit it off with the players at first," said Santín. "They didn't like him a whole lot. So I went around and I talked to Valle and I talked to Ajete. I said to them, 'Hey, this guy's a good guy.'"

Cubas's partner, Juan Iglesias, went along on some of the early trips and was amazed at how easy it was to talk to the players. In 1992, the year after Arocha defected, the Cubans returned to Millington, Tennessee, for another series against the Americans. Iglesias wangled a room at the Best Western on the same floor as the team. To Iglesias the trip was something of a lark. "One time we were downstairs in the lobby and there was this old man with white hair and a heavyset guy," he recalled. "They started taking pictures of us. So we turned around and started taking pictures of *them!* It was all a game to me. You know, it's funny, I realize that it's a serious thing but I looked at it totally the opposite of the way Joe did. Joe is all 007, cloak-and-dagger, behind closed doors and all that shit. But it wasn't like that at all. We started mingling with the players. The players would come to the room and we'd order pizza. We must have spent a week doing that. Then we'd get around to talking to them about defecting. They were like, 'No way! What, are you crazy?'"

Cubas and Iglesias were pitching the benefits of free-market capitalism, but they found that no one was buying. One night Iglesias struck up a conversation by the pool with a player named Juan Manrique. Eventually he invited the player up to his room, where he plied him with beer and Domino's pizza, then tried to close the deal.

"Look, why don't you stay," said Iglesias. "You'll be worth a lot of money in the big leagues."

"No, in Cuba I'm fine, I have everything I need," said Manrique.

"You're fine? How are you fine?"

"Oh, well, I've got my own apartment. I have a phone. I have a refrigerator. I have a fan."

Iglesias was stupefied. A phone, a refrigerator and a *fan?*

"Look, I don't know what it's like in Cuba, but that's nothing down here," he told Manrique.

Iglesias returned from Millington and told Cubas he wanted out of the defector business. He would continue to provide administrative support from Cubas's garage, he said, but Cubas would have to serve as the parnership's traveling salesman.

Part of Cubas's problem, at least initially, was that Domínguez had already cornered the market. It was a classic immigrant's story: Once Arocha had signed with the Cardinals, he referred the players who followed him to Domínguez, who soon found that he was running a full-time sports agency for Cuban defectors.

Joe Cubas and Gus Domínguez could not have been less alike. Cubas was short and rough. Part of his charm was his flagrant machismo, his sense of guerrilla theater. He made it seem as if he were part of a vast conspiracy that was bigger than money, bigger than baseball, and that led all the way to Fidel Castro's front door. "It's like he puts this web over your whole body and you become mesmerized," said René Guim, who later worked as Cubas's publicist. "He has this phenomenal way of wrapping everybody around his little finger with all that cloak-and-dagger shit and the mystery and the mystique and all the excitement." Ramón Batista, another Cubas operative, took it a step further: "Joe Cubas is one of those people who make you think he's God. But he is not God."

Domínguez, on the other hand, was mild-mannered and polished, a kind of Latin matinée idol. He liked the soft sell. He didn't want to force a player to make a life decision, a decision to abandon family and country, possibly forever, that he might later regret. "I never wanted to have it on my head that I influenced somebody to come, and then they break a knee or break their arm before they sign," he said. "The only thing I told all of them is that I was there to help. But I never said, 'Hey, stay, you'll get a lot of money.' " Later, after Cubas had stripped Domínguez of his monopoly, even Domínguez's friends said he might have been too timid for the business that he had fallen into.

In Millington, while Cubas and Iglesias were upstairs eating pizza, Domínguez had shown up with Arocha, who had come directly from a Triple-A game in Memphis. None of the Cuban players wanted to be seen with the notorious traitor, so Domínguez arranged a midnight meeting behind the motel. The players sat in the parking lot, drinking beer till dawn, listening with awe as Arocha described his new life as a professional ballplayer. The group was made up of some of the finest talent in modern Cuban history. In addition to Arocha, El Duque was there and so was Euclides Rojas. Also present was El Duque's best friend, Germán Mesa, a gregarious, spectacular shortstop.

The players had a million questions. How much money did he make? Where did he live? How was the food? How good were the Americans? "I just told them the truth," said Arocha. "I said, 'I'm in the minor leagues. They signed me for $15,000. My salary is $850 a month. But I'm happy.' " As it grew late, Arocha pointed out what a travesty it was that the players, all old friends, had to sneak around a parking lot at four A.M. to avoid being seen. "Look at me, even at this hour I can do whatever I want," he told them. "No one can tell me what to do. You guys, if they catch you with me, you know they're going to fry you."

Arocha made a suggestion: "Look, just get in the car. Let's get out of here."

The players fell silent. All had families back in Cuba. There was no way. Germán Mesa was the only one who eventually put Arocha's car to use: He took it for a spin around the block. It was your basic boxy rental, but Mesa came back euphoric, having driven such a magnificent piece of machinery. After a while, the group began to break up. El Duque, ever vigilant about his training, left first because he was pitching that night. Around six A.M., as the sun was coming up, the others returned to their rooms as well. Arocha and Domínguez drove back to Memphis. There would be no traitors on that trip.

CUBAS CONTINUED TO hemorrhage money. No one had defected. His wife, María, was beginning to ask pointed questions about a business that took him away for weeks at a time but produced negative income. But nothing was going to stop him: not Gus Domínguez, not creditors, not a hectoring wife, nothing. The following year, he traveled to San Juan for the Caribbean and Central American Games. He sensed that he was getting close. Cuba's vaunted sports system seemed to be on the verge of collapsing, and not just the baseball team. From the moment the Cuban delegation arrived, athletes sprinted for the exits as if someone had fired a starter pistol. It was a race for political asylum, a total free-for-all. White Mercedes sedans driven by anti-Castro exiles pulled up outside natatoriums and arenas, then screeched off with water polo players and weight lifters. Planes flew over stadiums with banners urging athletes to defect. By the end of the week, forty-five athletes—some 5 percent of the entire Cuban delegation—had defected.

The baseball team was the last to leave the island. Looking for stiffer competition beyond the preordained gold medal, the Cubans had agreed to an exhibition game against the San Juan Senators, a Puerto Rican winter-league club that featured several major-leaguers, including Juan González, Ruben Sierra, Carlos Baerga, and Javy López. I covered the game for the *Globe*, and it was one of those rare occasions where you could say without embarrassment that the air crackled with electricity. The mix of high political drama and a rare test for Team Cuba—as well as the sensory overload of Caribbean baseball—was overwhelming. A fifteen-piece salsa band warmed up the crowd from the roof of the home dugout. People were literally dancing in the aisles. Scouts from nearly every major-league club parked themselves behind home plate and aimed their radar guns at Lázaro Valle, whose fastball hit 97 three times. "Imagine that," said one scout. "A ninety-seven-mile-an-hour fastball and he can't pitch in the major leagues." The scene near Cuba's dugout resembled the front of the stage at Altamont. Every inning, club-wielding policemen plowed into the crowd to break up fights between foes and supporters of Fidel Castro. After San Juan won the game, 4–3, hundreds of people stood near the field, chanting, "¡Asílese! ¡Asílese!" (Take asylum! Take asylum!) and "¡Quédate aquí! ¡Quédate aquí!" (Stay here! Stay here!).

Incredibly, no one did. But Cubas, who had watched the scene, smiling, from the stands, believed the trip had been a success. Among other things he had gone out to dinner with a talented right-hander named Osvaldo Fernández. The pitcher hinted strongly that he was close. Other players, too, were beginning to confide that they'd had enough. "Gordo," said Rolando Arrojo, another pitcher, using the nickname the Cuban players had given the secret agent. "Gordo, I have no future in Cuba. I have no future." Valle continued to take money from Cubas, promising that he would soon be ready.

Cubas continued the dialogue all over the world, uncertain whether his prospects were promising or hopeless. At times they seemed both. At the 1995 Pan American Games in Argentina, a player sidled up to Cubas and told him he needed to follow him after the game. The agent immediately informed Santín, who was scouting for the Yankees, and the two men piled into Cubas's rental car and waited to trail the Team Cuba bus. "I had this tiny purple car, like one of those Hyundais," said Cubas. "Rudy and I could barely fit into this purple car. I didn't want to be seen, so we parked behind a tree and waited for the bus to come out. So out comes the bus, and then a second bus, and then a *third* bus. All three buses were fucking identical. And we didn't know which one was theirs. I'm going, 'Oh my god, which bus is it?'

"We follow the three buses for, like, half a mile, and then two go this way and one goes that way. I'm like, 'Fuck, which one do we follow? Okay, okay, *that* one.' So we follow the two buses, figuring the odds are with us, and we're going, and we're going, and we're going. It's like eleven-thirty at night. Finally, at around two in the morning, we finally get up enough guts to speed up and get right next to the bus. The buses we're following are *empty*! You know what time we got back to the hotel? Seven o'clock in the morning."

Cubas ran into the player the next day.

"Where were you? I waited three hours," the player complained.

"I told him what happened and he cracked up," said Cubas. Later that day, Cubas met with that player and two others, including pitcher Osvaldo Fernández, in his hotel room. The players now told him that they wanted to defect before the National Series in November.

Cubas took his road show to Japan. On the surface, the trip was a disaster—Cubas had borrowed another $15,000, only to be yelled at by El Duque Hernández—but the agent returned to Miami feeling optimistic. Among other things, Gus Domínguez had skipped the trip, and that had left an opening. Years later this would become Domínguez's primary excuse for having lost the defector market to Cubas. "The only reason Joe even got in the door is because we basically left it wide open," he would say. "I basically got tired of running around. You know the old saying: Out of sight, out of mind."

In Tokyo, Cubas met one more time with Osvaldo Fernández. The pitcher now said he wanted to defect when Team Cuba made its annual pilgrimage to Millington, Tennessee. Fernández was a *guajiro*, a country boy from the sticks. He sat attentively as Cubas diagrammed his future, explaining the third-country concept and free agency and Fernández's projected earnings. In truth, Cubas had no idea how much Osvaldo Fernández was worth. At that point the market didn't exist. But it all sounded good. True, Cubas was more broke than ever. True, his wife was threatening to leave him. True, the Miami construction industry was at a standstill, so he had nothing to fall back on. But he knew it was going to happen. He just knew it. Next trip, Joe Cubas told himself—if not his wife—next trip, for sure.

CHAPTER SIX

OUR MAN IN HAVANA

CUBAS HAD ANOTHER REASON TO BE OPTIMISTIC: HE HAD someone working for him on the inside. His name was Tom Cronin, and he was a middle-aged real-estate agent from Cape Cod, Massachusetts. In the rich history of subterfuge between the United States and Cuba, Cronin was as unlikely a mole as anyone could possibly expect to find. For the first fifty years of his life, he had never set foot in Cuba. His mastery of Spanish was limited to words like *sí, mañana* and *taco*. He was only a casual baseball fan, particularly for New England, the only place that could match Cuba in its passion for the sport. He was curious, though, an amateur photographer with a taste for adventure, and in 1995 he found himself in the middle of a caper that was beginning to play out like one of Graham Greene's entertainments.

Cronin first came to Cuba on vacation in 1991, walking right into the thick of the Special Period. Expecting to find the Havana of romantic lore, he instead discovered a population of undernourished zombies walking amid the ruins of a once-great city. What he noticed first were the lines; they snaked everywhere, dead-eyed people queuing up for hours for a roll of bread or a bus. Cuba was just beginning to make the conversion from a sugar-based economy propped up by the Soviets to one based on tourism. The dollar wouldn't be legal for another two years. One day, Cronin met a waiter who whispered to him: "I have some American dollars. If I give them to you, will you buy something for me?" Cronin agreed and met the young man when he got off work. "We walked all the way back to his house, and when we got there he had four single dollar bills hidden under his mattress," said Cronin. "I took him to one of the dollar stores outside the Habana Libre. I said, 'What do you want me to buy?' He said, 'Anything.' I said, 'You must need a hat or a shirt or something.' He said, 'Anything, I need anything.' "

Instead of being scared away, Cronin kept coming back. He felt like he had seen something extraordinary: a proud nation suddenly on life support after a tectonic shift in world history. "The whole situation was fascinating to me," he said. "It was like walking into the Heart of Darkness." He found the Cuban people amazing: beautiful and courageous in the face of their adversity. Despite the embargo and Castro's long-running rant against the imperialists, Cronin found that no one hated *him*. On the contrary, they welcomed him into their homes and offered what little they had. Because it was illegal under the embargo to travel to Cuba, Cronin took flights that connected through Jamaica or Montreal, and eventually Cancún. With each trip, he developed a circle of friends who led him into subterranean Havana, the city that existed beneath the probing eye of the state. There he found a wealth of opportunities, social and economic, including a thriving black market in which just about anything was up for grabs.

Cronin was walking in Old Havana one afternoon when he mentioned to a friend that he had collected baseball cards during his youth. "Oh, you like baseball cards?" the friend asked. The next thing Cronin knew he was sitting at a chemistry professor's kitchen table somewhere in central Havana. "The guy went into his bedroom and came out with a photo album that he plopped down on the table," said Cronin. "I was thinking, 'Oh, no, here we go.' I had seen some baseball cards floating around, all dog-eared cards from the fifties before the revolution. I knew they were essentially worthless. Then the guy flipped open the book and my mouth dropped open. My friend had to elbow me in the ribs to remind me not to act like I liked them. But there they were, two Babe Ruth cards, Goudey's, 1933 and 1934, in perfect condition."

Cronin wasn't yet an expert, but he knew enough to know that the cards were valuable. Before he left Cuba, he bought the two Ruth cards and a few others for $500, a small fortune on the island, especially in 1991. He turned around and sold the cards to a dealer in Boston for $3,300. Cronin thought he had stumbled on a gold mine. When he returned to Cuba he brought along his son, Jimmy, a recent graduate of Colby College, in Waterville, Maine, where he had majored in Spanish and philosophy. Jimmy Cronin had lived in Mexico and Spain and spoke Spanish fluently. Cronin figured his son could help him negotiate. In 1993, Cronin went back to see the chemistry professor. He wasn't disappointed: This time the professor laid across his kitchen table a 1933

Goudey card of Nap Lajoie, the Hall of Fame second baseman. In the memorabilia business, the card is legendary because the Goudey bubble gum company, in an oversight, never printed the card; it became available only on demand the following year. Cronin, who had been doing his research and knew the card's history, negotiated for two weeks. He bought the card for $600, then took it back to the Cape.

"I called up a dealer I know, a big-time memorabilia guy, and I told him what I had," said Cronin. "He says, 'I don't mean to disappoint you, but if you have that card it's a reproduction, because I know where every single one of those cards is.' I said, 'Well, this one might be real.' " Cronin had the card sitting on his desk when the dealer arrived. The dealer picked it up, took it out of the plastic and held it up, examining it closely.

"Where the fuck did you get this card?" he said finally.

"Never mind that," said Cronin.

Cronin put up the card for auction in New York, where it sold for $11,000.*

After that, Cronin scoured Havana. Word spread throughout the city of the American willing to pay hundreds of dollars for old American baseball cards. Collectors, most of them elderly, turned up at the Hotel Inglaterra (Greene's old haunt) in Old Havana carrying the detritus of a bygone era when Cuba and the United States shared the same sports heroes. But most of the cards were of little value. Among collectors, condition is everything, and the cards had been eroded by time, neglect and the heavy tropical air. The Cronins decided to quit while they were ahead.

"After that, the whole joke was, 'Screw the baseball cards, let's get the baseball players,' " said Jimmy Cronin.

THROUGH A FRIEND, Tom Cronin had met an English teacher whose main passion was the Industriales, the Havana "Blues." Cronin began to accompany the teacher to games at El Latino. The teacher, it turned out, knew several players, and after games they all would go out for dinner and a few beers. Among the teacher's close friends was the Industriales' shortstop, Germán Mesa.

Mesa was part of a long line of extraordinary Cuban shortstops stretching back to major-leaguers Zoilo Versalles, Guillermo "Willie" Miranda and Dagoberto "Bert" Campaneris. Many people believed that Mesa was the best of

*By 1998, the card was selling for $40,000.

them all. Once, René Arocha was sitting at his locker in the Cardinals clubhouse, talking with *Miami Herald* columnist Dan LeBatard about the wealth of baseball talent hidden on the island. After comparing Omar Linares to Barry Bonds, Arocha told LeBatard that he had seen only one player who was as fine a glove man as Germán Mesa.

"Who?" LeBatard asked.

"Him," said Arocha, pointing across the clubhouse at Ozzie Smith, the Cardinals' "Wizard of Oz."

In fact, Mesa had been a gymnast growing up, and before Industriales practices he liked to perform Smith's trademark back flip when he took the field. "But the coaches wouldn't let him do it in the games," said Euclides Rojas, Mesa's former teammate. "They thought he was imitating Ozzie Smith." It is widely known that Mesa prevented Rey Ordóñez from ascending to both Industriales and Team Cuba, in part because Ordóñez, who set a major-league record by not committing a single error in the last 100 games of the 1999 season, was not as good a hitter as Mesa. Built like a wisp of wheat, Mesa was a contact hitter who only got better after Cuba made the switch from aluminum bats to wood. His bunts stuck to the infield like putty dropped from the top of a building, and he could steal a base and even go deep when he had to. In his first thirteen seasons in the National Series he hit .280 with 99 home runs and 309 stolen bases. But many people believed that Mesa was also a better fielder than Ordóñez. The normal course of an evening at El Latino included seeing Mesa at least once stretched out behind second base, parallel to the ground, robbing some poor guy of a base hit. No one got rid of the ball quicker. For this Mesa had acquired a series of nicknames, the most common of which were El Mago (the Magician) and El Pulpo (the Octopus). Years after Ordóñez defected to the Mets, the Mesa-Ordóñez debate was still raging in Havana. In 1999, I saw two men nearly get into a fistfight above the first-base dugout at El Latino while everyone around them weighed in as if they were arguing about the death penalty. "I don't read much English, but I keep up on the Cubans in *Baseball America* and I saw they had Rey Ordóñez of the Mets as the best defensive prospect in all of baseball," Arocha told LeBatard in 1995. "They said he was the next Ozzie Smith. On the national team, Germán was so much better than Rey that Rey had to carry and shine Germán's shoes."

Mesa's best friend on Industriales was Orlando "El Duque" Hernández. The two players were inseparable, "like brothers," recalled El Duque. "We did everything together. On Industriales and Team Cuba we were always together." Before road trips, Mesa would stay over at El Duque's house behind the airport in Calixto Suárez. The players would hang out with their families and friends, watching Brazilian soap operas and eating, then walk across the parking lot the next day to catch their flight. El Duque was slightly more reserved than Mesa, more serious. Mesa was the prankster. Their personal connection extended to the field, where they performed the same ritual before every inning. After the ball had made its way around the infield, El Duque would always trade one or two tosses with his best friend at shortstop. Only then was he ready to pitch.

Tom Cronin met El Duque through Mesa and soon found that he was spending a lot of time around the players from Team Cuba. "It was just something to do," said Cronin. "But I was astonished that some of the biggest stars in Cuba—some of these guys were like Michael Jordan, you might say—and they're broke and they're hungry. So it started to become a ritual where after the game we'd go out and, you know, since they were hungry I'd feed them. It seems like an awkward, odd way to establish a rapport, but it seemed to work nicely. I was a real-estate broker from Cape Cod who couldn't speak Spanish. It was like, 'What would you be doing palling around with the highest level of ballplayers in Cuba?' But it just happened." New Englanders that they were, the Cronins pronounced El Duque's lyrical name "Dookie." On weekends, they would all crowd into a black-market taxi or Mesa's Lada and head out to the beach, Playa del Este, near where the pitcher Lázaro Valle lived. Valle and other players often joined them, and, with Cronin buying, the group would plow through chicken and cigars and Cuba Libres and beers, occasionally taking a dip in the ocean. All the while the Cronins watched with great curiosity as sunbathers treated the players with respectful remove. "That was the strange thing," said Jimmy. "They were totally public figures, but it wasn't a mob scene, like where if Mark McGwire went out to the beach it would be totally insane. People would go, 'Hey, El Duque,' pat him on the back, shake his hand, maybe a couple autographs and gawking, but nothing extreme." Jimmy, a Red Sox fan, had heard of one Cuban ballplayer: Luis Tiant. He certainly had never heard of these guys. Still wearing the long ponytail that he had cultivated in college, he regarded the experience as an interesting postgraduate vacation spent "speaking Spanish and hanging out with cool people."

Then, gradually, the conversations turned to the major leagues. "At first we didn't talk about it much," said Jimmy. "But the idea was always on the tip of everyone's tongues. They would be like, 'Imagine if we were still young, imagine if we didn't have families.' . . . That's what planted the seed with us."

Tom Cronin began to get the idea that perhaps he could make the same kind of score that he had with the baseball cards, only now with human beings.

But first he needed to do some research. One Sunday morning back on Cape Cod, he was reading Peter Gammons's baseball column in *The Boston Globe* when he came across the name of a Yankee scout named Bill Livesey. The name sounded familiar. Cronin turned to his wife, Judy, who had graduated (along with thirty-eight other students in her class) from Orleans High School on the Cape. "Didn't you go to high school with some guy who was with the Yankees, a scout or something?" Cronin asked. "Yeah, Bill Livesey," said Judy. And thus began a string of coincidences that led to the unlikely, avaricious alliance between a Cape Cod real-estate broker and a Miami sports agent, who both had the idea of selling Cuban defectors to the major leagues.

Dropping his wife's name, Cronin called Livesey, the Yankees scouting director. Livesey, in turn, put Cronin in touch with his director of Latin American scouting, a well-connected Cuban American named Rudy Santín. Santín put Cronin in touch with his boyhood friend Joe Cubas, who was already on the case. The more Cronin heard, the more encouraged he got. This could be fun, he thought, as he made his way down to Miami to meet with Cubas. The meeting took place at the Grove Isle Hotel. Cronin found Cubas secretive and slightly paranoid, concerned about who Cronin was and whether he really knew the players he claimed to know. Cubas was still smarting from the tongue-lashing El Duque had given him in Tokyo, and he didn't seem to believe that the pitcher would ever defect. But after several phone conversations they arrived at an understanding that Cronin would receive a percentage on any commissions earned by Cubas for players Cronin sent his way.

Tom and Jimmy Cronin returned to Havana in July 1995, this time with the sole purpose of persuading players to defect. From the start it was a full-court press. "We usually met for dinner, and then, after dinner, invariably, I'd get down to business," said Tom. "It was like, 'Okay, guys, you've had your chicken and rice, your stomach's full, you've had a little Coca-Cola.'" At times the Cronins would try to get Mesa and El Duque to meet in their hotel room, but the players were wary. They picked up the phone and checked for bugging devices, pointed up to the light fixtures and placed their fingers over their lips. "They would never, ever meet under a ceiling," said Jimmy. "It always had to be outside."

The Cronins began to speak in code whenever the subject turned to defections. Cubas was "the Big Guy." Germán Mesa was "Alemania," the Spanish word for German. El Duque was simply "Dookie." There was even a "Mr. X," a high-ranking Cuban baseball official who wanted to set up a pipeline to the major leagues, all at a tidy profit to himself, of course. But Cronin himself never believed he was taking a risk. "I felt like, 'I'm an American, I'm invinci-ble,' " he said.

The Cronins were now selling what had come to be known as the Joe Cubas Plan. Their pitch started with the basics: "We would ask them, 'Do you know what an agent is? Do you know what a *free* agent is? Do you know what a draft is?' " said Jimmy. "Then we'd ask, 'Does everybody know who Joe Cubas is?' They knew him as El Gordo. They didn't really like him much. They thought he was kind of shady. And we said, 'Yeah, he is kind of shady, always acting like a spy, making these quick phone calls and darting off. But that's why you need to trust us. Do you trust us? Yes? Well, if you trust us, you can trust Joe.' That was the whole triangle we were trying to create: 'If you trust us, you can trust Joe.'

"We would say to them, 'Listen, Joe's got a plan to get you to go to a third country to maintain your free-agent status. Now, I understand how with the money you guys are making now that it's difficult to understand, but we are talking about *millions* of dollars. We want to assure you that this is not danger-ous. We will pick you up at your hotel, then take you over to Joe's hotel and hand you over to him. And that will be the entire defection process.' We wanted to make sure they knew there weren't going to be any boats or anything dan-gerous like that.

"They would ask, 'What about our families?' And we'd say, 'Listen, you are going to have millions and millions of dollars. You are going to be able to buy anybody you want. You are going to have so much money you won't believe the power you're going to have. You'll be heroes in the United States, you'll be so high-profile that Fidel won't be able to touch your families back here.' "

That last claim, of course, was preposterous, as everyone, especially El Duque, would soon find out. But the Cronins were on a roll. Some players, like Omar Linares and Antonio Pacheco, clearly weren't interested. But most every-one else was listening attentively. At times as many as a dozen players attended the ad hoc sessions. The Cronins and Cubas were aiming toward Team Cuba's next trip to Millington, Tennessee. That's where it would all go down, they said. Just before the trip, the Cronins met again with the players at the Pan American Village outside Havana, where the players were in training. The meeting had one purpose: "We wanted them to know that we were going to be in Milling-ton, and that the fun and games were over," said Jimmy. "We told them, 'When you see us, you will know exactly why we're there, and that is for you guys to defect if you would like to.' "

The Cronins had one last talk with El Duque at 1830, a tourist restaurant and disco built like a castle above the water along the Malecón. El Duque seemed restless. He kept changing tables, looking over his shoulder. Eventually the three men took a stroll along the Malecón boardwalk, then came back to the restaurant and sat in the back, along the rocks just above the crashing surf. The lights from the restaurant shimmered on the water. In the distance, too far to be seen, too near to be ignored, was Miami, always Miami. Every day, every night, young men sat along the seawall, thinking their thoughts, staring north. What were they thinking, these young men who stared? El Duque had a lot of questions. "Where are you going to be in Millington?" At the hotel. "How will I get to see Joe Cubas?" We will drive you to his hotel. "How much money am I worth?" No one knows. "Are you sure you're going to be there?" Definitely.

The Cronins were sure they had him now. El Duque never came right out and said he was going to defect, but it seemed obvious. They were really going to pull it off.

As they drove back to their hotel, Jimmy Cronin turned to his father: "I think we got him," he said.

HAVANA TO MIAMI is a thirty-five-minute flight, but the Cronins had to take the circuitous embargo route through Cancún. Cubas met them at Miami International, then took them out to meet his parents. Whatever misgivings the agent may have had about Tom Cronin's involvement were apparently gone. Cronin was Wormold to Cubas's Hawthorne. They were both part of the same team, the Defection Team.

From Miami, Cubas and the Cronins flew on to Memphis, where they met up with two other charter members of the group: Juan Ignacio Hernández, Cubas's loose cannon of a cousin, and another exile named Ramón Batista. Hernández and Batista had driven tractor trailers together for a West Palm Beach freight company, and because of their expertise Cubas had assigned them the responsibility for the getaway car, a van that the agent intended to fill up with defectors.

Juan Ignacio was a big-talking, gluttonous man of action who bore a fleshy resemblance to the actor Jon Lovitz. Santín told Cubas that his cousin reminded him of Tony Montana, the cocaine cowboy played by Al Pacino in the bloody 1983 remake of *Scarface* ("You know what capitalism is? Get fucked!"). "Make sure you keep close wraps on that guy because he's liable to do *anything*," Santín had warned. Juan Ignacio cloaked himself in intrigue. He boasted incessantly of his daring adventures, legal and otherwise, which supposedly played out all across the Caribbean basin. He talked constantly about going to Cuba and pulling out the players himself. Santín was a baseball scout.

He didn't want the envelope pushed any further. "He was talking a lot of crazy shit," said Santín. "It got to the point where I said to Joe, 'This guy's either got big balls or he's flat-out crazy. Or both. You gotta watch him.' "

Batista was swarthy and beefy and made a menacing first impression of his own, but he was a teddy bear underneath. Batista couldn't be sure, but he thought he might be a distant relative of Fulgencio Batista, the dictator ousted by Fidel in 1959. He grew up with three-time heavyweight gold-medalist Teofilo Stevenson in a backwater sugar-mill town called Delicias in Oriente. He came to the States at eighteen only because his mother had begged him. Over the years, Batista had worked up an exile's frothing hatred of Fidel, and the scheme appealed to him on a number of levels. "I thought, 'This is one way to hurt Castro without killing anybody or having to shoot a gun,' " he said. "It was one way to put this fucker in his place without being in Cuba. Because I know that Castro loves his players like they were his babies. As far as the money goes, everybody likes money. I thought it was a decent way to earn some money, maybe a little risky."

With Juan Ignacio driving, the Defection Team pulled into Millington on a warm Tennessee night. The Cubans were due anytime but hadn't arrived yet. Millington was the site of the U.S. Olympic training center for baseball, a Memphis bedroom community that billed itself as "the Best Kept Secret in Tennessee." The town had more churches than motels and was deathly quiet. The Cubans were booked into the Admiralty Suites & Inn, a whitewashed two-story motel offering a free continental breakfast bar and HBO, down the street from USA Stadium.

Juan Ignacio pulled into a parking lot across the street from the motel and cut the engine. The Defection Team waited. The five men sat in the van, passing around Doritos, staring at the motel. One hour passed. Two hours. Where were they? Finally, at two A.M., the Team Cuba bus rolled into the Admiralty Inn parking lot and disgorged the groggy, disoriented players into the warm night. Cubas waited in the van while the Cronins ventured tentatively across the street to greet Mesa and El Duque. The players, dressed in their red, white and blue warm-up suits, seemed genuinely pleased to see them. The Cronins said they would pass by again in the morning, then returned to the van. Juan Ignacio drove the Defection Team back to its own headquarters, a Best Western about a half mile down the road.

It was around three A.M., but everyone was too wired to sleep. Cronin, sensing that the Joe Cubas Plan was about to become reality, began to think about what would happen after he turned the players over to the agent. What if

Cubas simply took the players, signed them to big contracts and then stiffed him? Certainly, from what he had seen of Cubas, it wasn't out of the realm of possibility. Somewhat sheepishly he knocked on Cubas's door. Cubas, too, was wide awake. "Look, Joe, I've been laying out a lot of dough on this thing," he said. "Before I bring these guys over I want to know that you and I have a deal. I need it in writing."

"I've got no problem with that," said Cubas.

Cronin went back to his room and pulled out a piece of stationery from the Miami International Airport Hotel, where he and Jimmy had stayed the night before. Cronin dictated; Jimmy wrote "because I have better handwriting."

I have decided to omit the name of one of the five players because he remains in Cuba and has never been linked to Cubas. Two of the players, Omar Linares and Antonio Pacheco, never seriously considered defecting.

Agreement of Association

The purpose of this contract is to define the referral commission agreement between Joe Cubas, president of Premier Sports Council, Miami, Fla. and Thomas Cronin of Orleans, MA. The above-mentioned parties (Cronin + Cubas) both agree to be legally bound to the following schedule: Cronin shall recommend and refer specific members of the Cuban national baseball team to Cubas as their exclusive agent. These players will include: Omar Linares, Germán Mesa, Orlando Hernández, Antonio Pacheco and ———— and possible others that Cubas may approve at his discretion.

In return for Cronin's services, Cubas agrees to compensate Cronin as follows: Cubas agrees to pay to Cronin ⅓ (one-third) of all commissions—monies earned as a result of major-league contracts involving the above-named players, with Cubas as agent.

Payments to Cronin shall be due and payable within 10 (ten) days of receipt of said commission to Cubas.

It is further understood that this is a legally binding and enforceable agreement.

Cronin took what was surely one of the most unusual contracts in the history of professional sports back to Cubas's room. The agent looked it over. The entrepreneurs then signed the contract. Jimmy Cronin signed as a witness. Everyone shook hands.

But Cubas still had his doubts about one of the players on the list: Orlando Hernández.

"There is no way you will get that Communist to come to this room," he said.

"Well, we'll see," said Cronin.

And thus everyone retired for the evening.

THE NEXT MORNING, Cubas sat in the van, training a pair of binoculars on the Admiralty Inn. He was seated on the passenger side, in the parking lot directly across the street from the motel. He picked up his cellular phone, called the front desk and asked to be patched through to Osvaldo Fernández.

"Hey, it's me, Gordo," Cubas said when the pitcher picked up.

"My God, where are you?" said Fernández. "Where *are* you?"

"Partner, I am right across the street. Go peek out your window."

Fernández parted the curtains about an inch. He peered outside. Juan Ignacio flashed the headlights. Cubas waved.

"Give me a minute, I'll be right down."

Ozzie Fernández had not been certain how he would react when this moment arrived. Back home his loyalty to the revolution had never been questioned. It was Fernández, in fact, whom the sports apparatchiks had chosen to fill Arocha's blighted roster spot in 1991. Fernández had grown up in Holguín, a lonely rural province in Oriente, a place where the revolution still enjoyed steady, if no longer overwhelming, support. The Special Period had hit the outer provinces especially hard, but Fernández had been able to use his position on Team Cuba to hoard cooking oil and extra rations of rice that he shared with his parents. The pitcher had a wife and a one-year-old baby girl. "I was the last person in the world they would have thought would ever defect," he said later.

In fact, Fernández's frustration had been building for years. He felt that *la lucha*, the daily struggle—the insane travel, the blackouts and the scarcity of everything—was eating away at him and everyone around him. At times, he looked in the mirror and felt like he was dying an accelerated death, aging two or three years for each one he lived. Every time he left the country with Team Cuba he wondered why every other nation was moving forward while Cuba remained frozen in time. "I had to travel outside Cuba for five years to see how bad things really were," he said. "If you don't leave Cuba you don't see it." He had been talking to Cubas off and on, working toward a decision. But one final incident had pushed him over the edge.

Before leaving for Havana to train for Millington, he pulled his old Muscovy into a Holguín brewery to pick up two cases of beer. Beer was rationed, but Fernández knew the manager of the plant and was able to get some on the side. "We were going to be in Havana for five days, and I was going to share it with [Orestes] Kindelan and Pacheco and the rest of the guys," he said. Before he left, he stopped by the park in downtown Holguín to say good-bye to friends. His trunk was open when two police officers walked by. "Suddenly they wanted to see the receipts for the beer, these two miserable guys," he said. "I had to go all the way back to the manager of the plant to get some receipts, but these guys still wouldn't accept it. They ended up confiscating the beer."

When Fernández arrived in Havana, the INDER held a pre-trip reception for Team Cuba. Castro's brother, Ramón, happened to be there, mingling with the ballplayers, as well as the president of the INDER, Conrado Martínez. Fernández had been indulging in the state's beer, a couple of six-packs' worth. "I was feeling no pain," he said. "I just vented on them." Fernández told Fidel's brother the whole story, not just the beer but also the squalid living conditions in Holguín and his terrible tiny apartment—the litany of complaints he had about the system. "He just nodded sympathetically," he said. "That's when I made up my mind. I mean, two cases of beer! I was already pretty sure I was going to do it—I had been talking about doing it—but that was the moment I decided. By the time we got to Millington my mind was made up."

Fernández walked across the street and hopped into the van. Juan Ignacio drove off. But even then it was unclear whether the pitcher had actually defected. The group went to McDonald's for breakfast, made small talk and then drove back to Cubas's room at the Best Western.

Fernández told Cubas he had decided to defect but still wanted to wait. "Why don't we do it tonight?" he said. "Let's just wait until after the game."

"What do you mean do it after the game? Ozzie, you're out. You are *out*. We did it. It's *done*. You're out."

"No, I want to wait until tonight, until after the game. I don't want people to know."

"Ozzie, the moment you step away they're gonna know. You're out. Why take the risk?"

Fernández thought for a moment. "Wait a minute. You're right. I'm out. I'm already out."

It was Cubas's big moment, the moment he had been working toward for three long, expensive years. He had staked his marriage, his entire family's future, his life savings and then some, on this peculiar moment in which a baseball player decided to abandon his country. One night, before he left for Millington, Cubas had sat down and tried to calculate exactly how much he had spent over the past three years. The total came out to something like $150,000. But now his days of debt and doubt would soon be over. He had his Cuban ballplayer. He was ready to cash in.

"Wait a minute," said Fernández.

The room fell silent.

"I want to go back and get my stuff. Let's go back and get my bags."

Cubas wanted to kill him. But back they all went, piling into the van to return to the Admiralty Inn. Cubas, Juan Ignacio and Batista waited anxiously as Fernández disappeared. Was he really coming back? The pitcher walked upstairs and opened the door to his room. Into his bag he stuffed what were now his entire life's possessions: clothes, his glove and his spikes, even his Team Cuba uniform. He then walked outside with his bags, into the sopping summer heat, down the stairs, away from his team and his country and his wife and his baby girl and everything that had come before. He looked straight ahead. No one stopped him, no one even noticed. He threw his bags into the van and hopped inside.

Juan Ignacio was just pulling out when Fernández spotted three other players walking across the parking lot.

"Stop! Stop!" yelled Fernández. The pitcher threw open the door of the van. "Hey, there's still room for three more in here," he said.

The players looked at his bags sitting on the floor, smiled nervously and kept walking. With no other takers, Fernández turned to Juan Ignacio. "Let's get out of here," he said.

BACK AT THE Best Western, Cubas was just beginning to celebrate his first big triumph when there was a knock at the door. Thinking it was the maid, Cubas flung the door open to find El Duque Hernández, Germán Mesa and the Cronins standing in front of him. El Duque extended his hand. "Here's your Communist," said the pitcher.

Tom and Jimmy Cronin had come by the Admiralty Inn that morning and found El Duque and Mesa hanging out in their room. Specifically, the players were lying in bed, smoking cigars and watching Mighty Mouse in a language that neither could understand. The Cronins took the players out shopping to soften them up, then drove them over to meet with Cubas. Along the way, one of them mentioned Cubas's remark about El Duque's supposed political leanings.

Cubas stood at the door, stunned. He was also alarmed. Ozzie Fernández, his meal ticket, was standing over by the air conditioner, nursing a beer, digesting what he had just done. "It was like you could hear a pin drop," Cubas recalled. "Everyone was just shocked. They looked at each other, and you could tell that El Duque was scared that Ozzie saw him talking to me and that Ozzie got scared that El Duque was there, too."

Cubas decided he better say something quick. "Above all, we are all Cubans here," he said. "We are all men. No one is going to snitch on anybody." Cubas turned to his new guests. "Duque and Germán, Ozzie has just defected. He's coming back to Miami with me." Then he turned to Fernández. "Ozzie, Duque and Germán are here to discuss a few things."

El Duque walked across the room and embraced his now former teammate. Later, people who were present would recall that the embrace seemed to go on for ten minutes.

"*Que dios te acompañe*," El Duque said, finally. May God be with you.

"Here was this Communist, who had exploded on me, and I've got Ozzie in my room," said Cubas. "My first thought was, Oh my God. But El Duque defused everything. I thought, This guy is unbelievable."

El Duque apologized to Cubas for the outburst in Tokyo. He said he had seen the Team Cuba technical director, Miguel Valdés, coming up behind him that day, and he didn't want Valdés to think that he and his brother Livan had been talking about defecting. With that, El Duque and Mesa plopped down on the bed like two buyers in town for a hardware convention.

Cubas, of whom it was said that he could sell sand at the beach, shifted into overdrive. He explained the Joe Cubas Plan once again. The plan was constantly being refined, and Cubas laid out the updated version. It was very simple. The players would be driven to Miami, then taken to the Dominican Republic to establish residency. There, they would play in the Dominican winter league to demonstrate their skills before major-league scouts. They would declare themselves free agents with the Commissioner's Office. A bidding war undoubtedly would follow, and the players would then sign contracts for untold millions of dollars.

Mesa was largely silent through the presentation, but El Duque had questions. He was especially concerned about the third-country idea. The Team

Cuba authorities were holding their passports. What were they supposed to do about passports?

Juan Ignacio cut in. "Passports? You want to see passports?" he said excitedly.

Then, like a manic watch salesman, he flipped open a briefcase to reveal about a half dozen passports, Dominican and Venezuelan. "He says, 'Here are your passports, we've got all kinds of passports,'" said Jimmy Cronin, who was translating the exchange for his father. "He's talking a mile a minute and he says, 'All we need are your thumbprints and you're good to go. We've got passports, we've got papers, we've got visas, we've got whatever you need. We know everybody there is to know.'

"As he's saying this you can tell these guys are starting to freak out," said Jimmy. "It just started to get really weird all of a sudden. These guys had legitimate concerns. Nobody had said anything about falsifying documents. And Juan Ignacio is just exploding on them. He's throwing out names of people he knows in the Costa Rican government, people he knows in the Dominican government. He was talking about planes that he could get and everything that he could do.

"You could tell he was losing them. I turned to Joe and I said, 'Joe, jump in there.' He says, 'It's not my problem right now.' Joe was just anxious to get the hell out of Dodge and get back to Miami. He didn't have time to build the trust with Dookie and Germán. It was his first player, his first defection, and now he had his guy and he was ready to go."

"Look," Cubas said finally. "That van downstairs is leaving for Miami. If you guys want to do it, let's go."

El Duque and Mesa said they weren't ready. El Duque was concerned about his daughters. He asked for a day to think it over. But Ramón Batista had already grabbed Fernández's bags and was carrying them downstairs. Fernández had told Cubas that he was anxious to leave Millington.

Tom Cronin was panicked, furious at Cubas. The whole Joe Cubas Plan, at least his role in it, was now collapsing before him. Worse, Joe Cubas himself didn't seem to care in the slightest.

"Joe, what the hell are you doing?" said Cronin. "We've got a plan here. We're going to be here for a few days. We're going to work on this thing."

"I'm out of here," said Cubas.

And so he was. The agent, his cousin and Batista climbed into the van with Ozzie Fernández and headed toward Miami. The Cronins, El Duque and Mesa were left standing in Cubas's room at the Best Western, surrounded by empty beer cans and half-eaten bags of chips.

For the Cronins, it was over. If El Duque and Mesa were going to defect—and, in the end, there is no reason to believe that they necessarily would have—they wouldn't now, not after that scene. "I don't understand why he couldn't have given us more time," El Duque told the Cronins after Cubas was gone. But it was clear that his heart was no longer in it. "We thought, Let's get out of this stupid fucking city," said Jimmy. "We had just lost the whole thing. We had let down Germán and we had let down Dookie, so we went home empty-handed, with just a good story to tell."

For Cubas, it was just the beginning. The drive back to Miami took sixteen hours. Fernández sat in the back, awake the entire trip, "thinking about what I had done. It felt like I was driving from the *campo* where I was born all the way to Miami. But it was done. I had made up my mind. They would have had to kill me before I went back to Cuba." That night in Millington, word spread quickly about what had happened. At this point, a baseball player defecting was no longer a total shock. The only difference was that this time Joe Cubas was involved. That night, and the next three nights, Team Cuba absorbed a terrible beating from Team USA, an unprecedented four-game sweep. But in Miami that wasn't the lead story. News of another defection hit the wires almost immediately. The city was buzzing.

Cubas called María from the road. "Hey, how are you doing, honey? We're on our way home. He did it. Ozzie defected."

"I know, I heard. Congratulations." Then she slammed down the phone.

CHAPTER SEVEN

THE FREE MARKET

CUBAS HAD NO SOONER DROPPED OFF OZZIE FERNÁNDEZ IN THE Dominican Republic (step 2 of the Joe Cubas Plan) than he received a collect call from the city of Monterrey in northern Mexico.

"Gordo, I'm ready," a voice whispered. "I want out."

Cubas misunderstood the urgency of the request.

"Well, when did you want to do this?" he asked.

"A *long* time ago," said Liván Hernández.

Liván and his half brother, El Duque, both inherited their father's ability to pitch. Beyond that, they had little in common. El Duque was formal, in manner and dress, with the self-discipline of a diamond cutter. His friend Mario Cobo described him perfectly: *el hombre vertical,* the vertical man. El Duque divided the world into two kinds of people: those who were serious about life and those who were not. "But you are a serious man," he would say imploringly whenever he perceived that someone he respected had strayed. On issues of right and wrong he could be as rigid as steel. Once, he and his friend Cobo took their families to the beach at Varadero, a good three-hour drive. When they arrived, only the famous El Duque had a room. The pitcher threatened to drag the entire group back to Havana unless the hotel came up with another room, which eventually it did.

Few would describe Liván Hernández as a serious man. Nine years younger than El Duque, he didn't meet his half brother until he was ten. He grew up on the Isle of Youth, an island fifty miles south of the mainland, infamous as the "tropical Siberia," where Fidel was imprisoned after Moncada. For a brief time in the 1970s, the original El Duque managed the island's edition in the National Series. When inevitably he moved on, Liván remained with his mother, Miriam Carreras, a typist in a government office, and an older sister, Yamile. Unlike El Duque, Liván was a natural from the start. Raised in the sports schools, both the EIDE and the ESPA, he threw with a classic, fluid three-quarters delivery. By his mid-teens, he was launching effortless, hopping fastballs in the mid-90s. His curveball was a dagger, hard and unexpected. He was not yet twenty when he made Team Cuba.

But many coaches on the island feared that Liván would never fulfill his vast potential. Miguel Valdés, the former technical director for the national team, once said of Liván: "He has tremendous talent, but he doesn't know what it takes to be an athlete." Rolando Núñez, one of the keenest judges of talent in Cuba, said the two brothers were like opposites: "El Duque has more guts than [Cuban independence hero] Antonio Maceo. He has an excess, well, not an excess, but an *abundance* of dedication. The other one is not dedicated. He's a skirt chaser. He drinks. I've always thought that if you could take Liván's talent and youth and mix it with El Duque's makeup, you'd have a pitcher who could win three hundred games in the major leagues." Cuban sportswriters I have talked to have almost total contempt for Liván, not because of his defection but because of his squandered potential. "Liván is an imbecile," said Michel Contreras, the sports editor for *Juventud Rebelde*. "But he has more natural ability than his brother. El Duque would love to have Liván's fastball."

Exactly what prompted Liván to defect remains something of a mystery. His father, who still returned to live with him occasionally, claimed that Liván fled his country over "a tube in a television set."

"It's true," said the elder El Duque, shaking his head. "The one we had on the island burned out. The local party president kept saying, 'Don't worry, I'll take care of it.' But he never did. Then Liván went to Japan and met Joe Cubas, and Joe Cubas bought one for him." El Duque said his son came back from Japan and broke the news to him in a park one afternoon. "He said to me, 'I'm going to sign with Joe Cubas.' I immediately sat down on a bench and opened a beer. What pain they give me, my sons! I kissed him and hugged him. It wasn't about politics. He just couldn't take it anymore. He defected for a tube in a TV set that the idiot president of the party kept promising him. The guy was the top government official in the province."

I asked Liván about the tube theory and he didn't exactly deny it. "Everybody in Cuba had the same problems," he said. "It wasn't just us. But the first thing was to find freedom. That was most important. Then to play in the major leagues and help your family." Liván lived in a cramped fifth-floor walk-up with his mother and his sister. He transported himself to the stadium on a Chinese-made bicycle. He earned the equivalent of $5 a month in a phantom job as an "electrician's assistant," even though he was rarely called upon to screw in a lightbulb. To get from the Isle of Youth to Oriente for a road trip required him to take a six-hour ferry trip, followed by a backbreaking twelve-hour bus ride. Most likely the TV tube was a symbol of accumulated frustration, the same myriad factors that lead someone to cross an ocean in an aluminum skiff or brave scorching deserts and mountain lions and *la migra* to sneak across an international border.

Liván's own quest for the American dream began outside a Monterrey industrial park late one September evening. Cubas had flown to Mexico immediately after getting the pitcher's call, bringing along a team of Juan Ignacio and Juan's wife, a blond Venezuelan named Teresa. The intrepid trio checked into the Holiday Inn, then went out to the Monterrey stadium, where Team Cuba was in training for the 1995 World Cup. Cubas took out an autograph book, placed a photo of himself between the pages and sent Teresa to make contact with Liván as he made his way to the team bus.

"She stuck out like a sore thumb standing between all those little Mexicans," said Cubas. "Liván walked right up to her and started flirting. Then she gave him the book. When he opened it up, she put the picture right in his hand. He nearly fainted. He says, 'Where is he?' And she says, 'He's right over there in that car.' Then she gave him a little slip of paper with the number that he could use to call us at the Holiday Inn. About eleven o'clock that night he called."

Team Cuba was staying in a dormitory on the outskirts of Monterrey. The area was so remote that Cubas needed to hire a taxi to guide him there. Another pitcher, Rolando Arrojo, happened to be with Cubas that night, making plans for his own escape the following year. Cubas had spent three years chasing promises, and now players were lining up to defect. That night, it was like a revolving door. Arrojo exited the rental car, walked inside the dormitory and announced to Liván that his car, sir, was waiting outside. "The thing is, you have to picture this industrial area," said Cubas, never one to underplay the drama. "It was a street, very dark, and he starts walking. You can see him walking and he's walking and he's getting closer, and then he starts to run." Later, Liván would say: "Men aren't supposed to cry, I know. I do. You worry about your family." The pitcher was bawling now as he made his way toward Cubas's car, which was parked on the far side of a frontage road. He was so distraught, in fact, that he nearly stumbled into oncoming traffic. A car screeched to a halt in front of the desperate, sobbing man. Liván looked up through his tears in horror. "I just didn't see it," he said later. "I was running across the street and I was nervous. How could you not be?"

They were two hours from the U.S. border, where Liván could have applied immediately for political asylum, but under the Plan that meant nothing. Cubas needed to get the pitcher to the Dominican Republic, where he had a prearranged agreement for Liván to play with a winter-league club, Escogido. Cubas wanted to get Liván out of Mexico as quickly as possible. The Mexican government maintained good relations with Castro, and the agent feared that the authorities might try to send the pitcher home. The next morning Cubas flew with Liván to Mexico City, then took him to the Dominican embassy. But getting the visa wasn't the slam dunk that Cubas had anticipated. After hours of wrangling he decided to send Liván with Juan Ignacio to a house Juan kept on Margarita Island in Venezuela. Liván at least could stay there on a tourist visa until the Dominican visa was sorted out.

RUDY SANTÍN, PRINCIPAL ARCHITECT of the Joe Cubas Plan, couldn't believe what was happening. It was exactly as he had dreamed. It was brilliant: The Cubans were walking right into the open arms of his boyhood friend, who was handling it all masterfully. "I couldn't have picked a better guy than Joe," Santín would say later. Better still, all the prospects would soon be Yankees.

Then George Steinbrenner intervened. So unnerved was the Yankee owner by his team's dramatic five-game loss to the Mariners in the 1995 playoffs that he launched a purge that was staggering even by his lofty standards. Steinbrenner backed up the proverbial truck in front of the Yankee front office. Jon Heyman, the veteran baseball writer for *Newsday*, counted fifty-four personnel changes—and those were *off* the field. Among the casualties were general manager Gene Michael, manager Buck Showalter* and Santín's boss, scouting director Bill Livesey. Santín could have stayed on, but he resigned out of solidarity with his mentor.

Santín's departure passed unnoticed in New York. But it would have later repercussions for the Bombers. Steinbrenner had unwittingly forfeited a monopoly in the burgeoning Cuban defector market, a blunder that still pained

---

*Technically, Showalter walked away after turning down a two-year contract extension sans his coaching staff. It was an offer apparently designed for him to refuse. When Showalter turned it down, Steinbrenner issued a press release claiming that the two sides had agreed to a mutual parting of the ways. Gene Michael stayed on as a senior scouting official.

Santín years later. "Oh, man, my whole plan went down the drain," he told me. "I was very, very frustrated. Steinbrenner would have eaten that stuff up. He *lives* for that kind of publicity. We would have had all those free agents. And everybody in baseball would have been bitching and moaning and he would have loved that even more."

Cubas, however, was still very much in business. He found that even without the Yankee pipeline there was plenty of interest. As terrible as Santín's luck had been, Cubas's was extraordinary. On July 5, 1991, the day after Arocha's groundbreaking defection, Major League Baseball had approved an expansion franchise for South Florida, home to 800,000 Cuban exiles. Two years later, the Florida Marlins played their first game at Joe Robbie Stadium. The team sold tiny cups of Cuban coffee and played salsa during the seventh-inning stretch. The first baseman was a slugger named Orestes Destrade whose family had fled Cuba when he was six. The Big O, as he was known, had been named after an uncle who was captured at the Bay of Pigs. He had hit 154 homers in four years with the Seibu Lions to become the most prolific slugger in Japan since the immortal Sadaharu Oh. The Marlins signed Destrade for $3.5 million, hoping he would be a bridge to the exile community and a power source in the middle of the lineup. But the pressure was too much for the Big O. He hit one homer in his first four weeks of the inaugural season, and by midsummer the fans were all over him. When the club released him the following year, he called it "a sayonara experience" and returned to Japan.

By 1995, Marlins attendance had dropped 35 percent and the team was desperately seeking new ambassadors for its community-outreach program. In that sense, Ozzie Fernández and Liván Hernández were like godsends. But to sign the players was going to mean a dramatic departure from the normal way of doing business in Latin America—not just for the Marlins but for any interested club. No matter how much he cloaked himself in the banner of freedom, no one was going to mistake Joe Cubas for Simón Bolívar. Players would later accuse him of bilking them out of thousands of dollars or simply abandoning them. Scouts would accuse him of soliciting, and quite possibly taking, bribes from major-league clubs. But Cubas and, of course, his puppetmaster, Santín, revolutionized how teams were forced to negotiate—at least in the niche market that Cubas inhabited.

Two decades after the landmark Messersmith decision, which brought free agency to baseball, the clubs were still basically operating under the plantation system in Latin America. In the Dominican Republic, scouts, agents and subsidized "bird dogs" funneled prospects as young as eleven into "academies," baseball factories where youngsters were either groomed for the United States or weeded out. Abuses, everything from underage signings (sixteen was the minimum) to poaching, were so common that the Commissioner's Office finally set up an oversight bureau in Santo Domingo. It was a huge, unruly business: By the late 1990s, Latin America was producing over 20 percent of all major-league players. Roughly half of that—one in ten major-leaguers—came out of the Dominican Republic, a nation with 3 million fewer people than Cuba and a monthly per capita income of $256.

In the "boatload mentality" of Dominican scouting, as onetime Rockies vice president Dick Balderson so classically described it to Marcos Bretón and José Luis Villegas in their book, *Away Games*, clubs sprinkled $3,000 bonuses on hundreds of prospects, hoping one or two would grow up to be Sammy Sosa or Pedro Martínez.

The Sosa negotiations, if they can be called that, were typical. Mike Lupica described them in *Summer of '98*, his diary of the unreal season when Sosa hit 66 home runs to Mark McGwire's 70. Omar Minaya, the scout representing the Texas Rangers, offered the prospect $3,000. Sosa, who was sixteen and representing himself, politely said no.

"You don't want to sign?" said Minaya.

"Four thousand," responded the willful boy, sitting next to his mother.

"Three thousand is what we generally offer."

"Four."

"Three thousand five hundred then," said Minaya.

The scout and the boy shook hands.

In Cuba, the business had been much the same before the revolution. One scout, Joe Cambria of the Washington Senators, dominated the island. Papa Joe, as he was known, dressed in white linen suits and Panama hats and scouted from a Cadillac convertible. Employing his own boatload mentality on behalf of the Senators' owner, Calvin Griffith, he signed a slew of players, including Zoilo Versalles, Camilo Pascual and Tony Oliva, most of whom received little more than their plane tickets. Mike Brito, who later became a legendary scout in his own right (he discovered Fernando Valenzuela in a northern Mexico backwater), said that when Cambria signed him in 1955 "all he did was fix my passport, which cost about twenty-five dollars." Brito described Cambria as "a short chunky guy who was always smoking a cigar, and when he talked to you, he always had one eye closed, like this."

Cambria handed out contracts like Chinese menus. One afternoon, the scout asked Brito if he wouldn't mind helping him with a tryout. When Brito protested that he had neither his glove nor his spikes, Cambria told him, "Don't worry, it'll just take a minute. We'll go across the street." The scout marked off sixty feet, six inches, on the Malecón boardwalk. Then he handed a catcher's mitt to Brito and a ball to the prospect, who was standing off to the side in his street clothes. It was the Havana equivalent of holding a baseball tryout in the middle of Times Square.

As traffic whizzed by, the prospect heaved five fastballs.

"That's enough!" shouted Cambria.

"He signed him right there," Brito recalled. "I forget the name of the guy. But what a scout this guy was. In street clothes!"

Some have described Cubas as Cambria's historical heir. But there are significant differences. The most critical is that Cambria was a scout, working for a team. Cubas was an agent, working for himself. Cambria wanted to keep contracts as low as possible, zero being the optimal number. Cubas wanted record-breaking deals. After René Arocha defected, baseball's peculiar cartel managed to hold down the market until Cubas came along and blew it open. In that respect, Cubas and Cambria were completely different animals. Cubas fully intended to take the players, who had spent their entire careers as tools of socialism, and turn them into instruments of the free market. If the Florida Marlins wanted to sign Liván Hernández—and they did in the worst way—they were going to have to pay top dollar.

"By creating the type of atmosphere that I created, and creating this type of platform for these players, I think I facilitated the clubs' mentality of getting closer to my mentality from a dollar-value standpoint," said Cubas.

Translation: I figured out how to stick it to them big-time.

CUBAS GOT A WHIFF of demand when he called up the Marlins' Al Avila from Santo Domingo one day. He wanted to know if Ozzie and Liván could meet with the team in Miami. "Not a problem," said Avila. "I'll talk to my people and we'll fly you in." In truth, Christmas was coming up, and Cubas was looking for free tickets home for himself and the players. But if the Marlins were that enthusiastic, Cubas figured, other teams might be as well. A few phone calls later, he had lined up an all-expenses-paid tour of the United States.

The tour was an eye-opener for Ozzie and Liván, both of whom had grown up in the sticks. It was also the birth of a market. The first stop was Texas and the Ballpark in Arlington, the Rangers' new $189 million stadium. The Ballpark was part of the new breed of stadium created for rich people but designed to feel homey. It had 120 luxury suites, two restaurants and a museum. One local writer waxed: "The corners evoke the belltower at St. Mark's in Venice; the columns and patterned brickwork are faintly Moorish, while the soaring arches might be remnants of a Roman aqueduct."

THE TEXAS RANGERS WOULD LIKE TO WELCOME OSVALDO FERNANDEZ
AND LIVAN HERNANDEZ TO THE BALLPARK IN ARLINGTON.

The greeting, in letters the size of a small apartment building, flashed on the megaboard as the players staggered onto the field. It was like the entire stadium had been reserved for them. "It was unbelievable," said Cubas. "They were both in shock. They were taking baby steps and I was leading them by the hand. I was loving every minute of it, too, this feeling of them wanting to overwhelm us." That night, the players and Cubas went to dinner with the Ranger front office, then prepared for the next leg of the journey: Miami.

Marlins owner Wayne Huizenga, the Blockbuster Video tycoon, sent his private Learjet. On board was the Marlins welcoming committee: Avila, manager Rene Lachemann, director of player personnel Gary Hughes and the legendary Tony Pérez. "I remember we left the hotel early, at seven or eight o'clock in the morning, and it was freezing, we were all sort of miserable," said Cubas. "Then we saw the plane. Even though I had coordinated it all, it was simply mind-boggling to me. It started to hit me that these guys were not only trying to woo the players, but also, to a certain degree, they were trying to woo me."

"They were flying us around like we were some kind of president," said Ozzie Fernández. "It was the first time I realized what it meant to be treated like a major-leaguer. It was emotional."

The plane's cabin was filled with swivel chairs and couches covered in rich, soft leather. Flight attendants came around with plates of shrimp and fresh fruit, ham-and-cheese hors d'oeuvres. At one point during the flight, Ozzie got up to go to the bathroom. He returned moments later, confused.

"*Oye*, Gordo, there's no toilet in the bathroom," he whispered.

Cubas went back to take a look. The bathroom was covered in gold, everything gleaming. But the agent couldn't find the toilet, either. He summoned a flight attendant.

"It turned out that the toilet was covered by a leather chair," said Cubas. "It was for a woman who wanted to make herself up. When somebody needed to use the bathroom, they would raise up the leather chair, this luxury leather chair, and there was the toilet."

A media horde, cordoned off, greeted the plane at Fort Lauderdale Executive Airport. A red carpet stretched across the tarmac to a podium where the visiting dignitaries—the two pitchers and their agent—would make opening remarks. It was like Reykjavík, only warmer. Both players remembered to thank Huizenga. "We worked on that on the plane ride," Lachemann explained to Peter Gammons. "You see, if you say Huizenga wrong in Spanish, it comes out a very bad swear word." Lachemann, in fractured Spanish, addressed the crowd as well: "We have here two of the best amateur pitchers in the world. And we hope to *firma la contracto*." The delegation then piled into waiting limousines for a pork-and-paella luncheon at Joe Robbie Stadium. Like the Rangers, the Marlins posted a megaboard greeting: BIENVENIDO, OSVALDO FERNANDEZ Y LIVAN HERNANDEZ.

It was obvious to everyone the socioeconomic factors at work: "We had to get one of them, it was as simple as that," said Louie Eljaua. "The whole thing was just snowballing. The Cuban community was sold on it. These guys were on the front page every single day. We had to sign one of them or we were going to get killed in our own city. It would have been a disaster."

So when Cubas asked for two suites at the Fontainebleau Hotel in Miami Beach, the Marlins didn't blink. By this time the agent and his wife, María, had separated. So Ozzie and Liván stayed in one two-bedroom suite, Cubas in the other.

That night the party moved on to Victor's Café, a famous Cuban eatery with a scaled-down replica of the Statue of Liberty towering over the parking lot. Upstairs in the private dining room a roasted pig sat at the end of a buffet table with a baseball in its mouth. The Marlins had invited the Cuban elite, some two hundred people: power brokers from the Cuban American National Foundation, former players like Pedro Ramos and Camilo Pascual, the entire Marlins front office. Peter Gammons, naturally, was there, and he found Liván, dressed in a new gray suit, gleefully weaving through the crowd, picking shrimp off the waitresses' trays. The pitcher still hadn't come down from the plane ride. "I didn't know there was such a thing as a private jet," he told Gammons.

On and on it went. Cubas and the players, this time in Huizenga's private helicopter, flew up to Melbourne for a team barbecue—"The steaks looked like cows," said Cubas—and a tour of the training facility. General manager Dave Dombrowski wanted to negotiate, but by then Cubas had figured out that he was the conductor of a runaway train. No way was he going to make a deal yet. Back in Miami, the players had one final dining experience courtesy of the Marlins: a luncheon at Larios, Gloria Estefan's restaurant in Miami Beach. Gloria herself couldn't make it, but she left each player a goody bag filled with a compact-disc player, autographed photos and CDs.

It was going to be hard for anyone to top all that, but the road show continued, mostly because Cubas didn't want it to stop. Every time the players landed, the media showed up, fanning public opinion, driving up the price. In Boston, it was the dead of winter, and the players arrived to see Fenway Park blanketed with snow, a blinking Christmas tree planted at second base. In New York, where the Yankees were now just another team trying to impress, Steinbrenner put up everyone in his Park Avenue suites. The next day, he ordered workers at Yankee Stadium to sweep the snow off the monuments so the players could tour the marbled pantheon of Ruth and Gehrig, Mantle and DiMaggio. In Toronto, the Blue Jays, bereft of such history, demonstrated the magical opening and closing of the roof at SkyDome, their once futuristic, now passé monolith.

Finally, everyone flew back to the Dominican Republic to get down to brass tacks. Cubas had decided to hold negotiations at the Plaza Naco Hotel in Santo Domingo. "Thanks for filling up the hotel," the desk manager told him when he went to check in. Nearly every major-league team had shown up. Cubas now had two other players, pitchers Larry Rodríguez and Vladimir Núñez, who had defected in Venezuela. The agent was negotiating for Ozzie and Liván while showcasing the new defectors in the Dominican winter league. "It was a circus," said Avila, who was part of the Marlins' negotiating team. "I remember that Dave Dombrowski was in Lizard Beach off Australia on his honeymoon, and we had to keep calling him. Huizenga's office, too. It was all because of the money. We were talking about big, big money."

No one was exactly certain what the benchmark was. Ariel Prieto, a defector who went into the draft that year and was selected by Oakland in the first round, had gotten $1.2 million. Hideo Nomo, a Japanese star, had signed with the Dodgers for $2 million, a record for a foreign player. Cubas bounced from room to room, writing down bids, going back and telling the clubs that, hard as it was to believe, they were *still* low. Everyone was stunned. It was all-out war. "I pride myself on always being prepared for any situation," Orioles general manager Pat Gillick said wearily as he withdrew, "but this is out of hand." The most furious bidding was over Liván, who everyone agreed was twenty-one and thus more attractive than Fernández, who was either twenty-seven or twenty-nine, depending on the source.

After three days, Cubas asked for final bids. The Yankees came in at $5 million for Liván. The Marlins bid $4.5 million.

There are many reasons why Cubas might have accepted the lower offer. There was Miami, of course, and everything that went with it. And there was a batch of incentive bonuses—all-star game, Most Valuable Player, and so on— that could have pushed the Marlins contract well over $6 million. It made perfect sense.

But Santín, who had taken a job with the expansion Tampa Bay Devil Rays after Steinbrenner's housecleaning, posed another interesting theory. He suggested strongly that the fix was in.

"Let's just say there was a friendship between me and Joe," said Santín. "And, at the time, the Yankees just weren't going to get those guys. They just weren't going to get them."

And so Liván Hernández, who had earned $5 a month as an "electrician's assistant," who most Cubans believed was nowhere near the pitcher that El Duque was, signed with the Marlins for $4.5 million over four years, including a $2.5 million signing bonus.

Osvaldo Fernández, the peasant from Holguín, had to settle for a $3.5 million contract with the San Francisco Giants, a surprising late entry into the fray.

Normally, the fee arrangement between players and their agents is relatively simple. Baseball differs slightly from other professional sports in that there are no restrictions on the size of commissions. The players association, champion of the free market, allows certified agents to charge whatever the market will bear. The average commission, according to the union, runs between 4 and 5 percent.

Cubas, of course, was no normal sports agent. He had operatives. He took risks. He had unusual hidden costs that stemmed from bouncing his clients from one country to the next. Before he even signed a contract, Liván had gone from Mexico to Venezuela to the Dominican Republic to the United States and then back to the Dominican Republic. Cubas passed along most of these expenses to his clients. He identified them vaguely as *gastos,* the Spanish word for expenses.

Shortly after Liván and Osvaldo signed, Rodríguez and Núñez, the latest defectors, signed with the Arizona Diamondbacks for $1.7 million and $1.5 million respectively. Based on a 5 percent commission, Cubas's total take on the four contracts should have been well over half a million dollars. The question of how much he ultimately took—and distributed to the people who contributed to his success—would be debated for years to come. The question would be debated bitterly, with disastrous, all-too-real results. Families would split apart and lives would be ruined over that question. The disputes that arose over the money were the root of all the evil that would follow.

It was the fallout that did most of the damage. The fallout was like Chernobyl. It spread all the way to Cuba, and a lot of people, including innocents like El Duque Hernández, would soon get scorched.

ONE OF THE FIRST disputes was over $137.

In Millington, Cubas had borrowed Ramón Batista's cell phone and run up a sizable tab. Batista, whose regular job was managing a trailer park, kept asking Cubas for the money. "I begged him for it but he just wouldn't give it to me," said Batista. He finally resorted to thinly veiled threats. "Listen, you better tell your cousin to pay me my fucking money," he told Juan Carlos Hernández, Juan Ignacio's brother. "He owes me a hundred thirty-seven dollars." A check arrived the next day.

Next up was Cubas's partner, Juan Iglesias. By now Iglesias had moved out of Cubas's garage and set up his own office, which Cubas would often use to communicate with teams. "I was like Joe's secretary for a while," said Iglesias. He, too, was waiting to get paid. Fifty percent was what Iglesias figured was due to him, having brought Cubas into the business as his partner.

"I called him up and gave him this spiel: 'Joe, I need the money, I'm getting married,' " said Iglesias. "I used getting married as an excuse because I know the way Joe operates. I knew he was bullshitting me like he was bullshitting everybody else."

Cubas handed him a $5,000 check. Iglesias was stunned.

"I say, 'Five grand for six months' work? Does that mean that I make ten grand a year? Are you *nuts*?' He says, 'Look, this is what I think is fair. You didn't do anything. I did all the work.' I said, 'You wouldn't have done *shit* administratively if it wasn't for me.' " Thus ended that relationship.

But where things really got ugly was with Juan Ignacio. Cubas and his cousin had grown up together, drifting in and out of each other's lives. Cubas, who was two years younger, often spent summers swimming and fishing with Juan Ignacio in Puerto Rico, where Juan Ignacio's father had a ranch. Compared with Cubas, who had spent his entire life in Miami, Juan Ignacio was a man of the world. Born in Cuba in 1958, he had moved with his family to the Dominican Republic as a toddler. His family later moved to Puerto Rico and, at fourteen, he became an American citizen. When his parents divorced he moved to Miami with his mother. By the time Juan Ignacio was an adult, he held citizenship in two countries and residency in a third, Venezuela, where his father had set him up with some land.

Juan Ignacio also had multiple professions. He was by turns a clothier and a truck driver in the United States. In Venezuela, according to his mother, he ran a car wash and, for several years, managed his father's land. According to Cubas, who has an ax to grind, and the Cronins, who don't, Juan Ignacio also talked about having dabbled in cocaine trafficking, an experience that apparently led to a stint in a Venezuelan prison. "He told us that he had done something like three years," said Jimmy Cronin. "He said that they had landed a plane on a secret airstrip, and they got caught with a bunch of coke. He was obviously hard-core, not a loser, but a shaker and a maker—the kind of guy who would try to run cocaine out of Venezuela and baseball players out of Cuba, the kind of guy who would run around with all those fake passports. It was insanity. He wanted to make sure that we knew exactly how crazy he was."

As if to prove his point Juan Ignacio started traveling openly to Cuba, apparently in defiance of his cousin. Once, while the players were still in the Dominican Republic, Ozzie and Liván filled a suitcase with clothes, dolls, shoes and more to send back to their families. When Juan Ignacio volunteered to take the suitcase himself, Cubas lit into him. "Are you fucking crazy?" he said. "You're going to get everybody in trouble and destroy these people's lives. You are related to me, and we just pulled *four* players out of Cuba. You're going to get your ass in trouble. You're playing with fire."

According to Cubas and Ozzie Fernández, Juan Ignacio assured them he wouldn't go. "Then one day I walk into the room and the suitcase is gone!" said Cubas. "I didn't notice it at first, then I thought, Where the fuck is the suitcase? Juan Ignacio had grabbed it and gone to Cuba. That's the way he was playing the game."

But Juan Ignacio also had been indispensable to his cousin. While Cubas was arranging visas in the Dominican Republic, Juan Ignacio had put up Liván, Vladimir Núñez and Larry Rodríguez at his home on Margarita Island for more than a month. He was constantly running errands for Cubas and the players, particularly for Liván, who was lonely and homesick and needed the attention. "He was like one of my best friends," said Liván. "He was always with me. He did everything for me. He took care of us."

The rift between Cubas and Juan Iglesias stemmed from the splits on the commissions on the four defectors. In hindsight, one obvious problem was that there weren't enough slices to go around. As Cubas's former partner, Juan Iglesias had been expecting half of the agent's commission. The Cronins, had it worked out, were expecting one-third. Juan Ignacio told friends that he and Cubas had agreed beforehand that their own split would be fifty-fifty. Someone's math was obviously flawed.

Cubas ultimately wrote Juan Ignacio a check for $116,000 (the $16,000 was for subsidizing the trip to Japan). It was a hefty sum, for sure, but Juan Ignacio was apoplectic. Where was the rest? He believed that Cubas owed him at least another $150,000. He went around telling anyone who would listen how his own cousin had screwed him. He had been stabbed in the back by family was how he put it.

Juan Ignacio's response was to become an agent himself, a maneuver that would put him in direct competition with his cousin. Although he had no clients, Juan Ignacio completed a lengthy application with the Major League Baseball Players Association, which placed it on file. He called his new agency the Caribbean Sports Council. Juan Iglesias had no experience as an agent, but he was apparently planning a full-service operation. When asked what services the Caribbean Sports Council planned to provide, he checked off boxes for contract negotiation, salary arbitration, financial planning, investment counseling, estate planning, tax planning and appearances/endorsements.

Asked to provide the names of players he currently represented, he responded: "N/A—at the moment."

Juan Ignacio listed as his partner Thomas F. Cronin.

Cronin, who later became engaged in a grueling federal lawsuit against Cubas, denied that he and Juan Ignacio "had formed an alliance or anything like that. There were players that he was chasing, there were players that Joe Cubas was chasing and there were players that I knew." But Jimmy Cronin said that Juan Ignacio approached him and his father about working together, combining the Cronins' connections (especially with El Duque and Mesa) with Juan Ignacio's derring-do.

Jimmy Cronin said the relationship was predicated on a simple logic that Juan Ignacio had formulated: "It was basically Joe screwed Juan Ignacio out of a ton of dough, and Juan Ignacio told Joe to shove it up his ass. So Juan came to us and said, 'Look, Joe fucked you, too. So why don't we both fuck Joe?' "

The Cronins thought that sounded okay.

CHAPTER EIGHT

A DEAL WITH
THE DEVIL (RAYS)

THE FEUDING COUSINS WOULD HAVE AN EPIC BATTLEGROUND: the 1996 Atlanta Olympics. Despite the mounting assaults on Team Cuba and the bleeding of its stockpile of talented players, the national team had agreed to a pre-Olympic tour of the South in advance of the inevitable gold medal. Cubas, for one, had high expectations. He told the media that he would need "a Greyhound bus" for all the defectors he was planning to bring back from Atlanta. Overnight, seemingly, Cubas had emerged as an odd national figure, a kind of agent provocateur who in one stumpy package combined the greed of professional sports with the unresolved (and, to most Americans, largely forgotten) conflict between the United States and Cuba. "His nickname is El Gordo, the Fat Man, and he is both agent and metaphor," wrote Steve Wulf in *Time.*

Before long, Cubas had hired his own press agent, a genial Castro-hater named René Guim (pronounced *Gimm*). Guim hadn't set foot in Cuba since 1960, his parents having spirited him from the island when he was ten. When Cubas approached him, he had just been made executive vice president at Greenstone Roberts, a prestigious Miami public relations firm. Guim ran the Latin American division from a plush waterfront office. A gentle, balding man, he liked to stand on his balcony at the end of the day, smoking a cigar, staring out at the straits, imagining that if he stared long and hard enough he could make out the homeland of his childhood.

For all of Cubas's deeds thus far, the stalking and the cat-and-mouse games, they paled in comparison to what he was cooking up for Atlanta. As Cubas became famous, his penchant for embellishment grew to epic proportions. Out of whole cloth, he made up a variety of death threats and attacks purportedly orchestrated by Castro. In perhaps his tallest tale, he claimed to have been chased and shot at by Zapatista rebels while helping three players defect in Chiapas, Mexico. "No CIA-masterminded plot to assassinate Cuban dictator Fidel Castro nor any U.S. sanctions against the island have worked as efficiently to gnaw at the foundations of the last stronghold of communism in the Western Hemisphere," Cubas wrote in *Sliding into Freedom,* the syrupy proposal for his unsold autobiography.

But Cubas's Olympic plan was no exaggeration. It was by turns breathtakingly real and perfectly illegal. The plot revolved around a right-handed pitcher, Rolando Arrojo, who had been flirting with defection for years. Arrojo was the real deal. In Cuba, his perennial rivalry with El Duque was like Seaver versus Gibson. Six-foot-four and as thin as the cane stalks of his native Villa Clara, Arrojo was a rangy country boy who employed multiple arm angles, similar to El Duque, but threw harder and with a certain disorienting chaos. In thirteen seasons in the National Series, he had compiled 154 wins, seventh on Cuba's all-time list. But Arrojo's moment was fast slipping away. Although he would later claim that he was twenty-eight, Arrojo, according to a multiplicity of sources compiled by Cuban baseball expert Milton Jamail, had turned thirty-two in May.

Over time, Arrojo had developed the same gripes about the System as most everyone else, but he was a timid man, and his desire to leave Cuba was tempered by his deepest fears. "From childhood I was taught that the United States was horrible, a big monster," he said. "They used to call it 'the Monster from the North.' They killed people on the street corners. They tore the limbs off people. They said that if you played professional baseball the team owners took all the money. The teachers told you that. Fidel told you that. Every book you read in school said that. It made you afraid."

Arrojo's fears subsided with repeated trips abroad, but the pitcher absolutely refused to defect without his wife and sons, who were eight and one. The pitcher had a cousin in Miami, an auto mechanic named Frank Triana. It was Triana who came up with the Ian Fleming solution to extricating Arrojo from Castro's grip. Triana, of course, was not only acting out of altruistic concern for his oppressed relatives. For his efforts the mechanic expected a hefty cut of one of those multimillion-dollar baseball contracts he had been reading so much about.

Triana's plan was to hire a smuggler to sail to Cuba, pick up Arrojo's wife and children under the nose of the Cuban coast guard, and then ferry them to a drop-off point in the Florida Keys. Once Arrojo had received word that his family was safe, the pitcher would defect. For sheer ambition and creativity, the plan was hard to top. It was also, of course, a federal felony; immigrant smuggling carried a maximum penalty of ten years in prison *per immigrant* plus a substantial fine. But no one would have to know about that aspect of Arrojo's defection.

Cubas was not unfamiliar with the smuggling trade. Back then, Miami was crawling with smugglers; one needed only to take a stroll down Calle Ocho— Little Havana's famous Eighth Street—to find any number of people willing to accept a dangerous assignment for a price. As Cubas's notoriety grew, the smugglers, recognizing a lucrative new market, began to come out of the woodwork to offer the agent deals to pull the valuable ballplayers out of Cuba.

"There were smugglers constantly calling us," said René Guim. "We'd get two or three calls a week. You could do a book on that alone."

Cubas decided to check around. Or, rather, he sent his operatives Guim and Ramón Batista to check for him. For Guim it was all part of the exciting cloak-and-dagger world that Cubas had drawn him into, a refreshing departure from his normal PR duties. Cubas was his only client who worked out of his garage, the only client who refused to discuss business over the phone. He was certainly the only client who would communicate with him in code ("The chicken is in the soup!"). Much later, Guim would conclude that he had been duped into participating in one of the great con jobs of all time: Cubas's self-invention as Baseball Agent 007. But at the time, Guim believed he had wandered into a dangerous world of smugglers and spies.

"One of these smugglers wouldn't stop calling; he kept telling us how he had a great track record," Guim recalled. "The guy even had references! He would say: 'The Fernández family in Hialeah, 887-blahblahblah; I brought over their aunt Roberta last fall.' The guy was unbelievable. Joe, of course, was such a chickenshit that he would never go to any of these meetings. He would always hide. So he sent me and Ramón out to meet this guy.

"The guy told us to meet him in the back of a shopping center in West Dade, off the turnpike, behind the Blockbuster Video place. So Ramón and I are sitting there in Ramón's Explorer, waiting for the guy to show up. We're just sitting there, talking about the weather, baseball, politics, whatever. About half an hour later, we're getting ready to take off, and Ramón suddenly says, 'What if this is a setup, and these guys are Castro's agents out to get Joe and they think Joe is in the car and they're ready to do us in?'

"So now Ramón and I are shitting a brick. I keep looking over my shoulder. Finally, the guy comes out of his car. We almost died laughing. He looked like one of the Three Stooges. He was so goofy, so weird-looking, it was obvious he couldn't hurt a fly. I turned to Ramón and said, 'Nah, this guy's not a killer.'

"The guy's house was about twenty blocks away. We get there and it's a beautiful house, with marble floors and all kinds of shit. The guy's got an electronic engineering degree hanging on the wall and a bunch of computers. I say to him, 'Hey, you're really into technology, aren't you?' He says, 'Yeah, I can build those things from scratch. I just toy around with them. But let's get down to business. It's real simple: You give me the person's name and telephone number. Tell them that a person—and I'll give you the name of the person—is going to contact them. Then my person will take him to a safe house. And three days later he'll be put on a boat. I have a little van. I go and pick them up in the Keys, and I bring them straight to your front door.'

"I look at Ramón and I go, 'Shit, piece of cake, man. How much?' He says, 'Well, normally I do this for twenty grand a piece. But since it's Joe Cubas I'll do it for twelve.' It still seemed kind of steep, so Ramón starts haggling with the guy! He says, 'We got a guy down in Hialeah that will do it for three thousand.' I felt like I was in one of those South American markets, one of those open-air markets where you're haggling with a guy over some chickens. So we go back and forth, and the guy finally says, 'Okay, look, nine thousand a piece. But as soon as I pull up to the door you got to have the cash in hand. I knock on the door and deliver the person, you gotta have the *cash in hand*. It's C.O.D, okay? C.O.D.'

"I say, 'You mean, collect on delivery?'

"And he says, 'No. Cash or dead.' "

That deal, alas, never came off. But for Arrojo's defection Triana and Cubas settled on a smuggler who, according to Guim, traveled under the code name "Santa Claus." Under the plan, Santa Claus would notify Cubas and Triana via a ship-to-shore phone line once Arrojo's family was safely in international waters, twelve miles off the Cuban coast. Cubas would then move in and execute the pitcher's defection.

His plan now set, Cubas moved to assemble his Olympic defection team. He replaced "that backstabber" Juan Ignacio with another cousin, a West Palm Beach bouncer named Ignacio "Iggy" Fong. The agent also brought along Ramón Batista, which proved to be somewhat awkward. Batista and Juan Ignacio were good friends—so close, in fact, that Juan Ignacio often introduced Batista as his *primo,* or cousin. After a while everyone, including Cubas, started referring to Batista as Primo, even though he was one of the few people around the defection racket who wasn't actually Cubas's cousin.

But Batista had his own complaints about how Millington had gone down. Juan Ignacio, who had recruited him, had promised him $20,000 and ended up paying him $10,000. For the Olympics, Cubas was offering $1,500 up-front and another $15,000 per defector. Batista, who was still managing the trailer park, did some quick calculating and immediately phoned his boss to ask for a vacation. How many seats were there on a Greyhound bus anyway?

For his part, Juan Ignacio showed up at the Olympics with his own new partners, Tom and Jimmy Cronin. Unlike Cubas, who spent much of his time skulking, Juan Ignacio and the Cronins liked to operate in the open. Cubas, they all believed, was a paranoid grandstander posing as a spy. Occasionally, the competing defection teams would bump into each other and snarl. "We'd see Cubas from afar, hiding, and we'd say, 'Hey, Joe, hiding in the bushes again?'" said Jimmy. "He'd tell us, 'You guys are fucking crazy. You're going to get yourselves killed.' We'd say, 'Right, Joe, just keep hiding in the shadows.'"

There seemed no limits to Juan Ignacio's brazenness. One night he and the Cronins feted Omar Linares, the noted revolutionary, in the middle of a hotel lobby in Columbia, South Carolina. Linares was about as much of a candidate to defect as Fidel Castro, but Juan Ignacio and the Cronins took their best shot regardless.

"He told us he wouldn't betray his country," said Jimmy, flabbergasted that a man would actually choose patriotism over money. "But he did ask us if we could find a part for his car. We were like, 'Dude, you're worth eighty million and you want us to repair your lousy two-thousand-dollar shitbox of a Russian car?'"

Cubas watched the scene from a second-floor landing. "They were all just sitting there, drinking beers and smoking cigars with Omar Linares and having a good old time. It was one of the stupidest, most idiotic things I've ever seen in my life. I was hiding up there, and as I peeked down I could see the Cuban security people taking everyone's picture. That was the last time I ever saw Juan Ignacio."

Paranoid or not, Cubas believed that they were all marked men. The Arrojo smuggling operation was in place, but Cubas needed a way to communicate with the pitcher. He sent his cousin Iggy, an unknown, to contact Arrojo. Arrojo was scheduled to pitch against Team USA one night in Zebulon, North Carolina. The tiny ballpark was packed. Iggy made his way through the crowd, descending toward the bullpen along the foul line, where Arrojo was signing autographs before the game. He carried a towel, folded to conceal the cellular phone that had been placed inside. He pressed against the railing, mingling with the autograph seekers, waiting for his moment. When no one was looking he passed the towel to the pitcher.

"Don't turn this on until you get back to the hotel," he said.

Arrojo looked as if he had been handed a ticking bomb.

"I'm Joe's cousin," explained Iggy. "I know you don't know me, but Joe's other cousin, the crazy one, he's here, too. Whatever he says, don't believe him."

Then he was gone.

THE ARROJO VENTURE had taken Cubas away from his other clients: Liván, Ozzie, Larry Rodríguez and Vladimir Núñez. The agent would say later that he had been distracted, but to many it seemed that he had simply abandoned the players after banking his commissions. Liván felt especially alone. He was twenty-one and had never lived apart from his mother. He had spent his entire life on the desolate Isle of Youth. He had possessed neither a driver's license nor a credit card. Now he was an instant millionaire in the United States of America.

For all the defectors, the transition from socialism to high-octane capitalism was so dramatic as to be comical. It was like passing through a door in the 1940s and emerging in the 1990s. After Ariel Prieto signed with the Oakland A's, he received his signing bonus, a $1.2 million check. Not entirely certain what the check was for, he shoved it in the back pocket of his jeans. "I didn't know anything about banks," he said. "I got the check on a Thursday and forgot about it. Then, over the weekend, I threw the jeans in the wash." By the time a friend had straightened him out, the check was a frayed mess but still barely legible. "When I got to the bank, the manager was like, 'What's this?' " said Prieto. "The check was all crumpled." After a few phone calls the bank accepted the check.

Dan LeBatard, the *Miami Herald* columnist, once accompanied René Arocha and Euclides Rojas to Publix, a southeast supermarket chain. Rojas had just arrived in Miami by way of Guantánamo. The three men took a stroll down the canned-foods aisle.

"I would buy this for my child," said Rojas, selecting a can. "This picture of a happy boy on the label tells me my boy would probably like the taste of this." The boy was pictured next to a dog. Rojas was holding a can of Alpo. "You have food for your dogs?" he asked.

"Yes," said Arocha, by now a veteran shopper. He pointed to the bones and the dog biscuits. "Look at all the things you can buy your dog. There is even separate food for puppies and old dogs."

The tour moved on to personal hygiene.

"This is to scrub your back with soap in the shower," Arocha explained.

"I haven't seen soap in months," said Rojas matter-of-factly.

Liván, too, was terribly callow. During the trip to Toronto to visit the Blue Jays, he walked into the hotel bathroom one day. Unable to locate the handle, he turned to walk away, only to be startled when the urinal suddenly flushed on its own. "I don't like it when people watch me going to the bathroom," he later groused to Juan Iglesias.

"He thought that there was someone behind the wall who watched and then flushed when you were done," said Iglesias. "He had never heard of one of those sensors."

For all his inexperience, Liván proved an insatiable capitalist. When he finally got his driver's license, he snapped up cars every three months. Among his purchases were a $40,000 Dodge Viper, a $130,000 Mercedes convertible, a $65,000 Porsche and a $100,000 Ferrari. "One time he went to buy a roof rack and he ended up buying a new car," said Iglesias. Liván was so fascinated by automobiles that on the day his $2.5 million bonus check arrived at the Marlins offices, he decided to wait until the next day to pick it up. Instead, he picked up a Toyota Land Cruiser that a dealer was giving him as part of a promotional campaign.

Liván's biggest obsession was fast food, a particularly dangerous habit in Florida, where the state motto should be: "Can I take your order, please?" As gifted as Liván was—and he was like a ballet dancer on the mound—the pitcher never had much of a body. Unlike his finely conditioned brother El Duque, Liván looked more like a plumber than a professional athlete. Arriving from Cuba, Liván was ravenous. "I ate everything I saw," he said. Soon, after an endless run on Big Macs and Whoppers, his weight had shot up forty-three pounds. In inverse proportion, he lost, by the Marlins' calculation, some 5 miles per hour off his fastball.

Liván wasn't happy. He had nearly made the major-league club out of spring training. In their last cuts the Marlins had dispatched him to Triple-A Charlotte, a good place to start but a letdown nonetheless. Charlotte, North Carolina, was not exactly a hotbed of Cuban life. Worse, the team lacked a Spanish-speaking coach. For a time Liván roomed with Euclides Rojas, who had snagged a minor-league contract despite his advancing age. "He was just sad," said Rojas. "He was very young, and I think he was used to living with his mother. Being away from his family and having fame were hard on him. This country's customs are so different. I've known Liván since he was a kid. He's a good person, but he was very, very naïve. He was still just a child."

"It was very tough for him in the beginning," said Al Avila. "People were trying to get to him. It's no easy task for a young man, twenty years old, when all you know is a fucking dictator, a country where there is practically no information, and all of a sudden you're thrown into this big old world. I mean, imagine what it was like for this guy. He just left Cuba, and now he's in the United States and he's got nobody. It's like, 'Who the fuck do I trust?'"

Liván called his mother back in Cuba daily. Unfortunately, he was unable to draw much sympathy from his agent. Actually, Liván could rarely get Cubas on the phone. The agent wouldn't return his own client's calls, which only added to Liván's frustrations. Off the field, the pitcher was bored, miserable and rapidly expanding, now packing 235 pounds on his six-foot-two frame. On the field, he was getting hammered. His record had fallen to 2–4 with a 5.48 ERA. He was relying almost exclusively on his curve, a difficult way to make a living as a pitcher. His frustrated coaches couldn't talk to him. "It always seems like something gets lost in the translation," said his manager, Sal Rende. After one disastrous outing, Liván was about to be removed from the game. Instead of handing over the ball, he winged it at the home-plate umpire, a transgression that drew him a suspension.

Desperate to get their $4.5 million man straightened out, the Marlins demoted Liván to Portland, Maine, home of the Double-A Sea Dogs. Initially, Liván fell into a deeper funk. Tom Cronin drove up from Cape Cod to visit him one afternoon with Juan Ignacio. They found the pitcher holed up like a recluse on the couch in his apartment, watching MTV and devouring potato chips for hours on end. "It was Juan Ignacio who finally got him off the couch," Cronin recalled. "He went to the store and got all kinds of stuff and came back and whipped up a huge Cuban meal. You could tell it made Liván feel better. The guy was hurting."

If Cubas wouldn't help Liván, Juan Ignacio was only too willing. The two men had grown close when Cubas deposited Liván in Venezuela while arranging the Dominican visa. Unlike Cubas, who seemed to view it as beneath him to manage his young clients' trivial affairs, Juan Ignacio was always willing to run errands, going so far as to drive Liván's car from Miami to Charlotte so the pitcher could fly ahead. Liván, in turn, believed Juan Ignacio was a genius in the fast-paced ways of capitalism. "He's very smart," Liván told me. "I think he's very, very intelligent. Above average."

But Juan Ignacio's most important role was as a courier, not just for Liván but for other defectors as well. For most immigrant groups in the United States, sending money home—the primary reason for *being* in the United States—is a simple transaction. Western Union and hundreds of other agencies will do it for a small fee. In 1996, because of the political situation, few such services existed between the United States and Cuba.* Juan Ignacio provided that service for Liván and the other defectors. The players would give him money and care packages filled with clothing and medicine and off he went, a giddy tourist toting horse-choking wads of $100 bills in his fanny pack. Once in Cuba, Juan Ignacio liked to travel in style. From the Isle of Youth to Holguín to Havana he sprinkled other people's money around the island, bestowing it upon the players' grateful relatives with cheerful, reckless abandon.

It was easy.

It was too easy, of course.

CUBAS, IGGY FONG and Ramón Batista slept in their clothes in Albany, Georgia, waiting for the call from Santa Claus. It came at exactly 1:51 A.M.

According to Guim and Batista, the smuggler called from the boat with the news that Rolando Arrojo's family was safely out of Cuba.

Cubas, Iggy and Batista walked out of their rooms at the Ramada Inn. The agent, who had recently reconciled with his wife, was driving María's car, a used black Mercedes. Iggy and Batista were driving the Cubas family van, a gray Ford Aerostar. The two vehicles pulled up outside a funeral home adjacent to the Quality Inn, where Team Cuba was staying. Cubas pulled off to the side. Iggy wedged the Aerostar between two hearses on the side of the funeral home, facing the motel. Batista got out of the van, walked up to Room 234 and knocked.

Arrojo opened the door. The pitcher was wearing gym shorts, a T-shirt and flip-flops.

"Let's go, we're ready," whispered Batista.

Arrojo hesitated. The pitcher had been waiting all night, but now he stood in the doorway of his room at the Quality Inn, paralyzed.

"C'mon, let's go, everything's okay," said Batista.

Arrojo inched his way into the night, shuffling toward his new life like a man walking the plank. In his nervousness he took nothing with him except

---

*Under the embargo, cash remittances to Cuba were limited to $300 every three months, a rule that, like most other aspects of the law, was routinely violated.

the clothes on his back, a decision he would later regret. Batista virtually had to lead the pitcher by his golden arm across the parking lot, step by step, toward the Mercedes idling in the dark some fifty yards away. "It was like he was in slow motion," said Cubas. "He was shitting a brick. You could tell he was scared stiff."

Iggy, sitting in the van between the two hearses, watched the scene unfold while communicating with Cubas via cell phone. "He's moving too slow," Iggy was saying to his cousin. "He's moving too slow. C'mon, Rollie, walk, walk! You're too slow. You're gonna get caught."

Cubas flashed his headlights and Arrojo broke into a dead run. Cubas threw open the back door and the pitcher scrambled inside.

"Go!" Arrojo yelled. "Go!"

Cubas sped away.

Batista walked back to the van with his eye on the motel to see if anyone intended to follow. For fifteen minutes, he and Iggy sat in the dark next to the funeral home, staring at the parking lot. The Quality Inn was quiet. Only the halls and the lobby were lit up. Nothing moved. The only sounds were the chirping of cicadas and crickets. Convinced that no one had seen them, Iggy and Ramón drove back to the Ramada Inn, where they met up with Cubas and Arrojo in the parking lot. By now it was around three A.M. Everyone embraced and traded high fives. Then Cubas and Arrojo got back in the Mercedes to begin the long drive to Miami.

Arrojo was numb. "I had a million questions and I couldn't answer a single one of them," he said. He was still feeling fairly queasy by the time they rolled into Miami. "I was so scared," he said. "I didn't leave the house for fifteen days."

Actually, Arrojo had another reason to be terrified: René Guim had set up a press conference in his honor at Victor's Café (the official restaurant of Cuban defectors). In terms of the defection itself, the press conference was sure to be celebratory. By and large, the Miami media, both Anglo and Hispanic, reflected the views of the community in which it served. Some reporters had flown back from the Olympics to cover the happy affair. But Arrojo was bound to get a few questions about his family.

Guim knew just how to handle it. "Look, if the questions get tough," he advised Arrojo, "just get emotional."

Arrojo followed the instructions to the letter. Not long into the press conference, someone asked Arrojo how difficult it was to leave his family behind in Cuba.

The pitcher wept.

"The guy broke out crying," said Guim. "And he had slept with his wife the night before. That day, in fact, when he left the house at six o'clock in the morning to do *Good Morning America,* he kissed his wife and kids good-bye."

The cover-up extended to Arrojo's immediate family. Cubas told Guim that when it came time to enroll Rolando Jr. in the third grade, Arrojo used an assumed name, enrolling him as Joe Cubas's son. Years later, Cubas and Arrojo, both aware of the criminal implications, would deny ever smuggling the pitcher's family into the United States.* But Cubas never bothered to keep it much of a secret. When the agent began to prepare the proposal for his auto-biography, he and Guim met with a Miami writer, Diane Montane, one night at La Carreta, a Cuban restaurant. Cubas, swollen with pride, was only too happy to recount his gripping life story. Before long he was spilling out the de-tails of the Arrojo smuggling operation.

"He recounted the whole story: the boat, Santa Claus, the cell phone going off," said Guim. "He was recounting the whole thing like he was 007. Sean Con-nery couldn't have played it any better that night."

At least part of the story later appeared in the proposal for *Sliding into Freedom.* As Cubas (and Montane) described it, Arrojo was reunited with his family in a tender scene in the Keys shortly after his defection. "When we got to Key West," Cubas wrote, "Arrojo's wife and kids were waiting at the entrance of the island inside a red pickup truck, and his eight-year-old boy started waving at his father. I didn't want the reunion to take place in the middle of a street, so we drove as a caravan to the nearest McDonald's. There, under the famous golden arches, Rolando Arrojo greeted his family for the first time in a free country. I would have laughed at the irony of this ad-perfect sight if I had not seen the kid's skinny fingers waving through the window.

"We have a saying that an angel flies over when there is silence. I swear I felt the biggest angel hovering over that boy and his father as they locked eyes and the child devoured his first American hamburger."

EXPECTING MORE DEFECTIONS, Cubas flew back to Albany, Georgia, after Arrojo's press conference. He arrived to a tense scene. The Cubans went ballistic after losing their number one starter on the eve of the Olympics. Days

---

*After receiving a $70,000 check from Cubas, Triana sued the agent for additional money related to Arrojo's defection. He reached an out-of-court settlement with Cubas in April 2000 and signed a confidentiality agreement not to discuss the case.

earlier Arrojo had throttled the Americans, striking out nine in seven effortless innings of an exhibition game. Now he effectively *was* an American, or at least a temporary resident. Even the normally supportive Cuban players were livid. "It was the way he did it," Lázaro Valle later told S. L. Price. "He betrayed everyone. . . . Even if he makes a hundred million dollars, he'll never be a hero in Cuba because he was like a Judas. He sold everybody out."

The Judas theme was a popular one. Castro denounced Arrojo as "a Judas who sold himself for twelve gold coins."

Even Arrojo had second thoughts. "I should have pitched," he told me. "But I had the opportunity to leave. They told us that in the Olympics we would be closely guarded and I didn't think I could get out. I felt bad after I did it. But they still won and here I am. I know they still talk shit about me, Fidel and all of them."

The tensions boiled over at the Albany ball yard. In some ways, it was a long time coming. For years now, Cubas, Gus Domínguez and dozens of major-league scouts had been trailing the Cuban players, seducing them, really, right under their minders' noses. The scouts and the agents had become a constant presence, following not only Team Cuba but also the talented "B" and junior teams. After a while the Cubans tried to keep the travel schedules secret, but it was impossible. Word would leak out and the pesky scouts and agents would appear again, inviting players up to their rooms, handing out cash and equipment, filling their heads with major-league dreams. And now Rolando Arrojo had defected on the eve of the Olympics.

Cubas's cousin, Iggy Fong, was standing next to the concession stand when one of the Team Cuba officials recognized him or at least thought he did. The official walked up and started yelling.

"Listen, you son of a bitch, I don't want you anywhere near these guys anymore, you hear me?" the official said.

Iggy was nonplussed. "What the fuck are you talking about, asshole?" he responded. "This is a free country. I'll go wherever the fuck I want."

Al Avila, who was scouting the Olympics for the Marlins, happened to be standing nearby. He watched as the argument developed into a shoving match, then a full-blown fistfight. "Suddenly I look over and these guys are going at it!" he said. "One guy shoved the other guy and then they were rolling in the aisles. It was really kind of a circus."

Miguel Valdés, the respected technical director for the Cuban national team, arrived just ahead of the Albany police. He quickly realized that the official had mistaken Iggy Fong for his infamous cousin.

"That's not Joe Cubas! That's not Joe Cubas!" Valdés was yelling.

The men were separated after the brief scuffle. In the end, no other players defected. The Cubans, of course, went on to win the Olympic gold medal, roaring through the tournament with nine straight wins. Before the finals against Japan, six U.S. marshals stood in front of the Team Cuba dugout. Two security officers guarded the bullpen. Fourteen officers stood on or behind the dugout. No one was certain whether the security was designed to keep the Cubans in or Cubas out.

Omar Linares belted three home runs in the gold-medal game, including one that landed in the left-field upper deck at Atlanta–Fulton County Stadium. Granted, Linares used an aluminum bat, but just four major-leaguers had reached the upper deck since the stadium opened in 1966. Linares batted .476 in the Olympics with eight home runs and 16 RBIs. He later said a major-league scout approached him in Atlanta and offered him $40 million to defect, a proposition the third baseman said he all but spat upon. The great El Niño called the three-homer game against Japan "the greatest night of my life."

Two weeks after Arrojo's defection, Cubas received a three-sentence missive at his garage-office:

July 25, 1996

Premier Sports Council
Miami, Florida

Attention: Joe Cubas

I wish to inform you from this moment forward that your services as "agent" will no longer be needed. I will soon inform you where you can forward all correspondence.

I thank you for your immediate attention with this matter.

Attentively,
Liván Hernández
Florida Marlins

The news of Liván's "second defection" was all over Miami. It was like an ugly family feud that had spilled into the open. In addition to firing Cubas, Liván had taken up with the agent's former business partner, Juan Iglesias, the author of the brutally concise termination letter. For days the word *backstabber* sailed back and forth across the city like a Frisbee. Amid the rhetoric was one particularly damning allegation: Liván claimed that Cubas had tried to charge him 25 percent of his earnings, a commission 20 percent above what most players pay their representatives. Cubas denied the charge, Liván and Iglesias insisted it was true. There the allegation stayed, never proven but part of the Cubas lore. In many ways the episode crystallized what many people had believed all along. If Cubas could take advantage of a recently arrived twenty-one-year-old immigrant, it only proved that he was using anti-Castro politics as a cover for his real motivation: blind greed.

By this point, Cubas's double-dealing and fiscal sleight of hand were fairly staggering. The agent was like a one-man tobacco industry with all the legal threats and lawsuits that his actions ultimately would generate. Through it all he righteously proclaimed his innocence. When Frank Triana sued him over the Arrojo affair, Cubas testified that he signed a contract with the pitcher's cousin to show that he was "an honest and decent human being" and never intended, as Triana apparently feared, to "stab him in the back."

The Arrojo deal was Cubas's nadir as a businessman. The pitcher, of course, could have simply stayed in the United States. Based on the market, he almost certainly would have netted at least a $2 million deal. Instead, Cubas dispatched Arrojo on a bizarre seven-month odyssey, all in the name of a contract that will stand as a monument to duplicity and greed, if not outright theft.

For starters, Cubas came up with a uniquely cynical solution to compensate Triana for the smuggling operation. Instead of paying Triana himself, as outlined in the contract, the agent intended to pay him through a dummy corporation whose coffers he would fill with Arrojo's money. In a sworn deposition, Cubas said that Arrojo was to contribute 5 percent of his earnings *on top of* the 5 percent commission the pitcher would pay to Cubas. It is unclear whether Cubas ever informed Arrojo of the plan to relieve him of an additional 5 percent of his income. Ramón Batista, who compiled the paperwork to set up the corporation in the Dominican Republic, said Cubas told him never to mention its existence to the pitcher.

Plans for the corporation fell apart when Cubas failed to obtain residency for Arrojo in the Dominican Republic. Unbeknownst to the agent, the political situation in the country had changed dramatically. That year, Leonel Fernández had succeeded Joaquín Balaguer as president, and the Dominican government's chilly relationship with Cuba had suddenly thawed.

Months passed while Arrojo, in an escalating panic, waited in Santo Domingo for his residency papers. It was left to Ramón Batista to baby-sit the pitcher while Cubas went off to work on other defections. "Rolando was getting desperate," said Batista. "His wife was back in Miami and she was going nuts. Every day he was crying like a baby and fighting with Cubas, asking him when his papers were going to be ready. Every day it was a different story. At one point Arrojo and I almost got into a fistfight. He thought I was lying to him. I said, 'Look, I just work for this guy. I'm just telling you what Joe Cubas tells me to tell you.'

"At that point I called up Joe Cubas in Miami. I said, 'Listen, this guy is desperate. We've got to do something.' So that's when Joe Cubas came up with the idea to get Arrojo out of the Dominican Republic and bring him to Costa Rica."

Actually, Cubas had three players who were stuck in the Dominican Republic: Arrojo and two junior stars, catcher Yalián Serrano and pitcher Osmani Fernández.

Serrano had defected at a junior tournament outside St. Louis. He did it on his own, but a relative in Miami brought him to Cubas, hoping the agent could land the boy a contract. When Serrano mentioned that he had a friend who might also want to defect, Cubas sent Batista to St. Louis with a cassette tape from Serrano imploring his friend to stay in the United States.

Osmani Fernández was a sixteen-year-old waif known to everyone by his nickname, "Capuro." Batista cornered him at a flea market one afternoon. He took him aside, pulled out a microcassette recorder and played the tape of Yalián Serrano urging his friend to defect. But, much to Batista's surprise, the boy politely declined. Batista asked him if he was sure.

"I'm sure," said Capuro. "I don't want to leave my parents."

A few days later, Batista approached him again. Again the boy said no. He didn't want to defect. "Then, as I was talking to him, Joe Cubas happened to call me on my cell phone," recalled Batista. "I said, 'Hey, Primo, I got the kid here with me. You want to talk to him? He says he's not going to defect. He wants to go back to Cuba.'

"So Joe starts to talk to Capuro, and Capuro starts crying. He's saying, 'No, I don't want to defect. I don't want to leave my mother and my father.' But Joe kept talking to him and talking to him and talking to him. Then finally he put Rolando Arrojo on the phone and Arrojo was talking to him." It was the rough equivalent of employing Mark McGwire to recruit a sixteen-year-old high school player to attend USC. Only the stakes were slightly higher.

"Capuro handed me the phone and he said, 'Look, if they want me to stay, I'm going to stay,' " said Batista. "I said, 'Well, jump in the car and let's go then.'

He cried all the way to Miami. He didn't want to leave his family. He was worried about whether he was ever going to see them again."

To reassure the boy, Batista called Cubas again from the road. The agent set up a three-way call between himself, Capuro and the boy's father back in Cuba. "That's when I told my father, 'I'm not going back,' " Capuro told Sánchez and me. "I told him I had defected in the United States. Then Joe Cubas got on the line. He says to my father, 'Sir, I don't know what your name is, but he is going to be in good hands. Don't you worry.' That's exactly what he told him. My father is a *guajiro* [peasant]. He doesn't know anything about this stuff. He just said, 'Thank you, I put my faith in you to protect my son.' "

Cubas had no idea whether Capuro could actually pitch, but he took the boy and Yalián Serrano to the Dominican Republic to play the third-country parlay. But the players found themselves in the same boat as their idol Arrojo. No one could obtain the residency papers necessary to sign a contract. The players lacked passports and the transit visas that would enable them to change countries. Really, they had nothing.

It is here where the adventures of Rolando Arrojo, et al., get particularly wild. Although Cubas would later deny it all, Ramón Batista's account is persuasive, because he also implicates himself.

"Cubas asked me how we were going to get them out," said Batista. "We had to figure out a way. A few days later he called me up and he said, 'Okay, I'm coming down there and we're going to take care of this.' So he came down and the first thing he did was come up with fake IDs: birth certificates and driver's licenses that the players could use."

Batista said he then helped Cubas set up yet another smuggling operation: this time from the Dominican Republic to Costa Rica. Armed with fake Puerto Rican birth certificates and driver's licenses, Cubas, Batista and the players set out to a private airport on the outskirts of Santo Domingo. There, according to Batista, they proceeded to buy their way out of the Dominican Republic.

"Arrojo was very scared," said Batista. "He was afraid we were going to get caught with the fake birth certificates and the driver's licenses and they were going to throw us all in jail. So I went to the guy at immigration and told him what we were doing. I said, 'What do we need to pay you to do this?' I can't remember what we paid him. I think it was about thirty-five hundred dollars. So he stamped the birth certificates and we went right through immigration and straight to the plane.

"It was a Navajo, a six-seater," said Batista. "We stopped in Jamaica to refuel, then we flew to Costa Rica. The pilot wanted to land in San José [Costa

Rica's capital]. But Joe stopped him. He said, 'No, no, no, we can't go there!' He knew we had the false IDs. We had to land somewhere where it was safe."

So it was that the motley crew—a Miami sports agent, his trusted operative and three Cuban baseball players, including a future all-star (Arrojo)—set down in the port city of Limón. Cubas and Batista were carrying their U.S. passports. The Cubans had the fake Puerto Rican birth certificates and driver's licenses. "We got to immigration and they asked us what we were doing there," said Batista. "We told them that we were going fishing, that we were there for a fishing tournament. We didn't even have any fishing poles. But it didn't seem like it mattered."

After spending the night in Limón, the players were driven to San José, where they eventually acquired their papers as residents of the Republic of Costa Rica.

FINALLY, IT WAS contract time. For this, Cubas was prepared. In fact, he had already laid the groundwork for something spectacular. Later, there would be more ringing denials all around, but the hearsay evidence is persuasive, coming from multiple sources. It starts with Cubas's confession to René Guim, his closest confidant at the time, that he had cut a preemptive deal to send Arrojo to the Tampa Bay Devil Rays for a staggering $7 million. Cubas added that he was especially pleased because in return the club had agreed to pay him $500,000 under the table.

"It just kind of blew me away," said Guim. "Here's this guy, he's trying to project himself as being the savior of the Cuban players, saying what an honor it is to help these guys reach their freedom, and all of a sudden he's talking about kickbacks. And I'm not talking about a couple of suits. I'm talking about big bucks." Guim said Cubas talked about the payoff constantly. "He boasted about it," said Guim. "He was going to make so much money on this because of all the money under the table."

The deal made perfect sense. Rudy Santín, Cubas's original silent partner, was now running the Devil Rays' Latin American scouting bureau. Santín was still seething over missing out on the first wave of defectors because of George Steinbrenner's capriciousness. An expansion team, the Devil Rays would make their debut during the 1998 season. Tampa was perfect: It boasted the second-largest enclave of Cuban exiles in the state after Miami.

Ramón Batista said he also became aware of the secret deal with Tampa Bay. While Batista was baby-sitting Arrojo in the Dominican Republic, Devil

Rays owner Vince Naimoli and general manager Chuck LaMar had flown down to meet with Cubas. Batista didn't attend the meeting, which he said took place inside the American Airlines lounge at the Santo Domingo airport. However, after the meeting broke up, Batista drove Cubas and Arrojo back to their hotel. "Joe was telling Arrojo exactly how it was going to work," said Batista. "Joe was explaining to Arrojo that he had a verbal agreement with Tampa Bay for seven million dollars."

A few days later, Cubas asked Batista to pick up a fax at the administrative offices of the Plaza Naco hotel, where Batista and Arrojo were staying. Lo and behold, the agreement appeared. "It was the agreement between Rolando Arrojo and the Tampa Bay Devil Rays for seven million," said Batista. Batista said he took the agreement to Arrojo to sign, then faxed it back to Cubas.

The deal apparently had one other interesting dimension. Later, Batista heard a rumor that Cubas had not only taken the $500,000 bribe but given a kickback to his boyhood friend Santín. Batista said he confronted Santín with the story. "Rudy told me, 'Ramón, it's true, but you can't tell anybody about that,' " said Batista. "He was actually pissed about it. He said that Cubas had promised him a hundred thousand dollars and only paid him twenty-five."

But Cubas had a dilemma. Once Arrojo had established residency in Costa Rica, the agent couldn't just come out and announce that the pitcher had signed with Tampa Bay without any other teams having a shot. The agent's only solution was to hold a tryout and go through the motions of negotiating. So with Arrojo as his star attraction, he invited every major-league team to attend a far-flung workout in Central America. Interest still proved to be high. Scouts from nineteen teams—over sixty scouts in all—descended on a rickety old stadium in downtown San José to watch Arrojo and the other defectors work out. Shortly afterward, the negotiations were opened and several teams began throwing money at Cubas.

According to Guim it was all an extravagant deception. "Everybody in his inner circle knew he had already cut a deal with Tampa Bay," said Guim. "The tryout was just a three-ring circus to make it look like a bidding war."

Sure enough, when Cubas announced the big winner, the Tampa Bay Devil Rays had prevailed, signing Arrojo to a $7 million minor-league contract, all the money to be paid in the form of a gargantuan signing bonus.*

---

*As an expansion team, the Devil Rays technically had no major-league roster. Thus the minor-league contract, for which Arrojo would be paid the standard minor-league salary of $850 a month.

When I asked Cubas about the alleged bribe, he flew into a tirade against Guim and Batista. By then, both men had left him, alleging that Cubas had failed to make good on thousands of dollars in unpaid salaries and expenses. Cubas was especially harsh on Batista, whom he called "a lowlife who has continuously turned on anyone who ever helped him." The Devil Rays and Santín also weighed in with denials. Devil Rays general manager Chuck LaMar said that the fact that the club showed up at the San José tryout to scout Arrojo proved there was no preemptive deal. LaMar said that the club made no payment to Cubas "under the table, over the table, or any kind of table."

As specific as the charges were, I did wonder whether Guim and Batista might have been grinding their extremely large axes at the expense of the truth. But it turned out that Cubas had guarded this secret about as fiercely as he had guarded the smuggling of Arrojo's family. Gordon Blakeley, the head of international scouting for the New York Yankees, brought up the Tampa Bay deal unprompted one evening during an interview, coincidentally, in Costa Rica.

Incredibly, Cubas had later tried to bribe the Yankees. He was unsuccessful, but Blakeley knew all about the Devil Rays' shenanigans.

"He took money from Tampa Bay," Blakeley stated flatly.

Although his figures on the alleged kickback to Santín differed from Batista's, Blakeley's understanding of the core of the scheme was the same: "It was five hundred thousand to Cubas and fifty thousand to Rudy," said Blakeley. "Rudy's a friend of mine. I guess he didn't think it was that big of a deal."

The other defectors were not as fortunate as Arrojo. Capuro, the reluctant sixteen-year-old, and his friend Yalián Serrano were thrown into the Arrojo deal for a few thousand dollars apiece. Both players lasted briefly in the Devil Rays' minor-league system before being released.

The last I saw of Capuro, he was working in a San José supermarket called Los Más por Menos (More for Less). He earned about $150 a month. He said he had tried for a while to contact Cubas, but the agent no longer returned his calls. He said he often thought about his arrival in Miami, and how Cubas had thrown his arms around him and called him "Capuro," as if he had known him all his life.

"He told me I was going to realize my dreams," said Capuro.

For his part, Ramón Batista was ashamed of his role in the episode. "It makes me feel terrible," he said. "I mean, I never would have imagined it would end up like this, where you promise a kid that you're going to take care of him for the rest of his life and then you just abandon him because he can't make it as a ballplayer and doesn't get a big contract."

THE OLYMPICS HAD been a disappointment for Juan Ignacio. His cousin had snagged another defector, the biggest yet. Even without the alleged bribe, Cubas's 5 percent cut from Arrojo's contract was a cool $350,000. The agent also incurred $249,370.38 in reimbursable expenses. A few of the expenses were rather conspicuous: $1,750 for "immigration documents and departure," $1,250 for "private plane," $5,000 "advance [for] F. Triana trip to Cuba." The bulk of the items, thirty-eight in all, were listed simply as "*gastos,*" expenses.

Juan Ignacio, on the other hand, had zero to show for his efforts. He determined that it was time to take bold action. He called up his old friend Ramón Batista. The two had had their own spat over money, but they remained close. "Whether he owed me money or not, I still loved him as a brother," said Batista.

Juan Ignacio asked Batista to meet him for breakfast in Miami. There, Juan Ignacio spilled out all his frustrations, how his cousin had burned him. Juan Ignacio had even had designs on representing Liván, but the frustrated pitcher instead decided to go with experience, signing on with Iglesias, who was also representing José Canseco.

Juan Ignacio told Batista that he was planning to return to Cuba. He told his friend how he planned to smuggle ballplayers off the island, then get them residency in Venezuela and sign them to big contracts.

"I was thinking maybe we'd go down together," Juan Ignacio suggested.

Batista declined. Too dangerous.

Juan Ignacio insisted that it would be easy. "Look at this," he said, lifting his briefcase from underneath the table. He pulled out a sheaf of documents and spread them before his friend.

"He showed me the papers and they were all fake," said Batista. "They were fake residency papers for Venezuela and Mexico."

Some of the papers already had names on them: One was for Orlando Hernández, the famous El Duque. Another was for Germán Mesa, the spectacular shortstop.

Batista tried to talk Juan Ignacio out of going. "Look," he warned, "Cuba is not Venezuela or the Dominican Republic or any other country. Cuba is Cuba."

"You're just chicken," said Juan Ignacio.

Batista sighed.

"Fine," he told his friend. "I'm chicken."

PART THREE

CHAPTER NINE

FIDEL, INC.

THE BLACK GOVERNMENT VANS PULLED UP IN FRONT OF THE Hotel Nacional around ten P.M. It was January 17, 1996, and Havana was warm and smelled of the sea. With some degree of mystery, word had passed to us that we were to gather in front of the historic hotel in formal dress to be taken . . . somewhere. We climbed into the vans and traveled mostly in silence, as the caravan snaked through the city, past the splintered buildings and the spooky ceiba trees and the shadow people who moved about in the dull, inadequate light.

We must have been early, because we drove in circles for some time before the vans finally stopped in front of the Palace of the Revolution. As a group we stepped into the quiet of the palace, a Soviet-style concrete mass. We walked up a flight of stairs and passed into a large, poorly lit anteroom, empty except for a cluster of ministers standing directly to our right. They included Carlos Fernández de Cossío, the Foreign Ministry's polished liaison to the United States, and Fernando Remírez, Cuba's representative in Washington. We formed to meet the receiving line, then circled toward the back of the room, where Fidel Castro stood waiting for us in a doorway.

Fidel wore his tailored combat fatigues like a three-piece suit. It was impossible to imagine the crisp green uniform flecked with even a speck of dirt, much less soiled by the jungles of the Sierra Maestra. Fidel was much taller than anyone had imagined—at least six-foot-two—with a thick chest and a soft, enveloping handshake. His hands, as Ariel Prieto so memorably described them, were indeed "about as big as that window." Our group was led by Joe

Moakley, the South Boston congressman, and consisted of an odd collection of New England business executives, environmentalists, *Boston Globe* editorial-page editor David Greenway and a few of Moakley's cronies from Southie. Phil Bennett, then the *Globe's* foreign editor, and I wangled our way in as official scribes of the delegation.

Fidel seemed to tower over us all. In my mind's eye, four years later, he remains larger than life. He welcomed us into the cocktail reception, grabbed a *mojito** from a passing tray and planted himself in the center of the room. There was very little mingling at this particular reception; everyone pressed forward to exchange a word or two with Fidel Castro, who was carrying on five conversations at once. By his side a young woman with short, dark hair and unwavering concentration translated seamlessly from English to Spanish and back again as Fidel fielded the rapid-fire questions that shot out from the crowd.

At one point he was asked about Mikhail Gorbachev. Fidel chuckled. Gorbachev, of course, had initiated the reforms that led to the collapse of the Soviet Union and the catastrophic destruction of Cuba's economy.

"I think he is someone who will spend the rest of time in limbo," he responded. "He will not go to hell. But I don't think he will get a visa to heaven."

One of the more interesting aspects of the evening was the way the Americans swooned over Fidel. Here was a man who had allowed the Soviets to aim nuclear missiles at the United States and, by many accounts, had been itching to pull the trigger. A man the U.S. government had tried several times to liquidate. A man whose troops had been aligned against the United States in proxy wars from Angola to Nicaragua. A man whose government had seized billions of dollars' worth of American property—BankBoston, which had a delegate in the room, lost six branches and saw its eagle logo dragged through the streets in a coffin. Yet history meant nothing next to Fidel's charisma and reputation; he was a living legend. The Cold War—regardless of what the State Department and the Miami exiles wanted to believe—could not have been deader at that moment.

Cuba itself was changing. The Special Period in Time of Peace continued, but the economy had bottomed out and had actually grown by a modest 2.5 percent the previous year. Out of desperation Fidel had launched his own tightly controlled reforms, none as aggressive as Gorbachev's but dramatic nonetheless. One move had turned the island completely upside down. In

---

*Cuba's national drink: a concoction of rum, seltzer, lemon juice, sugar and fresh mint.

1993, Fidel had legalized the possession of U.S. dollars. In the past, citizens had been thrown in jail for holding even a few bills, but suddenly, with a single decree, the greenback had been anointed king. Economically, it made perfect sense. Cuba needed hard currency to pull itself out of its free fall. But the move unleashed a world of contradictions. I could never quite get over the fact that Fidel had embraced a currency whose notes were signed by the secretary of the treasury, whose agency was charged with enforcing the trade embargo, which sought, by definition, to deprive Cuba of U.S. dollars.

After that nothing was sacred in Cuba. I once visited the Bay of Pigs, which was marked by a billboard as the site of THE FIRST MAJOR DEFEAT OF IMPERIALISM IN LATIN AMERICA. But when I went to find a hotel, it was like a bad commercial: If you want to spend the night on the hallowed ground of the First Major Defeat of Imperialism in Latin America, you better bring the imperialists' cash. Even the image of the late Che Guevara, who once described imperialism as "a carnivorous animal feeding on the helpless," was suddenly up for grabs. The government stamped Che's martyred visage on postcards, stickers, buttons, key chains, coffee mugs and, of course, T-shirts—all available only for dollars.

Over time the dollar acquired several colorful slang names, the most common of which were *fula, fao* and *eleggua*—a mythical child in Santería who opens all doors. Its legalization obliterated Castro's aspirations for a classless society. There were now dollar-haves and dollar-have-nots, the differences apparent on any city block. One afternoon in Trinidad, about two hours southeast of Havana, I walked into a musty bodega with Howard LaFranchi of the *Christian Science Monitor*. As shoppers palmed their yellowed ration booklets, we inspected the available inventory: a splintered cabinet filled with puck-hard crackers, eleven bars of unwrapped soap, four denuded cigars, a few bags of rice and beans, a ceramic lamp, one pair of dirty slippers and a wicker handbag. Dwindling rapidly were sugar and flour, which the woman behind the counter was scooping out of large white barrels ringed with flies.

"There used to be more: more cooking oil, more soap, more everything," one shopper told us. "Now it comes every once in a while, but you never know when. What happens is the people who have dollars can get whatever they want."

The woman said she occasionally received dollars from an uncle who lived abroad. When we asked where, she replied without irony: "Russia."

Directly up the block was the bodega's modern counterpart: an air-conditioned dollar store that resembled nothing so much as a socialist

7-Eleven. Familiar stickers indicated that the store accepted both Visa and MasterCard. The clean, well-lit aisles were lined with sardine tins, four types of pasta, two brands of beer, eggs, frozen meats, baguettes, chocolate sauce, flan, Gerber baby food and five kinds of soda. All that was missing were the Big Gulps, the microwave burritos and *Playboy*.

But what was truly unusual about Fidel's reforms was how they skewed the value of labor. Doctors, for example, were paid in pesos, and thus earned the equivalent of about $20 a month. Taxi drivers, bellhops and *jinateras* (prostitutes), meanwhile, could earn hundreds of dollars in tips alone. Cubans have a knack for coming up with the perfect joke to illustrate their surreal existence. One of the most popular at the time involved a drunk who pleads with a taxi driver to take him home one evening.

"I will pay you well," the drunk promises. "After all, I am a doorman at the Hotel Nacional. I receive all my tips in dollars." Thus assured, the cabbie ferries the drunk all the way to the other side of Havana. Along the way, the drunk passes out, so the cabbie has to carry him to the door. When he knocks, the drunk's wife answers.

"Here is your husband," the driver says. "He's drunk but he told me he was going to pay me well because he works at the Nacional."

"Oh, every time he drinks he has delusions of grandeur," says the wife. "He's really only a neurosurgeon."

If we could somehow get him alone, Phil Bennett and I were determined to ask Fidel about the reforms and what they were doing to the country. Our chance finally came around midnight, as everyone was finishing a sumptuous buffet of chilled shrimp, rice and beans, fried plantains and salad.

After finishing our meals, Bennett and I rose and walked across the room to request an interview with the Maximum Leader, who was seated next to Moakley. Bennett introduced us as gentlemen of the press.

The words were no sooner out of Bennett's mouth than Fidel was on his feet, leading us to the front of the room. Standing next to him, I now saw that his sixty-nine years showed. His skin was thin and translucent, and mottled with age spots. His tangled nest of a beard was dull and graying, but the questions seemed to energize him. As Bennett later wrote, he answered our questions "with the verbal thunderstorms that have simultaneously enthralled and worn down generations of listeners."

Fidel gently thumped me in the chest with the back of his hand when he wanted to emphasize a point. If he had one message, it was that Cuba was not going down like the Soviets. Gorbachev, he said, had "destroyed the whole history of his country." Yes, Fidel told us, the reforms were "irreversible." And, yes, they had created "privilege" contrary to the principles of socialism. And, yes, foreigners could even invest in the economy now. But he was in control at all times, he wanted us to know. "This is all under the control of the state," said Fidel. "It's not that we are handing over the country to foreign capital, nor are we going to put the country up for sale. We aren't thinking of selling the country. And the role of the state will remain important."

The interview lasted for about forty-five minutes. Fidel essentially kept coming back to the same point: that Cuba was surviving on its own terms. "We have managed to stop the free fall," he boasted.

I asked him, "Mr. President, when you talk to people on the street, they describe a country that has been divided into two unequal halves: those with dollars and those without dollars. How much does this concern you?"

"It's clear that all these openings bring differences," he said. "We know that. We prefer more equality. We prefer more justice." But he said he had no other choice. "We did not want to apply policies of a 'shock,' like those that have occurred in many countries of Latin America, that pushed hundreds of thousands of people into the streets, without protection. We have not closed a single school, not one hospital, not one day-care center, not a single home for the elderly."

The rest of the evening was like a lovefest. Shortly after our interview, Fidel, an avowed atheist, stood before the Americans and said: "We cannot be accused of being voluntary neighbors. It was nature that put us here. It was God. It was God who decided that we would be neighbors. What we know is that we cannot move away from each other, so we have to stay here and get used to it. We have to be friends."

Waiters then filtered through the crowd, handing out premium cigars. As everyone was lighting up—except Fidel, who had given up smoking years before as an example to the nation—Moakley reached into a bag and pulled out a variety of gifts for El Comandante. They were Boston Red Sox souvenirs. There was a Red Sox jacket, a navy blue cap with the familiar red *B*, a Red Sox watch, even a team pen donated by owner John Harrington (probably the one used to sign Matt Young).

"Are these Red Sox Communists?" asked Fidel, surveying the gifts with a smile.

Then members of the delegation crowded around him to shake his hand and get his autograph. A few people, aware of Fidel's past as a pitcher, had even brought baseballs for the Maximum Leader to sign. Suddenly, it was like a

BoSox Club field trip to the Palace of the Revolution. The aging former hurler stood there in the marbled hall in his military fatigues, signing baseball after baseball for the awed Boston executives as if he were Jim Lonborg.

Fidel was there at the door to see us out, and everyone got his picture taken with him. Fidel apparently had seen me checking my tape recorder and he asked, "Did you get it all?" I assured him that I had.

In all, it was a giddy night. Really, the only hint of political tension came toward the end of our interview. I decided to ask Fidel about two planes that had recently buzzed Havana. The planes, which originated in Miami, had crossed into Cuban airspace to drop thousands of leaflets over the capital, urging Cubans to rise up against their leader. Why, I asked Fidel, didn't the government respond?

"We have all the patience necessary," he warned. "But there are limits to our patience."

Bennett and I didn't think much of the remark. We buried it in the second to last paragraph of our story. "For now," we wrote, "Castro does not seem interested in looking for a fight."

A month later, two private planes again threatened to puncture Cuban airspace. This time, a pair of MiG fighters blew them out of the sky with heat-seeking missiles.

THE PLANES BELONGED to Brothers to the Rescue, a small group of Cuban American aviators who operated out of Opa-Locka Airport in northwest Miami. The group's leader, José Basulto, was a home builder and former terrorist who had entered Cuba as a spy before the Bay of Pigs, then walked through a minefield to reach Guantánamo after the operation failed. He founded Brothers to the Rescue in 1991 to aid the thousands of *balseros*, rafters, who foundered in the Florida Straits each year.

The group became a local sensation during the 1994 rafter crisis, the largest since Mariel. Basulto could hardly believe the desperation. On one occasion he spotted people floating on the roof of a cannibalized school bus. Wooden beams and Styrofoam kept the "vessel" afloat, and an old motorcycle engine powered it from the rear. It was total insanity. Whenever rafters appeared to be in distress, Brothers to the Rescue would drop handheld radios. If the rafters requested assistance, the pilots would alert the U.S. Coast Guard. Occasionally, the Brothers would attempt rescues on their own. Basulto once crashed his Cessna into a tree while trying to remove a sick child from a remote island.

The Brothers estimated that they had helped save more than 4,000 people. Then, in May 1995, the Clinton administration reversed the three-decades-old U.S. immigration policy toward Cuba. Cubans intercepted at sea would now be sent home rather than welcomed into the United States. The decision rocked Miami. The exile community accused Clinton of selling out to Castro to stem the tidal wave of refugees. There were several protests. One Miami radio station even invoked the community's benchmark for U.S. government betrayal: President Kennedy's refusal to provide air cover during the Bay of Pigs.

The decision also threatened to put Brothers to the Rescue out of business. Within days, the new policy slowed immigration to a trickle. When the group launched its search-and-rescue missions, the planes frequently encountered only vast expanses of open water. Over time Brothers to the Rescue would scale back its operations, selling off planes and flying symbolic missions just one day a week. But, at the same time, Basulto also discovered new ways of expanding the group's raison d'être.

As a young terrorist in the early 1960s, Basulto had once stood on the deck of a boat, lobbing 20-millimeter cannon shells into a Havana hotel in a foolhardy attempt to assassinate Fidel. He became a pacifist as he grew older, adopting the nonviolent teachings of Martin Luther King, Jr. The new activities of Brothers to the Rescue would fall somewhere between those two extremes. Basulto and his men began to play an escalating game of chicken with the Cuban air force, buzzing Havana and dropping anti-Castro leaflets before scurrying back to Miami. At the same time, the Brothers began to openly raise money for opposition leaders on the island, principally a dissident group called Concilio Cubano.

Concilio Cubano had been formed in October 1995 to unify some 5,000 dissidents inside Cuba. Historically, opposition to Castro had been weak and fragmented, undermined both by the government, which sent hundreds of people to prison, and by the exiles, who viewed the dissidents suspiciously for having remained in Cuba. Concilio Cubano sought to bring everyone together for the common goal of ousting Fidel. Organizers planned a historic conference in Havana to adopt a declaration of principles and a resolution for political change. In Miami, Basulto publicly announced a donation to the group, later disclosed as $2,000. "I think that was the straw that broke the camel's back when they decided to shoot us down," he said.

One prominent dissident later told me that Brothers to the Rescue had planned to sky-write CONCILIO CUBANO over Havana on the day of the scheduled conference. Basulto dismissed such reports as "a lot of bullshit. Actually, the plan for that day—and this was a decision made by the Support Group of

Concilio Cubano, of which we were just one of many groups—was not to do anything to distract attention from the main event." The flights that day, Basulto said, were "typical of two thousand such missions we conducted in the past."

It was February 24, a date that marked the beginning of Cuba's war of independence against Spain.

At 2:57 P.M. a Havana air-traffic controller spoke directly to Basulto, who was piloting one of three Brothers to the Rescue planes that day.

"We inform you that the area north of Havana is activated," the controller said.

It was a warning that the group's presence near Cuban airspace had triggered the launch of two Soviet-made MiGs.

"You are taking a risk," the controller warned.

"We are ready to do so as free Cubans," responded Basulto.

An independent investigation later determined that Basulto briefly entered the twelve-mile airspace boundary, then quickly retreated. The investigation also concluded that the three planes were outside Cuban airspace when the MiGs struck.

The attack was merciless. It was like shooting ants with an elephant gun. The streaking MiGs, traveling at speeds of up to 600 miles per hour, hit two of the three unarmed Cessnas—planes not much bigger than vans—with 230-pound heat-seeking missiles fired from under their wings. The Cessnas disintegrated instantly along with their four pilots.

"The other one destroyed! The other one destroyed!" cried one of the MiG pilots. "Fatherland or death! ¡Cojones [balls]! The other one is down, too!"

"We're next," Basulto said to his passengers. He wheeled his plane around and headed back toward Miami. Why he was spared is unclear. There is some indication that a MiG trailing behind him was low on fuel and aborted its mission.

Needless to say, the attack was an international incident. Among other things, it erased much of the goodwill that had been gradually building between the United States and Cuba. Clinton announced that he planned to sign the Helms-Burton bill, an absurd law designed to punish not only Americans but also foreigners who did business with Cuba. The incident was also a disturbing reminder that the enmity between the United States and Cuba—or at least Havana and Miami—remained potentially lethal. The Cold War, it now seemed, would go on forever.

By the time I arrived in Havana, two days after the attack, it was fairly obvious that it had been part of a larger strategy to crush Cuba's growing opposition. As I made my way around the city, I heard story after story of State Security agents bursting into people's homes, detaining some 120 dissidents planning to attend the first meeting of Concilio Cubano. In some cases the dissidents were strip-searched, then relieved of all documents pertaining to the event. Four of Concilio Cubano's leaders were arrested: Leonel Morejón, the group's thirty-three-year-old president, was charged with "disobedience," as was Lázaro González Valdés, a thirty-six-year-old member of the organizing board. Jesús Ramón Marante, a thirty-seven-year-old doctor, was sentenced to a year in prison for the illegal sale of medical supplies. Roberto López Montenez, forty-six, got fifteen months for "slandering the Maximum Leader."

The conference was postponed indefinitely. At least sixty opposition figures later went into exile. Elizardo Sánchez, the island's most prominent dissident, called it "the largest wave of repression we've seen in the last thirty years."

I left Havana in a terrible mood. Unlike in the Moakley visit, just weeks earlier, I had seen not the legendary, benign Fidel but the face of totalitarianism. I couldn't wait to get out. Havana is often that way. The first week is wonderful and exotic, a whirl of *mojitos* and salsa and laughter and baseball. But by the second week, the city closes in on you. There is no real information. The eight-page morning newspaper delivers platitudes and lies. The two-channel television is worse. Your best friends can't enter your hotel because of obscene laws designed to separate the natives from the tourists. At the same time the government is preaching socialism, it has its hands in your pockets, gouging you of every last dollar in your possession. People have to cup their hands or lower their voices or raise their eyes to the heavens or invent a secret code when they want to speak freely. And, of course, the ridiculous embargo makes everything worse. Credit cards issued by American banks are useless in Cuba, so you have to walk around with wheelbarrows of cash. I can't begin to count the number of times I've run out of money in Havana and had to rely on the kindness of others. It happened that very trip, in fact.

I left on the first flight out. I can't remember the exact time, but it was barely light when I got to the airport. I had forgotten to close out the account on my state-administered cell phone, so I wandered over to the state-administered cell phone trailer across the parking lot. This was a couple of years before the big airport expansion. The international terminal was still a glorified hangar packed with the requisite ticket counter, baggage claim area and bar. Suitcases in hand, I strolled across the empty parking lot and walked up to the trailer, which of course was closed at that early hour.

As I turned around, a man was walking toward me. He was dressed in gym shorts and a T-shirt and looked like he had just come from a run.

"Don't you remember me?" said Orlando "El Duque" Hernández.

I had met El Duque only once. I had interviewed him at his home behind the airport one afternoon, shortly after Liván had defected. I wasn't even aware that Liván had a brother, but a Cuban friend had quickly filled me in. The then commissioner of baseball, Domingo Zabala, told me generally where I could find El Duque. So one afternoon, I asked a taxi driver to take me out to the airport. We drove around for about twenty minutes before some friendly neighbors led us to the house.

The modest house was blue and immaculate, a cutoff throw from Terminal 2. The back fence was nearly on the runway. El Duque wasn't home yet, but his wife, Norma, asked us to wait in the living room while she got us refreshments. She came back with plastic glasses of lemonade, and we made small talk until El Duque suddenly burst in the door, apparently home from baseball practice.

He couldn't have been happier to see us. One of the pleasures of working in Cuba is that you can usually drop in unannounced and expect to be received warmly. We sat in his living room and talked about his brother's defection, of which he professed no prior knowledge, even though he had been sleeping in the same room. El Duque said that he had no interest in defecting—not that he would have confessed this. He said the INDER had begun to hand out cash bonuses to help players make ends meet in the new dollar economy. "They are aware that many of us could be millionaires, but not in our own country," he said.

Then he said something that has stayed with me ever since: "*Yo sé que la palabra más bonita en el mundo es el dinero, pero creo yo que las palabras como lealtad y patriotismo también son muy bonitas.*" ("I know the prettiest word in the world is *money,* but I believe that words like *loyalty* and *patriotism* are very beautiful as well.")

El Duque has since disavowed such blather, saying the comments were made under the duress of an authoritarian system. But I am convinced that he believed those words, at least in that moment.

By the time I bumped into him at the airport, however, his life had taken a dramatic turn for the worse. He sounded like a lot of people I had spoken with that week, people whose lives were suddenly turned upside down by the government. El Duque said the authorities had been progressively turning up the heat on him. He had been interrogated several times, and the government kept insisting that he was responsible for Liván's defection. Worse, they had determined that he was a defection risk himself and were threatening to pull him off Team Cuba, which was in training for the Atlanta Olympics. He said the officials had falsely claimed that he was injured and that his performance had suffered. He said his arm was fine.

"I don't know why they're doing this to me," he said pleadingly. "I've had every opportunity in the world to defect and I never did."

I had to catch my plane, so we shook hands and I started to walk back across the parking lot. I told him I'd look him up when I got back to Havana. Neither of us knew that in the intervening months his life would become a waking nightmare.

NOT A MONTH LATER, El Duque got the unceremonious boot from Team Cuba. The news came over the state-run television one night. "We were just sitting around Orlando's house drinking beer, and they started announcing who had made the team," said Roberto "Pelusa" Martínez, the pitcher's close friend. The announcer started with the position players, and someone noticed that he had skipped El Duque's best friend, shortstop Germán Mesa. "That's when we started to wonder," said Martínez. "They're listing the pitchers and someone yelled, 'They didn't mention El Duque!' " Everyone stared at the television in disbelief. "It was so strange, I can't even begin to describe it to you," said Martínez. "We were sure it was a mistake."

But it was no mistake. The next day, the players confirmed through the INDER that, in fact, they had been left off the team for Atlanta. It was as if the Yankees had decided to waive Roger Clemens and Derek Jeter before the World Series without any explanation. Of course, everyone knew the unstated reason: The INDER was concerned that El Duque, lured by his brother's $4.5 million contract, would follow him to the major leagues and bring his best friend, Germán Mesa, along with him.

"I don't understand why I have to pay for my brother's sins," El Duque told me as his life began its descent into hell.

The decision was a blow on a number of levels, not the least of which was financial. Suddenly, El Duque was cut off from the cash bonuses that the INDER had started handing out for victories in international play. He was also cut out of the players' creative moneymaking schemes. In a country where the dollar had become all-powerful, that money was critical. It enabled him to provide scarce essentials for his family: soap, cooking oil, toilet paper. "At least they were able to wipe," said El Duque. He was still allowed to play for Industriales, but now he derived his entire salary from a job as a rehab counselor at the Havana Psychiatric Hospital. He earned 207 pesos a month, approximately $8.75.

Fortunately, he had an alternative source of income: Liván. From the moment he cashed his $2.5 million bonus check from the Marlins, El Duque's younger brother had started sending money home. The pitcher had to be fairly discreet about it. Once, Liván told a writer for USA Today how pleased he was to be able to send money to his family. The story appeared in the paper's sports section, a harmless immigrant's tale, until the U.S. Treasury Department saw it and fired off a letter to the Marlins. The letter informed the team that one of its players had violated the U.S. trade embargo and ordered him to cease and desist at once.

From then on, Liván remained relatively circumspect. "That's private," he said when I asked him about the remittances. But the same could not be said of his faithful courier, Juan Ignacio. By all accounts, Cubas's portly cousin roamed the island like he owned the place, a nubile friend often in tow. His appointed rounds took him out to the Isle of Youth, where Liván's mother and sister and occasionally his father resided, and also to Havana to visit El Duque.

Juan Ignacio's lack of discretion was mind-boggling. He made his deliveries like an emissary from Publishers Clearing House. Tom Cronin made one run with him in the spring of 1996, shortly before the war between Juan Ignacio and Cubas split the defection industry into partisan factions.

Cronin was staying at the Hotel Valencia in Old Havana when he heard a knock at the door. "You know how it is in Cuba," he said. "You go to bed at four in the morning; you're not getting up at seven or eight. But it must have been about eight when I get this knock. One of the women who works at the hotel is yelling, 'There is a man downstairs to see you!'

"So I go downstairs and Juan Ignacio is sitting there having breakfast with his girlfriend. She was this young thing, very attractive, probably about nineteen. She was hot. I say, 'What are you doing here?' He says, 'Oh, I just thought we should have a talk. I'm here to see El Duque.' I said, 'Oh, really?' I started thinking to myself, Wait a minute, now he's trying to horn in on Dookie and me.

"He told me that he had ten thousand dollars from Liván and that he was going to deliver it to Dookie. He said that he was going over to his house by the airport. I decided that I better go with him. So we get out there and we're talking with Dookie, and now Juan is saying, 'You know, Dookie, Tommy gets a third of the commission when you defect. And when you talk to Joe Cubas, you gotta tell him that I want a third, too, because I'm the one who gets all the visas.'

"Then Juan Ignacio reaches into his fanny pack, this bulging blue fanny pack that he carried with him. He always had it locked. He unlocks it and he yanks out this huge wad of hundred-dollar bills. It was typical of the way he operated. He loved the big scene. It's funny, because sometimes he would take precautions, driving here, driving there, trying to keep people off his trail. Then other times he was totally irrational. He liked to play the part of the big operator. Of course, all you have to be is American and you're a big operator in Cuba."

Once, during a visit to the Isle of Youth, Juan Ignacio got a yearning to rent an airplane to fly across the gulf to pick up his girlfriend. "He just suddenly had to go to Havana," said Arnaldo Hernández, the original El Duque. "They charge you something like five hundred dollars an hour just to take you, wait awhile, and then bring you back. He said, 'C'mon, let's go and we'll pick up my girlfriend and bring her back.' I said, 'I don't think so.'

"He was crazy," said Arnaldo Hernández. "He was always going around handing out money. He'd hand out eight thousand here, eight thousand there. We'd go somewhere and he'd order a pack of cigarettes. He'd pay for it with a twenty and tell the workers, 'Here, take this twenty and get yourselves some shoes.' I'd say, 'Listen, Juan Ignacio, what the fuck is wrong with you?'

"He just fucked around too much. He tried to pass himself off as some kind of big shot. Once he took me to a store. He says to the guy, 'Give me all the jeans you have. Everything.' He must have spent something like a thousand dollars that day. Then he filled up the car with clothes and went around handing them out to everyone on the island."

Delivering wads of cash on behalf of Liván Hernández, traitor to the revolution, was more than enough to get Juan Ignacio in trouble. But he also began to explore his own business opportunities. He met with players in their homes, handing out money and urging them to defect. In most countries, of course, recruiting baseball players is a business, not a crime. But in Cuba, after so many high-profile defections—most carried out by Juan Ignacio's own cousin—it was dangerous, felonious behavior. Anyone around the Cuban baseball scene at least knew that. Whether Juan Ignacio understood the gravity of what he was doing is not entirely clear.

On August 10, 1996, Juan Ignacio landed at José Martí International Airport in Havana. By then he and Cubas were blood enemies, and he had formed his unofficial alliance with Cronin. The timing of his arrival could not have been worse. Just weeks earlier, Rolando Arrojo had defected in Albany, Georgia. Although Juan Ignacio had not been involved, Cuban authorities could not have known the intricacies of his familial war with Cubas, who, of course, had helped Arrojo escape. Besides, if Cubas is to be believed, Juan Ignacio had been photographed on the same trip, smoking cigars in a motel lobby with Omar Linares, whom Juan Ignacio and the Cronins had been trying to recruit. On top of that were the political tensions still simmering after the Brothers to the Rescue episode and the Helms-Burton law—HEIL HELMS! read a Havana billboard. It was the tensest period in U.S.-Cuba relations since the end of the Cold War.

There is no evidence that Juan Ignacio took any of this into consideration. Once again he arrived in Havana bearing gifts. El Duque was expecting him. "He had eight thousand dollars and a bag full of clothes and sneakers for us," said El Duque. "We waited for him for hours but he ended up coming on a later flight." Once he arrived, Juan Ignacio could have walked across the parking lot to El Duque's house. Instead, he made a beeline for the rental-car office. To a visitor, it may appear that there is a plethora of distinct businesses that serve Havana's tourism industry. The rental-car agencies go by different names such as Gaviota and Transautos. There are five-star hotels like the Melia Cohiba and the Nacional, four-star hotels like the Habana Libre and Sevilla, three-star hotels like Neptuno and Tritón, and so on. Seemingly, there is a wealth of diversity. In reality, all are part of the same entity: Fidel, Inc.

As he filled out the forms Juan Ignacio began to openly discuss his plans with the rental-car agents. Many were friends of El Duque, so Juan Ignacio may have felt comfortable around them.

"He was talking a lot of shit," said El Duque, whose astonished friends later recounted the scene for him. "He shows up and he starts saying how he's there to get me and Germán Mesa out of Cuba. I mean, the rental-car place is run by Gaviota, which is run by the Ministry of Interior." El Duque paused. He laughed and shook his head. "Brother, he was an idiot," said El Duque. "He was just plain stupid."

Back when he worked for Cubas, Juan Ignacio often drove the defection vehicle. Now, working for himself, he decided to enlist his own chauffeur: yet another cousin. His name was Alberto Hernández, but everyone called him Lingote (pronounced Lin-go-tay), "pig iron." "All the fuckers around here call me Lingote," he explained cheerfully. "Since I'm heavy, that's what they call me." Lingote lived in a farming community called San Nicolás, about forty-five minutes east of Havana. In hindsight, there was a certain macabre symbolism about his selection as Juan Ignacio's driver: his day job was driving a hearse for the local San Nicolás funeral home.

As one of his first assignments, Lingote ferried Juan Ignacio out to Sancti

Spíritus, a city in the central highlands. An international eighteen-and-under baseball tournament was in progress, and Juan Ignacio told Lingote he wanted to watch the United States play Venezuela. Lingote figured he and his family could make a minivacation of it. He decided to take along his wife, Marisel, and their ten-year-old daughter, Yusmila. Juan Ignacio supplied the car, the one he had rented at the airport from Gaviota, still loaded up with the clothes and shoes he was to deliver to El Duque.

When the group pulled into Sancti Spíritus, they discovered that there was no game that day. The U.S.-Venezuela contest was scheduled for the following morning. With time to kill, they decided to spend the night in nearby Trinidad, a quaint coastal city to the south. It was a lovely evening. Juan Ignacio took Lingote and his family out to a nice dinner on the water at one of the tourist restaurants and paid for their hotel room.

The next morning, with Lingote at the wheel and Juan Ignacio riding shotgun, they drove back to Sancti Spíritus for the game. It started at ten. By noon it was brutally hot, and the United States had won. When the game ended, Juan Ignacio drifted down to the field to see a coach he knew on the Venezuelan team. Lingote went back to the concession stand to get his family some cold drinks. "I was standing there in line and somebody says to me, 'Hey, where is that guy who was just with you?' " Lingote recalled. "I said, 'Where is he? He's right over there, that's where he is. Where else would he be?' They said, 'No, they just arrested him right over there.' "

Lingote turned around to see his cousin in the parking lot, surrounded by five security agents dressed in green military uniforms. "It turned out we were being followed," said Lingote. "They had been sitting in their cars waiting outside the field. They weren't policemen. They were agents with immigration and State Security."

Juan Ignacio was on the verge of tears as he stood surrounded by the agents. The men hustled him into an unmarked sedan and drove away, first to the immigration office in Sancti Spíritus, then to Villa Marista, the State Security headquarters in Havana.

The agents told Lingote he could keep Juan Ignacio's rental car and drive his family back to San Nicolás. He did exactly that, then hunkered down inside his home and waited, terrified of what would happen next. His wait lasted four days, at which point there came a knock at the door. Lingote, too, was then taken into custody. He was driven to Villa Marista, where he encountered his cousin Juan Ignacio, dressed in blue prison attire, sobbing uncontrollably in a cell.

It remains unclear why the Cuban government chose to arrest Juan Ignacio at a baseball tournament in the country's interior. Months later, a Sports Ministry official told me that the authorities had been tipped off by the enraged parents of Juan Ignacio's teenage girlfriend, who had informed them about his endeavors. The official said that Juan Ignacio had been so brazen that he had tried to recruit Cuban players right there on the field. Lingote said that wasn't true. "No, no," he said, "he wasn't after the juniors. He was after El Duque and Germán."

That much at least is clear. After arresting Juan Ignacio the agents confiscated all his possessions. That included thousands of dollars of Liván Hernández's earnings as a major-league baseball player, clothing, athletic shoes, credit cards, four rings, a cellular phone and battery charger, a pocket translator, a calculator, a spiral-bound notebook, house keys, matches, cologne, photos of his wife, Teresa, and his five children, a U.S. passport, six pens, a pair of Oakley sunglasses and a black briefcase.

The authorities were particularly interested in two documents that were found in Lingote's possession. Juan Ignacio, they said later, had told Lingote to guard the documents "with his life." The documents were work visas from Venezuela, already made out in the names of their intended recipients: Orlando Hernández Pedroso and Germán Mesa Fresneda.

"I didn't even know he was carrying those papers," said El Duque. "It was just a moment of stupidity on his part. If you have an improper document in your possession in Cuba, it's worse than getting caught with drugs in the United States. If I had known I would have said, 'Compadre, tear that shit up. I don't need those documents to get out of Cuba.' "

ON AUGUST 13, 1996, Tom Cronin arrived in Havana. Years later, he would recall the date exactly. It was Fidel Castro's seventieth birthday. It was also the day Cronin's escapades in Cuba lost their playful innocence.

Cronin took his usual route: Boston to Miami, Miami to Cancún, Cancún to Havana. The forty-five-minute AeroCaribe flight from Cancún landed nightly at Terminal 2, directly across from El Duque's house. Cronin stepped out of the plane into the sopping Caribbean heat. He walked across the tarmac, into the immigration lounge, a spartan room with dirty linoleum floors and a video monitor looping silent images of Cuba's main attractions: Varadero beach, the Tropicana nightclub, cigar rollers, gorgeous women.

Cronin got in line. He knew the routine by heart. In a nod to the embargo, the immigration agent would wave him through without stamping his passport. It was the Cubans' method of helping Americans travel to the island illegally. It no longer seemed strange to Cronin, this anachronistic dance of the Cold War. It was all part of Cuba's exotic allure. Cronin stood in line and thought about his plans for the evening. After clearing customs, he would take a cab to his usual domicile, the Hotel Valencia, then look up Juan Ignacio, who had arrived ahead of him.

Years later Cronin denied that he and Juan Ignacio were partners, despite considerable evidence to the contrary. In addition to the fact that Juan Ignacio had listed Cronin as his partner on his agent application with the Major League Baseball Players Association, there had been a series of phone calls between Cronin's home on Cape Cod and Juan Ignacio's home in Venezuela in the days leading up to the fateful trip. The phone records would later surface in a federal lawsuit Cronin filed against Cubas. Cronin was trying to argue that he had been partners with Cubas, and not Juan Ignacio, and thus deserved one-third of Cubas's commission from El Duque's contract.

Cronin handed his passport to the immigration agent, dressed in the green military uniform of the Ministry of Interior. The process seemed to be taking longer than usual. "The guy looks at my name, then he looks at me, then he's looking at my name again," said Cronin. "Finally I said, 'Is there a problem?' And he says, 'Yes, there is a problem.' There was a South African guy standing in line behind me and he says, 'Oh, don't worry about it. You know how these third-world countries are, they just want twenty bucks for the visa.' And I said, 'No, I think it's a little more serious than that. Believe me, I do this all the time and this has never happened.' Well, then the security boys showed up and they escorted me off."

At this point I asked Cronin what seemed to be an appropriate question: "Were you shitting your pants?"

"Well, I was a little concerned. But I started arguing with them. I said, 'Hey, let me talk to the guy who's in charge here.' I didn't know what the hell was going on. So I just kept arguing with them to let me in the country. But they never told me what was happening. They just took me off to an unused area of the airport and I stayed there all night long."

At one point, Cronin asked a woman if he could use the telephone.

"No," she said.

"Listen, I'll give you twenty dollars if you just let me use the phone."

"No."

"Why? What's the problem?"

"It's you. You are a big problem."

"They had taken my passport away," said Cronin. "So I sat there all night, awake, wondering what the hell was going on. By five or six o'clock in the morning it started getting light out, and I kept asking, 'C'mon, what is going on here?' Then, around seven o'clock, without saying much of anything this big guy came along with my passport. I said, 'I want my passport back.' He said, 'You just come with me.' Another guy came along and they walked me back out to the tarmac, one on each arm. There was a Mexicana plane out there with the stairs down. The big guy marches me right up the stairs and he says, 'You are now leaving the country.'

"I said, 'Hey, where's my passport?' Then he literally pushed me into the plane. I turned around and said, 'I want my passport!' He said something quickly in Spanish and then he gave it to the stewardess.

"When I got to Cancún I called my wife. I said, 'You're not going to believe what happened.' And she said, '*You* are not going to believe what happened! I've been worried sick about you. I got a call from Joe Cubas asking where you were. He said Juan Ignacio had been arrested in Cuba. He wanted to know if you knew anything about it.'

"So I called Cubas. He wanted to know what I knew. All I knew at that point was that Juan Ignacio had talked to me before he went to Cuba. He said he had a very good friend who was a Cuban coach in Venezuela. Apparently Juan had befriended him, he was with the Venezuelan junior team and Juan wanted to go see him. That's all I knew."

Cubas told a slightly different story. He said Cronin called him from Cancún, hysterical: "He's says, 'Joe, you gotta help your cousin. You gotta help Juan Ignacio. You gotta help him. Joe, you gotta believe me, we were doing it all for you, Joe. We were going to get the players for you.' It was all a bunch of bullshit."

Regardless, it was clear to everyone that the game had changed dramatically. Certainly, Tom Cronin wasn't going back to Cuba anytime soon.

"My only crime was hanging around ballplayers," insisted Cronin. "I didn't think that was a crime."

CHAPTER TEN

CRIMES AGAINST BASEBALL

$\int$ TATE SECURITY RELEASED LINGOTE AFTER A WEEK OF INTERRO-
gation, convinced that he had nothing to do with Juan Ignacio's alleged crimes.
"They kept asking me about the visas, but I couldn't tell them a thing," Lingote
said. "I was just the driver. I would stay in the car and he would go off and work
on his things." Lingote returned to San Nicolás, thankful he had escaped punishment. He resumed his life driving the hearse. Every Monday afternoon he
traveled to Havana to visit his cousin, confined to a cell in Villa Marista. Frequently, he found Juan Ignacio shivering with grief, unable to comprehend
what had happened. "He would cry and cry," said Lingote. "You can imagine
the trauma he was going through. We suffered, too, just thinking about him in
there. But he was never mistreated."

While Juan Ignacio sat in jail, the government began to compile its case
against him. There were plenty of people to interview. During his two years
with Cubas, and then on his own, Juan Ignacio had managed to contact nearly
every top player in Cuba. In addition to El Duque and Mesa, he had wooed two
players from Pinar del Río: right-hander Pedro Luis Lazo and outfielder Daniel
Lazo, who shared the same last name but were not related. Pedro Luis was the
more valuable of the two, a hulking fireballer in the mold of retired major-
leaguer Lee Smith. The players told investigators that during the pre-Olympic
tour, Juan Ignacio bought a Hitachi videocassette player for Pedro Luis and a
Toshiba color television for Daniel. He then urged them to defect. The players
took the gifts but not the bait.

From the beginning, one of the key witnesses was a chunky catcher named
Alberto "Albertico" Hernández. Boyish, with wavy brown hair, a sizable head

and an innocent smile, Alberto Hernández was an average hitter with a deadly arm. He was known to throw out runners from his knees. His nickname was the "Pride of Holguín" because he had been the first player from the province to make Team Cuba. Inside the local stadium, sports authorities erected a glass-encased Pride of Holguín shrine to house his trophies and medals, including two Olympic golds. "We all wanted to be Alberto," said Juan Carlos Bruzón, a young player from Holguín. "Kids playing in the street argued over who got to be Alberto."

Alberto Hernández grew up in Gibara, a wind-lashed fishing village perched atop a hill overlooking the sea. His father, Juan Hernández, was a former third baseman and hard-core revolutionary who worked for twenty-one years in the Ministry of Interior. Alberto, too, had unyielding faith in the revolution. He regarded his success as a tribute to socialism in general and Fidel in particular. Holguín is a poor province far out of the mainstream, but Alberto and his wife, Zaily, lived relatively well. The INDER gave the catcher a two-bedroom apartment and a Lada, and what he didn't have he was able to pick up abroad, most important, medication for his mother, who suffered from Parkinson's disease.

Alberto came under suspicion because his best friends were Osvaldo Fernández, Cubas's first catch, and Rolando Arrojo. While Arrojo was shuffling out of the Quality Inn in Albany, Georgia, his roommate Alberto was hunkered down inside, pondering what he would tell team officials. He pleaded ignorance—"I was sleeping"—but somehow word got around that he had been spotted earlier in the day in Cubas's car. Cubas, by his own admission, had been "hammering" Alberto to defect, but the catcher had refused. It was more than Zaily and his family. Alberto was torn between the growing realization that he could have a better life outside Cuba and an upbringing that forbade him even to harbor such treasonous thoughts.

"It was so hard," he said. "You think you lived a life that was on the right path. You made sacrifices. You played for love and not for money. You were away from your family. You always represented your country. You did the right thing. I was blind. My eyes had been closed."

After Juan Ignacio's arrest Alberto received a call ordering him to report immediately to the Sports City, the INDER's national headquarters in Havana. He had no idea what to expect when he pulled up at the squat, circular building after the long trip from Holguín. "They had me there for eight hours," he said. "They *interrogated* me, these three guys from State Security, all dressed in green. They were pissed because Arrojo had defected. They wanted to know how I knew Juan Ignacio. How *long* did I know him? Where did we meet? Had he visited me? I told them that I knew him like all the players knew the scouts. He visited me in Cuba every year. We talked about baseball. But I never said I would defect.

"After that they left me alone for about a week. I stayed with my in-laws in Havana. Then State Security came to get me again. They put me in a black car and drove me to a house on the road out to Guanabo. I was there from eight A.M. until five A.M. They would interrogate you for two hours at a time. Then they'd leave you in the room with some six-foot animal watching over you. When you went to take a piss, the guy would stand there and watch you holding your dick.

"They cursed you. They said I was a contact for Joe Cubas, and that I was a contact for all the Cuban players who defected. They said I was still in contact with all the defectors. They kept reminding me that my father had worked for the Ministry of Interior for twenty-one years. They thought every word out of my mouth was a lie. They wanted information. But I still thought everything was going to be okay. I knew that Omar Linares and Pacheco and all the others had met the scouts and talked to them. I thought it was normal."

As the government pressed Alberto, El Duque and Germán Mesa were getting the same treatment. El Duque was questioned twice. One afternoon, security agents pulled him off the practice field at the Sports City. He was taken to "some kind of house for diplomats," he recalled. "They kept me there for twelve hours, in my uniform. They kept offering me food, but I refused to eat it and that would piss them off even more. They asked me about Juan Ignacio, but what was I going to say about Juan Ignacio? He was a friend of mine. All he ever did was help me."

At this point it may be helpful to consider the Orwellian logic of the events now unfolding. A flamboyant thirty-eight-year-old man is being held for recruiting baseball players. In the course of the government's investigation, certain players have fallen under suspicion for a crime that they *might* commit. That crime is choosing to leave their desperate island-nation, its economy reduced to ashes, to play a game they love for millions of dollars against the toughest competition in the world. The players are being pressured to testify against the man who tried—unsuccessfully—to persuade them to commit this terrible crime. The players are also being pressured to testify against one another. No one would deny that Juan Ignacio's methods and motivations were less than pure, but it certainly seemed, as his mother later wrote in a plea for the pope to intervene: "His was not the act of a criminal yet that is how he is being treated."

And now it was about to get worse. Much worse.

ON OCTOBER 28, 1996, Juan Ignacio Hernández Nodar—Case No. 572—came before the Popular Provincial Tribunal, Havana, Cuba. The courtroom, No. 4, was located near the Capitolio, an immense replica of the U.S. Congress erected before Fidel gave the gringos the boot. The witness list comprised the far-flung relatives of the traitor Liván Hernández and some of the finest ballplayers in Cuba, if not the world. The list included El Duque; Germán Mesa; Arnaldo Hernández, the original El Duque; his ex-wife Miriam Carreras, Liván's mother; Pedro Luis Lazo; Daniel Lazo; Alberto Hernández and, of course, Juan Ignacio.

As they filed into the court, people were shocked at Juan Ignacio's appearance. Seated at a wooden table next to his lawyer, Camilo J. Loret de Mola, he was a pitiful sight. In the two months since his arrest, he had gone from being a plump, garrulous party animal to a gaunt, almost spectral presence in the room. He was sallow and haunting. His blue prison uniform sagged off his body. He looked like he had been crying for days, which, of course, he had. He sat before a panel of five judges—three women and two men—mournfully awaiting his fate. "You had to see him sitting there, dressed in blue," said Arnaldo Hernández. "We kept asking ourselves, 'What kind of crime did this man commit?' "

There was no publicity of this trial of the century. And, as Cuba has yet to pass any sunshine laws, there is no available documentation of what was said. But it is possible to piece together a rough outline of what occurred through the recollections of people who attended and the memorable sentencing documents, later released to Juan Ignacio's family.

The first witness was Orlando "El Duque" Hernández. The state had amassed considerable evidence that the most successful pitcher in the history of the revolution had visited the defendant several times. El Duque already had been kicked off Team Cuba over the Liván affair, and the government apparently figured that he and the other players would turn against Juan Ignacio in an effort to save their careers.

Over the next two years, El Duque would be tested in a variety of settings, from the streets of Havana to a tiny Bahamian island to the mound at Yankee Stadium. Yet no single act of bravery would compare with his performance in the courtroom that afternoon, a performance recounted again and again by his friends and family and even Juan Ignacio's relatives. The prosecutor, Angel Aguión Menéndez, pointed to the defendant. "This man who sits before the tribunal, do you consider him a friend or an enemy?"

"I consider him a *compañero*," responded El Duque.

"You are referring to this citizen?"

"Yes, *compañero* Juan Ignacio."

In most Spanish-speaking countries, the word *compañero* has several meanings: companion, partner, mate, among others. In Cuba, the word has but one meaning: comrade. The word is invoked almost universally in the revolutionary sense, and now El Duque Hernández had applied it to a U.S. citizen on trial for alleged crimes against the state. It was, at the very least, professional suicide.

"I knew he was fucked, but I had nothing against him," said El Duque. "[The prosecutor] asked me if he was a friend or an enemy, and so I called him a *compañero*. And that's what he was. I told them how once my daughter was sick and I spent the whole night looking for medicine for her. Juan Ignacio showed up at eight o'clock in the morning with the medicine. That morning he took my daughter's pain away. She was colicky and he helped her. How could I have anything against this man?

"Later, at the end of the trial, they mentioned me. They said, 'El Duque Hernández called Juan Ignacio Hernández Nodar a *compañero*. He must have his reasons for this.' I told them what my reasons were. It was all bullshit."

"El Duque was a man," said Juan Ignacio's mother, Marta Nodar.

The second witness was Germán Mesa.

Friend or enemy, the prosecutor asked.

Enemy, said Mesa. In that moment, the long friendship between El Duque and Germán Mesa began to dissolve.

The trial continued like a scripted movie of which everyone knows the outcome. A procession of witnesses followed. The Lazos recounted how Juan Ignacio had presented them with the illicit TV and VCR in South Carolina. "I was witness number six," said Arnaldo Hernández. " '*¿Amigo o enemigo?*' I said Juan Ignacio was like a brother because we even shared the same last name." Alberto Hernández was terrified when he took the stand. "I was the eighth witness," he said. "They read my declaration back to me. I looked at Juan Ignacio and he looked at me. He looked so different. He was gaunt and thin. He was going bald. My testimony only took eight or nine minutes. They asked me what my connection was to Joe Cubas. How did I know him? How did Juan Ignacio get my in-laws' address, that kind of thing." As soon as Alberto finished he bolted from the room.

There was never any doubt that Juan Ignacio would be convicted. The only question was how many years. The state made it clear in stultifying detail that the crimes were of the utmost seriousness. They represented, the government wrote, a "pronounced social dangerousness which affects the public order and the development of sport in our country, whose motive was to profit by consciously and deliberately living parasitically off the enormous efforts of the working people to develop sport for the masses."

The sentencing documents stated that the government considered Juan Ignacio a Cuban citizen, even though he had left the country when he was two. In the end, that distinction was lethal. It meant that he had committed crimes against his own people. It probably meant the difference between Tom Cronin being hustled onto a plane back to Cancún and Juan Ignacio landing in jail. The government even managed to link the crimes with the trade embargo. "The accused, having been born here, unscrupulously took advantage of our condition as an underdeveloped and blockaded nation, attacking the dignity and the capacity of resistance and loyalty of several of our acclaimed athletes," the judges wrote.

The charges went on and on. The Venezuelan work visas were the smoking gun, although the government acknowledged that neither El Duque nor Mesa had known about them.

In effect, Juan Ignacio was about to pay not only for his own crimes but also for those of Joe Cubas. "It is proven that since 1995 the accused JUAN IGNACIO HERNÁNDEZ NODAR dedicated himself to the capture of high-performance Cuban athletes in order to function as their representative before professional baseball teams outside the country," the judges wrote. Never mind that Juan Ignacio had not one client while Cubas was making millions. Cubas is never mentioned by name, but the documents read like an official government critique of his relentless stalking of Team Cuba. It's all there: the Japan excursion, the gifts, the walking-around money. At one point Juan Ignacio is cited for slipping $20 to Alberto Hernández. If not for his incessantly capitalized name— "the accused JUAN IGNACIO HERNÁNDEZ NODAR"—one could have easily concluded that it was Joe Cubas who had been on trial. Juan Ignacio even ended up taking the fall for Arrojo, even though he had nothing to do with the pitcher's defection.

The exact nature of Juan Ignacio's alleged crimes was bewildering. The Cuban government charged that he had committed "five counts of illegal departure." Illegal departure apparently meant that he had encouraged El Duque, Mesa, Alberto Hernández and the two Lazos to flee the country. At that point, of course, none had departed—legally or illegally. The best that could be determined was that Juan Ignacio had committed several high crimes against baseball.

His sentence was fifteen years in prison, three years for each player.

"There are two classes of criminals: political and common," said Juan Ignacio's mother, Marta Nodar. "Into what category does Juan Ignacio's crime fall? Is he a political prisoner or a common criminal? He hasn't killed anyone. He hasn't robbed anyone. He must be a political prisoner. . . . His only crime was touching Fidel's ballplayers, his favorite sons."

Marta Nodar had learned from her other son, Juan Carlos, that Juan Ignacio had been arrested. He called her at work one day from Santo Domingo with the disturbing news. "He said, 'Mom, don't be frightened when you hear this, but my brother was arrested in Sancti Spíritus at a baseball game,'" she recalled. "I went crazy." She immediately left the Miami hospital where she worked as a medical assistant. "I got in the car and turned on the radio and it was already on Radio Mambí: 'A Cuban American citizen has been arrested . . .' When I got home I called Cuba."

When she finally saw Juan Ignacio again, he had been tried, convicted and incarcerated at Combinado del Este, a huge concrete prison east of Havana. "It was the most terrible experience of my life," she recalled. "I had never been inside a prison. I was sixty years old. I hadn't been to Cuba since we left in 1960. Thirty-eight years later I had to go back to deal with my son's case. I hadn't seen him in a year and a half. I cried and cried. We talked about his children. And then we cried again. If he had no hope of coming out he would have hanged himself."

By the time Sánchez and I met with her, Marta Nodar had visited Juan Ignacio several times. It was a Saturday afternoon, and we sat in her immaculate two-bedroom apartment in Miami. Mottled light crept into the room through the half-drawn shades. Marta was still wearing a pink satin housecoat thrown over her nightgown. Her living room was crammed with knickknacks: gingerbread houses, porcelain owls, tiny angels perched atop a Bible resting on a glass coffee table. Every few minutes or so, one of the knickknacks would come alive and play the theme from *Love Story*.

In an effort to win her son's release, Marta had written letters to Pope John Paul II, Fidel Castro, President Clinton, Secretary of State Madeleine Albright, El Duque and Liván Hernández, John Cardinal O'Connor, newly elected Venezuelan president Hugo Chávez and Fidel's good friend Gabriel García Márquez, among others. She said she had recently attended the Ibero-American Summit in Havana in an unsuccessful attempt to personally deliver a letter to Fidel at an exhibition baseball game. So far she had gotten little response.

"My son was dumb," she said, sobbing quietly. "He walked into the mouth of the wolf. Joe Cubas was smarter. He did it all from here."

Later, during a visit to Cuba, I managed to get a message to Juan Ignacio at Combinado del Este. I told him about this book and asked if he would be willing to recount his story in writing. Two months later, a letter arrived at my apartment in Manhattan.

The letter was short on details but filled with compassion and gratitude. I had heard by then that Juan Ignacio had gained back much of his weight along with his good spirits. In the letter, at least, he was philosophical. He called his case "the biggest injustice in the world. But I have faith in God and I know that someday this nightmare is going to end and I will be back at the side of all my friends. I want you to please deliver this message to the two people who I consider, not even friends, but more like two older sons: El Duque and Liván."

In an obvious reference to the money that drove a wedge between him and Cubas, Juan Ignacio denounced "that person who betrayed (double-crossed) me. Because I thought, as I always have thought and believed, in the word between men and not what you put in *black and white* like everyone does in our country. But I am old-fashioned that way. And to this day that person has been able to walk away with all the money and the applause, and look where I am.

"Today as I write this I have spent 1,317 days in prison. I don't know how many I have to go. Steve, if you see El Duque and Liván, I want you to make sure that you tell them that I am very proud of them. If this is the price I had to pay for them to triumph, it was worth it."

AFTER THE TRIAL, everyone scattered. El Duque and Mesa, though no longer members of Team Cuba, were still part of Industriales, the defending National Series champions. The season was to begin the following month. The players were preparing for a trip to Mexico to play in a tournament before returning for opening day. Alberto Hernández returned to Holguín, relieved that the trial had ended with his career still intact. He ordered up a pig on the black market to roast for his homecoming meal.

Not surprisingly, the trial had hit the sports system like an earthquake. There were certain to be aftershocks, but no one knew where or when they might strike. The president of the INDER was a Communist party lifer named Reynaldo González. He knew relatively little about sports, but that was not necessarily a prerequisite for his job. The INDER president was a political appointee. He held a seat on the Council of Ministers, which was headed by Fidel. As INDER vice president, González had dealt with much of the fallout from the defections. He had held several meetings exhorting the players to resist the twin evils of treason and temptation. He had ascended to his new position after Fidel named his capable predecessor, Conrado Martínez, mayor of Havana.

"From the beginning, Reynaldo was not a very popular guy," said a Sports Ministry insider. "He was a bureaucrat with a huge beer gut and absolutely zero charisma. He was just a typical, narrow-minded Communist bureaucrat, someone who really didn't have any vision at all of sports."

One of González's contributions involved a scheme by which the INDER rented out players to other countries, notably Japan. The plan was basically a gambit to scare up hard currency. But it also gave veteran players an opportunity to earn a few thousand dollars abroad. González didn't invent the controversial plan, but he introduced a new wrinkle: In addition to turning over 80 percent of their earnings to the government, the players also would have to retire from Cuban baseball to avoid the ruination of "revolutionary morale."

The González plan thus led to the momentous "retirements" of some of the country's greatest players. Lázaro Junco (pronounced *Hoon*-coh), a Herculean slugger from Matanzas, reluctantly hung it up to play in Japan. Junco had hit 405 homers and was a provincial icon, so naturally the locals wanted to mark his passing with a Lázaro Junco Day. "It was one of the saddest things you've ever seen," a friend reported. "The stadium was packed, and they brought out Lázaro Junco on the back of a black 1959 Cadillac convertible and drove him around the field. Here was this huge black guy, propped up in a Cadillac, crying like a baby. He didn't want to retire but he needed the money."

The rent-a-player plan ultimately failed for a variety of reasons. Among other things, it did nothing to neutralize the magnetic pull of major-league baseball. Really, none of the strategies devised by Reynaldo González and the INDER proved effective in combating the defections. The situation, in fact, was growing worse, gathering its own momentum as players learned about the money to be made in the States. From the government's perspective, it was an epidemic. Ballplayers defecting on the eve of the Olympics? *Gusano* sports agents gallivanting around the island with Venezuelan work papers? Nothing the INDER had tried—not revolutionary speeches, not tighter security, not secret travel itineraries, not even the carrot of playing in Japan—had managed to stop the northward tide.

Now it was time to try the stick.

The word went out for El Duque, Germán Mesa and Alberto Hernández to report immediately to the commissioner's office at Estadio Latinoamericano. Even after the horrors of Juan Ignacio's trial, the players could only guess at why they had been summoned. El Duque and Mesa kicked it around and concluded that the INDER would probably give them stern warnings about trying to defect when Industriales traveled to Mexico. The players devised a plan to allay the authorities' concerns: "We decided to tell them that we didn't want to travel to Mexico if they didn't have any confidence in us," said El Duque.

Alberto was in Holguín and had to fly in for the meeting. Mesa drove his state-issued Lada. El Duque borrowed a friend's sputtering Muscovy. El Duque had worked in the same building for ten years. He didn't need to think about where he was going. He wheeled the Muscovy out onto Avenida Boyeros, past the turnoff to Lenin Park, past the Sports City, chugging along until he could make out the lights of the stadium above the Havana neighborhood of El Cerro.

For style and comfort, Estadio Latinoamericano is strictly utilitarian, perhaps a couple notches below Milwaukee's County Stadium. Built originally as the Gran Stadium of Havana, where the Cuban professional league lived and died, it acquired a new identity after the revolution, standing now as a 55,000-seat monument to the socialist experiment. Concrete light stanchions lean precariously over the outfield. Immense works of propaganda frame the center-field scoreboard. One sign reads: SPORT IS FOR PARTICIPATION, SPORT IS FOR THE PEOPLE. The other, in right field, is a familiar etching of Fidel and his triumphant comrades beneath the slogan: MEN OF STRONG BODY AND SPIRIT.

The stadium derives most of its personality from the people who attend its games. There is nothing quite like watching a game at El Latino. For one peso (about five cents, up from the previous price: *free*), vendors push the tiny tickets—raffle tickets, really—through barred windows. Inside, the aroma of coffee and cigarette smoke drifts over the crowd, spread out over splintered wooden seats and concrete slabs. Milton Jamail described it perfectly in his book *Full Count:* Cuba is a nation of 10 million managers. Everyone in attendance knows the game cold. Wherever you sit, men—almost exclusively men—engage in deep conversations and heated arguments over the finer points of baseball. In this setting, El Duque Hernández, master of his craft, was a legend. For a decade, he had wowed the world's most knowledgeable fans with his guts, style and smarts. And now Reynaldo González and the INDER had invited him back to El Latino one last time. As his close friend Osmany Lorenzo later put it, "It was like murdering someone in his own home."

The baseball commissioner's office is located in the bowels of El Latino, not far from the statues of Martín Dihigo and Adolfo Luque, the greats of the Cuban game. It is a concrete room, nondescript in most every respect except that it sits directly beneath the grandstand of a baseball stadium.

"It was about eight o'clock in the evening," said El Duque. "Germán and I both got there around the same time. They brought Germán in first. When he came out, he looked at me. Then he dragged his finger across his throat."

El Duque thought the sign meant only that he and Mesa had been cut from the Mexico trip. He still had no idea what he was in for. He entered the room. Seated behind a desk were Raúl Villanueva, the INDER vice president, and Domingo Zabala, the commissioner of baseball. Conspicuous in his absence was Reynaldo González.

El Duque later recalled it as perhaps the saddest moment of his life, after his brother Arnaldo's death.

"We have some news for you," said Villanueva. "You have been suspended for life from all levels of organized competition."

El Duque sat frozen in his chair. He realized immediately that he had just been told that he would never play baseball again. He asked for an explanation but none was forthcoming. Villanueva portrayed himself as an innocent messenger carrying out orders.

El Duque staggered out into the streets of El Cerro. Outside the stadium, the neighborhood is a shadow world. El Duque got back in the Muscovy and cranked up the engine. "I didn't want to go home," he said, "but I had no place else to go."

A few hours later, Alberto Hernández pulled up. The stadium was empty except for the light coming from the commissioner's office. Alberto knocked tentatively and walked inside. Domingo Zabala was seated behind his desk. He had been waiting all night and got straight to the point.

"He said he had orders from Reynaldo González to suspend us permanently from revolutionary baseball," Alberto recalled. "He said that at six the next morning the news would be made public. I told him that I didn't agree with the suspension. He just said that he had his orders. I realized at that point that there was no point in arguing with him. By the next morning it was all over the news."

When Kenesaw Mountain Landis banned Shoeless Joe Jackson and seven other members of the Chicago White Sox for fixing the 1919 World Series, he took into consideration the impact on the nation. For months, the scandal had been playing out in all its grotesque manifestations on the front pages of U.S. newspapers. Because of baseball's place in the culture, the confessions of the ballplayers had shaken America to its core. "As the impact of the confessions sank in, the American people were at first shocked, then sickened," wrote Eliot Asinof in *Eight Men Out*. "There was hardly a major newspaper that did not cry out its condemnation and despair. Henceforth, the ballplayers involved were called the Black Sox. But the scandal was a betrayal of more than a set of ball games, even more than of the sport itself. It was a crushing blow at American pride."

Seventy years later, Major League Baseball had to rent out a ballroom at the New York Hilton to announce the banishment of Pete Rose. The decision followed the release of a 225-page report that chronicled Rose's gambling in excruciating detail. In the packed, dramatic news conference that day, Commissioner A. Bartlett Giamatti, who once wrote that "to know baseball is to continue to aspire to the condition of freedom," stood before the nation and announced gravely: "Yes, I have concluded that he bet on baseball." The following morning I flew out to Cincinnati, where Rose had made his legend. It was as if the president had been assassinated. There was almost no one out on the streets.

And now, in 1996, how would the Cuban Sports Ministry explain to the public that the great El Duque, the incomparable El Mago and the Pride of Holguín had been banished from the national sport? And for what, exactly? In a country where nearly 10 percent of the population lived in exile, would the INDER say that the players had been suspended for aspiring to play abroad? In a country where 50 percent of the population lacked access to dollars, the currency necessary to buy everything from tennis shoes to toothpaste, would the government say the players had been punished for accepting money from their relatives and friends? What would be the explanation for something inexplicable?

The official announcement took the form of a single anonymous statement. It appeared on the front of the sports section of *Granma,* the official newspaper of the Communist party. It was also read over the radio.

At the risk of losing readers, I run the statement here nearly in its entirety as a document of a time when baseball players were branded as traitors for dreaming of playing in the major leagues. One helpful hint: The historic news of the players' banishment appears in the second-to-last paragraph. The article was published as a rectangular block of text beneath the following headline, perhaps the worst in the history of journalism:

Information from the INDER

Publicly it has been reiterated and it has been known by our people for many years that foreigners, Mafia elements of Cuban origin who reside outside the country, principally the United States, have dedicated themselves, in a gross, shameful and unacceptable manner, to stalking, pressuring and making tempting offers to Cuban athletes, all with the wretched purpose of inciting desertions and the betrayal of the fatherland.

The principal manifestation of how these people operate expresses itself in a permanent harassment of the country's athletes, principally ballplayers and boxers, wherever they travel, with the purpose not only to persuade them to desert but also to prejudice the sports results and the image of our country.

These inciters use all means at their disposal, including limitless material and financial resources, to bribe and corrupt.

These unscrupulous activities have resulted in the following known cases: René Arocha, who has loaned himself out as a collaborator, sending messages and inciting others to desert; Osvaldo Fernández, who like Arocha has participated in the inciting and stalking of Cuban athletes to commit treason; Liván Hernández, who has maintained contact with his brother Orlando Hernández and Germán Mesa, inciting them to desert and making offers; Vladimir Núñez and Larry Rodríguez, who are also traitors; and Rolando Arrojo, who after a long period of conspiring in close contact with the ballplayer Alberto Hernández, committed treason, like the others, against the Cuban people.

It is worth mentioning that these Mafiosos also organized and carried out the clandestine departure from the country of the families of Osvaldo Fernández and Rolando Arrojo.

All of these athletes have sold their dignity, abilities and athletic development in a disgraceful manner and without any respect for the people and the Revolution, which has given so much priority and resources to the practice of sport.

Our authorities have decided to act in a firm and systematic manner in the adoption of measures that will permit us to neutralize these condemnable activities and protect our athletes and the Cuban State from unscrupulous mercenaries of this type.

As a result of these new measures, on the 12th of August, on the occasion of the World Junior Baseball Championships, JUAN IGNACIO HERNÁNDEZ NODAR was arrested at the baseball stadium in Sancti Spíritus, while carrying out his work seducing young ballplayers. Hernández was born in Cuba, naturalized in the United States and is a resident of Venezuela.

Through investigations it has been convincingly demonstrated that this individual first collaborated in these activities as a representative of known trafficker Joe Cubas, who has dedicated himself to seizing, bribing and corrupting Cuban athletes. Recently, this individual (Juan Ignacio) has participated in and has been the direct author of the organized attempts to cause our athletes to desert.

Systematically, Joe Cubas and Juan Ignacio Hernández Nodar attended events where our teams participate, fundamentally abroad, to carry out their work approaching and capturing those athletes to whom they issue invitations, gifts and promises, offers that in an overwhelming majority of cases were rejected.

The investigations recently carried out have proven that Hernández Nodar has committed multiple and repeated violations of the law, including those involving migratory documents illegal in third countries and continuous activities of incitement, seizure and bribery.

This said citizen has been placed at the disposition of the tribunals and the full weight of the law will fall upon him.

Our country will never permit our athletes to succumb to these efforts to profit from them or corrupt them in an effort to convince them to desert. The strength and sweat of the people, so many of whom fight for and support the development of a healthy and dignified sport, cannot be damaged by shameless people like those mentioned.

It is evident that these mercenaries are associated with the counterrevolutionary Mafia of Miami. Their shallow goals are also able to count on the complicity and support of the authorities of the United States, who have permitted the entry of the deserters into the country without visas, without passports and also without any legal status and who have made it possible for the athletes to compete and sign contracts with professional teams.

These Mafia groups have used conspiratorial methods in their illegal activities, false documentation, entry and illegal exit and other violations of the law.

As our Commander in Chief has said, our people deserve athletes with a dignified and patriotic attitude. Lamentably, although isolated, there exist cases of athletes who have been receptive to these siren songs, athletes who dream of "paradise" and have sold their dignity and the affection of the people for a fistful of dollars.

It has been proven that the ballplayer Alberto Hernández has been at the center of a good part of these activities; in some form he knew of the proposals of other athletes who deserted; he linked himself to these mercenaries; he served as an intermediary between [the mercenaries], the deserters and their relatives; he was close to the desertions themselves, which were carried out with all the disgraceful conduct that constitutes a true betrayal of the people. The ballplayers Orlando Hernández and Germán Mesa also had close links with the subject who has been detained. They accepted [gifts] liberally from him and did not reject proposals to desert and they requested that Hernández Nodar help them to prepare to abandon the country in a fraudulent manner.

The condemnable attitude of these three players makes them unworthy of participating in organized events of Cuban sports at any level, much less serving as advocates and representatives of our revolutionary fatherland.

Taking into account the gravity of their disloyalty it has been decided to suspend them permanently from all organized sporting competition in the country.

Independent of how their conduct hurts the purest sentiments of our people, the enormous majority of our revolutionary athletes stand firm and faithful at the side of the Revolution, the Party and their Commander in Chief. They are motivated by the healthy pride and the satisfaction given to them by all the Cuban people.

As if the previous evening at the stadium hadn't been bad enough, El Duque opened up the newspaper to learn that the government had labeled him a mafioso, a criminal and a traitor. "That really hurt," he said. "Mafioso? Fuck, mafiosos have money in their pockets. They have loads of money and fancy cars. I was traveling around in a Muscovy, and it wasn't even mine. I had no money. I didn't have shit, and they were calling me a mafioso. Mafiosos wear suits. I wore jeans."

El Duque had tried to shield his family from the crisis. His mother, María Julia, had not even been aware of Juan Ignacio's trial. That morning, she flipped on the radio and heard it all. She felt that she could hardly breathe. "I was inconsolable," she said. "They were calling my son a mercenary and a traitor. It was all over *Granma*. It was strange: the night before I had been crying all night. I didn't know why. You know how sometimes mothers can tell when something bad is going to happen?"

María Julia turned to a friend. "One of my sons is dead," she said, still sobbing. "And now my other son is living dead."

IF THE GOVERNMENT had been counting on public support, it was sadly mistaken. In the United States, the Black Sox scandal and even the Rose affair had touched a nerve. The scandals, each in their own way, seemed to reflect something terrible lurking inside the culture. The Black Sox scandal foreshadowed the roaring, decadent twenties. The Rose affair came at the end of the self-absorbed, greed-ridden eighties. "There was something almost prophetic about the scandal," Asinof wrote of the Black Sox. "The 1920s, a decade of unprecedented crime, corruption, and immorality, were just beginning. 'Say it ain't so, Joe . . . say it ain't so.' It was like a last desperate plea for faith itself."

But to most Cubans, the banishment of the players reflected something entirely different: the bizarre and dangerous obsolescence of their own government. "It was an unbelievable miscalculation," a well-informed Cuban friend told me. "They turned the players into martyrs." Outside the government, I have never once heard anyone defend the decision. Not long after the suspensions, I went down to Havana's Central Park, where dozens of men gather each afternoon to argue about baseball. The fans were seething. Their criticisms were thinly disguised complaints about the government itself. "Baseball in this country is run by a mafia," one young fan said, turning the state's own terminology on its head.

A few days after the suspensions, the INDER called a meeting of Industriales players at El Latino. Most of the players had seen the statement in *Granma* or had heard it on the radio. It was hard to conceive of El Duque and Mesa as traitors. "We all found it so strange," said Roberto Colina, a first baseman. "It was so sudden. They were key players on Industriales. These guys won championships for us. But we didn't know anything. We knew that they had been suspended and that was all we knew."

Now, the INDER had a different message: "They came and said that they were sorry about it all," said Colina. "They started talking all this shit about how they regretted it because Germán and Duque were such tremendous people, how they contributed so much to the history of baseball in Cuba. They told us it was just all too bad and we had to keep up the fight with the players we had. I mean, our team was decimated."

After the meeting, the team left for Mexico. The trip was a perk for having won the title the year before—behind El Duque and Mesa, of course. The tournament, in the Mexican state of Tabasco, would serve as a tune-up for the National Series.

Shortly after the team's arrival, Colina received a call in his hotel room.

"I'm here," said Joe Cubas.

Colina packed his bags and walked downstairs. Cubas and Ramón Batista were waiting in a rental car with the engine running. Colina hopped inside and bid farewell to his team and his country. By the end of the week, five Industriales players had defected. "A few more and we would have had enough to field a team," said Colina.

CHAPTER ELEVEN

BANNED IN HAVANA

CAUGHT UP WITH EL DUQUE A FEW MONTHS LATER. WHAT LIT-
tle information there was about his suspension I had read on the wires. After
clearing customs, I walked across the parking lot to the last place I had seen
him: the state-run cell phone trailer. I figured someone there might know
where to find him. Looking back, it seems like one of those moments where life
is scripted.

"Can you tell me where I might find the pitcher El Duque Hernández?" I
asked a woman seated in front of the trailer.

She simply pointed. Walking toward me along the airport frontage road,
alone on this blinding afternoon, was the man himself. We embraced, although
at the time we hardly knew each other. I think it had something to do with the
fact that I had known El Duque, however briefly, before he had lost everything
and had still come back to see him. My reasons were professional, of course: I
wanted the story. But El Duque seemed moved. The Cuban press wouldn't
touch him. No one had heard his side.

It immediately became clear that El Duque's life had been reduced to its
most basic elements. His marriage was history; already teetering, it had collapsed under the weight of the scandal. He had moved out of his state-issued
house across from the airport and was now living with his girlfriend, Noris
Bosch, in a dank windowless shack built out of gray cinder blocks. Norita, as
she was affectionately known, was slender, with wavy black hair cascading over
her shoulders. A dancer with the National Theater, she had once appeared in
a televised performance called *Humo*, or Smoke. Her parents had built the

cinder-block room as an extension to their own tiny house, also out near the airport. A corrugated aluminum roof kept out the rain in El Duque's new home. Inside stood an old stove, a bed and little else. The only decoration was an odd photo of the pitcher, winding up on the airport tarmac, preparing to throw a pitch in front of a jetliner.

El Duque's vast circle of friends had dwindled to a precious few. Later, it would be said that many of his friends abandoned him. This was only partially true; many people, for obvious reasons, were afraid to be seen with him. But it is accurate to say that his friends now were his *real* friends. Many had known him since childhood. They went by nicknames like Cebolla (Onion) and El Yayo and Lache. "I had a lot of friends before the sanctions," he recalled, chuckling. "And then suddenly I had a few. You could count them on two hands. I had been the king, and now I was just El Duque."

One of his best friends was a brilliant former schoolteacher named Roberto Martínez. He was known, even to his wife, as Pelusa, slang for someone with thick, fluffy hair. Pelusa, who indeed had thick, fluffy hair, picked up the nickname as a shaggy-haired baby. "My students and coworkers thought it was my real name," he said. "They would call me Professor Roberto Pelusa." Pelusa taught high school, left to work as an administrator for a state-run food distributorship, then, as soon as it became legal, opened his own business selling sandwiches and coffee out of his house in Boyeros.

Pelusa's entry into incipient capitalism made perfect sense. He was hardly a counterrevolutionary, but he held grave doubts about Cuba's moribund economic system. In 1982, seven years before the fall of the Berlin Wall, he had the audacity to predict the collapse of communism in his high school Marxism class. His thesis was that the system lacked the efficiencies of capitalism. When Pelusa told me this story I had a hard time believing him, so he gleefully pulled his eighteen-year-old report card out of a closet. "Needs to work at educating himself in the principles of our Revolution and the superiority of socialism over capitalism," his instructor wrote.

Pelusa and El Duque had gone through rough times together, including the deaths of Pelusa's father, who suffered a heart attack, and El Duque's brother. "You don't just measure your friends by how much they make you laugh," said Pelusa. After the suspension, El Duque turned again to his friend. "He showed up at my house, crying," Pelusa said. "He didn't know what to do. I mean, think about it: They told him he had to stop doing what he was born to do. It was his reason for being, and they had taken it away from him."

The ban on El Duque covered all state-sanctioned competition. Pelusa played ball on the weekends, and he got El Duque involved in two neighbor-hood leagues: Saturday hardball and Sunday softball. I took in one of the Sat-urday games at El Globo, a glorified cow pasture out near Vladimir I. Lenin Park. The scene reminded me of the stories of Joe Jackson bouncing around semi-pro leagues under assumed names. El Duque played under his own iden-tity, but he was forbidden to pitch because no one could possibly have hit him. Instead he managed a team called Río Verde and played the infield, primarily second and third. The outfield fence was a piece of wire stretched from foul line to foul line. Behind the backstop, seven lean cows grazed in a field. The crowd consisted of a few dozen shirtless neighborhood kids perched atop a concrete wall.

El Duque played the languorous games with the same intensity he later displayed at Yankee Stadium. He even wore an official-looking Yankee pullover someone had sent him from the States. Before the game, he made his ragtag ball club run wind sprints. He argued with umpires and exhorted his players to hustle. But the game never quite rose to his level of seriousness. Once, a player hit a pitch off the handle, snapping his aluminum bat in half. The barrel went flying up the third-base line, settling near the coach's box. A search ensued for another bat. No one could find one. As El Duque pulled his team off the field, one of the players sped off to find a replacement.

"Game postponed for lack of bats!" yelled El Duque, feigning an an-nouncer's voice.

"How romantic," grumbled one of his teammates.

But the government was serious about enforcing El Duque's ban. His soft-ball team, Baluarte, played in a city league sponsored by the INDER. At some point the Sports Ministry heard that El Duque had secretly resumed his career. It dispatched an official out to the softball field one afternoon to announce that the team was employing an unauthorized third baseman.

The team manager was Lázaro Vichot, known to everyone as Lache. He was a heavyset man who spoke like a street preacher and threw a nasty curve-ball despite, or perhaps because of, the handicap of being born with two fingers on each hand. Lache was also missing several toes. His right ankle ballooned grotesquely, as if his circulation had been cut off by an elastic band. Lache had played baseball with El Duque since childhood, a physical marvel to his friends. Now he stepped forward to speak with the INDER representative.

"I simply said that if Orlando 'El Duque' Hernández doesn't play then there *is* no softball here," said Lache. "I told him, 'In our opinion, he has done nothing wrong for you to erase him from the face of the earth as a ballplayer.'" The official left, never to be seen again. El Duque continued to play.

For his part, El Duque betrayed not the slightest doubt that he would return to organized baseball. He defied the government with his optimism. His only concession to the crisis was chain-smoking: He'd suck a black-market Marlboro to the nub, then flick the butt into a puddle and light up another. Other than that, he trained harder than ever. He ran every morning along Avenida Boyeros, one of the busiest streets in town, as if to show everyone he had not been defeated. "People would tell me, 'I just saw your son running in Boyeros. He shouted "¡*Todo bien!*" and kept running,' " said Maria Julía. El Duque threw to anyone who would catch him. Sánchez went looking for El Duque one afternoon and was drawn to a group of boys gathered at the end of a dirt road. As he moved closer, Sánchez saw that the kids were gathered around El Duque, who was tossing fastballs and sweating through his old Team Cuba warm-up jacket.

"I have to train every day without fail," El Duque said as the reporter introduced himself. "If I don't, I'm defeated. I'm finished. I keep the arms and the legs strong. My mind is strong. I *know* I will pitch again. ¡*Sí señor!*" He then unleashed more fastballs, including a dozen or so to Sánchez.

El Duque's status in those days was murky at best. The public still loved him. The government had erased him. Once, El Duque and Sánchez went to see Punto y Coma (Period and Comma), a controversial comedy troupe known for poking fun at the Special Period. As El Duque walked in the door, one of the comedians recognized him.

"Look, here comes El Duque Hernández, the great pitcher!" he announced.

The crowd cheered wildly.

"Hey, *chico*, shut your mouth," another comedian chimed in. "You'll get us suspended as humorists."

Later, Sánchez accompanied El Duque and Noris to a Havana nightclub, La Tropical, to see the famous Manolín, El Médico de la Salsa (the Salsa Doctor). The outdoor nightclub, off the beaten tourist path, was jammed. As El Duque made his way toward the entrance, people shouted his name and stopped to shake his hand. At the door, however, a police officer asked Noris for identification. When she couldn't produce it, he detained her. It was an uncomfortable scene. It was as if the officer was trying to get to El Duque through his girlfriend. Finally, a club employee intervened and allowed the group to enter through a VIP section in the back.

The nightclub pulsated with warm-up music. El Duque sashayed through the crowd, which was tugging at him, shaking his hand, yelling out his name. He well knew the song booming over the speakers: "Nothing's Wrong with El

Negro" by Los Van Van. El Duque danced and sang along. He belted out Juan Formell's lyrics as if he were singing to the entire city, to the entire country, to Fidel Castro himself:

> *Look, Negro, you're a ghost*
> *'Cause you're burned up*
> *You got torched, burned up!*
> *All Havana says so*
> *The talk is everywhere*
>
> *Without thinking I approached her*
> *Come here, touch me and see*
> *I've got a lot of fight yet in me*
> *Nothing's wrong with El Negro*

I once asked El Duque if he really thought he would pitch again.

"Hope," he said seriously. "That's what I have for breakfast every morning."

WORKERS DISMANTLED THE Pride of Holguín shrine to Alberto Hernández shortly after the mafioso article appeared in *Granma*. The workers took the trophies and the medals, the golds from Barcelona and Atlanta and the World Cups and the Intercontinental Cups and the Pan American Games and loaded them up in cardboard boxes. "They shit all over it and wiped their asses with it all," said Alberto. "Please put that in your book."

In some ways, the sanctions hit Alberto harder than El Duque and Mesa. In Oriente, where Fidel grew up and the revolution began, there remained large pockets of commitment to the government. It seemed counterintuitive: The Special Period had raked Oriente like a tornado, leaving the rural provinces in a permanent state of deprivation. But there was something about the history and the isolation and the poverty that bred a higher degree of revolutionary fervor. For Alberto that fervor cut both ways. Before the scandal he had been an icon. "For me, communism represented only the best in the world," he said. After the scandal, "I was a traitor to my country. I was nobody."

Actually, worse than nobody. Alberto and his family immediately became targets for the local Committee for the Defense of the Revolution. The CDR was a neighborhood watchdog group assigned to monitor revolutionary vigi-

Orlando "El Duque" Hernández with President Fidel Castro of Cuba during the celebration of Castro's sixty-sixth birthday, August 13, 1992. *Author's collection*

Banned from official competition, El Duque channeled his competitiveness into weekend pickup games. Here he argues with an umpire during a game at El Globo field near Vladimir I. Lenin Park, Havana. *Jorge Rey*

During his banishment, El Duque (above) continued to throw to anyone who would catch him. He is seen here playing catch with his friend Osmany Lorenzo (out of camera range) near his home in Havana as neighborhood children look on.
Ray Sánchez

Former best friends: El Duque with shortstop Germán Mesa, "The Magician." *Author's collection*

Cape Cod real estate agent Tom Cronin (right) with Germán Mesa in Havana. Cronin tried unsuccessfully to persuade Mesa to defect.
Courtesy Tom Cronin

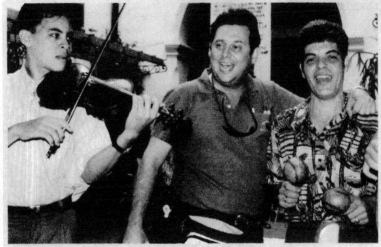

Juan Ignacio Hernández Nodar (center) joins the house band for a song at the Hotel Valencia in Old Havana, four months before his arrest in 1996. Note the fanny-pack, from which Hernández distributed money for Liván Hernández. *Courtesy Tom Cronin*

El Duque (right) with his older brother, Arnaldo, before a youth-league game in Boyeros. The boys' mother, María Julia Pedroso, carried this weathered photo in a ceramic bowl when she departed Cuba after the 1998 World Series.
Courtesy María Julia Pedroso

Catcher Alberto Hernández in the dugout during his unsuccessful major-league tryout, February 1998, in San Jose, Costa Rica. Alberto, who defected with El Duque, ended up playing two seasons in Taiwan. *René Guim*

René Guim, El Duque, and the pitcher's great-uncle Ocilio Cruz in the dugout before the Costa Rica tryout. Cruz, known to everyone as "Tío," financed El Duque's escape. *Courtesy René Guim*

After signing a $4.5 million contract with the Florida Marlins, Liván Hernández purchased a new car every three months. These included a $40,000 Dodge Viper, a $130,000 Mercedes convertible, a $65,000 Porsche (pictured), and a $100,000 Ferrari. *Courtesy Juan Iglesias*

Orlando "El Duque" Hernández in Costa Rica, February 1998.
René Guim

In Havana:
El Duque, Roberto
"Pelusa" Martinez,
and Osmany
Lorenzo, pictured
next to Lorenzo's
Russian-made
Muscovy sedan.
Osmany provides the
caption: "In Cuba
with Pelusa and El
DK washing our
inseparable friend
'El Moskovich.'"

Courtesy
Osmany Lorenzo

El Duque unleashing a pitch during his victory over the Cleveland Indians in Game 4 of the 1998 American League Championship Series, pulling the Yankees from the brink of elimination.
John Keating,
NEWSDAY

Arnaldo Hernández Montero, the original El Duque, looks over a magazine featuring his son Orlando at an athletic facility off Havana's seaside Malecón.
Angel Franco/Visión Fotos

El Duque embracing a
fellow Cuban exile, first-
base coach José Cardenal,
after defeating Cleveland
in the 1998 ALCS.
John Keating, NEWSDAY

Joe Cubas in Miami,
May 2000.
David Bergman

The late John Cardinal O'Connor at his Manhattan residence with
El Duque, shortly after the cardinal intervened to bring the pitcher's
family to the United States. *Cesar Alvarez, Northeast Hispanic Catholic Center*

lance—a nest of spies in the barrio. After the *Granma* article, the CDR convened an emergency meeting. The president held up the article and spoke to the assembled masses: "Look at everything the revolution has given to Alberto Hernández! And now he betrays us! He is a traitor! He cannot serve as an example for our children!"

Shortly after, dozens of CDR members assembled outside Alberto's apartment building for a *repudio*, a public repudiation of alleged traitors. The demonstrations, which occur nationwide, usually amount to a lot of shouting. Occasionally rocks are hurled. Now the people shouted at the treasonous catcher's apartment: *¡Traidor!* (Traitor!) *¡Mafioso! ¡Gusano!* (Worm!) Alberto, Zaily, their five-year-old son Albertico and infant daughter Jessica huddled inside. It was terrifying, and what could be done? These *were* the authorities. Unlike El Duque, who responded with defiance, Alberto became immobilized. He gave up baseball entirely. His weight ballooned. "You realized that they can erase you in an instant," he said. "I was afraid to go outside. I just stayed at home with my wife and my kids and my mother. I never went out."

"It was like psychological torture," said Zaily. "In the building where we lived, one of our neighbors was a party leader. Suddenly he wouldn't allow his kids to play with our son. His son and my son had been best friends and now they couldn't play together. Our friends were afraid to visit us. They stopped coming by our apartment."

The local branch of the INDER gathered Alberto's former teammates to discuss the crisis. Julio César Villalón, a pitcher, said an INDER official waved the *Granma* article during the meeting. "He said that this could not be tolerated," said Villalón. "He said that Alberto had to serve as an example. He said, 'Who agrees?' We all raised our hands."

"It was the biggest scandal we ever knew," said Juan Carlos Bruzón, another player from the province. "People couldn't believe it. Not Alberto. He had done so much for the province and the country. How was it possible? There were always huge parties whenever Alberto came home. Then, after he was suspended, the same CDR that had praised and celebrated his achievements was now staging an *acto de repúdio* against him.

"In a way I'm glad this happened to him," said Bruzón, who later defected. "Thanks to the way the state handled this, we all began to realize that the same thing could happen to us. We weren't free. We became aware that if we were going to realize our dreams we had to get out of Cuba. This scandal was our education. It was the biggest lesson of our lives up to that point. We saw who Alberto had been. People loved him. The state loved him. And then suddenly they turned their backs. We realized it was all hypocrisy. The repercussions over what they did to Alberto were felt all over Cuba. All the players in the provinces felt the same way. You'd arrive in a town and that's all the players were talking about."

After months of being ostracized, Alberto and Zaily decided to move to Havana, where Zaily's parents lived. They figured that people in the city would be more tolerant. They set out to rebuild their lives. The couple lived mostly off their savings: a few thousand dollars tucked into a stocking deep in a closet at Zaily's parents' house. Alberto spent most of the day indoors. In an effort to show that he had repented, he even joined his tormentors: the local Committee for the Defense of the Revolution. He attended the meetings and listened to the CDR members discuss the problems of a revolutionary community. "I didn't want anyone to suspect me," he said. "I was just trying to avoid problems. I didn't want anyone to think that I was a *gusano*."

Zaily clarified: "He joined the CDR because he was afraid."

Alberto saw none of his former teammates, not even his fellow traitors. El Duque rarely came around and Alberto didn't seek him out. Germán Mesa, too, had cut himself off. His performance at the trial had turned everyone against him. There were whispers—they would later become shouts—suggesting that he was the one who had fingered Juan Ignacio. A few days after the suspensions El Duque suggested to Mesa that they appeal directly to Fidel. Surely the Maximum Leader would understand and make things right. Mesa refused. Over time the two players, former best friends, stopped talking to each other entirely. Their lives diverged. In the face of the same extraordinary circumstances, El Duque and Mesa chose opposite paths.

One afternoon I asked El Duque if he would take me to see Mesa. He politely declined, but one of his friends, Osmany Lorenzo, offered to drive me. It was a sun-drenched weekday afternoon. When we pulled up at the house it looked like the occupants had moved. The windows were shuttered, the shades drawn tight. There was no answer at the front door. We went around to the side and knocked again. We circled the house and were getting ready to leave when the front door finally creaked open. Peering out was Germán Mesa, Cuba's answer to Ozzie Smith.

Mesa recognized Osmany and invited us in. The house was dark, illuminated only by the sunlight creeping around the shades. Mesa's living room was like a museum to his now-dormant career. There were trophies and medals everywhere: on the shelves, on the television, on the floor. Mesa wore gym shorts and was shirtless. Despite the layoff, there wasn't an ounce of fat on him.

He looked like he could have turned his Wizard of Oz back flip on the coffee table. He wore a cast on his left forearm, from an injury he said he had incurred playing basketball. Osmany introduced me and said I was hoping to interview him. Mesa couldn't have been nicer, but he declined. He said the timing wasn't good. He didn't want to antagonize anyone. He and Osmany sat for about forty-five minutes, catching up on old friends and old times. I listened, and then after a while we got up, shook Germán Mesa's hand and drove away, leaving perhaps the finest shortstop in the history of Cuba sitting alone in his living room.

IT WASN'T UNTIL LATER that the incredible symmetry became apparent. At the time, it all seemed like a magnificent collision of events, an international pileup. It was hard to make sense of it all. Only later did the events take shape as perfectly formed episodes, each seemingly dependent on the one that preceded it.

For as the Cuban government was attempting to destroy one Hernández, another was coming alive. Liván had suddenly caught fire. It was like a brushfire that began in Portland, Maine, and spread through the amazing summer of 1997, engulfing Miami and then leaping across the straits to consume broad swaths of Cuba itself.

Liván's turnaround could be traced to a minor-league manager named Carlos Tosca. He was the skipper at the time of the Portland Sea Dogs, the Double-A team to which Liván had been demoted after his disastrous, bloated Charlotte run. Tosca was slight and bespectacled and had the manners of a kind pediatrician, the position his father had held in Cuba before the revolution. Tosca came to the States with his mother when he was eight, expecting his father to follow within a month or two. "I didn't see my father again until I was a senior in high school," he said. "He became a political prisoner. They walked in one day and said he was supporting the American CIA and they put him to work in a camp."

After Charlotte, where Liván couldn't even communicate with his manager, Carlos Tosca was a revelation. He had the patience of Job, the empathy of shared experience and he could speak the language. But Tosca had his work cut out for him. The pitcher he inherited was an overweight malcontent who had lost his fastball at Burger King. "I heard he discovered the drive-through window and that was about it," said Tosca. Liván had the arm of a young Dwight Gooden and the mound presence of a Little Leaguer. "He was pouting; his whole body language was not good, not professional," said Tosca. "You could read him real easy on the mound, which is not something you want in a pitcher. Also, the strength and conditioning program was a problem for him. One day I told him, 'I don't care if you weigh three hundred pounds. But you're supposed to be throwing ninety-six and you're throwing eighty-nine. Just show me ninety-six and I'll stay off your back.' "

Gradually, Liván started to lose weight. Tosca called him "Flaco," the Spanish word for skinny, and that buoyed him even more. He fought off the urge to swerve his Porsche off the highway toward the shining beacon of the Golden Arches. "He began to like what he saw in the mirror," said Tosca. "It's sort of like a guy who starts to work out and all of a sudden he feels pumped. I think it was trust more than anything. I think it was the realization that he was going in the wrong direction. Maturity is something that you can't rush. He started to understand that he had to make some adjustments."

Liván's talent suddenly began to emerge, and it was frightening. His fastball, a blistering dart, crept back into the mid-90s, making his hammer of a curve even more effective. The Marlins called him up in the middle of 1997, which was turning into a surprisingly strong season for the four-year-old franchise. In many ways, the Florida Marlins were an aberration of modern baseball. The team's honeymoon in South Florida had lasted but a year, after which the players strike of 1994 wiped out one-third of its entire season-ticket base. When play finally resumed, the Marlins found themselves playing in an environment that owner Wayne Huizenga likened to "drinking in an empty bar"— even on good days. After the team's fourth season, Huizenga declared that he intended to prove "once and for all whether this region can support baseball." He set out to assemble the best team that $89 million could buy. He threw his Blockbuster Video money at free agents like Bobby Bonilla, Alex Fernández, Moisés Alou, among others. He gave Gary Sheffield a $61 million contract extension. By the end of the season, with the Marlins headed for the World Series, Huizenga was still groaning. "We're losing our ass here," he said. A year later he staged one of the biggest fire sales in the history of sports.

It was an incredible run while it lasted, though, led by Cuban defector Liván Hernández, age twenty-two. On June 28, Liván got his first major-league win: 4–2 over Montreal. By July 31, he was 5–0. By mid-August he was 7–0. On August 31, he beat Toronto and became the first major-league rookie to begin a season 9–0 since Whitey Ford did it for the Yankees in 1950. As the Marlins staged their $89 million "miracle," Little Havana succumbed to Liván Mania. People cleared the streets to watch him pitch. At Versailles, the famous exile restaurant on Calle Ocho, he ate his dinners behind a rope line. He was on top of the world, almost literally. During the playoffs—the Marlins sneaked in as a wild-card team—I visited Liván at his $300,000 apartment on the twenty-second floor of a Miami Beach luxury building. Contrary to what I had heard, he hadn't entirely given up fast food. His agent, Juan Iglesias, brought up a Burger King breakfast on a carton tray and, with his free hand, introduced me. "I'm only talking about baseball, not politics," Liván warned. But he did give me the nickel tour of his new millionaire's life. His walk-in closet—a riot of shoes and fancy suits—would have qualified as a one-bedroom apartment in Manhattan.

When I tried to bring the conversation around to his brother's suspension he said: "I don't think it's fair, but I don't want to comment on that." Liván never had much enthusiasm for interviews, but by the time he returned to Miami he had pretty much shut it down. People like me were always pestering him to talk politics, a no-win proposition for a high-profile defector with family back on the island.

Later, I caught up with him in the Marlins clubhouse. He was wearing pressed blue jeans, a black Hugo Boss T-shirt and tennis shoes as white as bleached flour. I asked for his reasons for defecting and he said: "The first was to seek freedom, the second was to try to help out my family and the third was to play baseball in the major leagues."

"What does freedom mean to you?" I asked.

He sighed impatiently. "*Freedom* is a word that every Latino and every American knows. It means the same in Spanish as it does in English. It's the freedom to do whatever you want, everything that you would ever want to do. This is the point, nothing more and nothing less."

End of interview.

Such were the ironies of the Brothers Hernández: Liván lived in the United States but he was afraid to talk; El Duque lived a few blocks from the Havana airport but he couldn't leave.

IN OCTOBER I WENT back to Cuba to watch them bury Che Guevara, thirty years dead.

Che was the Argentine physician who joined forces with Castro in Mexico City. He arrived in Cuba on the infamous Granma expedition, rose to the rank of *comandante*, then became Fidel's right-hand man. After serving as minister of industry and head of the Central Bank, he launched a campaign to export the Cuban revolution to other countries. In 1967, at age thirty-nine, he was captured and executed while trying to ignite a revolution in Bolivia. The Bolivian army amputated his hands and buried the rest of him in a secret grave.

Che was the revolution's uncompromising martyr, an enduring image for millions of international leftists. In Cuba, children were indoctrinated with his heroic tale from the moment they learned the hymn "*Todos seremos como el Che*" ("We Will All Be Like Che") as young *pioneros*. There were Che study groups where people gathered "to discuss his ideas and read his words," as one participant explained. In his definitive biography, *Che Guevara,* Jon Lee Anderson wrote that when Che died, his eerie resemblance to Jesus Christ moved Bolivian peasants to clip locks of his hair. The Cuban government later deified him as a secular saint. "The veneration is practically the same as in the church. It is as if he's Saint Che," one Catholic priest told me. "He is presented as more than a human being. He is a man to be imitated, to be venerated."

Thirty years after his death, forensic experts dug up Che's remains in Bolivia. The bones were shipped to Cuba, where they lay in state for six days in a circular hall inside the Plaza of the Revolution. Thousands lined up to view the tiny coffin, draped with the Cuban flag. Despite the impoverished condition of the revolution (including reforms that Che almost certainly would have regarded as craven), people were clearly moved. "It is almost difficult to express how I feel about him; he is like a god," said the man from the Che study group. "His word is the word of the revolution."

Among the people *un*moved by the Che phenomenon was Orlando Hernández. El Duque and his friends wanted no part of the Che festivities. All of them still loved Cuba to the bottoms of their souls, but their low regard for the revolution at that point was obvious. When they referred to the Maximum Leader, for example, it was as "Fifo," a canine nickname. One Saturday, El Duque and his friends invited me to play baseball at El Globo. I begged off, explaining that I had to work. What could I possibly have to do on a Saturday afternoon, everyone wondered? I told them I had to go down to the Plaza of the Revolution and look at Che Guevara's miniature casket.

Everyone found this hilarious. As I said good-bye, El Duque's friend Osmany Lorenzo called out:

"¡*Oye,* Fainaru!"

"What?"

"*Todos seremos como el Che.*"

El Duque and Osmany were like soul mates back then, brothers, more than friends. They were the Cuban odd couple. El Duque was tall, black and elegant. Even in disgrace he left a wake in his path. Osmany was average, white and slovenly. He frequently went shirtless, allowing his impressive gut to spill over his cut-off jeans. But he and El Duque shared much in common. Both, in their own way, had been banished from the System and left to their own devices.

Osmany's devices were considerable. He was an expert at working the exploding black market, where there was real money to be made. From the very beginning, he had figured out how to tap into the new dollar economy. He learned the system from the inside, using a family connection to win a highly coveted slot at one of the "tourist schools," institutes where Cubans were trained for jobs in the dollar-denominated tourist sector. Osmany studied hard, but even back then he was running scams. To avoid making the four-hour commute from his home in Matanzas, for example, he slept inside a Havana hospital room courtesy of an intern he knew. "He gave me a medical gown that I would put on every night, like I worked at the hospital," he said. "I'd go up to a room on the top floor and sleep. In the morning I'd put my gown back on and walk out the door."

Osmany eventually secured a job as a butler in the government's diplomatic residences for distinguished guests. He waited on the likes of Gabriel García Márquez and Daniel Ortega. He played dominoes with former Mexican president José López Portillo. He worked later at the Varadero beach resort, fell in love with a *jinatera* (prostitute), then followed her back to Havana after she was kicked out of Varadero for hustling tourists. Shortly after his return, he latched on to his most lucrative position yet: bartender at the José Martí International Airport.

"Tourism in Cuba is an organized Mafia. Everyone steals," he said. "When I worked at the airport it meant that I had access to everything: tips, gifts, clothing, bottles of liquor. Some days I made twenty dollars. Other days I made fifty. I lived with my girlfriend from Varadero and she was in love with me. She was very faithful. I used to keep the money behind an electrical outlet inside the wall." Eventually, he saved enough to buy a small house for $4,000. The house stood across the airport parking lot, on the same street as El Duque's. Osmany also bought a faded red beater of a Muscovy from a retired military officer. "The guy had fought at the Bay of Pigs, but he got caught up in the Special Period and he had to sell his car," said Osmany. "He wanted forty-five thousand pesos. The dollar was still illegal, and when I tried to pay him in dollars he told me, 'No, it's forty-five thousand Cuban pesos.' So I exchanged the dollars with a friend. Then I went back with a huge sack of bills and said, 'Here's your forty-five thousand pesos. You can spend the next two hours counting it.' "

By 1993, Osmany's life was nearly ideal. The dollar had been legalized, and now he was like a legitimate businessman. "If you had access to dollars you were fine," he said. "I was thirty years old. I had my own house. I had a job." Then, one afternoon at the airport, he turned on a boom box that sat behind the bar. Inside, someone had left a cassette tape. It was a live recording of Guillermo Alvarez Guedes, a popular exile comedian who had gathered a ton of material at Fidel Castro's expense.

Coincidentally, Alvarez Guedes and Osmany hailed from the same small town, Unión de Reyes in Matanzas. The septuagenarian comedian had released some thirty albums and sold hundreds of thousands of tapes in Latin America, but none—legally, at least—inside Cuba. Now, suddenly, Alvarez Guedes's voice was booming over the bar of the Havana international airport. He was telling the following story, one of his favorites:

> Fidel is making one of his speeches at the Plaza of the Revolution. He is telling the masses, "Last year we promised you this, and last year we promised you that." He's promising things like he always does, he's going on and on, and as he's talking there's a guy walking through the crowd selling ice cream. The guy's yelling, "¡*Coco y piña!* [Coconut and pineapple!] ¡*Coco y piña!* ¡*Coco y piña!*"
>
> So Fidel goes on. He's saying, "Next year we promise you that you will be even better off. We will cultivate this, and we will cultivate that." And all through the speech the guy keeps yelling, "¡*Coco y piña!* ¡*Coco y piña!*"
>
> Finally, Fidel yells, "Who is that shouting '*Coco y piña*'? Bring him over here. I'm going to kick him in the ass so hard he's going to fly all the way to Miami."
>
> The next thing you hear is 150,000 people, all yelling, "¡*COCO Y PIÑA! ¡COCO Y PIÑA! ¡COCO Y PIÑA!*"

"I put that tape in twice," said Osmany. "There was this young guy at the airport who worked for State Security. He walked up and he said, 'Give me the tape.' He escorted me to the other side of the airport and then State Security interrogated me. They wanted to know why I had played the tape. What I really wanted to tell them was that I put in the tape because it's true. I just thought it was funny. I was trying to liven things up. People laughed when they heard it."

The joke cost Osmany his job, but not his livelihood. As disappointed as he was, in some respects it was the best career move he ever made. It freed him up to work the black market full-time. He was perfectly situated: His airport connections were still intact and deliveries were easy. He spent much of his day sit-

ting around the house, listening to his favorite band, La Charanga Habanera,*
a controversial group known for its lyrics about *putas* (whores), women who
dated dollar-toting tourists, consumption and materialism in a changing land.
Unlike their predecessors, revolutionary balladeers like Silvio Rodríguez and
the other *nueva trova* artists, Charanga gave voice to the new Cuba and new
men like Osmany Lorenzo. In the Charanga vernacular, Osmany was a *papir-
riqui con güaniquiqui:* a sugar daddy with greenbacks, flush and comfortable.
All day he received valuable contraband through his back door: American cigarettes, Hatuey Beer, ham-and-cheese sandwiches delivered direct from the
airport lounge. My personal favorite was the jet fuel: It came delivered in barrels that sat in his rock-strewn backyard. Osmany explained that the fuel could
be used in some of the old Muscovys that tooled around the capital. He resold
the items using his connections throughout Havana, often with the help of his
new partner, El Duque Hernández.

Osmany and El Duque were already well acquainted. They had met at the
airport when both were gainfully employed, and they saw each other frequently as neighbors. But their respective punishments drew them even closer.
"When you are a figure like El Duque, you have many doors that are open to
you," said Osmany. "They say to you, 'Here, take this for your home. Here's
some gas, some food, anything you want.' But now they started shutting all
those doors on him. It was painful to watch. You can't really describe how brave
the man is, the strength that he has. I don't know what I would have done if I
had to deal with even half of what he went through.

"After we started having our problems, we always hung out together. Of
the twenty-four hours in the day, we were probably together for twenty. We
thought the same way. You could probably say that we came to the same realization about the System at the same time.

"We did what we had to to survive. We sold gas. We sold sandwiches. We
sold ice cream. We bought ice cream from Copelia[†] from distributors. It was
stolen, of course. We sold it at the airport. We made a little money. We paid fifty
cents for each and sold them for sixty. Orlando would help me sell. We sold the
stuff together.

*In July 1997, the government suspended La Charanga Habanera for six months after a
raucous appearance at the XIV Youth and Students World Festival. Charanga arrived by
helicopter and made several sexual jokes; the lead singer threatened to drop his pants. The
government denounced the appearance as a capitalist concert and suspended the entire
band.
†Cuba's version of Baskin-Robbins, only better.

"Once we were *boteando,* using my car as a taxi. We were standing in front of the international terminal and some policemen were there. One of the cops says, 'You're El Duque, no? I know you're running a taxi. I'm going to hunt you down.' That was humiliating that day. The guy was famous, an Olympic champion, an example for the Cuban people, and now the cops were harassing him. Before they used to protect him. When he was famous everyone looked out for him. Now they were his enemies."

El Duque was reliant on Osmany in part because his own financial situation had turned dramatically south. His courier Juan Ignacio was in jail. Liván, under pressure from the U.S. Treasury Department, had stopped making shipments. El Duque's only other source of income was his job at the Havana Psychiatric Hospital, where he worked as a rehabilitation therapist. Before the suspension, the job had been basically a front to preserve his amateur status, but now he needed every one of the 207 pesos (about $8.75) the hospital paid him each month. To his credit, El Duque never minded the work. The patients, clad in beige uniforms, gathered around for their morning calisthenics in varying states of coherence. El Duque led the patients through their paces in a concrete courtyard next to a baseball stadium where he was no longer allowed to pitch. "It is decent work that helps people," he once told me. "It's humane work. But it's not baseball."

Liván's meteoric rise was another source of strain for El Duque. Certainly, he was proud of his younger brother, but it was an awkward situation, bizarre even. By mid-October, Liván Hernández and the late Che Guevara were battling it out for the hearts and minds of the Cuban people; and, truth be told, Che was taking a beating. Word of Liván's success had spread rapidly across the island. There was no official news, of course, but Cubans followed his exploits via Radio Martí—the U.S. government propaganda station—relatives in Miami and clandestine satellite dishes thrown together with smuggled parts and kitchen appliances. "All El Duque hears is Liván this, Liván that," said El Duque's cousin Joel Pedroso in the dugout one afternoon at El Globo. "He's had it with Liván. That's all anybody talks to him about. Look at Liván's life. And look at El Duque's. Is it fair? El Duque's fucked. What did he do?"

One night, El Duque, Noris, Osmany and I gathered at Osmany's house for dinner. Beforehand, Osmany and I ventured out in the old Muscovy to do some Cuban-style shopping. For $10, some guy pulled a side of beef out of his refrigerator, hacked it up with a cleaver and then wrapped the meat in a recent edition of *Granma.* Another guy pulled some ripe plantains out of his garage. On the way home, Osmany stopped at a bodega and used his ration booklet to pick up some rice and beans. I bought a bottle of Havana Club at one of the dollar stores. Then we went back to the house, where Osmany whipped up a massive feast.

After dinner we were all sitting around drinking rum and watching Brazilian soaps on one of the state-run channels* when a teenager appeared at the door.

"Duque! Duque! Are you in there?"

The kid was talking so fast I couldn't understand him. Slowly, though, I began to decipher the urgent message: Liván had struck out fifteen Atlanta Braves in Game 5 of the National League Championship Series in Miami. "It's a record!" the kid kept yelling. "It's a record!" Indeed it was. It was the most strikeouts recorded by a pitcher in LCS history. It was two shy of the postseason record set by Bob Gibson. Liván had outdueled Greg Maddux, perhaps the finest pitcher of his generation. The Marlins beat the Braves, 2–1. With the Elton John song "Levon" booming out over Pro Player Stadium, Liván retired 17 of the last 18 batters, including slugger Fred McGriff, who looked at strike three for the final out.

Within minutes of the last out in Miami, Osmany Lorenzo's living room in Havana was filled with jubilant neighbors. They clinked their beers and pumped their fists and whooped it up and traded high fives. I glanced over at El Duque. It is difficult to describe what I saw. It was a man both grieving and celebrating in the exact same moment. I'm pretty sure he was crying. Exactly what he was thinking I don't know, but a few minutes later he motioned Osmany and me outside.

We stood under a red-and-white awning that made Osmany's house look vaguely like an Italian restaurant. El Duque then asked me to contact the baseball agent Joe Cubas. He wanted me to tell him that he was ready to get out. He would do whatever it took, he said. He asked me to please deliver the message to the agent as soon as possible. I told him I would. Journalistically, I suppose I had crossed some kind of ethical boundary. Nowhere in the reporter's handbook will you find a passage about delivering messages for ballplayers who wish to be smuggled out of their country. But it seemed like the right thing to do. It also seemed like an incredible story. I told El Duque that not only would I deliver the message, I wouldn't mind going along with him.

I SPENT THE REST of the week covering the Che memorial. Fidel gave workers the day off to watch the casket paraded through the streets. Hundreds of

*Cuba has two channels: 2 and 6.

thousands of people stood impassively as Soviet-made jeeps pulled Che and his fallen comrades in a high-speed cortege though the capital. It was night when Che finally arrived in the city of Santa Clara, where Fidel was to preside over his interment. I drove out with Brook Larmer of *Newsweek*, but instead of watching the burial we ended up spending most of our time talking to the families of eleven dissidents who had been rounded up before the ceremony. The dissidents' apparent crime was staging a hunger strike to protest the detention of other political prisoners.

Before making the two-hour drive back to Havana, Larmer and I pulled into a Servi, a state-run gas station/mini-mart. The station was like a neon UFO that had landed in the middle of a blacked-out neighborhood. Thousands of people were still milling about in Santa Clara, where Che had led the historic final battle against Batista. As we gassed up the car, a man wearing a Florida Marlins cap approached. He seemed slightly drunk and proceeded to speak.

"Are you journalists?" he asked.

"Yes."

"All this stuff with Che, it's all manufactured, you know. It's just a publicity stunt. It's manufactured, staged. Me, I see a black future for Cuba."

"Oh?"

"Yes. I am a political opponent of this regime. The Cuban people are lambs. This is the silence of the lambs. [But] they couldn't brainwash me. Listen, I'll give you my name, my address, I'm not scared."

The gas-station attendant, dressed in his green Servi coveralls, stood listening to this curious monologue. After a couple of minutes he could stand it no longer. It was then that a political debate broke out over the hood of our rental car. The debaters were a tipsy Florida Marlins fan and a gas-station attendant.

"Hey, are you a politician?" the attendant said with disdain. "If this were really a tyranny, you'd already be tossed into prison."

"Well, you'll probably report me," the man responded.

"No, no, you have the freedom to talk here."

"But I can't go to the ballot box and vote, can I?"

"Why not? We have elections."

"They're not really elections. There's no candidate except for Fidel."

"You say there are all these people who are not in agreement with the government. But they don't ever do anything. In Chile, or Argentina, if people don't like the government, they take a flag and go out in the streets. But I've never seen you in the streets."

"I'm talking about human rights. Animals don't know what those are."

"Are you calling me an animal? There's no tyranny here. The majority of Cubans love their president. He's the most charismatic figure in the world. There are people who know nothing about Cuba, but everybody knows Fidel Castro. And look what he's done! No other country in Latin America is so developed."

"Yeah, you're a gas-station attendant at the Servi. You have a little bit of status so you can say these things. You don't know that Cubans are the least-informed people in the world."

"I'm very informed."

"What do you read? You get everything you need to know from *Granma, Trabajadores* and *Juventud Rebelde*?"

"Yes, those are enough for me."

Just then another car pulled up and the attendant walked away. The man shook our hands and stumbled off into the shadows. Larmer and I drove back to Havana, thus ending the alternative fall classic.

A few days later my newspaper, *The Boston Globe,* summed up the week that was in Cuba. The editorial appeared beneath the headline MAJOR LEAGUE PARANOIA:

> They buried Che Guevara's bones in Cuba last week to hosannas from the Communist Party press, but Cubans were telling foreign reporters that they cared much more about the brilliant pitching of their native son, Liván Hernández. . . . The regime of Fidel Castro, as if enacting an allegory of its own obsolescence, has branded Liván Hernández a traitor for defecting to the enemy. And to complete its self-portrait as a police state hopelessly entangled in its own paranoia, the regime banned Liván's brother, Orlando Hernández, from Cuban baseball for life. . . . All the melancholy themes of Castro's political dotage are on display in his petty persecution of El Duque. If the old revolutionary and onetime pitcher himself had not lost touch with his people, he would have crowed patriotically over the exploits of every Cuban ballplayer who made it to the majors. . . . The tale of Cuba's two pitching brothers should have taught the maximal leader a lesson he has long refused to learn: that a system which succeeds at distributing poverty equally without creating wealth will never be major league.

CHAPTER TWELVE

FELIZ NAVIDAD

THE FLORIDA MARLINS WENT ON TO WIN THE 1997 WORLD SERIES, beating the Cleveland Indians in seven games. The Most Valuable Player, naturally, was Liván Hernández, who won Games 1 and 5. When his miracle run ended, Liván fell to the grass at Pro Player Stadium and pounded himself in the chest. He then took the stadium microphone and bellowed, in practiced English, "I Love You, Miami!" Miami, of course, loved him back and then some. Liván danced through the ticker-tape parade with a sliver of confetti stuck to his cheek. He was the honored guest at all the parties. The mayor, Joe Carollo, awarded him the keys to the city, then, unbeknownst to Liván, slipped the beloved pitcher into one of his paid political ads for reelection.

I watched the Series in awe from Mexico City, feeling a little like Albert Brooks in *Broadcast News*. Suddenly, I was giving a lot of briefings about "Liván's brother" back in Cuba. A spate of stories appeared about the so-called Brothers in Arms: one living the American dream, the other a Cuban nightmare. It was good theater. I also kept my promise to El Duque and reached out to Joe Cubas as soon as I got home. I decided to go through his friendly press agent René Guim. After Guim was satisfied that we were speaking over a "secure" phone line, I told him: "I'm really calling more as a friend than as a reporter. I just got back from Havana. El Duque wanted me to let you guys know that he's desperate to get out. He wants Cubas's help." I did add, of course, that I'd be interested in covering the escape from the inside, should something develop. Guim said that he would speak with Cubas and get back to me immediately.

It was another month before I heard from him again. Only much later did I get an explanation. Guim said he tried to call Cubas on his cell phone, but the agent, as was his wont, was ducking his calls. Deciding it couldn't wait, Guim phoned Ramón Batista, the agent's go-to guy. Batista told me he relayed my message. "I remember Joe was with his family somewhere around Disney World when I talked to him," he said. "I said, 'Listen, Gordo, there's a newspaper guy in Mexico City who says that he's talked to El Duque and he wants you to help get him out.' "

By then, Cubas didn't need the work. He had made a killing on Rolando Arrojo and now people were coming to *him*. It seemed like every rafter who washed ashore arrived with a baseball glove and a request for an audience with Joe Cubas. The agent could pick his spots and, according to Batista, he no longer wanted anything to do with El Duque Hernández. It all went back to his feud with Liván. "He told me, 'You know what? Tell El Duque to go fuck himself,' " said Batista. " 'He'll fuck me the same way his brother did. Let the nigger drown.' So I called René back and I told him that Joe didn't want to help El Duque."

Cubas, of course, denies this as part of a smear campaign later waged by Guim and Batista, his disgruntled former employees. And, in fact, it does appear that Cubas, at least briefly, showed interest. Guim said Cubas changed his mind after being approached by one of the smugglers who continued to pester him. "This time it was a guy who had a speedboat," said Guim. "It was going to be scientific and camouflaged and nothing could possibly go wrong. The guy told us that he was all ready to go.

"That's why I called you," Guim told me. "Joe couldn't remember your name, but he says, 'Hey, get ahold of that guy from *The Boston Globe*. See if he'll line us up with El Duque.' It was like he was sending somebody out for a quart of milk. You know, 'Go to Cuba, pick up a few things.' "

I received the frantic message on my answering machine in Mexico: "Hey, this is René Guim. Listen, buddy, you gotta get your ass back to Cuba as soon as possible. We got a guy that's going to pick up El Duque, and we want you to go in and tell him where he has to go. You gotta call me back as soon as possible because this is all going down in the next few days."

I called Guim from Brownsville, Texas, where I was working on a story about the U.S.-Mexico border. Guim set up a conference call. As Cubas explained it, the plan sounded pretty vague. He said an unnamed smuggler would pick up El Duque somewhere along the Cuban coast. My role would be to fly to Havana and instruct El Duque where he needed to be and at what time. I would then have the option of leaving the island on my own or tagging along with El Duque on his journey north.

As crazy as it now seems, I gave it some thought. On the one hand, I wanted to help El Duque. His cause was plainly just. I was also salivating over the opportunity to write a firsthand account of his escape. I suppose I should also admit that, like everyone else in this Le Carré novel come to life, I was enjoying my turn playing spy. Without question, it was like no story I had ever covered.

On the other hand, I was well aware that Juan Ignacio was serving fifteen years for baseball-related activities. I was getting married the following month, and the thought of spending my honeymoon in a Cuban jail was hardly appealing. I also wondered about the potential embarrassment for my employer: GLOBE REPORTER HELD IN DEFECTOR SCAM. I told Cubas that I at least needed to talk it over with my boss. He wouldn't hear of it. *No one* could know. We went around and around on this issue, never resolving it, vowing to talk again soon.

In the end it didn't matter. I never got another call. The plot apparently fizzled. According to Guim, the smuggler "took about ten thousand dollars of Joe's money and he never saw it again." As far as I know Cubas never made another attempt to help El Duque escape. The next time we all saw the dissident pitcher, he had found an alternative route out of Cuba.

THE MASTERMIND WAS a tall, barrel-chested man named Ocilio Cruz. He was María Julia's uncle, and thus El Duque's great-uncle. But everyone—relatives and friends alike—simply called him Tío, the Spanish word for uncle.

Tío lived in Miami, where he was president of Florida Patrol Security Detective, Inc. A strapping private investigator, he operated out of a two-room suite on Biscayne Boulevard, a few blocks north of *The Miami Herald.* Tío was sixty-six and drank only whiskey, because beer, he said, put the weight on. He looked about fifteen years younger than his age, which was why most people assumed he was actually El Duque's uncle.

"God has treated me well," said Tío, spreading his arms wide. "Look at me: I'm a former political prisoner."

With his bald pate and his bulk, Tío had an intimidating presence, but it dissolved whenever he smiled, which was often. He was the only member of El Duque's family who was intensely political. As a young man he had been a sergeant in the Batista military. After the dictator fled in 1959 he found work as a security guard at the Havana bus terminal. He never abandoned hope that the

Batistianos would return to power, however, nor did he stop doing his part to try to make it happen.

After hours, Tío formed an anti-Castro terrorist group with his fellow guards at the bus station. As he explained it, "We were trying to convince people that the country was headed in the wrong direction. We did a lot of subversive activities. We did everything. But we never killed anyone." The band of counterrevolutionaries operated until the fall of 1960, when the police discovered a cache of explosives in the trunk of a car near the Tropicana nightclub. "We were infiltrated by someone with the new government," said Tío. "He gave up the entire cell, all eight of us. We each got different sentences. I got fifteen years."

Tío was sent to Presidio Modelo on the Isle of Pines.* Less than a decade earlier, Fidel had been sent to the same penitentiary for the attack on Moncada. How the political tide had turned. Tío found himself surrounded by hundreds of opponents of Fidel's new regime. He was assigned to cellblock number 20, where he lived with three other inmates in a concrete room designed for two. "I wouldn't wish those fifteen years on anyone," said Tío. "But having conviction is the most important thing in life. If you believe in the cause then you accept the consequences."

Tío's fondest memories of prison were playing baseball. Growing up he had been a power-hitting first baseman, and to pass the time he and the other inmates played in the prison courtyard. As a small act of defiance, the prisoners divided themselves into the teams of the disbanded Cuban professional league: Almendares, Havana, Cienfuegos and Marianao. "One time we had a problem because they wanted us to change the names of the teams," he said. "They wanted us to call ourselves the Azucareros [Cane Cutters] or Industriales or Constructores [Builders]. We didn't play ball for a week until it was resolved.

"I managed and played first base for Almendares," he said. "We played for packs of cigarettes. The batting champion and the best pitcher would get one hundred packs. Our families brought us T-shirts and we had people inside paint logos. Some had scorpions for Almendares, or lions for Havana. . . . There was a guard tower behind second base. If you hit the tower and it was caught it was an out, so you always tried to hit down on the ball. The games started at one, always one o'clock. The prisoners would surround the field. They used to argue a lot. They were loud."

Tío was released in 1975. He had served his entire sentence: fifteen years.

---

*The island was renamed the Isle of Youth following the revolution.

Concerned about his criminal record, he spent the next five years trying to find a legal route off the island. Fidel ultimately provided it. In 1980, a group of Cubans sought asylum at the Peruvian embassy in Havana. In his angry response to the crisis, Fidel opened the floodgates at the port of Mariel. Over the next five months, 125,266 people crossed the Florida Straits. The almost biblical exodus led President Carter to declare a state of emergency in South Florida, which was forever transformed.

"I arrived alone," said Tío. "I stayed with some neighbors from Cuba for a while and I got a job at a gas station. Then somebody told me about security work. I said, 'What's that?' They said it was what we call a *sereno*, a night watchman. I knew a guy who had a security agency, a police colonel under Batista. I asked him, 'Colonel, do you have any work?' So he gave me a job. We watched car dealerships at night. Then after a couple years I decided to start my own agency."

By 1990, Tío was so proficient he had landed a job as a bodyguard for Jorge Mas Canosa, founder of the Cuban American National Foundation. It was the rough equivalent of protecting Cuba's president-in-exile. In Miami, Mas, a telecommunications mogul, was widely viewed as the successor to Fidel—once Cuba was liberated, of course. Among other things, he used the foundation to almost single-handedly direct U.S. policy toward Cuba. Mas and the foundation retained their outsized political power by carpet bombing Washington with political donations. Over time, the foundation established what one research institute described as, "dollar for dollar, arguably the most effective" lobbying group in the country.

Jorge Mas often traveled like a head of state, and certainly he was protected like one. Tío became a member of his security team. He helped protect the exiled leader against potential assassinations orchestrated from Havana, where Mas was considered the *capo di tutti capi* of what Fidel frequently referred to as "the Miami Mafia."

"If somebody wanted to get to him they had to go through us," said Tío. "We were always armed and ready. I kept a pistol in my waistband and a shotgun in the car wherever we went."

Tío eventually returned to running his security business full-time. In Miami, where espionage is a flourishing industry, there was plenty of work. Tío employed a couple dozen security guards and handled his own cases—marital infidelities, tracing, small-business protection—on the side. He earned enough money to buy a gold Lincoln Continental and a comfortable house. He regularly sent money to his family back in Cuba. As a former ballplayer, he also kept close tabs on his grandnephew, El Duque.

Tío had tried repeatedly to convince El Duque to defect. He told him, "The biggest dream of my life is to watch you pitch in the major leagues. You have the ability, son, you can make millions." After Liván's defection, his entreaties became more desperate. "I begged him, 'Orlando, please leave,'" said Tío. "They're not going to let you out of Cuba now because of Liván.' But he wouldn't do it. He always said he would never leave his daughters." A year later, Tío was passing a newsstand in Miami when he glanced down at the headlines. "It was right there in the paper," he recalled. "It said: 'Orlando "El Duque" Hernández has been suspended from baseball for life.'"

Tío knew immediately what he had to do. He was motivated not by money but by blood and personal history.

"I had lost my youth in a Cuban prison," he said. "I wasn't going to let that happen to Orlando. I had to get him out."

THE FOYER OF Tío's office displayed a photo of him with Bill Clinton at a Cuban American National Foundation fund-raiser. "I hope neither of you are Republican," he said politely as Sánchez and I walked through the door. The security business was apparently slow this hot afternoon. Tío sat behind his desk, bathed in air-conditioning, watching a Spanish-language soap opera on a corner television. He lowered the volume as he turned to the subject of our visit: his plot to help El Duque escape from Cuba.

"These are the secrets of war," said Tío.

As Tío described it, his campaign to liberate El Duque was like a journey into Miami's Cuban American underworld, a veritable Stop & Shop for smugglers and spies. It was an environment in which Tío, with his security connections, was not entirely unfamiliar. His first stop was with "a friend of a friend" who specialized in forgeries of immigration documents. "I went over to his place and he told me it would be eight thousand dollars a head," said Tío. "I would give them the money and then they would handle the rest. But when I told him that it was El Duque Hernández, he told me to forget it. He said that everyone at the airport would know El Duque. He was too well known."

Within a short time, it became obvious that El Duque had only one way out. His suspension had effectively turned him into a prisoner of Cuba's unforgiving geography. The island itself is 777 miles long, 117 miles wide at its widest point, and stretches across the Caribbean like a giant crab claw. The distance between Havana and Key West is just 106 miles, but in between lies shark-infested waters, the powerful Gulf Stream and notoriously volatile weather. For those wishing to escape, however, Cuba does have a few advantages. Its periphery is pocked with thousands of hidden cays, secluded beaches and tiny islands. For the Cuban coast guard, it presents a challenge not unlike the U.S. Border Patrol's task of protecting the varied 2,000-mile frontier with Mexico. There was really no way to stop the smugglers, many of whom used cigarette boats, global positioning systems and satellite phones. The Cubans could only hope to get lucky on occasion.

After abandoning the false-document plan, Tío began to plot El Duque's escape by sea. Gradually, he and El Duque formulated their plan through letters because "it was too dangerous to use the phones," Tío explained. "We'd use code words like 'the business.' He would write, 'How is the business going?' I'd write back and say, 'I'm going to send you some money for a restaurant now that you're not playing ball.' I had a contact who went to Cuba. He was the one who delivered the letters for me. He had people going down there all the time."

Tío allowed Sánchez and me to examine the letters but said they were too personal to print. Suffice it to say that the letters reflect the growing desperation of a man willing to risk his life to play baseball again.

It was in one of these letters that El Duque passed along the name of a potential smuggler: René Valle. El Duque apparently got his name through Valle's relatives in Boyeros. He advised Tío to visit the experienced smuggler in Miami and set up an attempt as soon as possible.

What happened next is not entirely clear. Tío said he provided Valle with a $25,000 speedboat in the fall of 1997 and organized an expedition to pick up El Duque in Pinar del Río, off Cuba's western coast. "That was the area he knew," said Tío. "He had done this many times before. It was a profession for him. But this time he got caught. He was inside Cuban waters when they captured him. He declared that he was fishing and had drifted off course. They locked him up and after five months they put him on a boat back to the U.S. This is what I heard."

Tío lacked many specifics about this failed adventure, so Sánchez and I set out to find René Valle to get the full story. We located him one afternoon at his split-level apartment in Miami. His wife answered the door and, after we identified ourselves, motioned us to the couch. Valle was on the phone, shirtless, seated at the kitchen table in gray gym shorts. He seemed to be arguing with a client over a construction project for which he was seeking payment. Specifically, he was threatening to run over the project with his truck. "You know me!" he was screaming. "If I have to kill somebody, I will. I don't care if I get killed, but somebody's going to end up dead!" He then slammed down the phone and turned to us.

"*Buenas tardes*," he said pleasantly. "How can I help you?"

As gently as possible, we told Valle that we had heard he might have been involved in an attempt to smuggle El Duque Hernández out of Cuba. Valle, to our amazement, confirmed that one afternoon in the summer of 1997 he had received an unexpected visit from "El Duque's uncle." Tío told Valle that he had the backing of unnamed baseball people who would finance a smuggling operation. Valle then launched into a long, rambling story about how he had spent 1993 to 1995 in a Cuban prison for trying to smuggle out members of his own family. He said the Cuban coast guard had impounded his boat, seized his passport and charged him with illegal entry into the country of his birth.

For that reason, he said, he had turned Tío down. His ordeal in Cuba had been hell, he told us. Even after he was released, he had been unable to leave the country because the Cubans still held his money, his boat and his passport. He said he finally made it back to the States as a common rafter.

Valle said Tío had a hard time taking no for an answer. When he refused, he said, Tío became angry.

"What, are you afraid?" he quoted Tío as saying.

"Yeah, I'm afraid," Valle said he responded. "There's no way I'm going back to jail."

Tío later insisted that Valle had accepted the mission. And, as Tío pointed out, few people would admit publicly to committing a federal crime, no matter how noble the cause. Tío himself knew he was on shaky ground. "This is a very delicate matter," he said. "It's illegal, you know. But I was prepared to go to jail."

After the Valle episode, Tío moved on. "I didn't do or say anything about it," he said. "I knew there would be other attempts. So I just let it go. My wife saw him later and said hello. But we never saw him again after that. I went by his house one day but they said he had moved."

WHATEVER REALLY HAPPENED, the plan's failure led Tío to change his strategy. He now wanted to hire a boat inside Cuba to deliver El Duque from the island. His reasoning was that an ostensibly legal vessel would have an easier time making it past the coast guard. Once El Duque was in international waters, the plan went, he could transfer to an American boat that would bring him in to Miami.

Because of his own past, Tío was reluctant to travel to Cuba to make the arrangements on his own. For this latest plan, he paired up with a man who went by the nickname El Argentino (the Argentine). The one time I met him, El Argentino introduced himself as Jorge Ramís. He said he was an Argentinian businessman who lived in Miami. Beyond that, he declined to elaborate. As

Tío explained it, El Argentino's role was to act as a liaison between Miami and Havana, delivering messages and money during the preparation of El Duque's next attempt, In return he would be allowed to represent El Duque if and when the time came to negotiate his major-league contract.

Looking back from the perspective of three World Championships, such an arrangement seems perfectly logical. But at the time it was a pipe dream. It was now December 1997. El Duque was a desperate man. He had not played organized baseball in fourteen months. In October, while Liván was making history, he had turned thirty-two.* Cubas had shown little inclination to get involved, and Tío's efforts, thus far, had failed. El Duque and Osmany had tried several times on their own to line up a boat, with disastrous results. They combed the beaches of Pinar del Río, El Duque wearing sunglasses to hide his identity. They looked outside Havana. "The name of one place we went was Boca Jaruco; we tried to leave from there many times," said Osmany. "The place was off a mountainous road. You have to go around the mountains to get to the sea. You had to cross a river and then go around the mountains. But we never got the boat there. This was so hard. You have no idea how hard it was. Everybody leaves Cuba in boats and rafts and I couldn't find one to get us out of Cuba."

Osmany had a standard line to keep El Duque's spirits up: "During all of the attempts, every one, I used to tell Orlando, 'Don't worry, we'll be munching at McDonald's in Miami in an hour.' "

Once, at the beginning of November, El Duque and Alberto Hernández set out for Santa Clara. The players were to be picked up at a predetermined safe house and then taken to the water for a midnight voyage north. Alberto kissed Zaily good-bye, perhaps forever, and headed out. He met up with El Duque at the prearranged location. "We sat there up in the mountains, waiting for hours," said Alberto. "But it didn't happen. It all fell through." The players crept back to Havana in the early morning darkness. "When Alberto walked through the door I couldn't believe it," said Zaily. "I thought he was gone."

In mid-December, El Duque and Alberto were summoned again to Villa Marista, the Havana headquarters of the Ministry of Interior. The players were taken to separate rooms. Both were told that the government was aware of their latest escape attempt. Alberto said a State Security agent warned him that he was now forbidden to set foot in Santa Clara, the crossroads for a number of

---

*Even back then, El Duque was telling people he was twenty-eight. I happened to be around for his birthday, and when people asked him how old he was, he continued to say twenty-eight. Remarkably, his birthday had not affected his age in the least.

launch points on the northern coast. He said the agent told him that he and El Duque could expect to be watched so closely that Havana would feel like it was the size of a *centavo*, a penny.

El Duque said the low point of the meeting was when an agent told him flatly: "You will never play baseball again."

"I told him, 'I'm going to play baseball again before I die, even if I have to play in Haiti,' " said El Duque. "His response was the same response they always gave you: an ironic little laugh and the face of victory. The look of having defeated you, the enemy. But you cannot claim victory while the enemy is still standing."

Osmany Lorenzo was waiting outside in the Muscovy when El Duque finally emerged at nine P.M., fourteen hours after entering the building. "They say at Villa Marista that everybody sings," said Osmany. "When he finally came out he was both happy and sad. He was happy that they didn't break him. He had spoken his mind. But he was sad because he knew it was finally time to go.

"We had to leave now, there was no other way," said Osmany. "We were in too deep. We were trapped. There was no way to get him out legally. Somehow we had to escape. People on the street, total strangers, were coming up to him and telling him, 'Duque, you have to get out of here. You have nothing.' "

El Duque had never been very religious but now, in his desperation, he sought divine intervention. In Cuba the dominant religion is Santería, a syncretic mix of Roman Catholicism and Yoruba, an African faith. The religion evolved as imported slaves combined the religion of their Spanish masters with their own. Often mistaken for voodoo, Santería combines the rituals of Catholicism with a kind of gory mysticism so out of the mainstream it is often reduced to stereotypes (for example, Pedro Cerrano, the Cuban defector who sanctifies his bats in the movie *Major League*). But to its millions of practitioners, Santería is as real as the sun.

Like Catholicism, Santería is composed of different orders. In this, his darkest hour, El Duque turned to Palo Mayombe, a branch imported to the Caribbean from the Congo in the 1500s. Carlos Galdiano Montenegro, a Brazilian whose family has practiced the religion for two hundred years, offered the following description in his book *Palo Mayombe: The Dark Side of Santería*:

> There is a sharp distinction between Palo Mayombe and Santería. The religion of Santería uses the forces of light. The initiated members of Palo Mayombe use the forces of darkness to achieve their goals and magical spells. Palo has its own priesthood and set of rules and regulations.

The power of many Palero priests is so strong that they can take a man of obscure origins and turn him into a very powerful world figure in a relatively short period of time. Many of the most notorious and famous Latin American and Caribbean political leaders have been linked . . . with the practice of Palo Mayombe in order to keep them in power. It is believed that a Palero can make or break you by saying just a few incantations and performing a few minor rituals.

El Duque refuses to discuss his baptism into Palo Mayombe other than to acknowledge that it transformed his life. Later, in New York, he gave much of the credit for his success to a *palero* priest named Carlos, or Carlito. The pitcher frequently consulted with Carlito in Havana via cell phone. Enrique López Oliva, a religious historian in Cuba, said El Duque's reticence to discuss his initiation almost certainly stemmed from a vow of secrecy, the violation of which reputedly causes initiates "to lose everything: success, friends, even their health."

The initiation into Palo Mayombe can vary, but certain rites are universal. The ceremony is held over an iron kettle or terra-cotta bowl filled with sticks from the ceiba tree, pieces of wood, a crucifix, human bones and, often, dead animals such as a goat or a rooster. The cauldron sits in a white circle of pulverized eggshells, surrounded by candles. The ceremony is conducted by the *palero,* who begins by invoking the spirit of Zarabanda, divine messenger of the Palo Mayombe underworld:

> *O mighty spirit, Zarabanda*
> *I call your spirit from the north (taps three times in front of the cauldron)*
> *I call your spirit from the south (repeats)*
> *I call your spirit from the east (repeats)*
> *I call your spirit from the west (repeats)*

The initiate then calls upon Zarabanda "to encircle my body with a ring of powerful fire to protect me from my enemies and to balance nature in my favor." He requests that Zarabanda help him fight off his enemies to avoid the "capture of my soul" and to "balance the scales of justice in my favor." He accepts several amulets from the *palero,* the most common of which "allows an individual to escape the law or authorities." According to Galdiano's book, "[The amulet] contains earth from mountains, from crossroads, from four jails and four police stations. It is to be carried by the person at all times."

The centerpiece of the Palo Mayombe initiation ceremony is the *rallamiento*—literally, a scratching. "They take a knife and with the knife of the *palero* they draw your blood," said Lázaro Montero, a Cuban expert in Santería and Palo Mayombe. "It is to strengthen you. In Palo there is a belief that through *rallamiento* you receive special powers so you can go anywhere and not be seen. You become invisible."

El Duque never flaunted his religion or discussed it in great detail. But he obviously gave great weight to its influence over his improbable life story. Later, when he traveled with the Yankees, he erected makeshift shrines in his hotel rooms to Changó, a Santería diety. The shrines usually consisted of a variety of offerings: candles, a sunflower, a burnt Cuban cigar, red wine and, always, a miniature replica of the Statue of Liberty.

Months after his escape Sánchez and I were sitting with El Duque in a restaurant in San José, Costa Rica. El Duque was talking about his deliverance from Cuba in spiritual terms. Sitting at the table, he rolled back his sleeve to reveal his right shoulder, still bearing the dark thin scars of the *rallamiento* that he believed had propelled him from the world of the unjust.

TÍO SENT EL ARGENTINO down to Cuba with $4,000. The money was to be used to find a boat and a crew to carry El Duque out of Cuba. El Duque, in turn, entrusted the task of finding the boat to his friend Osmany Lorenzo, master of the underground economy.

Osmany had a well-connected friend in Santa Clara who went by the nickname El Chino. El Chino, in turn, knew a fisherman in the northern port city of Caibarién. The fisherman was known, more conventionally, as Juan Carlos Romero. He was a thirty-one-year-old Cuban navy veteran and part-owner of a thirty-foot boat that he used to fish the waters off Villa Clara every weekend.

By Cuban standards Juan Carlos and his wife, Geidy, lived well. Juan Carlos held a number of jobs, only one of which was legal, and he made a decent living selling fish on the black market. What he didn't sell he and his family ate. He owned a German motorcycle and a beat-up Lada, and his modest home contained a color television, a VCR and a ceiling fan. His only fear was that the government might drop in one day and ask how he had come to own such valuable possessions working in a tannery, his official job.

Back then, Caibarién was a mecca for rafters. Situated at the midsection of the northern coast, it was one of the closest points in Cuba to the United States. The town's principal industry was fishing, but a significant percentage of the population also supported the *balseros* who set out by the hundreds from the nooks and crannies of the ragged coastline. The town was awash in all manner of watercraft, many of which were under construction out of view of the authorities.

Osmany and El Chino showed up at Juan Carlos's house unannounced one afternoon. They came with a proposition. "They told me that if I got a boat for them they would guarantee that I and my family would get into the United States," Juan Carlos said. "They also promised me a job when we got there. Osmany was really like El Duque's mouth and eyes back then. He told me that El Duque was trapped in Cuba and that he couldn't get out. He said he had tried and tried many times and he had always failed. He wanted me to help get him out."

Juan Carlos told Osmany that he needed a day to think it over. He spoke with his wife and decided it was a no-lose proposition. He felt certain that he could meet his part of the bargain, which was to navigate El Duque through Cuban waters, then ferry the ballplayer to a meeting point near a Bahamian island called Anguilla Cay. In addition to the $4,000 payment, Juan Carlos was attracted by the promise of a new life in the United States. And he believed that El Duque could deliver. Although he had never met the famous pitcher, he had heard about the vast riches bestowed upon Cuban ballplayers in the States.

Now that Juan Carlos had agreed, Osmany wanted to see the boat. "They had very specific orders about the boat," said Juan Carlos. "They insisted that it had to be a good boat. It had to be secure. If El Duque arrived at the beach and said, 'I'm not getting on that boat,' then the whole thing was fucked."

Juan Carlos took Osmany down to the beach. The boat was bobbing in the water several yards offshore. It wasn't a yacht, but it wasn't a wreck, either. Juan Carlos and two friends had bought the wooden fishing vessel for 50,000 pesos, about $3,000 at the time. The boat measured about thirty feet from stem to stern and was powered by a 480-horsepower diesel engine that Juan Carlos said had been made in either Germany or Argentina. An enclosed cabin, with room to accommodate several people, dominated the deck. The cabin rose about ten feet and supported a platform from which the boat was steered. From the stern fluttered a small red, white and blue Cuban flag mounted on a pole. So secure was the boat, in fact, it had already made one voyage to Miami to drop off a group of rafters—a far more arduous journey than to the Bahamas—and had returned to Caibarién unscathed. Osmany, suddenly a nautical expert, gave the boat the once-over.

"When do we leave?" he asked.

Juan Carlos said he needed a few days to prepare. Osmany returned to Havana and gave El Duque a positive report. All that remained, really, was to complete the passenger list. There was El Duque and Norita, of course; Juan Carlos and his wife, Geidy; Joel Pedroso, El Duque's stocky cousin; and Alberto Hernández, who readily signed up when El Duque approached him with the latest plan. Osmany was undecided: His primary interest was El Duque. "I knew it would have hurt if ten or twelve years later I was sitting around in Cuba, thinking that one of my friends could have pitched in the major leagues," he said. "I knew that my life was going to be more or less the same, but this was an opportunity that Orlando couldn't pass up."

In addition, the crew would include Juan Carlos's two partners in the boat. Their role would be to drop off El Duque and the others in the Bahamas, then return to Cuba. The boat was too valuable to ditch. The men took Tío's $4,000 not only as payment for services rendered but also as insurance in case the boat was impounded or lost.

After the Villa Marista episode, El Duque was concerned about tipping off the authorities. He firmly believed that State Security was monitoring his movements. The latest plan had come at a propitious time, however. The island was absorbed in feverish preparations for the visit of Pope John Paul II, now just a month away. Rumored for years, disbelieved and denied, the papal visit had finally been confirmed with all its historic implications. John Paul's pivotal role in the collapse of communism in Eastern Europe had been well documented. Cuba, of course, was hardly Poland, and Fidel was a far cry from the Soviet puppet Wojciech Jaruzelski. But still. . . . Two thousand foreign journalists, including all three American network news anchors, planned to descend on the island.

Cuba was the only Spanish-speaking country to elude the frail, aging pope, and for good reason. Fidel himself was a former altar boy, baptized, raised and educated within the Catholic church. While fighting in the Sierra Maestra, he had worn a cross on the lapel of his uniform and often traveled with a priest, Reverend Guillermo Sardiñas, who baptized scores of children with the rebel leader standing as godfather.

After the revolution, however, Fidel moved to diminish the church's role in a newly atheistic society. Nearly three-fourths of some eight hundred priests either fled or were deported. For three decades, "believers" were banned from the Communist party and, thus, most state-sanctioned jobs. Fidel's relationship with the church was as complicated as the man himself. He continued to invoke Christianity as a philosophical underpinning of the revolution, even as he dismissed his own past. "If somebody were to ask me when I held religious beliefs, I'd have to say: never, really," Fidel told the Brazilian priest Frei Betto.

Even then, he persisted in expressing solidarity with the church teachings: "I believe Karl Marx could have subscribed to the Sermon on the Mount," he said.

The run-up to the papal visit was equally complex, a strange dance of conflict and concession between church and state. In Santa Clara, where the first of four papal masses was to be held, the government first proposed that John Paul preach before an immense machine-gun-toting statue of Che Guevara, the atheist martyr. The church, not surprisingly, refused. The government also severely restricted the church's access to the state-run media, which meant that almost all promotion for the papal visit would have to take place within the church.

Fidel did grant a few concessions, however. One of the biggest was the reinstatement of Christmas as a national holiday. For nearly three decades, the government had treated December 25 as any other day. Even during the early stages of the revolution, government propagandists had banned Santa Claus, replacing him with a revolutionary figure named "Don Feliciano," and revising a popular Christmas tune with new lyrics: "Jingle bells, jingle bells, always with Fidel." Now, it wasn't exactly Macy's in Havana, but as the day approached, tiny plastic trees began to appear in the dollar stores. Many people placed the trees on top of their television sets and their coffee tables, wrapping them up in strings of cheap lights. Families gathered food for traditional Christmas dinners. Some planned to attend Midnight Mass, another novelty.

But for El Duque and his supporters, the resurrection of Christmas was not just a religious and historical event. It was also a unique opportunity to camouflage their getaway. "The first authorized Christmas: What better day was there than that?" said Tío. "We knew that people would be celebrating and drinking a lot. And with the pope coming, we figured that the government's guard would be down. People would be traveling all over, celebrating Christmas, so they would be less likely to question anybody."

So now the date was set: December 25, 1997. El Duque betrayed his plans to no one, not even his mother. On December 24, he dropped by to see María Julia at the old house in Wajay. María Julia was on her way to spend Christmas Eve with her ex-husband. El Duque was with Norita, and they suggested that on the way they all go over to see Alberto Hernández, who was having Christmas Eve dinner with his family. For Alberto, who had told everyone about his intended escape, it was a farewell meal as well.

"It was near where I was going, anyway," said María Julia. "When we got there Orlando said, 'Mama, let's stay and have dinner.' Albertico had cooked. So we ate and I met Albertico's wife and their children. I remember Orlando told me at one point, 'Mama, relax, you're so tense.'

"After dinner they drove me over to Pedro's house. The apartment is on the fourth floor, and everyone was out on the balcony. When I went out there, Orlando was still downstairs. He was dancing in the street and causing all kinds of monkey business. He was yelling this and he was yelling that. He was saying good-bye and I didn't even know it."

On Christmas Day, El Duque and Noris attended the wedding of Ernesto Bazan, an Italian photographer. Bazan had met El Duque during shooting assignments for *Natural History* and *Newsweek*. He invited the pitcher to attend a wedding reception for him and his wife at a renovated guest house in the Havana neighborhood of Buena Vista. The reception started at two P.M. There were about fifty guests, many of whom had flown in from New York and Italy. To most of the foreigners, El Duque was unrecognizable, one of perhaps twenty Cubans in attendance. But he was spotted immediately by Tom Miller, an American who wrote about baseball in his book *Trading with the Enemy*, and Miller's Cuban wife, Regla Albarrán.

"I had never met him before," said Regla, "but I had always been drawn to him. He was such a respected athlete. Tom and I had watched Liván pitch for the Marlins in Miami, and we used to talk about how El Duque was supposed to be much better. We knew El Duque would fascinate American baseball fans. So we saw him at the reception and we mentioned this to him. We said we enjoyed watching him pitch, that we were honored to meet him. We didn't talk about conflicts or the suspension. He seemed very relaxed. He didn't seem pressured at all."

At one point Miller suggested that he would like to interview the pitcher. "He said, 'Sure,' " Miller said. "He invited me to stop by his house sometime in the near future. I said I was going to be in Cuba for another week or so. He said, 'When you're in the neighborhood there are a lot of bad restaurants but there are a couple of good ones, too.' Then he wrote down the address. A lot of good it did me."

Miller kept the note, though. "What do you think I could get for it on eBay?" he joked. "I have a theory about El Duque and that party," added Miller. "There were dozens of foreign journalists there. He knew that. He wanted to make a presence. It was all a cover."

El Duque and Norita sat mostly by themselves. A few people stopped by to say hello. The reception featured a traditional Cuban meal of pork chops, rice and beans. Waiters and waitresses fluttered over the tables, delivering beer and wine, *mojitos* and rum punches. "It was one drink after another," said Regla. "We were all drunk." El Duque sat back, sipping orange juice and sucking on his Marlboros.

After a while, someone turned on a boom box, and people got up to dance.

El Duque and Norita eventually joined in. Later, Regla, who had seen many of her own friends flee the island, was struck by how relaxed the couple looked, as if it were just another afternoon in Havana. "I could never have imagined that he was planning to leave Cuba immediately," she said. "He was just so relaxed, almost serene."

On the party went, the house filling with salsa and laughter and smoke. The music was familiar: the throbbing rhythms of Los Van Van (the Go Gos), for decades the most popular band in Cuba. Founded by bassist Juan Formell, the band derived its name from the early ambition of the revolution, lifting it from a government slogan exhorting the masses to a record sugar harvest. Over time, Los Van Van essentially provided the soundtrack to the revolution. Its songs described the essence of Cuba's tortured identity. Inside and outside the island, Cubans projected onto Los Van Van their own visions of what Cuba had become. For members of El Duque's generation, the band represented their music, their culture. For many older exiles, Los Van Van was Fidel Castro's house band. In 1997, in an effort to bridge these two worlds, Los Van Van traveled to Miami for the first time. The band's mere presence sparked violent protests.

El Duque and Norita danced. One particular song stood out. It was a Cuban classic, Formell's exaltation of Afro-Cuban culture, of Santería and its saints: Changó, Obatala, Eleggua, Yemaya. . . . The lyrics describe one man's plea to Orula, the Santería god of wisdom, to help him and the Cuban people through difficult times. The song is essentially an eight-and-a-half-minute prayer, building to a plaintive, hypnotic wail for redemption: *Ay, dios, ampárame* (O God, protect me!). Only El Duque, for whom music seemed an extension of his very being, could have grasped its full significance:

> *Look, the hour has come for you to analyze this well.*
> *You say you're the king.*
> *So show me your crown.*
> *Show it to me!*
>
> *If tomorrow I should die,*
> *I will always follow you in heaven.*
> *My God, help me.*
> *Protect me. Protect me.*
> *O God, protect me.*

By seven P.M. El Duque and Norita were gone.

———

EVERYONE GATHERED near the on-ramp to the National Highway for the five-hour journey to Caibarién. El Duque, Norita, Alberto and Joel Pedroso piled into a late-model Chevy. Osmany had ditched the notorious red Muscovy and gone ahead with a friend. He planned to pick up another player, Jorge Luis Toca, who had indicated he also wanted to go. El Duque wore a baseball cap pulled low over his eyes. A mysterious amulet hung from his neck. The plan was to arrive in Caibarién by daybreak, since Juan Carlos had set the launch for seven A.M.

At first, Osmany had been opposed to leaving in broad daylight, if only because everyone left Cuba under the cover of darkness. But Juan Carlos knew what he was doing. He had spent the preceding days monitoring the movements of the coast guard. He knew that the boats patrolled at night and rested during the day. He also had calculated that it took exactly ten minutes to ride his bike from the launch point to his house in Caibarién. That was critical: Juan Carlos wanted to confirm that the coast was clear, then pedal back to the house, where the group would then set out for the boat en masse.

In the waning hours of Christmas, the National Highway was pitch-black. Unnoticed, the cars slowly made their way through the warm night, careful to avoid being stopped. No one spoke much. It was early morning when the group stopped in Santa Clara to pick up a late entry: a thirty-five-year-old hustler named Lenin Rivero.

Lenin's father had given him his patriotic name. "It was the start of the revolution," Lenin explained, "and everybody was caught up in the promise. Many fathers were calling their sons Lenin, Fidel, Ernesto, Vladimir. They were all linked to the revolution and the Soviet Union." Later, though, Lenin was arrested for trafficking in dollars. He did some time in jail. By the time a friend mentioned that he was organizing a trip to the United States, Lenin was eager to leave, even though he knew no one on the trip.

Lenin agreed to trade his '58 Oldsmobile in return for his passage. "I asked my friend, 'What if they send me back?'" said Lenin. "He said, 'Well, then you get your car back.' So I said okay."

Lenin waited at a tourist stop on the side of the highway in the predawn. The car pulled up beside him. "When I got in the car it was the first time I had met everyone," said Lenin. "I mean, I had seen El Duque on TV many times. But I had never seen him in person.

"It was very tense when I got in the car. I remember asking something, although I don't remember exactly what. But they obviously weren't in the mood for questions. It might have been something like, 'Are you El Duque?' They ignored me like I wasn't there. They must have been afraid. Then Orlando said something like, 'Shut up, don't ask so many fucking questions. Let's get out of here.' I didn't say another word after that."

Osmany, failing to locate Toca,* also joined the group in Santa Clara. El Duque and Alberto were now driving through the province that the government had declared off-limits. The players hunched down in their seats. The group was off the main highway, heading northeast toward Caibarién. One of the organizers, who will remain nameless, drove ahead on a motorcycle. Each time the group was about to enter a town, the motorcycle would speed ahead to scout for police. "It was stop-and-go the whole way," said Lenin. "Every time the motorcycle went ahead, we would pull over, lift the hood and check the engine like we had broken down. Then we waited until the motorcycle came back and said all clear."

It was around five A.M. when the group pulled up to Juan Carlos's house. Juan Carlos and Geidy had been up most of the night, partying and saying good-bye to their families. The group parked about a quarter of a mile from the house to avoid suspicion. Juan Carlos then hopped on his bicycle and rode down to the launch point: a secluded campground called Conuco Cay.

Juan Carlos and a friend had arranged a signal. The friend, a fisherman, agreed to watch for the coast guard that morning. If the area was clear, he told Juan Carlos that he would fly the Cuban flag from his boat. Juan Carlos pulled a pair of binoculars from his backpack. He stared out at the water. "I saw the flag," he said. "When I saw it I rode my bike back home. Geidy was standing in front of the house. I left the bike and we got in the car."

As they made their way toward the boat, El Duque and the others tried to meld into the floorboards, their caps pulled over their faces. It was still very early, and there was almost no one on the streets in the soft morning. At that hour Caibarién was a sleepy fishing village: low-slung houses, the smell of the sea, the occasional clomping of a horse-drawn carriage on the buckled streets. The launch point, Conuco Cay, was just outside town. Occasionally people camped there, but now it was empty, a secluded knoll of palm trees and shrubs and heavy grass running toward the beach. The group was able to drive up almost to the edge of the shore.

As daring and dramatic as the escape surely was, it should be noted that such acts occur in some form *every single day:* Mexicans fording the dangerous

---

*Toca defected by boat the following year and later signed with the New York Mets.

Río Grande; Haitians packing themselves into floating death traps; Chinese crossing oceans in suffocating cargo containers. All with the same goal: a better life. To get to the boat, El Duque and the others had to wade into the water. And so, after some hesitation, into the water they all went: two of the finest baseball players in Cuba's history, their friends and companions, and a few others just looking for a way out of the national malaise. At the last minute, Osmany had decided to tag along, if only to see how it all turned out. He seemed like the most relaxed member of the group. The others were tense, quiet and determined. Alberto, by his own admission, was petrified. It took him a few moments to muster up the courage to wade into the great unknown. He was grossly overweight from the fourteen-month layoff, and when he went to climb onto the boat he tumbled awkwardly into the water. "This boat is a piece of shit," he said, indicating that he might not go. Norita looked back at him. There, in the water, she offered up some hard words of encouragement.

"We've made our decision," she said. "Better to drown than to turn back now."

PART FOUR

CHAPTER THIRTEEN

THE GANG THAT COULDN'T SHOOT STRAIGHT

Soaked from the waist down, El Duque, Noris, Osmany and Joel piled into the cabin and hit the floor. Alberto and Lenin lay facedown on the deck. Geidy took a seat out in the open with Juan Carlos's anonymous partners. Juan Carlos climbed to the top of the cabin and began to ease the boat out of Conuco Cay. To anyone who happened to notice, the boat would have appeared to be heading out on a routine fishing expedition—a little later than usual perhaps but not surprising after the first legal Christmas in twenty-eight years. "We took the same route that we always took on fishing trips," said Juan Carlos. "I was roaming around like we were looking for fishing zones." In the distance stood a Cuban coast guard cutter, too far away to be threatening. Gradually, after about an hour of phantom trolling, Juan Carlos maneuvered the boat in the direction of the Bahamas.

"There was dead silence as we floated away," said Osmany. "No one moved. No one said a word. We kept our heads down. I thought it was the last time I would ever see Cuba. And I had to keep my head down. I couldn't look. It was sad. That was the hardest part."

Just off Caibarién, a group of tiny islands that are part of the Sabaná Archipelago blocks the path to the open sea. Juan Carlos chose among several narrow channels that run between the islands. It was low tide, and as he gingerly made his way the boat struck bottom and became stuck. Climbing down from his perch, he jumped into the shallows and gave the boat a push, jarring it loose. Within minutes, the defectors had made it past the archipelago, past the critical twelve-mile international limit, out of Cuba, heading north at speeds between six and eight knots. The weather was unchanging: balmy and pristine, as if lifted from a travel brochure. The water was bright aqua in places, with dark shadings of coral mass. Occasionally, a marlin leaped into the air. "It was *calma blanca*," said Juan Carlos. "The calmest navigational conditions there are."

By the time he yelled that it was safe to come out, however, most everyone was too queasy to move. Packed on the floor of the sweltering cabin for the better part of four hours, El Duque and the others had gotten seasick. When they finally emerged, it was to empty their stomachs over the side of the boat. Alberto, too, was pale green after baking on the deck. "Imagine lying there for four hours without moving," he said. As the travelers leaned over, retching, Juan Carlos held them by the waist to keep them from tumbling overboard. He sprinkled cold water over El Duque's and Alberto's heads. In retrospect, it should have been a moment of relief, jubilation even, the beginning of a new life. But the celebration was tempered by a tableau of contorted faces and prostrate bodies scattered across the deck.

Within a few hours everyone had recovered sufficiently to prepare for the next stage: the transfer at Anguilla Cay. The boats were to meet at five P.M. between the Santaren and Nicholas Channels, not far from the uninhabited island. Using navigational charts, Juan Carlos had given El Argentino and Tío precise coordinates for the spot where the transfer would take place. The hardest part, it had seemed to everyone, would be getting out of Cuba. Once that was accomplished, it was a matter of loading everyone onto a speedboat and eluding the U.S. Coast Guard long enough to make a landing at Key Biscayne. Tío, who had poured $50,000 into El Duque's freedom thus far, stood by with rented vans. He planned to take the group directly from the beach to the Krone Detention Center, an INS way station, where El Duque and his companions would then be processed and admitted into the United States as political refugees.

Like clockwork, Juan Carlos maneuvered the boat near Anguilla Cay at around five P.M. In total, the trip had taken about ten hours. The passengers surveyed their surroundings. Nearby was the island—islands, actually, an uninviting strand of rocks rising out of the sea. The main island was a sliver, perhaps eight miles long and several hundred yards wide, carpeted with palmettos and dull brush. Along the edges were intermittent patches of white sand, but it was hardly Club Med. Anguilla Cay was a desolate speck rising in the middle of a void. Wind-lashed and exposed, it looked like it might easily disappear in a heavy storm. But where was the other boat? Juan Carlos pulled out his binoculars and stared toward Miami, a good seventy miles away. He saw a desert of vacant sea. As the afternoon passed, the crew became fearful that something had gone terribly wrong. They had not prepared for this. Confident that Tío would easily complete the back end of the Cuba-Anguilla-Miami double play, El Duque had packed little more than his cigarettes. He wore jeans, a dark shirt and tennis shoes. Noris wore a Yankee jersey that Ray Sánchez had given El Duque as a gift. She, too, carried little. Osmany had brought two cans of Spam. The best-prepared crew member was Juan Carlos Romero, who had the presence of mind to cart along ten pounds of sugar and a tank containing several gallons of drinking water. That and Osmany's Spam represented the entirety of their provisions.

It was getting dark now, and Juan Carlos's partners needed to get back. Soon people would notice they were missing. They wanted their return to Cuba to be as inconspicuous as possible. The crew decided to get off the boat and wait. It could not be long now. The boat drew next to a beach on the south side of Anguilla Cay. Once again everyone piled into the water. Juan Carlos grabbed the sugar, the drinking water, a few blankets and a tank of diesel fuel and set them on the sand. His two partners remained on the boat, waiting, hoping that they would not have to abandon the group. After an hour, however, they reluctantly headed back. Slowly, the fishing boat disappeared into the immense darkness. El Duque and the others sat on the beach, listening to the engine trailing off, until the only sound they heard was lapping surf. Now they were totally alone.

Knowing that the transfer might take place in the dark, Osmany had brought along an unsophisticated beacon: a 35-millimeter camera with a built-in flash that a tourist had given him as cab fare. Now, with everyone clustered on the sand, squinting to locate the tardy rescuers, Osmany aimed the camera into the night. He snapped at every odd sound or movement he detected or thought he detected. Everyone chimed in, shouting, "Osmany, over there! Over there!" For hours, Osmany flashed the camera at ghosts until finally, after midnight, the wind kicked up, the starlit sky glazed over and it began to rain. Osmany flashed with greater urgency now. He raised the camera and fired off dozens of trigger-happy blasts that picked up the rain like a strobe. "I was desperate," he said. "We were stranded on a fucking island. I just wanted somebody to see us."

"Hey, Osmany, don't play around with the camera," said El Duque, crouching in the sand. "We're gonna need that camera. You're gonna break it if you keep flashing so much."

Osmany kept shooting. The boat had to be out there somewhere, he figured, searching in the dark. The last thing he wanted was for it to turn back.

That would be even worse. *Flash! Flash! Flash!* Then, as El Duque warned him yet again, Osmany shot off a flash and the rain-slicked camera slipped from his grasp, tumbling into the sand at his feet.

"It got all wet," said Juan Carlos. "There was sand all over it and it just broke. The flash wouldn't work anymore. The camera was fucked. We were fucked. Now we had no way to signal a passing boat.

"Orlando started yelling, 'Osmany, you fucking shit-eater! You're always playing around! Now look what you did! Now they won't see us!' "

"The camera was the only instrument we had to generate light," said Osmany. "Everyone had been telling me to leave the camera alone, don't use it too much. As soon as they warned me, it broke. Orlando was yelling, 'You are so fucking stupid! I've been telling you for the longest time, "Don't play with the fucking camera!" ' "

"Joel was cursing Osmany, too," said Geidy. "And we were all trying to fix the camera. But we couldn't bring it back to life."

"Everybody took turns tapping it, trying to shake the sand out of it," said Juan Carlos, "but there was nothing. No flash."

When the bickering finally ended, the exhausted group fell silent and stared into the dark. The rain eventually stopped and, one by one, everyone fell asleep on the tiny beach at Anguilla Cay.

RISING EARLY THE NEXT morning, the group could see exactly how alone they were. For miles around there was nothing but water. After passing around thin slices of Spam and sugar water, the group began to explore. Wandering the shoreline, they discovered a rafter's graveyard. "There were candles and boat engines and wrecks—all the people who had been there before us," said Alberto Hernández. "You wouldn't believe the stuff. It was everywhere." Juan Carlos tied a scrap of white cloth to an old engine to signal a passing boat. Then they all began to scavenge. There were discarded tarpaulins to sit on and tents to keep out the rain, now coming in sporadic squalls. Everyone foraged for dry wood. Juan Carlos discovered a charcoal stove. He sparked a fire using a splash of diesel fuel, the wood and El Duque's lighter. "So many people had stopped on the island that whatever you needed to survive was there," he said.

The group found pots and pans, but of course there was no food to cook. Alberto came upon a solution. Midway through the second day everyone was famished, and he suggested that they peel off the conch shells that had fastened themselves on the rocks. The women, Noris and Geidy, were repulsed by the idea and continued to subsist on sugar and water, but the men were game. Juan

Carlos used a pocketknife to pry the shells from the rocks. The conch was then tossed into a pot of boiling seawater and eaten from the shell.

Every couple of hours or so, El Duque grasped the amulet he kept around his neck. "It was like a small cloth bag he had," said Geidy. "It was red. It was a Santería thing. He wouldn't tell us what was inside. It was a secret. He would take it out and walk away to pray. Norita would encourage him. She would tell him, 'Go ahead, ask them to help us. Say a prayer for us.'"

The group alternated from hope to despair and anger. One moment, El Duque would be cursing Tío and El Argentino for stranding them all. The next he would be speculating that it must be the bad weather that was keeping them away. He insisted that the boat was still coming.

But it wasn't. After receiving confirmation of El Duque's departure from Caibarién, Tío and El Argentino had set their plan in motion. Tío headed to Key Biscayne to await his grandnephew's arrival. El Argentino, meanwhile, dispatched a boat toward Anguilla Cay. "We had two people heading out to pick them up in a launch," said Tío, "but the boat started taking on water as soon as it left Miami. They jumped into the water in life vests as the boat was sinking. The plan was to pick them all up and deliver them to Key Biscayne, but that didn't happen. We were waiting out there and they never showed up. If we had a millionaire working with us, we could have sent another boat. But I was doing it all alone."

The exact nature of the boat's failure—why, where and when it occurred—has never been adequately explained. Even Tío, who orchestrated the escape, offers scant details. By the time I saw El Argentino, a few days later, the story of El Duque's escape had already taken on a life of its own and bore little resemblance to reality. I haven't seen him since.

Regardless of how the second boat was waylaid, though, it was the defector equivalent of Bill Buckner allowing Mookie Wilson's ground ball to pass through his legs in the 1986 World Series. Tío was now facing a desperate situation. He knew that El Duque and the others were out there, waiting and exposed. He had to get them. But how? For help, he turned to Brothers to the Rescue, the volunteer aviators now better known for their confrontation with the Cuban MiGs. "One day out of the blue we got a call to provide assistance for this group," said José Basulto, the Brothers' leader. He agreed to help, albeit reluctantly. Basulto was annoyed that so much urgency had been attached to a ballplayer while so many thousands had faced similar danger. The caller even offered a reward. "I said, 'I'm sorry, we don't take money to find anybody,'" said Basulto. "I said, 'This organization is financed by the community and we don't work on behalf of specific groups.' All this for a stupid baseball player."

Convinced that the group might be in danger, however, he agreed to make an attempt.

Brothers to the Rescue knew Anguilla Cay like the back of its hand. The island is part of an unimpressive chain known as the Cay Sal Bank. The bank basically consists of a few dozen rocks standing between Cuba and South Florida in the remote southwest of the Bahamas. The rocks have names like Muertos Cays (Dead Man's Cays), Dogs Rocks and Double-Headed Shot Cays. The Brothers had been rescuing rafters from the area for years. The plane made several passes over Anguilla Cay in search of El Duque but found nothing. The search team then moved on to nearby islands, figuring that the group had taken refuge elsewhere. Still nothing. After scouring the area, the planes finally returned to Miami.

What the Brothers didn't know was that El Duque and the others were hiding behind the palmettos. They believed—incorrectly—that if the U.S. Coast Guard picked them up they would be sent back to Cuba. It is here that the bizarre and contradictory U.S. immigration laws come into play in the El Duque saga. Under the 1994 agreement between Fidel and the Clinton administration, you may recall, Cubans intercepted at sea were to be sent back except in cases of demonstrable persecution or medical need (the floating child Elián González, for example). Under the 1966 Cuban Adjustment Act, however, rafters who reached U.S. soil were still welcomed as political refugees. Anguilla Cay was a worthless, uninhabitable spit of land, but because that spit was Bahamian territory, El Duque and the others would be taken to neither Cuba nor the United States. The Bahamian government would decide their fate.

The group did not know this, however, so they hid in the bushes until the planes were gone. "The plane passed overhead twice," said Osmany. "We thought it was the Coast Guard so we hid."

As the hours passed it occurred to everyone that there was an outstanding issue that needed to be addressed: the explanation for their arrival on the Cay. What would they say, exactly, when asked how they got there? Everyone agreed that the real story was inadequate. It would lead the Cuban authorities directly to the two men who went back with the fishing boat. If El Duque declared publicly that a boat had dropped him off, State Security would eventually figure it out and go after Juan Carlos's partners. "We couldn't just give away the people who dropped us off," said Geidy.

"No, we agreed that we needed a story," said Juan Carlos. "We couldn't just say that we fell out of the sky."

For those seeking an explanation for why El Duque's escape later became such a mystery, this is where it all began. "There's a saying in Cuba: A lie repeated many times becomes the truth," said Lenin Rivero. "That is so true. That's what happened with us. We made up this story, stuck to it, and eventually it became true for us and the whole world."

"Orlando practically made up the whole version," said Lenin. "He said, 'We're going to say that Juan Carlos was the *patrón* of the boat.' He told me that I was going to say that I organized the trip. He stood there and told each of us exactly what we were going to say. He had a lot of it laid out in his mind. We all added a few details here and there."

In the lie's original form, the fictitious vessel was a twenty-foot sailboat that Juan Carlos had built in Caibarién. The story went that the boat began to take on water after leaving Cuba. Nine hours later it staggered into Anguilla Cay, then sank. That would explain the absence of the boat if anyone bothered to ask. The group sat on the beach, embroidering the great lie. "Everybody agreed on it," said Juan Carlos. "It was El Duque's story but we all added our own little embellishments as we went along." It seemed like a harmless enough stretch, a necessary fib to protect the people who had helped get them out of Cuba. Within a year, though, a story that had begun as a thread would emerge from the media rinse cycle in the form of an Armani suit.

Nights on the island were cold. Everyone huddled around the fire, which was now burning constantly. The group passed the time with small talk. Osmany told some of his favorite jokes. ("The biggest joke was my body odor," he said. "I hadn't showered in days. Nobody wanted to stand near me. None of us had showered, but my body odor must have been different.") El Duque talked about his dreams of playing in the major leagues, the riches he would make. Eventually, the talk came around to the players' real ages. Like El Duque, Alberto was well into his thirties. El Duque's cousin, Joel Pedroso, was a young catcher, but he had little experience and needed all the help he could get. From the beginning of time, Latin American ballplayers have been shaving years from their ages. The problem in this case, they all realized, was that U.S. immigration would undoubtedly request identification if and when they were processed into the country.

There was a tidy solution for that, too. What if they didn't have any identification? And so it came to pass that one more piece of fiction was concocted on the deserted island. No one could recall who got the idea first, but as they sat on the beach one evening El Duque, Alberto and Joel pulled out their various pieces of identification: driver's licenses, ID cards, "all the papers they used in Cuba to keep track of us like dogs," said Alberto. Together, the players held up the documents and pitched them into the campfire.

"We burned everything," said Alberto. "We threw our identities into the fire."

BY DAY THREE, the group was playing baseball, using planks as bats and chunks of old buoys as balls. There was nothing else to do except wait and hope. The chance that Tío's boat was coming was growing dimmer. It also seemed less likely that the group would be discovered anytime soon. It was December 28, 1997: the dead week between Christmas and New Year's. They figured that even the U.S. Coast Guard would be taking it easy. With little food and a dwindling water supply ("water, water, everywhere, nor any drop to drink"), the situation had become precarious. Not all-out panic, but moving in that direction. At one point, Osmany and El Duque took a long walk together. After a while, Osmany stopped to rest but El Duque kept going, searching for any sign of hope. Osmany sat on the beach, watching his friend walk and walk along the shore until he become a dot on the horizon.

The general mood was darkening when, suddenly, out of nowhere, a helicopter appeared. The group's first instinct was to hide again. But when everyone considered their predicament, they decided otherwise. Bursting out onto the beach, the group jumped and waved their arms. The helicopter stopped and hovered within a few hundred yards. The pilot waved in acknowledgment then flew off.

"The helicopter left and then we waited," said Juan Carlos. "We expected to be picked up. We spent the whole day waiting. Night came and nothing. Everyone was getting desperate. During the first hours of the morning we all went out to check. We looked around. Then, coming from the east we saw a Coast Guard boat getting closer and closer."

Actually, it was Joel Pedroso who first spotted the boat. El Duque's cousin had wandered off into the bushes to relieve himself. "When he saw the boat he just took off running," said Osmany. "He was still holding his pants. He didn't even stop to wipe. He just ran, shouting, 'There's a boat! There's a boat!' When we saw him, he was running toward us, trying to put on his pants."

The group waved as the boat drew closer. Because of the shallow reef encircling the island, it stopped about two hundred yards from shore. The cutter then lowered an inflatable raft with a small engine, and the raft motored within about twenty yards of the beach. As the castaways waded into the water, the raft made three trips to ferry them to the cutter. Osmany, Joel and Lenín went in the first group, Norita, Geidy and Juan Carlos in the second, El Duque and Alberto in the third.

Shortly after, the group was transferred to another boat: the *Baranof,* a 110-foot Coast Guard cutter based out of Miami. Used primarily for search-and-rescue and to interdict immigrants and drug smugglers, the *Baranof* was on a routine five-day patrol of the Florida Straits. The boarding officers guided the Cubans to the stern, where the group sat in the open air. The weather was miserable: rain, with choppy seas. A Coast Guard officer brought blankets, coffee and rice and beans, which Alberto immediately spit up. Juan Carlos happened to glance at the American flag rippling in the wind. It indicated that the boat was headed north.

"They're taking us to the United States," he announced, to everyone's relief.

Then, without warning, the boat shifted directions.

Juan Carlos made another announcement.

"We've changed directions," he said. "We're heading toward Havana."

"What?"

"Look at the flag: We're headed back to Havana."

It was true. Upstairs, the Coast Guard had three other Cuban rafters in custody. It appeared that they were all being sent back. El Duque leaped out of his seat. He summoned the first American he saw. He asked Geidy, the only member of the group who spoke passable English, to inform the officer that he was the brother of Liván Hernández, the famous pitcher. Then he tried to drive home the point himself.

"Liván bro-ther, Liván bro-ther," said El Duque in halting English. "Baseball. Baseball. *Pelota.* Baseball."

The ship's translator, Irving Puig, arrived on the scene. El Duque repeated his message.

Puig, a son of Cuban immigrants, turned to boarding officer Allen Bandrowsky.

"Hey, this guy says he's Liván Hernández's brother," said Puig.

Bandrowsky was from Cleveland. Two months earlier, he had watched Liván shackle his beloved Tribe in the World Series.

"Oh, yeah?" said Bandrowsky. "Tell him I'm an Indians fan. He's not getting any sympathy from me."

In truth, the only thing that mattered was where El Duque had been picked up. On that score, Anguilla Cay saved him and the rest of the group. The other rafters had been rescued at sea. In the cold-blooded language of applied immigration policy, they had been caught "wet foot" and were headed back to Cuba.* El Duque's group of eight had been found on Bahamian soil, pitiful as

---

*Cuban immigrants who reach U.S. soil are "dry foot" and thus eligible for asylum.

it was. They would be taken to the Bahamas, whose authorities would then decide how to dispose of them.

That was a relief, obviously, but it also meant more time on the roiling seas. The refugees were placed in a narrow upstairs passageway. As the boat rocked, everyone became violently ill. Rain and surf pelted them so relentlessly that at one point Osmany nearly fell over the railing. "The Coast Guard wasn't paying any attention," he said. "They didn't really care. If I fell they wouldn't have given a shit. It would have been, 'Oops, there goes another Cuban rafter.'" As Juan Carlos pulled him back by his belt, Osmany turned around and threw up all over him. "It was awful," said Juan Carlos. "The vomit was all over my legs. Our feet and our pants were soaked in seawater and vomit. The vomit was sloshing back and forth in the water." The castaways were eventually brought inside.

The boat tried to dock in Bimini, but the weather was too rough. It ultimately pulled into Freeport. There, El Duque and his companions finally set foot on land. They were whisked from the dock to the airport, where a wire-service reporter took a brief statement and issued the first dispatch on the pitcher's escape. Then the group was flown to Nassau.

There, the situation wasn't much better. Leaving the small plane, the men were handcuffed and separated briefly from the women. Then they were all taken by bus to the Carmichael Road Detention Center, a bleak holding facility on the outskirts of Nassau. El Duque and his companions joined hundreds of wayward immigrants: Cubans, Haitians, Dominicans, all living in cramped, rat-infested dorms. A double chain-link fence topped by barbed wire surrounded the squalid compound. Armed guards manned the exits. "I felt like a criminal," said Geidy. "Norita and I were crying uncontrollably. We were so scared. I couldn't eat, and I hadn't eaten in four days. All I had had was water and sugar."

The group knew little at that point, but one piece of information was particularly disturbing: The Bahamas, it turned out, had a repatriation agreement with Cuba. If the law was to be followed, El Duque and his companions would soon be sent home.

AFTER SPENDING CHRISTMAS vacation in Los Angeles, my wife, Erin, and I were flying to New York when I got the news. As embarrassing as it is to admit, I was checking my voice mail from the plane. There was a frantic message from René Guim—back then, most of René's messages could have been described as "frantic"; such were the times. When I called him back, the details were still sketchy. He said it had been confirmed that El Duque, Noris and Alberto were in the Bahamas, but the government was threatening to deport them. There also seemed to be five other defectors, but no one was certain who they were. I figured Osmany had to be among them. I dictated a brief story from the plane and then booked a flight to Nassau for the next morning.

I pulled up at the Bahamas immigration office just after noon. It was an oddly cheerful building, pink, its parking lot filled with broadcast vehicles topped with satellite dishes. A receptionist informed me that I had arrived just in time for the press conference. Suitcases in hand, I walked up to the third floor. There, in a small conference room, was the entire Miami press corps, a camera crew from CNN, the wire services and reporters from *The New York Times* and *The Washington Post*. Also present, standing toward the back, were Joe Cubas and René Guim. Separate from them and looking strangely uncomfortable were Tío and the thin, dark-haired man known as El Argentino.

I couldn't have been there for more than two minutes when the door flew open and in walked El Duque. We fell into another dramatic embrace—a Cuban defector and the unbiased Latin America correspondent for *The Boston Globe*—in a scene captured, much to my chagrin, by CNN. Behind El Duque trailed everyone else: Noris, Osmany, Joel, Alberto, Juan Carlos, Geidy and, finally, Lenin. El Duque, his great-uncle and Joel came together in the middle of the conference room, their sobbing heard over the clicking of photographers.

"Thank God you've made it," said Tío.

"Yes, we have," said El Duque, burying his head into his great-uncle's shoulder. "Forever."

Amazingly, no one looked worse for the wear. El Duque had an eye infection that he said he had picked up before he left Cuba. He wore a Charlotte Hornets pullover and looked a little thin. Everyone else was fine, so much so that they then proceeded to field questions from the media.

The first questions were about baseball. How's the fastball, Duque? Would you like to play on the same team as your brother? Finally someone asked something to the effect of: "So, how did you guys get here?"

Out poured the now famous Robinson Crusoe medley: the fictitious twenty-foot sailboat that Juan Carlos supposedly had constructed with his own bare hands; the water gathering ominously in the bottom of the boat; the four oars with which the men had so gallantly rowed for dear life; and finally, land ahoy! At that point there was no mention of sharks or bad weather—that would come later—and the boat was most assuredly a sailboat, not a "rickety raft." Except for a few minor embellishments, their account of the four days on

Anguilla Cay was much the same as it is here. Their enthusiasm for the lie, though, bordered on breathless: "This is the guy who built the boat!" Osmany told me by way of an introduction to Juan Carlos.

Like everyone else, I lapped it up and wrote it for page one of the *Globe.* Who could have imagined that someone would fabricate his own shipwreck?

After the press conference, Cubas walked up to speak with the players. Neither Tío nor El Argentino tried to stop him. Cubas's feud with Liván, and by extension El Duque, was miraculously behind him. The agent's first move was to press $500 into Alberto's palm. "That's to help you guys eat," he said. He then gave specific instructions on how they should comport themselves. Their case needed to be public, he said. They needed to keep pressing for political asylum whenever possible. They were political refugees. Cubas's goal was to shame the Bahamians into holding the players until he could devise a way to get them out. The press conference was his idea. Under extreme pressure, bucking an international treaty, no less, Cubas's performance that day was masterful. No one could have handled it better. Certainly, one could quarrel with Cubas's business practices and his scruples, but it was impossible to question his skills as a man of action. Earlier that morning, Cubas had wanted to get a message to El Duque and Alberto at the detention center. The guards wouldn't let him inside. Cubas thus scribbled a note on a page of René Guim's Day-Timer, ripped it out and wrapped the note in a $100 bill. He handed the bribe to one of the guards, who took the money and eagerly delivered the message to the players.

Now, after the press conference, the Bahamians announced that no deportations would take place while the cases were being evaluated. It was, at least, a temporary reprieve. Everyone descended to the parking lot, where the group of eight was loaded onto an orange bus that looked like a Disneyland shuttle. The group's destination was not Tomorrowland but the Carmichael Road Detention Center. Everything in the Bahamas was cheerful, even the bus that took you back to jail. The defectors seemed in good spirits despite the resumption of their confinement. Osmany heckled me from the bus. "This could have been you," he kept saying. "This could have been you."

El Duque then pointed at El Argentino, standing off to the side with Tío. "That's our representative," he told me. As the trolley sped off, I went over and introduced myself. El Argentino didn't seem to speak much English. He said he was a family friend and a businessman in Miami. I asked him if he had any experience as a baseball agent. He said no but that he didn't think that would be a major problem. What a circus! El Duque was incarcerated in the Bahamas, but here he was holding press conferences. He already had an agent, albeit one who did not speak English, had no experience and went by the nom de guerre El Argentino. Meanwhile, across the parking lot stood the infamous Joe Cubas, sweating under the hot sun. I walked over and asked if he, too, was representing El Duque. He said that, yes, in fact, El Duque and Alberto had asked him to represent them "on certain matters." He declined to say what those matters were. He said he had to go. At that very moment in Miami a couple hundred people were gathering in his backyard to celebrate New Year's Eve.

What happened next is like a primer on the power of the Cuban exile community in this country—at least at the time. One of the smartest decisions the players had made upon arriving in Nassau was to place a call to the Cuban American National Foundation in Miami. Ninoska Pérez, the foundation's spokeswoman, and her assistant Mariela Ferretti were just getting ready to walk out the door. "We were getting ready for the new year," Pérez recalled. "It was a little before five and the phone started ringing just as we were about to close the door. I never like to leave when the phone is ringing. So we go back and Mariela picks up the phone and she says, 'You have a collect call from the Bahamas.'

"This is very common, you know. There are a lot of Cubans detained in the Bahamas and they like to call us. I thought, you know, it's New Year's, and they're lonely, so I pick up the phone and the guy says, 'This is El Duque. I'm Liván's brother.' I said, 'Oh my God!' I talked to him and I asked him if they were okay, and he told me who was there with him. I tried getting Liván on the phone but he wasn't answering. At least I was able to call the press. It was amazing because in fifteen minutes we had press from all over the world calling."

Within hours the Miami media had filled up the flights to Nassau, so quickly in fact that Cubas had to barter with a television station to get a seat. The foundation also called on one of its members, Gerardo Capó (pronounced Cah-po), a Miami developer who happened to be vacationing in the Bahamas. Capó had vast holdings in Nassau, and he called the Bahamian foreign minister, Janet Boswick, and bought some time for the players. Capó said that if he hadn't been in the Bahamas, "El Duque would have been back in Cuba, right then and there. His plane was leaving at nine-thirty the next morning." The combined pressure from Capó, Cubas and the media had cowed the Bahamians into ignoring their own repatriation agreement with the Cuban government.

Now that the deportation had been stayed, the Cuban American National Foundation shifted its considerable influence toward the U.S. government. It mobilized its all-star team of anti-Castro hard-liners: Florida senators Connie Mack (the grandson of the legendary Philadelphia A's manager) and Bob Graham; South Florida representatives Ileana Ros-Lehtinen and Lincoln Díaz-Balart; and Senator Robert Torricelli and Congressman Bob Menendez of New Jersey. The politicians, in turn, began to press the State Department's Cuba desk. Within hours, El Duque's predicament had become a cause célèbre. The Clinton administration scrambled to respond, much of the activity flowing through Lula Rodríguez, the State Department's deputy assistant secretary of state for public affairs. A political appointee, Rodríguez had twenty-five years' experience in Cuban-American relations—she had even helped process refugees from Mariel—and she knew most everyone involved. Vacationing with her assistant, Sue Walitsky, Rodríguez converted her Miami home into a kind of State Department South. She fielded dozens of frantic calls from Liván, his agent Juan Iglesias, Capó and representatives from the INS, the White House and the State Department.

The decision took all of one day. The U.S. government extended "humanitarian parole" to El Duque, Alberto and Noris. The other five defectors were on their own. Rodríguez told me the government invoked a provision in U.S. immigration law that grants asylum to unusually gifted applicants. The same provision had been applied to dancer Mikhail Baryshnikov and Soviet dissident Aleksandr Solzhenitsyn, among others. Certainly, the players deserved asylum: Their claims were airtight. But the swiftness with which the U.S. government had moved was staggering. When the Cuban exile community and its surrogates shifted into high gear, U.S. government bureaucrats worked on New Year's Eve to secure visas for two baseball players. The decision was announced a few hours before midnight.

I immediately took a cab over to the Carmichael detention center. When I pulled up, El Duque was standing alone in the courtyard, behind the double chain-link fence. He was bathed in floodlights, idly smoking a cigar that one of the Bahamian guards had given him. I yelled the news through the fence.

"The U.S. government gave you a visa."

I'll never forget this: His immediate response was neither joy nor surprise but concern for his friends.

"What about the others?" he asked.

"No. It's just you, Norita and Alberto."

"If the others aren't given them as well, it's still not great news," he said.

He was still standing there when I left, his cigar smoke drifting into the warm night. We wished each other a Happy New Year. It was now about ninety minutes until midnight and I went to find a hotel. I figured my chances were slim. People were already staggering through the streets with noisemakers and half-quaffed bottles of champagne. The cab pulled up at a Marriott. I went to the front desk, which was covered in colorful streamers. The sound of slot machines emanated from the casino. The desk clerk was wearing a glittery pointy hat. She informed me that, in fact, there were a few rooms available. Fantastic, I said, how much? Four hundred dollars, she responded cheerfully.

Back in Miami, Joe Cubas barely made it home in time. Exhausted, he walked through his living room to the backyard. The New Year's Eve party was in full swing. Slowly, people began to notice that the host had arrived. The El Duque drama had been all over television. Cubas began to work the crowd, shaking hands, apologizing for his lateness. Then one of his guests started to clap, and then another, until Cubas was standing in his own backyard, awash in applause over his latest coup. "To be a man of action in Miami," wrote Joan Didion, "was to receive encouragement from many quarters."

It was New Year's Eve 1958, of course, when the dictator Fulgencio Batista stepped aside. In Havana, supporters of Fidel Castro took to the streets, ransacking Shell stations and government newspapers and, finally, the casinos of the mob-run hotels. Slot machines and craps tables were reduced to kindling and pitched into the bonfires that raged in Old Havana. The dictator and the mobsters and the gringos fled by air and by sea, leaving the island to Fidel and the Cuban people. Now, thirty-nine New Year's Eves later, Fidel Castro was seventy-one years old. As Cuba celebrated another anniversary of its spent revolution, El Duque Hernández, once one of its proudest symbols, stood in a Bahamian jail, smoking a fat cigar, quietly contemplating his American future.

THE NEXT MORNING, New Year's Day, El Duque, Noris and Alberto walked out of Carmichael with tears in their eyes. The five others watched them leave, their fingers threaded through the chain-link fence. Also looking on were dozens of other rafters who had drifted to the Bahamas in much the same fashion. Many had been there for months. As television cameras filmed El Duque's exit, one refugee held up a towel bearing a hand-scrawled message: FREEDOM FOR ALL THE CUBANS.

"I can't even look back," said El Duque as he boarded a black van.

They were driven to the Atlantis Resort and Casino, where Gerardo Capó assumed responsibility for their welfare. Capó didn't know the players, but they were Cuban and that was enough for him. Like many people who were drawn into the El Duque saga, he felt a moral obligation to assist fellow Cubans. He also relished the opportunity to strike against the man who had altered his fate forever. "Every time you can do something against the Castro regime you should not hesitate," he said. "I knew this meant a lot to Castro. El Duque was poor. El Duque was black. He represented everyone who Castro tells the Cuban people doesn't stand a chance in the United States of America."

Capó's story is the story of thousands of people in Miami, the strivers who transformed an American city overnight. He was eighteen when he came to the States, five months after Batista's downfall. Like everyone else, he figured that he and his family would be returning to Cuba any day. "We thought it was going to be a short exile," he said. "It has lasted forty-one years."

Capó worked first as a messenger, netting $32.50 a week. He gave $25 of that to his parents. He then quit his job to join the impending Bay of Pigs invasion. "I went to see my father and told him I was enlisting," said Capó. "He said, 'Where are you going?' I said, 'I'm going to fight like a good Cuban.' He says, 'You think you have ten minutes to talk before you leave?' Then he started to lecture me without telling me not to go. He told me exactly what was going to happen. He told me all these guys are going to get killed. The ones who are not killed are going to jail. He said we weren't going to get any backup." Dissuaded by his father, who had correctly forecast the invasion's outcome, Capó helped the cause by running arms shipments into Cuba in rented planes.

By 1964, with American efforts to topple Castro in disarray, Capó and his father borrowed money to open an appliance store in Little Havana. By the following year, business was booming, so Capó's father, also named Gerardo, sold the store and put his money into a housing development in the Dominican Republic. No sooner had they arrived in Santo Domingo, however, when an uprising broke out and U.S. Marines swept in to prevent a "second Cuba" in the Caribbean. The Capós lost everything. Thinking they would be evacuated to Miami, they were flown instead to Puerto Rico with "about eighty Dominican cents in our pockets."

The Capós had been exiled yet again. Instead of returning to Miami, they set out to rebuild their lives in San Juan. Capó's father worked as a cashier in a Cuban restaurant. Capó made sandwiches. Eventually, they went into business selling garbage bins for $145 apiece. "People used to have these fifty-five-gallon drums that they kept outside with the flies and the stench," he said. "Ours were enclosed. It kept the flies out. We used to call it the Magic Box." The Capós made a killing on Magic Boxes. Then they invested in real estate—first in Puerto Rico, then in Miami. By the time Capó's and El Duque's paths crossed, Capó was taking a vacation from his job running Ameri-Housing Corp., which built six hundred homes a year in Dade County alone. Capó lived in one of his twenty-five-story condominium developments. He called it Capo Bella.

Capó listened as El Duque and Alberto described their perilous escape, the botched pickup on Anguilla Cay. "These people who were going to pick them up out there, I call them the Gang That Couldn't Shoot Straight," said Capó, laughing. "They wanted to be his agent, but they didn't know the business. They couldn't speak English." Capó set up the players in one of his town houses as they tried to figure out how to get their friends out of the Carmichael detention center. Once again El Argentino was of little help. The players were still fuming over his lame explanation for the Anguilla Cay debacle. Now the entire deal was unraveling.

"The guy wasn't serious," said Alberto. "First he told us the boat sank. That wasn't good enough—I mean, we were out there for four fucking days. Then he didn't do anything to get us out of jail, and suddenly he shows up and says, 'I'm your agent.'

"When we got out of jail Orlando asked him about the others. He didn't have an answer for that, either. Orlando said, 'Look, you have to get those five people out of jail.' He said, 'No, let's leave now and we'll see what we can do for them later.' Orlando said, 'We're not moving.' Orlando asked him, 'What would you do if those people were sent back to Cuba?' He said that he would cry for the rest of his life. Orlando said, 'Well, you won't have to cry. We're going to resolve this now.'

"We needed somebody with more clout. That's when we decided to call Joe Cubas. I was the one who called him."

It was the return of El Gordo. On January 2, Cubas flew back to the Bahamas. Capó sent a limousine to meet him at the airport. The limo took Cubas to the Atlantis resort, where the players and the agent quickly struck an agreement. The feckless El Argentino was out. Cubas was in. Even Tío had to agree that it was the right thing to do. At the last minute, Liván, fresh off his appearance as grand marshal in the Orange Bowl parade, tried to warn off El Duque from dealing with his former agent. But El Duque realized that there was perhaps one man in the entire world with the skills to liberate his friends from the detention center and then set about negotiating a major-league contract.

Cubas had his work cut out for him. The Bahamian government, which had already violated its agreement with Cuba, was refusing to release the remaining crewmembers without a guarantee that Cubas would take them immediately to a third country. In this respect, however, the government's interests intersected with his own. As usual Cubas was practicing his own special brand of venture humanitarianism. He wanted to take El Duque and Alberto to a third country as soon as possible to register the players as free agents. Among other things, that would mean discarding the hard-won U.S. visas. And that is exactly what the players did.* Lula Rodríguez, who had worked nonstop to procure the visas, said she was not "hurt or disappointed," but the decision infuriated others in the U.S. government who, of course, had worked overtime on New Year's Eve to stave off El Duque's deportation.

No matter. Within a week Cubas had secured seven visas from not one but two countries: Costa Rica and Nicaragua. He preferred Costa Rica, but the Nicaraguan visas came in first. He used them to persuade the Bahamians to release the five remaining refugees. On the morning of January 7, Osmany, Joel, Juan Carlos, Geidy and Lenin walked out of the Carmichael detention center, their arms raised in triumph. They were loaded into the festive orange trolley and taken to the Nassau airport, where a Learjet waited on the tarmac.

The plane was scheduled to leave in the early afternoon. Cubas, in possession of the Nicaraguan visas, had routed the plane to Managua, but he actually wanted to go to Costa Rica. The Nicaraguan visas, secured by Lincoln Díaz-Balart, the South Florida congressman, were only temporary. In Costa Rica, the players stood a far better chance of establishing residency, and thus, reaching the ultimate goal, free agency, the key to untold millions. Cubas still had not received confirmation from the Costa Rican government, however, and neither the Bahamians nor the charter company was about to release a planeload of undocumented Cubans to a country that had not authorized their arrival.

Cubas stalled through the afternoon. If the plane didn't leave soon, the Bahamians finally told him, they planned to throw everyone back into the detention center, including El Duque and Alberto. The charter company, meanwhile, was threatening to pull its plane back to Florida. Cubas was pressing René Guim in Miami, who in turn was pressing the Costa Ricans to produce the letter of authorization. "Cubas had this guy working for him in Costa Rica to get the letter, and the guy was drunk!" said Guim. "He's saying, 'But *Don Reneeeeee, por favooooor.*' Finally I said, 'Listen, you got twenty minutes to send me this fucking letter.'

"Finally, the letter comes in," said Guim, "but it isn't signed and it doesn't have the seal. I fax it over to Joe at the executive center at the Nassau airport. Joe says to me—well, what he said was—'I can't give this to these nigger bastards. They'll throw it in the garbage. You gotta doctor it up.'

"So I take the letter, take out a pen and sign it myself. Then I took one of those In-Out stamps that they have in every office. I stamped the letter, smudged the shit out of it and I faxed it back to Joe. Joe says, 'It just came

---

*Noris used her visa to fly ahead to Miami with Capó.

through. Looks good. Looks good. Okay. We got it! We got it! We're on our way.' At the same time I've got Murray Chass of *The New York Times* on the other line, waiting for the story. I'm telling him, 'Okay, Murray, they're just about out of there.' "

Cubas gathered everyone on the tarmac. Inside the plane were several bottles of champagne that Guim had ordered up from Miami. Cubas pulled out a bottle and eight glasses and popped the cork right in the middle of the tarmac of the Nassau international airport. The group raised a toast to the end of their ordeal. Then everyone piled into the plane.

But, incredibly, it wasn't over. The Bahamians wouldn't let Cubas change the flight plan. The plane had to go to Nicaragua, they insisted. The government didn't know anything about Costa Rica and, at that point, didn't care. The charter company, meanwhile, was demanding another $3,000 for delays. Cubas got out of the plane. "It was complete chaos," he said. "The Bahamian immigration guy is saying, 'You are going to Nicaragua, *now!*' And I'm trying to convince the pilot to fly to Costa Rica."

On the spot, Cubas devised a solution as only he could. First, he asked Guim to pay for the Learjet. Guim dutifully complied, whipping out his own Visa card. Then Cubas lied to the Bahamians and said the plane was flying to Nicaragua. At the same time, he showed the pilot the doctored letter of confirmation from Costa Rica and asked him to change the flight plan when the plane refueled in Jamaica.

And that, according to Cubas and Guim, is what happened. The plane took off, refueled in Kingston, then continued to San José, Costa Rica. Inside were several more bottles of champagne. The group drained each and every bottle before drifting off to sleep in the plush leather chairs. The defectors had arrived in the Bahamas on a thirty-foot fishing boat, subsisting on Spam and sugar water. They left in a Learjet, sipping champagne. For El Duque, if not the others, it was a sign of things to come.

CHAPTER FOURTEEN

FREE TRADE

THE PLANE TOUCHED DOWN IN SAN JOSÉ TO A MOB SCENE. THE Costa Rican press had been waiting since the middle of the afternoon. Now it was one A.M. The defectors cleared customs without incident—in fact, they were simply waved through—but the atmosphere outside the airport was like the final scene in *The Year of Living Dangerously*. Hundreds of onlookers, porters, cabdrivers and seething journalists were gathered outside the terminal. As soon as the Cubans appeared, the crowd surged forward, pinning everyone against the building. A television camera butted Cubas in the back of the head, nearly knocking him to the ground. The agent's burly associate, Ramón Batista, had been awaiting the group's arrival and now he thrust himself into the mob, cracking heads as he went. One by one, he pulled the group into vans idling at the curb.

Cubas set up headquarters at the Hemisferio, unquestionably one of the oddest hotels ever built. It was strictly low-rent, two stars at most, with a dimly lit lobby and a barren café. But what gave the Hemisferio its charm was that not a single room came equipped with a window. It was like renting out a room at Manhattan Mini-Storage. This would be everyone's home for the next month. As he would all along, Tío footed the bill, slapping down his credit card for the $40 rooms, an additional $20 for three square meals a day.

From the very beginning, it was clear that El Duque was a changed man. He had never really lost his confidence, but now that he was out of Cuba, away from the eternal punishment that had defined his daily life, the difference was startling. He was still flat broke, ensconced in a Costa Rica fleabag, but he acted as if he already had won. One day Ray Sánchez accompanied El Duque to a shopping mall. For days the pitcher's story had been on the front pages of the local dailies and the TV news. As he practiced his salsa steps on the concourse of the mall, strangers stopped to ask for his autograph. El Duque danced over to the shoe store, to the department store, to the music store, piling up shopping bags as he went. Joel and Osmany, too, shopped till they dropped, trailed by Tío, wielding his fungible magic card. Costa Ricans have a saying for living life to the fullest: *pura vida*, pure life. As Tío pulled out his credit card yet again, he muttered, "*Puro tarjetazo*," pure credit.

That night, decked in their new clothes, the entourage moved on to La Beny, a nightclub–restaurant–strip joint owned by a Cuban exile. The complex was like a pocket of Havana, circa 1957, in the middle of San José. It spanned two city blocks and was named after Beny Moré, the legendary mambo king. El Duque and his entourage began at the claustrophobic strip club. A buxom waitress approached the table. El Duque wanted a Cuba Libre, a rum-and-Coke, the translation of which is "free Cuba." The pitcher smirked, then ordered up a "Mentira con Hielo"—a Lie on the Rocks. The table of exiles, young and old, exploded.

"Finally," said El Duque, still laughing, "I am free."

Across the street was the nightclub. El Duque walked through the door to a standing ovation, as if he were a head of state who had dropped in unexpectedly at the opera. There were some 200 people, mostly exiles, gathered in the garish, smoke-filled room, its walls draped with red velvet curtains. Bottles of Havana Club sprouted from the circular tables, also covered in red. The band, a ten-piece salsa troupe, was already onstage, and the lead singer invited El Duque to say a few words to the crowd.

To more applause, the pitcher sauntered to the front of the room, Mentira con Hielo in hand. Stepping onto the elevated stage, he grabbed the microphone and belted out the lyrics to "La Bola," a Médico de la Salsa number:

> Now I am the king
> Like it or not
> I am the king

But could the king still pitch? That, of course, was the big question. As El Duque was enjoying his freedom, Cubas was working the phones. The agent wanted to set up a major-league tryout as quickly as possible. Within a short time, it became obvious why Cubas had been so desperate to bring the players to Costa Rica: He had turned the tiny Central American republic into a migratory clearinghouse for his clients. Cubas had defectors *stockpiled* in Costa Rica, free agents all. In addition to the recent arrivals, he was sitting on a promising catcher, Francisco Santiesteban, who had defected in Colombia, and an outfielder, Osmany Santana, who had defected in Mexico, among others.

Cubas had the Costa Rican immigration process wired. It took El Duque and the others a day to gain their residency papers, a process that normally took months. Residency, of course, enabled the players to declare free agency. Cubas achieved this miraculous transaction with the help of the minister of labor, Farid Ayales, whose sister, Sandra, coincidentally held a high-ranking position in the Immigration Ministry. Farid Ayales was so accommodating that he later threw a raucous party to help the Cubans celebrate their new immigration status. Exactly how the visas were procured was unclear. With rumors of impropriety thick in the air, the Costa Rican government later opened an investigation into whether the Immigration Ministry had improperly handed out visas to more than a dozen Cuban ballplayers, including El Duque and Rolando Arrojo.

At this point, Morley Safer and *60 Minutes* were hanging around San José—not for El Duque but for Cubas. The newsmagazine was preparing a profile on "the Great Liberator," fresh off his latest triumph. The El Duque tryout would provide the perfect backdrop for the agent's star turn. Cubas had sent out invitations to all thirty major-league clubs. Attendance was expected to be high. After Liván Hernández's performance in the NLCS and the World Series, the words *Cuban ballplayer* now held the same power over Major League Baseball that *Internet stock* later held over financial markets. The words were enough to cause sober-minded baseball scouts to travel to the ends of the earth on a moment's notice.

For his part, El Duque could scarcely believe that he might play baseball again. "What's to come in my life doesn't matter as much as the fact that I will pitch again," he said. "If I pitch in the big leagues, I will be living out my greatest dream. It would be like being born again." To help prepare for his tryout, El Duque asked René Guim, who was flying down from Miami, to bring him a plaster bust of Santa Barbara, the Roman Catholic saint. In the complex relationship between Catholicism and Santería, Santa Barbara is the equal of Changó, the Santería god of war. Practitioners of Santería believe that Changó masquerades as a woman, as Santa Barbara, within the Catholic Church. El Duque wanted to make certain that Guim brought along special candles to properly venerate Santa Barbara before his big tryout.

Guim was already hauling down a lot of stuff. Ever helpful, though, he made the rounds of the Santería stores in Miami. He picked out a nice $200

Santa Barbara and transported the idol to Costa Rica as part of his carry-on luggage.

NOT ALL THE DEFECTORS shared in the excitement over the impending tryout. The futures of Juan Carlos, Geidy and Lenin were far less promising. True, Cubas had helped get them out of the Bahamian detention center, but now that they were all in Costa Rica, the Great Liberator wanted little to do with anyone who couldn't play. A few days before the tryout, Cubas sent Ramón Batista to gather up Juan Carlos, Geidy and Lenin at the Hemisferio. Batista drove the refugees and their scant personal belongings to an empty apartment, for which Cubas had paid the first month's rent. Disoriented and penniless, the three were left to begin their new lives.

Obviously, this had not been the original plan. In exchange for providing his thirty-foot fishing boat and safe passage out of Cuba, Juan Carlos had signed on to the escape as a means of bringing himself and his wife to the United States. He believed, with justification, that he had fulfilled his end of the deal, delivering El Duque and the others to Anguilla Cay. But Juan Carlos's plan fell apart while awaiting the arrival of the ill-fated second boat. Now, due to the vagaries of the market for Cuban baseball players, he and his wife found themselves in Costa Rica, desperately scouring the want ads, a daunting process they of course had never faced in Cuba.

Cubas, who had nothing to do with the escape, couldn't have cared less about their predicament. He greeted the concerns of Juan Carlos, Geidy and Lenin with total disdain. "Those three have come here with such mistaken minds," he told Dan LeBatard of *The Miami Herald*. "My father came here with nothing, eating crackers and cat food, and he never asked for anything. You aren't owed anything here. You must earn it. Let them drown."

El Duque didn't offer much sympathy either. The pitcher, at times, could be overwhelmingly generous, but the same stubbornness and glacial pride that got him through his travails in Cuba often created conflicts. Quite simply, he never believed he was wrong. His falling out with Juan Carlos was not his finest hour. One evening, in a scene witnessed by LeBatard, Juan Carlos showed up at the Hemisferio to try to talk things out. El Duque autographed a baseball for the man who had helped spirit him out of Cuba, but then an argument ensued. El Duque apparently believed that Juan Carlos should have been grateful, not indignant, because the pitcher could have abandoned him in the Bahamas after receiving his American visa, the one he opted not to use.

"I don't want to be divided," Juan Carlos said finally. "Please. We need to be united. Like we were on the boat."

As Juan Carlos pleaded, El Duque picked up a wooden box, extracted several dominoes and spread them across the table. He strung the dominoes together, stacked them, idly playing solitaire as Juan Carlos continued his soliloquy. On at least a half dozen occasions El Duque had tried to escape from Cuba before Juan Carlos managed to pull it off. But that was apparently forgotten. After fifteen minutes Juan Carlos gave up and walked away.

"Didn't hear a word he said," said El Duque.

Juan Carlos eventually made it to the United States, securing passage on a flight to New York, then declaring political asylum once he landed. Before he left Costa Rica, Sánchez and I visited him one evening at his home, a converted storage room in the back of a garage. Juan Carlos occupied the space with Geidy and their infant daughter, Karla Jane, who had been born in San José. To enter the apartment, one had to walk through the garage, through the lingering smell of exhaust fumes and past several cars, to finally reach the metal front door. Juan Carlos was working as a night security guard for a few hundred dollars a month. "I still watch El Duque on TV," he said. "I still root for him. I get emotional. I want him to win."

Still, his anger over how he had been treated consumed him. He had filed a lawsuit against the pitcher for nearly $1 million, a suit he had about as much chance of winning as the Costa Rica lottery. He was incredulous over how El Duque and the others had turned on him. "When we got to Anguilla Cay they all thanked me; if they didn't kiss my ass it was only because I didn't let them," he said. "They said they had tried so many times to escape and finally I made it look so easy. The promises and guarantees stopped when we got to Costa Rica and he became a free agent. Then he treated us like dogs."

As we were all getting ready to leave Juan Carlos fetched a .38-caliber revolver out of a drawer, loaded it with a fistful of bullets and shoved it in the back of his jeans. With the handle of the gun sticking out of his waistband, he leaned over to kiss Karla Jane, who was standing up in her playpen. He then kissed his wife good-bye and headed out into the night to make a living.

FOR ALL THE HYPE and preparation, the tryout wasn't much. As a safe haven, as a vacation spot, as the birthplace of ecotourism, Costa Rica is a wonderful country—but not exactly a baseball hotbed. The workout had to be held at a broken-down stadium, Antonio Escarré, in the middle of a San José slum. The field was only a slight improvement over El Globo, the cow pasture where

El Duque had played out his sandlot exile. It took all the effort the players could muster to whip the field into shape.

René Guim threw together some press passes for the big event, but they weren't really necessary. The media consisted of *The Boston Globe* (me), *Newsday* (Sánchez), the Associated Press, the Costa Ricans and Morley Safer, working his way around the field with a *60 Minutes* crew. Cubas, dressed in a glossy tracksuit, knocked around a few fungoes while the stopwatch-wielding scouts stood around in groups. After batting practice, there was a game: the defectors versus a motley collection of Costa Rican collegians, a couple of whom appeared to be little more than three feet tall. Afterward, the scouts retired to the palatial San José Marriott, where they sipped beers and racked up Marriott points and chewed over the day's events on wicker chairs overlooking the mountains.

There wasn't much to discuss, really. To say the least, El Duque was an unusual prospect, having arrived from Cuba by way of a deserted island. But to the scouts who had assembled, the lack of information about him was nearly as unusual. In many respects scouting is like stock picking: There are no guarantees, but the more information the better. It is usually done through an exhaustive series of evaluations in game situations. The process, filled with checking and cross-checking, is designed to minimize mistakes and surprises. By the time the teams, agents and trade publications have pored over the mountainous data, the prospects have been dissected like so many IPOs.

As El Duque burst upon the scene, Major League Baseball, like many other American industries, was in the midst of revolutionary change. The arrival of new teams (the Marlins, Rockies, Diamondbacks, Devil Rays, plus their minor-league affiliates) had diluted the game's talent pool and created a chronic shortage of skilled labor, especially pitchers. The shortage, in addition to inflating scores and lowering the quality of play, had caused most clubs to expand their scouting departments well beyond U.S. borders. The entire office of Marlins' scouting director Al Avila, for example, is covered with maps, like a bunker inside the Pentagon. Baseball's globalization extended not only to traditional hotbeds like the Dominican Republic and Venezuela, but also to previously untapped markets like South Africa and Australia, even Russia. In many ways, the game was a typical industry seeking out cheap foreign labor to help meet expansion needs.

Cuba was the impenetrable exception, however. Major-league teams were dying to get in, but age-old hostilities always got in the way. In addition to his roles as president of the Republic, president of the Council of State and president of the Council of Ministers, Fidel Castro effectively also served as Cuba's president of baseball. As Juan Ignacio's fifteen-year prison sentence and El Duque's banishment demonstrated, Fidel suffered neither scouts nor agents gladly. The U.S. trade embargo only played into Fidel's hands, contributing to Cuba's voluntary isolation. Federal law prohibited teams from doing business on the island. The Commissioner's Office had even expanded the embargo to include the Canadian clubs, the Toronto Blue Jays and the Montreal Expos.

In many ways Cubas was simply a middleman, a market maker who brought teams and players together. Occasionally, however, the clubs would take matters into their own hands. It was an open secret that major-league scouts regularly traveled to Cuba to evaluate potential defectors; one even tried to bring in a radar gun. But the Los Angeles Dodgers set the standard for sheer audacity. In the spring of 1999, Sánchez and I sat down at Dodgertown, the Dodgers' spring training complex in Vero Beach, Florida, to interview a defector named Juan Carlos Díaz. To our shock and amazement Díaz told us that his first encounter with the Dodgers had actually taken place inside Cuba.

In the film noir scenario described by the first baseman, a scout named Pablo Peguero had traveled to Cuba as a tourist in 1996. He then held secret, videotaped tryouts for several prospects. The image of a Los Angeles Dodgers scout hitting fungoes in Havana—just months after Juan Ignacio's arrest and imprisonment—was almost too mind-boggling to fathom. But it got even better. Díaz told us that Peguero then hired a young woman to pose as his Dominican girlfriend to secure him permission to travel to the Dominican Republic. Once Díaz arrived in Santo Domingo, the club stashed him at its baseball academy and signed him for $65,000. As the big finish, Pablo Peguero and his boss, Ralph Avila, then ordered Díaz to lie about the elaborate scheme. If anyone asked, Díaz was to say he was a native of the Dominican Republic. The plot was eventually revealed when Díaz and another player, outfielder Josue Pérez, filed a grievance with the Commissioner's Office saying that they had been signed illegally. The commissioner ruled in favor of the players, declared them free agents and fined the Dodgers $200,000. Baseball stopped short of disciplining Peguero and Avila only out of concern that the U.S. Treasury Department would open an investigation into possible violations of the trade embargo itself.*

Among other things, the Dodger episode revealed the real truth behind the so-called Cuban Mystique. It was simply white-hot demand chasing scarce,

---

*Díaz signed with the Red Sox for $400,000. Pérez signed with the Phillies for $850,000. The Commissioner's Office later suspended Peguero and Avila, who had since retired, for one year for signing a Dominican player, Adrian Beltre, before his sixteenth birthday.

highly skilled labor. Because the Cubans were so rarely seen, scouting and signing them was a crapshoot, a risky investment for neither the faint of heart nor
the poor. As the market began to spiral, it was taken over by the elite "big-
market" teams who could afford to take multimillion-dollar gambles. "You'll
never see the Pittsburgh Pirates, the Milwaukee Brewers or the Minnesota
Twins at one of my workouts," Cubas sniffed. And he was right.

El Duque was like a case study in how the strange market worked. When
he arrived in Costa Rica, he had not pitched competitively in nearly two years.
Even before his banishment, he had been more impressive inside Cuba than on
the international circuit, so few scouts had seen him at his best. In San José, just
six weeks after his adventure at sea, he donned a blue jersey with the words
GRACIAS COSTA RICA stitched across the front and pitched a total of five innings
against a collection of Costa Rican urchins. On the basis of those five innings,
the scouts—sixty-two showed up—would have to make their multimillion-
dollar decisions.

As El Duque dusted off his fastball, the scouts aimed their radar guns from
behind home plate: 88, 90, 89, 90, 91, 89—an average major-league heater at
best. He unveiled the biggest leg kick since Juan Marichal and a variety of interesting curves, but to many scouts he was a disappointment, certainly not
worth the money that Cubas would be asking. What made it worse was that no
one had any idea how old he was. Cubas listed him as twenty-eight but no one
believed that. "He might be a middle [reliever] who could help you out in
spots," one scouting director told me. "But I'll tell you one thing: He's not half
the pitcher that his brother is." Several teams left the country after El Duque's
first outing, a two-inning stint that took all of ten minutes.

"That's $2.5 million per inning," cracked one scout as the performance
ended.

Scouting is an interesting profession, though. Anyone can read a radar
gun. The most successful scouts are those who can project well beyond what
everyone else sees. One scout who stuck around was Gordon Blakeley, the vice
president of international scouting for the New York Yankees. Blakeley was a
tall blond man with a perpetual tan from watching thousands of games. He
was a baseball careerist. Like most scouts he had begun as a player, reaching
Triple A as a third baseman with the Alan Trammell–Lou Whitaker generation
Detroit Tigers. When he was finally cut loose he went home to Southern California, picked up his teaching credentials, coached high school for a few years
and then returned to professional baseball as a member of its most itinerant
profession.

Blakeley loved scouting; more than anything he believed he knew how to spot winners. He had seen El Duque before the suspension and had formed strong opinions about him. "I loved the guy," said Blakeley. "Always. Every time I'd go to see him he would strike out the first batter, and then the next batter, he'd throw at the guy's head. They'd be intimidated the whole game. I never saw him lose. I mean, he never threw that hard: ninety, ninety-two. Stuff? Average to slightly above average fastball. Average to slightly above average hook. But he could flat fucking pitch for your ass."

When Blakeley heard that El Duque was out of Cuba, he could hardly contain himself. "I went ballistic," he said. "This was my guy." In fact, he went directly to Yankee owner George Steinbrenner. "I told him, 'This is *the* guy,' " said Blakeley. "I said, 'This is the ace of the Cuban game. He's better than any of these guys that have come out so far. This is a guy who's dominated Cuba for a long time.' So George said, 'Okay, get your ass down there and see what's going on.' "

Blakeley attended the Costa Rica workouts with Lin Garrett, the club's vice president of scouting. He was unfazed by many of the concerns of his peers. Blakeley stood behind the backstop along with everyone else, watching El Duque plow through the hapless collegians. To him, it didn't matter who El Duque was facing. It didn't matter that his curveball was a little flat. It didn't even matter how old he was. "I'm just sitting there thinking, Oh shit, he's still got his fastball. Oh shit, he's still healthy." Garrett wasn't immediately sold. To all appearances, here was a stylish pitcher with average stuff and undetermined age. He seemed like just another guy. "No, this is not just another guy," Blakeley corrected him. "This is El Duque." Before long Garrett was convinced as well.

The scouts went back to Tampa and typed up their report. From the distance of three World Championships (and counting), the document reads like an oracle of the Yankees' immediate future. In terms of raw ability, Blakeley and Garrett described an average pitcher who received above-average marks for poise and instinct.

Then came the remarkable summary:

PHYSICAL DESCRIPTION (INJURIES, GLASSES, ETC.):
A physical specimen, med-lge frame, muscular yet loose and flexible, proportional, an athlete, phy. mature, strong, Dave Stewart look, reported to be 28 yrs old but may be 32—body is 25. Seen in Costa Rica.

TOOLS AND ABILITIES:
Very easy, loose and free arm, TQ (three quarters) to LTQ (low three-quarters) angle, sudden violent leg lift (Len Barker) then goes easy

with the arm—ball gets in on you (Rivera), FB (fastball) 88–92 with sink or bore/sink or riding life or occ. straight. LTQ angle CB (curveball)—has occ. hump but plus rotation—will vary angle, depth and velocity, threw all strikes, located away but will come inside with a high rider, mixes pitches well, very confident, poised, athletic and strong, likes being out there, likes the attention, enjoys the game, AKA: El Duque, movement grade is based a lot on the description.

WEAKNESSES:
Saw chg (changeup) only in the pen—palm ball type grip—has turnover life and arm speed but not a good pitch—has a big hump in it and two much "white" showing in the rotation, will have no problem picking up new way to throw pitch; Saw 2 games for a total of 5 inn's, 2nd outing was not as sharp, was underneath and a little flat, but has been away from the game 1 to 2 yrs. Age is not a factor. Saw several type CBs, but would like one a little harder.

SUMMATION:
3–4th starter on 1st div club now; has a unique presence about him—more than just confidence, like him, high interest.

Blakeley and Garrett went to the famous Yankee brain trust: Steinbrenner, vice president of scouting Gene "Stick" Michael, vice president of baseball operations Mark Newman, organizational pitching guru Billy Connors and thirty-year-old Brian Cashman, who had recently been promoted by Steinbrenner to become the second-youngest general manager in major-league history. The scouts went for the hard sell. Blakeley knew exactly which buttons to push with Steinbrenner. "He's a winner," he told the Boss. "And I think he'll sell tickets. I don't know if he can help us in the rotation within the next year, but he's perfect for New York."

Garrett, having gotten over his early reservations, was even more confident: "I think he can help us this year," he said.

The Yankees were under no illusions about El Duque's age. "We told the Boss flat out how old he was," said Blakeley. "I said, 'Look, they list him at twenty-eight, but he's really thirty-two.' And then Lin said, 'You know what? His body doesn't go to that. He's a great athlete. He could pitch maybe five or six years for us.' "

Now the price tag came up.

Blakeley told Steinbrenner he thought El Duque would cost at least $6 million, maybe more.

The Boss didn't flinch.

"Okay," said Steinbrenner. "You got him. Go get him."

THAT, OF COURSE, was easy for Steinbrenner to say. The Yankees' play for El Duque was a classic example of the team's financial superiority over its competitors. The Bombers, of course, have always been rich. In 1920, owner Jake Ruppert purchased Babe Ruth from the Boston Red Sox for $100,000 and a $300,000 loan—the collateral was Fenway Park—"an amount the club could not afford to refuse," Sox owner Harry Frazee said at the time. But by 1998 the Yanks were less a sports franchise than an empire. Since 1973, when Steinbrenner bought the club from CBS for $10 million, its value has risen to an estimated $500 million. The Yankees' annual revenues dwarfed those of all other teams. The primary reason was neither attendance nor merchandizing but a $493.5 million television contract the club signed with the Madison Square Garden Network in 1988.

Inside baseball the Yankees' financial clout had brought the game to the brink of hysteria. The problem was self-evident: The Yankees had more money to spend on draft picks, free agents and, of course, thirty-two-year-old Cuban pitchers who washed up in the Bahamas. "Baseball is broken . . . it can't last in the present environment," wrote Bob Costas, the respected broadcaster, in *Fair Ball*, his well-reasoned 177-page plea for restructuring. More interesting than the problem, however, were the proposed solutions, most of which bore a strong resemblance to the straitjacket economic system from which El Duque Hernández had just been liberated.

One of the more amusing ironies of the El Duque saga was that the pitcher arrived from Communist Cuba to a heated debate over how to redistribute baseball's enormous wealth. Noted capitalists such as George Will, who in real life would never support policies such as revenue sharing and draconian taxes to aid the poor, proposed turning baseball into a welfare state, all in the name of parity. By escaping Cuba, where he had earned $8.75 a *month*, El Duque had positioned himself to benefit from one of the purest forms of free-market capitalism: free agency. And yet some of capitalism's biggest boosters were working to undercut that right. Why? So the Pittsburgh Pirates, Montreal Expos and Kansas City Royals would have a better shot of going to the World Series.

Fortunately—for El Duque, at least—the debate had not gotten that far. The Yankees were free to pursue him with all their economic might. In fact, the decision to sign him would ultimately hinge less on money than on the results of another adventure in free trade: a $12.8 million disaster called Hideki Irabu. The Yanks had signed Irabu the previous year, making the tall Japanese right-hander the most expensive international player in history. Irabu possessed a 100-mile-per-hour fastball and a reputation as the "Japanese Nolan Ryan." But the goodwill generated by his signing had roughly the shelf life of a California roll.

For starters, Irabu's contract proved more complicated than NAFTA. His Japanese club, the Lotte Marines, first worked out a deal with the San Diego Padres, but the pitcher, guided by agent Don Nomura, a sort of Japanese Joe Cubas, announced that Irabu would pitch only for the New York Yankees. Negotiations thus ensued between the Yanks and the Padres. Steinbrenner ultimately forfeited $3 million and two prospects (Ruben Rivera and Rafael Medina) just to gain the rights to Irabu, who then received a whopping $8.5 million signing bonus.

Irabu missed spring training. When he finally showed up, he displayed occasional brilliance, his fastball indeed conjuring up images of the fabled Ryan Express. After the Yanks rushed him to the bigs, his much-anticipated debut drew an enormous walk-up; the club sold $80,000 in Irabu T-shirts alone. But more often than not Irabu was a doughy, sullen presence around the Yankee clubhouse and a complete riddle on the mound. For all his ability he often pitched with the bewildered expression of someone who had taken a wrong turn at the concession stand and wandered out onto the field. He finished the 1997 season buried in the bullpen, supporting a 7.09 ERA and Steinbrenner's unmitigated wrath. "I've got about seven dozen Hideki Irabu T-shirts I am giving to the Little Sisters of the Blind," the Boss fumed to the *New York Post.*

Despite the Yankee riches, the Irabu debacle hung over the El Duque negotiations. In the Darwinian world of George Steinbrenner, another botched international signing could mean everyone's head. Brian Cashman, the new GM, broached the subject with Blakeley one day. Cashman had started with the Yankees as a security department intern, breaking up fights and writing up fans for smoking pot. He was just weeks into the toughest job in sports, for which he had signed a one-year contract. His predecessor, Bob Watson, had resigned with high blood pressure from Steinbrenner's unrelenting verbal barrage. Signing El Duque was certain to wreak havoc on the Yankee payroll, already on an inexorable path toward $100 million.

"Cashman said to me, 'You know, Irabu's not pitching that well. Maybe we ought to back off and not sign somebody like this,' " Blakeley recalled. "I mean, Cashman's the GM. It was like, 'Do we really want to stick our necks out?' "

Blakeley responded with the speech of his life. "I said, 'Are we going to be afraid? So we fail on Irabu, if, in fact, we fail. Does that mean we're scared, so when the next guy comes along we're not going to take him?' And Cashman agreed with me. He said: 'You're dead fucking right. Just because we're convicted on this other guy, let's not back off.' "

It was a critical moment for the Yanks. Cashman had set the tone of his tenure, entrusting his scouting department with a critical personnel move, even though he had never seen El Duque pitch. Cashman said the scouts' reputations "spoke for themselves." Blakeley's commitment alone was enough to persuade him. "Gordon said to me, 'You can't be shy; if you believe in something you have to go for it,' " Cashman said. "He said, 'You may make mistakes along the way, but if you hesitate you could miss out on the next Cy Young Award winner.' "

"That speech," said Cashman, "may have changed the course of the 1998 season."

Negotiations for El Duque began in "the Bunker," a conference room at the Yankees training complex in Tampa. Cubas knew he couldn't get Irabu money, but he at least wanted to surpass $7 million, the benchmark Arrojo had set for the Cuban market (the fact that there was such a thing as a "Cuban market" was testimony to Cubas's success). When the Yankees came in significantly lower, Cubas, with typical theatrics, stormed out of the room.

"You're not going to sign him," Cubas told the Yankee brass.

Mark Newman turned to Blakeley.

"Trail his ass," said Newman.

So ordered, Blakeley followed Cubas to Melbourne, Florida, where Arrojo was scheduled to pitch an exhibition game. He then followed the agent to West Palm Beach, where Cubas was to attend a family wedding. He followed Cubas all the way to Miami, where the two men ended up at Versailles, the famous Cuban restaurant on Calle Ocho. Cubas thought the atmosphere might loosen up Blakeley, along with the agent's wallet. It didn't. Cubas wanted $8 million. The Yankees weren't close. At that point, the agent later asserted, "Gordon was starting to get on my nerves."

With spring training in full swing, the gamesmanship picked up. Cubas's main problem was that no other team wanted El Duque as badly as the Yanks. His solution was to stage a phantom bidding war. He first asked Ray Sánchez to plant a story in *Newsday* that the Cleveland Indians were close to a deal. Sánchez refused. He then pulled René Guim out of a Miami Heat game to plant a story that the Disney-owned Anaheim Angels had prepared an offer—part baseball contract, part movie deal. Guim leaked the story to the Associated Press in Los Angeles. "Joe later told me it wasn't true," said Guim. "After he cut the deal with the Yankees he told me it was all bullshit." Finally, Cubas baited the Yankees publicly. With palpable indignation he called up Murray Chass, the respected baseball writer for *The New York Times,* and ripped into the club for tactics that he himself was engaged in. "The Yankees are attempting to negotiate through the press," Cubas raged. "I'm fed up with these people and how they handle things. George is leaking it on purpose to scare others away. If they think they are going to corner me into a deal with those tactics, they're going to have a rude awakening when they see I'm about to cut a deal with another club. There was an opportunity here, and they're letting it slip away with dirty tactics."

The strategy, about as subtle as a lead pipe, seemed to work. Steinbrenner, seemingly oblivious to the fact that the agent had bullied him, unloaded on "his baseball people," according to Chass, and the Yankees began to bid against themselves. The Angels deal, particularly the purported Disney movie, was a concept, not an offer. The Indians had some interest, but they were nowhere near the Yankees. The Yanks ended up offering more than twice as much as any other team. "We did a tremendous job of evaluating the player," said Cashman, who, at Cubas's request, stepped in to close the deal. "We didn't do as good a job evaluating the market."*

In the end Cubas couldn't crack the Arrojo barrier, but he came close enough: $6.6 million over four years. El Duque received a $1 million signing bonus. It was a major-league contract, which meant that the pitcher would be placed immediately on the forty-man roster. For El Duque, who made 207 pesos a month in Cuba, his contract was worth the equivalent of 162,500,000 pesos. I talked to him briefly from Mexico just before the deal was announced. "It doesn't really seem real," he said.

But before it was over, Cubas had one additional piece of business he wanted to attend to. At this point the agent's reputation for bending the rules was known far and wide. In the tight-knit world of agents and scouts, the allegations surrounding Rolando Arrojo's deal with the Devil Rays—the alleged $500,000 bribe, the alleged kickback to Rudy Santín, the phantom tryout— were an open secret around the game.

Even so, Blakeley was taken aback by the agent's next request. As Blakeley understood it, Cubas wanted the Yankees to pay him an additional $500,000

---

*By the following year, El Duque was widely regarded as the biggest bargain in baseball.

under the table to complete the deal for El Duque. The proposition directly mirrored what Blakeley had heard about Arrojo and the Devil Rays, but he was still stunned. It was one thing to hear rumors about payoffs and side deals. It was another to be hit up for an actual bribe. In his two decades as a scout Blakeley had never fielded such a proposition.

"He said, 'What do you think about paying me five hundred thousand dollars to get this deal done?' " Blakeley recounted. "I said, 'We're not gonna do that.' Cubas said, 'Well, I could pay you fifty, under the table, and nobody would ever know.'

"I mean, you think I'm going to whore myself to him?" said Blakeley. "For fifty grand? For five million I might. Shit, if I'm going to rob a bank, I'm gonna take a big wad. I'm not going to take fifty. I mean, seriously. I've worked twenty-one years in this game. I've never taken a dime from anybody."

THE COSTA RICA TRYOUTS produced two other signings: catcher Francisco Santiesteban went to the Seattle Mariners and outfielder Osmany Santana went to the Cleveland Indians. El Duque's cousin, Joel Pedroso, was never a real prospect, so it wasn't surprising when he failed to get a nibble. For Alberto Hernández, though, the tryout was a nightmare, like one last punishment by the Castro government.

In peak physical condition Alberto almost certainly would have merited a contract. But he was hardly in peak physical condition. Unlike El Duque, who had stayed in shape during the dog days of his banishment, Alberto had allowed his skills to atrophy cowering inside his apartment. He was at least twenty pounds overweight when he took the field. The scouts openly scoffed at his age, listed at twenty-five. Alberto's powerful arm and his command behind the plate were still in evidence, but his deterioration became obvious as soon as he took a few swings.

In Cuba, Alberto had never used a wooden bat in competition. Now, as he took batting practice, he looked like he was trying to hit with a log. He popped up pitch after pitch. Things got worse during the first exhibition game. Lugging out a grounder, Alberto pulled his hamstring and collapsed in the dirt. El Duque and another player helped him off the field as he swooned with pain. For the next couple of days he iced his injury in the hope that he could give it one more shot. Finally, with just a few scouts still hanging around, he hobbled to the plate in batting practice and clubbed three homers into the dilapidated houses beyond left field. But by then it was too late.

After the teams passed him over, Alberto held out hope that Cubas could find him a job. Instead, in a familiar refrain, he lost contact with his agent and grew to despise him. To make ends meet he got a job working in a San José auto repair shop. El Duque helped him pay the rent on his one-bedroom apartment. Periodically, Alberto tried to reach Cubas, who he said never returned his calls. "Fuck Joe Cubas," he said a year after the tryout. "If you see him, tell him his *primo* [cousin] is dying of hunger down here in Costa Rica. I thought he was a friend but it really wasn't like that. It was all business with him."

Gus Domínguez, another Cuban American agent, finally took on Alberto's case and found him a job in Taiwan. It wasn't ideal, but at least the catcher was playing ball again. Trimmed down, Alberto played two seasons in the Taiwanese League. He made $7,500 a month. Then, in the middle of his second season, his team informed him that he had been released. He returned to San José, Costa Rica, which he had thought would be a rest stop on his way to the major leagues but instead turned out to be his home in exile.

CHAPTER FIFTEEN

THE BLUE LINE

IT WAS ST. PATRICK'S DAY 1998 WHEN EL DUQUE MADE THE REQ-uisite appearance at Victor's Café. The press conference at the Coral Gables eatery had become a ritual of the Cuban ballplayers' diaspora. Outside stood the scaled-down replica of the Statue of Liberty. Inside stood dozens of denizens of the exile press. Before the festivities began, someone tapped me on the shoulder and led me to a back room. There, sipping soft drinks and beam-ing was the now familiar gang: El Duque, Noris, Tío, Cubas and René Guim. El Duque wore a new white shirt buttoned at the collar. He was so well groomed it looked like he had polished his head. His fairy-tale life was such that all I could do was laugh and congratulate him. Guim passed around photos from Costa Rica while we all waited for the press conference to start.

El Duque cried through much of the event, so overcome was he by his ar-rival in America. Half the questions were about politics, of course, and the pitcher deflected them with remarkable aplomb. "Let's not waste our breath," he said at one point when asked about Fidel. Another reporter drew a tongue-in-cheek comparison between the two dictators, Castro and Steinbrenner. As everyone laughed, El Duque, bewildered, turned and asked, "Who is Stein-brenner?" Cubas lunged for the mike. "There is no comparison!" yelled the agent, his sense of humor abandoning him. "George Steinbrenner is a busi-nessman who is simply looking out for the interests of himself and his ball club. Fidel Castro is a traitor to the Cuban people!" The room erupted in spir-ited applause.

After several minutes of this politically correct banter, Liván Hernández suddenly burst into the room. The brothers had not seen each other in almost three years—not since Liván staggered onto a frontage road in Monterrey, Mexico, to rendezvous with Cubas, with whom he no longer spoke. Liván pushed through the crowd, his diamond stud earring picking up the TV lights. Amid the snapping of cameras and more applause, the brothers embraced. Liván kissed El Duque's shiny head, which was now buried in his shoulder. By the time El Duque looked up, his face was a mask of joy and relief. He blinked into the cameras and rubbed his wet eyes. He could hardly speak. Finally, someone asked Liván if he had any advice for his brother. "*Sí*," he responded. "I would tell him not to eat too much McDonald's."

That night, Tío threw a party at his house. Liván didn't show, apparently because he didn't want to stand near Cubas for too long. In the middle of the room was a huge rectangular cake with WELCOME TO AMERICA EL DUQUE spelled out in vanilla icing. In the streets a gauntlet of humming TV trucks made the gathering feel like a Hollywood premiere. The gala's official photographer, hired at the last minute by René Guim, was Alan Díaz, who later snapped the famous shot of a helmeted, goggled and armed federal agent moving to seize six-year-old Elián González. I never got near the guest of honor, who was sitting on a stool in Tío's playroom, surrounded by hundreds of well-wishers.

Among other things, the drawn-out reception had delayed El Duque's arrival in Tampa. Cubas and the Yankees had come to terms on March 7. It was now ten days later, a full month into spring training, and some officials were growing uneasy with the delays. "I'm sure the first thing he wants to do is kiss the ground and say thank God he finally made it here," said Brian Cashman. "But he has to understand that only one part of his dream was freedom. The other part was to play in the major leagues. Every day we wait to get him over here is another day that pushes that dream back." But Steinbrenner, whose opinion was the only one that counted, was unconcerned. "If I came across that gulf on a rowboat, I'd want to be with my family for at least a day, too," said the Boss, in what may also have been the first recorded mangling of the great escape.

The morning after Tío's party, El Duque and Cubas flew to Tampa and made their way over to Legends Field. For the uninitiated, walking into a major-league clubhouse is an eye-popping experience, even during spring training, like being admitted to an inner sanctum. The carpeted room is usually immaculate and, by definition, major-league. The cubicles are filled with a baseball cornucopia: jerseys, spikes, tissue-wrapped balls, batting gloves, caps and so on. There is often a spread of cold cuts and fresh fruit catered by eager attendants. The half-dressed players lounge on sofas or director's chairs in front of their cubicles, watching sports or chatting or giving interviews. To someone like El Duque, who spent an entire decade sleeping in dank stadiums and washing his own uniform, the experience was a revelation. "He just gasped," said Cubas, who virtually led the pitcher by the hand. "There was everything, all nicely stacked, all these boxes just for him. He had running shoes, he had shower slippers, he had spikes—everything he needed was just sitting there waiting for him. He couldn't believe the size of the television sets. He was just overwhelmed."

One thing became clear immediately: El Duque was not Hideki Irabu. The differences were born partly of circumstance. Irabu, for example, needed a full-time interpreter to communicate with his teammates. El Duque did not. The first player he met, the Panamanian pitcher Ramiro Mendoza, knew how to speak his language. Several players and one coach—Cuban exile José Cardenal—also spoke Spanish. In addition, the organization had learned from the Irabu experience and knew to bring El Duque along slowly. But the major difference was in the pitchers' personalities. Irabu's diffidence, whether cultural or innate, had been off-putting to players and sportswriters alike. To some, he lacked self-esteem. El Duque, of course, was the most confident man on the planet. He also seemed to understand intuitively what it meant to be a Yankee. He came to his first workout as if he had won a raffle to be a Yankee-for-a-day. After one drill he darted around the infield, eagerly scooping up baseballs while his bemused fellow pitchers looked on. "He looked like a kid on an Easter egg hunt," said Buster Olney, who covered the team for *The New York Times.* Within moments the thirty-two-year-old rookie was cradling a dozen baseballs in his arms.

For the Yankee beat writers, El Duque's arrival was a godsend. As a rule, spring training produces a month and a half of boring, speculative stories. The last couple of weeks are particularly tedious. By then all the stars have been written up, the team is basically set and all that's left are features exploring the third-catcher dilemma and the middle relief. Well, here was a story of note: a crafty right-hander of undetermined age who had arrived on a boat. Nothing about El Duque was normal. He wore his stirrups to his knees, as if he had stepped out of the 1920s. His windup was a complex artifice of incredible deception, a throwback to Satchel Paige, Juan Marichal and the great one himself, El Tiante. Jack O'Connell, the veteran baseball writer for *The Hartford Courant,* stood outside the bullpen, watching El Duque nearly knee himself in the chin.

His pitches seemed to come from everywhere except behind his back. He wasn't throwing very hard, but every pitch was on target. The catcher, Joe Girardi, never moved his glove. Three months earlier El Duque had been stranded on a deserted island. Now he was painting the corners at the Yankee training camp. "A lot of guys were just looking at each other saying, 'Who *is* this guy?' " said O'Connell, who has covered the game for more than two decades. "You could just tell immediately that he was a big-league pitcher.

"After Irabu, who was such a hostile guy, there was this warm feeling all around him," said O'Connell. "It was just completely different. People treated him like a next-door neighbor. I remember while he was throwing there was a bunch of people watching from up on the catwalk. Just as I looked up, there was this one woman, and out of nowhere she yells out, 'Welcome to America!' I don't know if El Duque understood what she said, but he touched his cap and he kept throwing. It was a touching moment."

On that first day, the Yankees allowed Cubas onto the field to help El Duque get acclimated. But the pitcher didn't need any help. "It was like he had been there before," said Cubas. Every important figure in the organization save for Steinbrenner turned out to watch him toss. Billy Connors, the organization's pitching specialist, took one look at El Duque's socks, his cap pulled low over his eyes. "Oh, I love that," he gushed to Cubas. "That old-fashioned throwback type thing, I just love that." A few minutes later Yankee manager Joe Torre showed up.

"How's he throwing?" Torre asked.

"He's in perfect shape," said Cubas.

Torre stood there, arms folded, watching El Duque paint the black with pitch after pitch. The manager turned to Cubas. "Keep 'em coming," he said, smiling. "Keep 'em coming."

As the writers began to chronicle this amazing tale, there were still the nagging questions about El Duque's age. "I don't know where the discrepancy comes from," El Duque said during his first encounter with the media. "I am twenty-eight years old. I was born October eleven, 1969, as told by my mother." The Yankees, even though Blakeley knew better, went along with this benign fable. No one thought it unusual, really, age-doctoring being a Latin American baseball tradition. The team already had one veteran, Venezuelan infielder Luis Sojo, who looked like he might have turned the double play with Rogers Hornsby. The issue was deflected somewhat when a team physician announced that El Duque was the fittest athlete he had ever examined. But the inquisitive beat writers kept pushing. Was he twenty-eight or was he thirty-two? Brian

Cashman said not to worry. The team had studied the matter thoroughly and had come to a definitive conclusion.

"We carbon-dated him and found out he was twenty-two," said Cashman.

THE 1998 YANKEES broke camp two weeks later. El Duque stayed behind for extended spring training. The plan was to start him in the Gulf Coast League and go from there. El Duque started twice for Tampa, a rookie league club composed mostly of teenagers and rehab projects. He was literally a man among boys. It quickly became obvious that he needed stiffer competition, so the Yanks jumped him to their Triple-A team in Columbus, Ohio.

"I wasn't sure what was going to happen," said El Duque. "I had been out of baseball. I hadn't pitched for two years." Cubas sent along Ramón Batista to look after him, as he had for Rolando Arrojo, but El Duque needed no such coddling. He lived the life of an ascetic as he pursued his major-league dream. By night he went to the ballpark and honed his craft. By day he hung out with Batista, watching soaps and pining for his daughters. From the beginning, that was the downside to El Duque's new life. He often referred to baseball as "the son I never had." But his separation from Yahumara and Steffi (after tennis star Steffi Graf) was painful. He combed the malls for toys and clothes, which he dispatched to Cuba along with money for his family. He frequently asked Batista whether he would ever see his daughters again. Batista, who went years without seeing his own father, tried to assure him that he would.

The competition at Triple A—one step from the majors—is stiff and cut-throat, but El Duque waltzed through the International League as if he were merely passing through, which of course he was. In his debut, a 1–0 win, he struck out 10 in seven innings against the Toledo Mud Hens. In his second start, he struck out 11 in six innings to beat the Indianapolis Indians. "He's a man on a mission," said his manager, Stump Merrill. El Duque was 3–0 when he traveled to Rochester to play the Red Wings, a Baltimore Orioles affiliate. The game was a preview of his not-so-distant future. A small contingent of Cubans showed up with drums and Cuban flags, and before long, fans were snaking through the grandstand in a conga line, chanting, "*Du-que! Du-que!*" After beating the Red Wings 4–2, El Duque reached over the dugout and plunged his hand into the clamoring crowd. He signed autographs for an hour. "I have no words to describe the rush of emotions I feel," he told a reporter.

The Yankees were suddenly faced with a decision much sooner than expected. Cashman had said repeatedly that the club was not counting on El

Duque until 1999, and yet here he was banging on the door. By the end of May he was 6–0. The only thing keeping him in Columbus was the solid Yankee rotation: David Wells, David Cone, Andy Pettitte, Ramiro Mendoza and Irabu, who had temporarily rebounded at 4–1. The club had an opportunity to call up El Duque on May 28 after the demotion of reliever Willie Banks. Still cautious, Cashman summoned Todd Erdos instead. But the team couldn't wait much longer. A few days later, Wells, the corpulent lefty, complained of a sore shoulder. This time Cashman called El Duque to fill the temporary spot in the rotation.

El Duque's moment had arrived. But for a pitcher who had spent part of his career in Communist purgatory and another four days stranded on an island, it couldn't be that simple. Wells, it turned out, was fine. El Duque wasn't needed after all. He had no sooner arrived in New York than the Yankees were preparing to send him back to Columbus. Then David Cone walked into the clubhouse with a bandage on the tip of his right index finger.

Cone was one of the grittiest, most intelligent pitchers of his generation. Two years later, he dislocated his left, nonpitching shoulder diving for a bunt and was pitching again within days. On this night, however, Cone recounted an unfortunate accident. He had bent over to pet his mother's Jack Russell terrier, a four-month-old puppy named Veronica. Veronica responded by taking a nip at Cone's pitching hand with teeth "as sharp as hypodermic needles," slicing open his finger. "Oh, well, you might as well tell the truth about these things, as embarrassing as it might be," Cone told reporters. "I should only miss one start, but considering we're talking about El Duque here, the name Wally Pipp did pop into my mind." Pipp was the Yankee first baseman who sat out with a headache one afternoon in 1925. His temporary replacement, Lou Gehrig, played the next 2,130 games.

"Two men, one mound, one angry puppy," wrote Ian O'Connor of the *Daily News*. "Stephen King could not have done any better."

So El Duque went back to the hotel and waited. The Yankees booked him into the Hilton in Fort Lee, New Jersey. The following day, Sánchez called to see how he was holding up. He caught El Duque eating his traditional pregame meal: spaghetti plain, no sauce. The pitcher made it sound like it was any other day. Asked if he was nervous, he seemed almost offended. He compared the experience to Cuba. "Why should I be nervous?" he said between bites. "I've pitched when it was packed at Estadio Latinoamericano."

El Duque arrived at Yankee Stadium at 3:30 P.M. It has been decades since they built stadiums that conform to the personality of their cities. Even the newer, retro models, impressive as they are, exude an antiseptic sameness, like the open-air shopping malls that often surround them. Buildings like Fenway Park, Yankee Stadium and Dodger Stadium are part of a dying breed. Fenway is like Boston: quaint, cranky, *small*—"a lyric little bandbox of a ballpark," John Updike famously wrote. Every year a new Red Sox player drives right past it. Yankee Stadium is like New York: colossal, intimidating, looming over the Major Deegan Expressway like a gray giant. Its history is the history of legends. On Opening Day 1998 Mike Lupica followed Joe DiMaggio back to the stadium. The Yankee Clipper had made his first appearance in 1936. Now he was to throw out the first ball. A thin blue line marks the path to the Yankee clubhouse. Lupica, in his book *Summer of '98*, described the great DiMaggio as he followed the blue line "in the direction of another Yankee season, part of more than a line painted into the Stadium floor, part of the most famous line in the history of the sport, one that goes back to Babe Ruth."

And now El Duque Hernández, fallen hero of the Cuban revolution, was walking the blue line. He followed it through the catacombs of the stadium, beneath the exposed insulation and the air-conditioning ducts and the swarming cables until he arrived at the black clubhouse door. His white cubicle was on the left side, third from the front wall. Inside he found the most distinctive uniform in sports. The Yankees, in addition to introducing the world to pinstripes, were also the first team to make permanent use of numbers. The team's tradition is so rich that many have been retired—out of 1 through 10, for example, only 2 (Derek Jeter) and 6 (Torre) are still active—and veteran players often have to switch when they arrive. El Duque did not. He was able to keep 26—the number he wore with the Industriales of Havana and the Cuban national team.

For some exiles, this preference came as a shock. In modern Cuban history perhaps no symbol is more provocative than the number 26. To revolutionaries, the number represents the 26th of July Movement, the name adopted by Fidel Castro's rebel army in memory of the 1953 attack on Moncada. To exiles, it symbolizes the date when their world began to come apart. On the fringes of the community, people began to phone in to radio talk shows. They wondered aloud whether this pitcher might be a closet Communist, or worse, a spy sent by Fidel. El Duque wore the number because his father had worn it—no more and no less. He tried to set the record straight. "For all those *viejos* [old-timers] in Miami who call me a Communist because I wear the number twenty-six, they need to know that it has nothing to do with the 26th of July Movement," he said. "To hell with those *viejos*."

INSIDE THE TUNNEL leading to the field hangs a blue-and-white sign with a quote from DiMaggio: I WANT TO THANK THE GOOD LORD FOR MAKING ME A YANKEE.

El Duque passed beneath the sign and bounded up the dugout steps onto the field. The stadium seems even bigger from within, a stage for all of New York. El Duque jogged alone on the warning track. It was still light out and fans were beginning to trickle in. Because El Duque's arrival had happened so fast, amid such confusion, there wasn't much time to generate a walk-up. The opponent, the expansion Tampa Bay Devil Rays, didn't help. The attendance would be 27,291, larger than normal for a weeknight but well short of Irabu's debut, a near sellout. But the fans were vocal. Some carried Cuban flags. As El Duque started to got loose, cries of "¡Libertad! ¡Libertad!" could be heard from the upper deck.

Somewhere between Columbus and New York, El Duque had lost his glove. Before he headed out on the field, an attendant handed him a new one, a black Rawlings. El Duque tried out the mitt. "It was very hard," he said. "I softened it up with a little water and just said, 'Let's do it.' At that point, the glove didn't matter. I was pitching at Yankee Stadium. The glove was the least of my worries. I had a job to do, not only for me but for my family, my friends, for all Latinos and all Cubans."

Warming up in the bullpen with his brand-new glove, El Duque had a sudden epiphany: "God has granted me an opportunity to pitch in the major leagues." He wept. It was a cool Wednesday evening, June 3. Under his jersey El Duque wore a long-sleeved navy turtleneck, a white interlocking NY on the collar. As he walked across the outfield toward the mound, Bob Sheppard, the voice of God at Yankee Stadium, was announcing the starting lineup: "And pitching, number twenty-six, Orlando 'El Duque' Hernández, number twenty-six." Joe Girardi had warmed up the pitcher in the pen and now he returned to the Yankee bench. How did he look, David Cone asked? "He's a little short," replied Girardi, implying that El Duque might have trouble slipping his modest fastball past major-league hitters.

El Duque removed his cap for the national anthem, the symbol of everything he had been taught to despise. Once again his eyes welled up with tears. The pitcher's head glowed slightly beneath the stadium lights. As organist Eddie Layton wrapped things up on his Hammond, El Duque turned to face the plate. He commenced to toss warm-up pitches to his catcher, Jorge

Posada—lightly at first, then harder. His expression was blank, devoid of fear. The first batter was Quinton McCracken, a switch-hitter batting left. He stepped into the box.

El Duque unleashed a fastball straight down the middle. McCracken took the pitch for strike one.

Up in the press box, Jim Kaat and Ken Singleton were settling in for the MSG telecast. Both had been accomplished players, of course, before becoming broadcasters. Kaat won 283 games, primarily for the Minnesota Twins. Singleton was a switch-hitting outfielder for the Baltimore Orioles who finished his career with 246 homers and 1,065 RBIs. The two former greats watched this curious debut with obvious anticipation.

El Duque's second pitch was a tumbling curveball. It reminded Singleton of the hands on a clock. "Looks like a nice twelve-to-sixer, straight down," said Singleton, taking El Duque's measure.

As McCracken worked deeper into the count, MSG put up a graphic to tell fans a little more about the new Yankee hurler. The bio seemed to raise as many questions as it answered:

> Orlando Hernandez
> "El Duque"
> 6'2" 190
> 28 years old?
> M.L. debut
> Defected from Cuba, December 26, 1997
> 129–47 career with Cuban National Team
> Banned from playing 10/96 for planning to defect

On a 2–2 pitch, El Duque struck out McCracken with a diving fastball.

"From the boat to Costa Rica to the minor leagues to the big leagues to a strikeout of his first batter!" said Kaat.

"They say he is a very poised guy who knows how to pitch," added Singleton.

The next batter was Miguel Cairo, a right-hand-hitting second baseman. El Duque whipped a sidearm fastball that seemed to shoot out of the third-base dugout. Cairo took it for a strike. Cairo slapped the next pitch to left, where Chad Curtis made an easy running catch.

The third batter was Wade Boggs. I had the privilege of covering Boggs on a day-to-day basis in the mid-1980s, when he was still a hitting machine for the Boston Red Sox. Off the field Boggs was like a compendium of daytime talk shows: palimony suits, admissions of sexual addiction, even ghosts. The third baseman saw apparitions of his late mother at the foot of his bed and once told a reporter that he had willed himself invisible to escape a mugging. On the field he was an artist. He always looked like he could flick the ball wherever he wanted. In my favorite Boggs story, told by Joe Morgan—the ex–Sox manager, not the Hall of Fame second baseman—Boggs was hitting during a spring training game, fouling off pitch after pitch, as he often did. Finally, a fan on the third-base side yelled out, "Hey, Wade, hit one to me!" "On the very next pitch, Boggs hit one over and the guy caught it," said Morgan. "It's just chance, but what are the odds of that, a billion to one?"

Boggs was now thirty-nine and chasing 3,000 hits at the end of his brilliant career. He was 167 short and had left the Yankees, with whom he had finally won a World Series, to pursue the milestone in Tampa, his hometown. The crowd rose to a standing ovation as Boggs strode to the plate. El Duque stepped off the mound in deference to the great hitter. When Boggs finally dug in, El Duque curved him and he hit an innocuous fly for the third out. El Duque walked off, perfect in his first major-league inning. His face still impassive, he pulled off his cap and wiped his brow with the back of his hand, stepping over the foul line for luck. A few of his new teammates met him at the top of the dugout.

The second inning went much like the first. Fred McGriff, the ever dangerous Crime Dog, was the first batter. El Duque started him off with a curve that snapped over the plate for a strike. McGriff, a left-handed hitter, flinched, as if the pitch had startled him. El Duque's strategy was unconventional. "In a sense he was pitching backward," Buster Olney wrote in the *Times*. "The majority of his contemporaries set up their off-speed pitches with their fastballs. Hernández was setting up his fastball with his off-speed pitches." El Duque came back with a sinking fastball and McGriff beat it into the ground for the first out of the inning. The next hitter was Paul Sorrento, a journeyman slugger. El Duque whiffed him with a plummeting curve in the dirt.

MSG flashed another graphic, the scouting report on El Duque:

- Dangerous Curves Ahead [a nod to the pitcher's myriad curveballs]
- Changes arm angles
- No fear

"Can you imagine where he's been?" said Kaat, his admiration growing. "Just pitching a little big-league baseball game can't be much pressure at all." With each strikeout, fans pasted placards on the front of the mezzanine: El

DuKKKK. One fan in the upper deck unfurled a Cuban flag the size of a parachute. In the Yankee dugout, Torre as usual was stoic, his face betraying nothing. The pitching coach, Mel Stottlemyre, sat near him, watching El Duque put on a clinic. The slightest hint of a smile creased Stottlemyre's face.

By the third, it was clear that the entire stadium was falling in love with El Duque. Kaat was especially enthused. McCracken came up again with a runner on third and two out. He topped a pitch in front of the plate. El Duque took three long strides, corralled the ball as if he were chasing down a stray cat, then wheeled and fired a dart to first for the out. "You can tell he has had a lot of good instruction in Cuba," said Kaat, the winner of sixteen Gold Gloves.

Part of the excitement was that here, at last, was an artist. By 1998, baseball was producing waves of cookie-cutter hurlers, many of them mediocre. The buzzword of the age was "mechanics," a meaningless cliché for fundamentally sound pitching. Every time a pitcher gave up a 400-foot homer he had to go back and work on his "mechanics," as if there were a special garage where pitchers went in for a tune-up. The relentless pursuit of mechanics was driving individuality out of the game. But here was El Duque, fundamentally sound in every respect, mesmerizing hitters with style *and* substance. Kaat took note. "You don't see a guy that's kind of liberated and creative, who's just out there," he said. "Because he's been a successful pitcher for a while in Cuba, he's taking the same approach even though they're big-league hitters."

By the fourth, El Duque was pitching with such confidence that he piped a fastball to McGriff, who pounded it 379 feet over the right-field wall. El Duque walked off the field at the end of the inning, disgusted, down 1–0. But the Yanks unloaded on left-hander Tony Saunders, a sort of poor man's Tom Glavine, for five runs in the bottom of the inning. El Duque coasted the rest of the game, throwing nothing but strikes to everyone except McGriff. "He looks, with his motion and his demeanor and his pace, that if he had to he could pitch eighteen innings," said Kaat. El Duque ended up going seven. He gave up 5 hits, walked 2 and struck out 7.

After Mike Stanton got the final out, preserving the 7–1 win, El Duque bounded back onto the field to greet his teammates. In the background, Frank Sinatra was crooning the opening lines to "New York, New York." The Yankees play the song after every game; after big wins, the fans often join in. The words had never seemed more appropriate:

> *Start spreading the news*
> *I'm leaving today . . .*

Torre retrieved the lineup card from plate umpire Larry McCoy and handed it to El Duque, who was already palming two game balls. As he walked off the field, El Duque bumped into Posada. The catcher went to shake El Duque's hand. El Duque threw his arms around him. The pitcher and catcher walked off the field with their arms around each other, like the groom and his best man staggering into the night at the end of a bachelor party. El Duque wore a padded Yankee jacket. Posada had his mask propped up on his helmet. The crowd above the dugout roared as the two men disappeared into the tunnel.

"What a story," said Singleton finally.

A few minutes later El Duque and Posada appeared on the MSG postgame show with Al Trautwig. El Duque started by thanking Cubas. Posada handled the translation.

"Joe Cubas has been like a father for me in the United States," said El Duque. "I think that without him it would not have been possible to be where I am now."

Trautwig wanted to know how the Yankees had received him.

"The team gave me a big welcome in spring training and now one more time they have shown me that they are not only great sportsmen but humanitarians as well."

Was he nervous?

"No, not nervous. I simply knew I had a responsibility; I had an obligation to myself, to my family, to the Hispanic community and also to the team. The responsibility was big, because I was taking the place of David Cone, an experienced pitcher, one of the best. I love how he pitches but I also want to thank the team and the great support they gave me. It is true what they say: This is a team sport."

The brief interview over, Trautwig thanked Posada for his time and began to send it back to the booth. But El Duque interrupted.

"Excuse me. Just before we say good-bye." Once again, the pitcher burst into tears. "Excuse me, I'm a little emotional. I want to dedicate this game to my mother and my two daughters and my entire family in Cuba, and my family here in the United States. And to all the Hispanic community and all the Yankee fans."

As Posada translated, poorly, El Duque lowered his head and wiped the tears with his pitching hand.

Trautwig wished El Duque luck. The broadcaster signed off to the sound of El Duque, a tiny microphone still attached to his jacket, sobbing.

Downstairs, Sánchez and I waited with the rest of the media. Coincidentally, both of us had transferred from Mexico City to New York that spring, and now El Duque was joining us. I thought about how many times in my career I had referred to an athlete as "a warrior" or "great in the trenches"—any number of clichés. Daily sportswriting lends itself to hyperbole: There are only so many ways, after all, to describe a home run. Words like *ironic* and *tragic* are employed routinely, even when the matter is neither. And now through the door came El Duque Hernández, banished from the game for no good reason, forced to abandon his children and his country, having hidden on the floor of a fishing boat and crossed an ocean to fulfill the most basic child's dream: to stand on the mound at Yankee Stadium, victorious.

BURIED IN THE HOOPLA was the Yankees' record, now 40–13. El Duque's debut, among other things, was an ominous development for the rest of the American League. The Bombers had already looked unstoppable, and now out of nowhere another frontline starter had materialized. The rotation was so strong, in fact, that Torre's first inclination was to send El Duque back to Columbus. The manager was satisfied with his rotation. After the game, he told the media he planned to follow the one-day plan unless ordered to do otherwise, a transparent reference to George Steinbrenner.

Sure enough, the Boss flew in from Tampa the following day and everything changed. El Duque wasn't going anywhere. The odd man out, ultimately, would be Ramiro Mendoza, the versatile right-hander, who would be exiled to the bullpen. From a baseball standpoint, the move was debatable, especially given the history of Yankee flameouts. From a show-business standpoint, it was unassailable. "You can say what you want about [Steinbrenner], but the man does have an idea what he's doing," said Buster Olney. "He's made hundreds of millions of dollars. He buys the team for ten million dollars and now it's worth, what, six hundred million? George, the first thing he's always said is that star quality is important. And El Duque has star quality. If you're a fan, and you're sitting in Westchester County and you're deciding whether or not to go see the game, would you rather see Ramiro Mendoza or the Cuban defector who came over on a boat? The guy with a funky delivery, with the hat curled down and the socks pulled way up high. George understood that immediately."

The beat writers went to get Mendoza's reaction. In the past, similar Steinbrenner power plays had been enough to unleash weeks of unrest in the Bronx.

"I'd rather be a starter, but the bullpen is okay," said Mendoza. "The important thing is to win."

That quote could have been the mantra of the 1998 Yankees, the most understated juggernaut ever built. As great teams go, the Yanks were virtually anonymous. The club would win 114 games in the regular season and 11 more in the playoffs, but it placed not one starter on the American League All-Star Team. Position by position, the 1998 Yankees were no match for the teams to which they were constantly compared: the '27 Yankees, the '61 Yankees, the '76 Reds. They lacked the larger-than-life sluggers of yesteryear: Ruth and Gehrig, Mantle and Maris, Reggie. Missing, too, were the colorful personalities—Billy Martin, Catfish Hunter, Graig Nettles—who once made the team a constant presence on the back pages of the New York tabloids. The Yankees didn't even have a real power hitter, an unthinkable notion at Yankee Stadium. For these reasons and more, the club was often dismissed as somehow less impressive even as it racked up win after win after win.

But rooting for the Yankees in 1998 was no longer like rooting for U.S. Steel: It was like rooting for Microsoft. The team operated with a bland corporate efficiency that meshed perfectly with the user-friendly New York of Mayor Rudolph W. Giuliani. The renovation of the Yankees mirrored the renovation of Times Square. The team was less interesting perhaps, less controversial, with a decidedly richer clientele, but it had been restored to its previous grandeur. In a season when Mark McGwire hit 70 home runs and the three-run homer had become accepted managerial strategy, the Yankees won with pitching and defense and the subtleties that make baseball the greatest game.

In an era of appalling selfishness all across the sporting landscape, the Yankees were a *team*. Torre, a wise and decent man, set the tone. He seemed immune to the absurdities that had plagued previous Yankee skippers. He was particularly adept at keeping Steinbrenner at bay. When the Yankees fell behind the Braves, 2–0, in the 1996 World Series, the Boss, apoplectic as usual, summoned the coaching staff for one of his patented tirades. "We all go up to his office and he's saying, 'How is it possible? We lost two games to Atlanta *here*! The Series is over! How are we going to beat them at home?' " recalled José Cardenal, the team's then first-base coach. "Joe said, 'George, let me tell you something: We travel tonight and we're off tomorrow. We're going to win three in a row in Atlanta, then we're coming back here and win another one.' George was saying, 'Oh, yeah, sure, sure.' Well, that's exactly what happened, man, I swear to God."

Torre later wrote that the prediction was "nothing more than an educated guess, of course, but I used it to calm down George."

In 1998, Steinbrenner was still the wild card in the otherwise tranquil Yankee universe. The threat of an eruption loomed constantly, particularly for the

beat writers, who were forced to monitor the Boss's mood swings like volca-
nologists. "It's like we all have nuclear warheads aimed at each other," said
Olney of the *Times*. For years, the primary instrument of Steinbrenner's des-
potism was a red phone that sat on the desk in the manager's office. When the
phone rang after a Yankee loss it was the ultimate room clearer. Lou Piniella
once ripped the Steinbrenner hotline clear out of the wall. The lava flowed
from the owner to the manager to the players to the tabloids, eventually engulfing the team.

But Torre was "the man who slayed the meanest boss in the business," said
Tom Verducci, a *Sports Illustrated* writer who assisted Torre with his autobiography. Part of it, as Torre himself pointed out, was that Steinbrenner, as he
headed toward seventy, was mellowing. Another factor was that the owner, to
an increasing degree, had taken his spats out of the public eye. Behind the
scenes he directed most of his fury at his young general manager, Brian Cashman. But Torre clearly had Steinbrenner's number. He neutralized the Boss so
effectively that he eventually wrote a management book loosely based on the
subject: *Joe Torre's Ground Rules for Winners: 12 Keys to Managing Team Players, Tough Bosses, Setbacks, and Success.*

The hot-button phrase, of course, was "Tough Bosses." Torre penned three
separate chapters on that subject alone. "George has not had a negative influence on our clubhouse," the manager wrote in a chapter titled: "Dealing with
Tough Bosses III: Deference, Distance, and Dialogue: Striking the Balance." "If
anything, he motivates people by challenging them. With the volatile Yankee
teams of the seventies and eighties, players and managers would overreact to
every slight, which led to a media feeding frenzy. Beat writers and broadcasters
never had to worry whether they would have something to report the next day.
The stories would go on and on, because people never knew how to keep it
under control."

It wasn't that the Yankees were homogeneous. On the contrary, the clubhouse was filled with diversity. "Take a look at their pitching rotation, for example," observed Bob Elliott, the veteran *Toronto Sun* writer. "David Wells, a
California surfer whose mom used to hang with the Hell's Angels; David Cone,
one of the original night crawlers; Andy Pettitte, a devout Christian; Orlando
Hernández, who arrived in the U.S. after fleeing Cuba on a raft; and Hideki
Irabu, the Nolan Ryan of Japan, with a $12.5 million U.S. deal."

But every player bought in to Torre's philosophy, turning the clubhouse
into a black hole for controversy and news. Cone, the thirty-five-year-old
pitcher, acted as a sort of corporate spokesman—part sage, part spin doctor.

Bernie Williams, the graceful center fielder, occupied the most prominent cubicle in the room, the spacious "Mattingly Corner," where he kept an impressive array of amps and guitars. Yet his zone of privacy was so vast that Mark Kriegel of the *Daily News* described him, in his eighth season, as "something of a shy stranger." Derek Jeter, the amazing shortstop, was a cheerful blank slate. Right fielder Paul O'Neill, an immense talent, was known for trashing batting helmets and water coolers, but he kept the media at a comfortable distance, even though his sister, Molly, was a *Times* food columnist. "There's nobody in that clubhouse who's gonna leak you a story," said team broadcaster Michael Kay, who once made a living off the Yankee turmoil as a nearly unbeatable beatman for the *Post* and later the *Daily News*. "The stars on the team are one-hundred-percent baseball players, just very professional. They don't celebrate on the field, they don't do the high-five stuff, they don't stand and watch home runs. It's really a different team for this day and age. I've heard a lot of opposing players say, 'You know, you want to hate their guts so much because they have everything going for them. But you can't, because they're such good guys.'"

Buster Olney of the *Times* marveled at how the players consistently shielded one another from controversy. Olney was the perfect beat writer to chronicle these new Yankees, a writer of great style and nuance. Olney knew tranquillity when he saw it: He grew up on a 120-acre dairy farm in Randolph Center, Vermont, where the cows (1,000) outnumbered the people (400). Olney's family didn't buy a television until he was sixteen. Randolph Center had but one general store, Floyd's, where every Sunday the Olneys received *The New York Times* and *The Boston Globe*. It was after meeting legendary columnist Red Smith at a prep-school dinner that Olney decided to become a sportswriter. But his baseball sensibilities were shaped by a weekly diet of Peter Gammons, who raised beat writing to an art form while covering the Red Sox for the *Globe* in the 1970s.

Gammons later became a well-known television analyst. But he set the standard for an entire generation of baseball writers, combining exhaustive reporting with passionate prose, often at a Herculean rate of three and four stories a day. In his hands, the Red Sox, an interesting, if cursed, franchise, became a kind of macabre summer serial. His game stories were less news accounts than essays on the daily drama of the Olde Towne Team. It is probably safe to say that no one has covered baseball like Peter Gammons in 1978. When the season came down to one apocalyptic game between the Red Sox and the Yankees, and it seemed like the entire world had stopped, Gammons led his advance with the opening lines of *A Tale of Two Cities*: "It was the best of times, it was the worst of times, it was the age of wisdom, it was the age of foolishness, it was the epoch of belief, it was the epoch of incredulity, it was the season of Light, it was the season of Darkness . . ."

In the same classic story, Gammons wrote that a particular Luis Tiant curveball "looked as if it had been prepared by a team of chefs, surgeons, locksmiths, belt-buckle artisans and bartenders."

Like his idol, Olney, at thirty-four, was an obsessive reporter who served up a seamless blend of exclusive information, analysis and liquid prose. By his own admission, he was a relentless "seamhead," a kind of baseball nerd. During the season, he often looked like he was working on three hours' sleep. He developed his polished style covering hundreds of games over constantly shifting time zones under the most brutal deadlines in journalism. He began his career in Nashville with the now defunct *Banner,* covered the San Diego Padres for the *Union-Tribune,* then moved on to Baltimore to cover the Orioles for the *Sun.* When he was hired to cover baseball for the *Times,* which was expanding its sports section after years of neglect, he was struck by how different the Yankees were from the Bronx Zoo of his childhood memory.

The Yankees were far more cohesive than the Orioles, an underachieving team dominated by one man, Baltimore icon Cal Ripken, Jr. Olney admired Ripken's strength and endurance. But he believed that the shortstop's all-consuming pursuit of Gehrig's consecutive-games record, which he broke in 1995, had divided the team into self-absorbed factions. In 1996, Olney was standing in the clubhouse when an image of Barry Bonds appeared on a television monitor. Brady Anderson, the O's center fielder, was watching, and he turned to Olney and commented, "What a great player."

"Second best player I've ever seen," said Olney.

"Well, who's the first?" Anderson asked.

Olney pointed across the clubhouse at second baseman Roberto Alomar.

"So he says to me, 'That just shows you don't know anything about baseball.' And I said, 'Well, actually, Brady, the guy's a great defensive player, he can do a lot of things.' And he said, 'No, you don't know what you're talking about. Barry can do this and this and this.' And I said, 'Brady, I'm entitled to my opinion.' Then he got in my face, screaming, 'You don't know shit about baseball! You don't know anything about baseball!' And this is his *teammate.*"

Later that year Alomar was ejected for spitting at umpire John Hirschbeck. The act was reprehensible, for sure, but both men had been under tremendous pressure and Hirschbeck seemed to have instigated the argument. Alomar's teammates left him twisting in the wind. The writers went to Ripken, the elder statesman, hoping for some perspective. "It was nothing. 'No comment,' " said Olney. "Because you've got to maintain the iron. You've got to be the Iron Man. You've got to be pristine. If I'm covering the Yankees and that happens, Cone's out front, Jeter's out front saying, 'Hey, you know what? Robby's a good guy. Maybe he just overreacted a little bit. It's an unfortunate situation. But I think Hirschbeck has some accountability in this matter. . . .' It's just two totally different situations."

Olney noted how the Yankees policed themselves. "I'll give you an example: They get into a game, a really hot Sunday afternoon, and the umpire is Greg Kosc. So Kosc makes some bad calls. He's having a bad day. He's obviously affected by the heat. He's got cold towels wrapped around him. Posada had been called out on a couple of pitches, and after the game he just torches him. He says, 'This guy's out of shape. He's fat. What kind of crap is this?' Posada's relationship with umpires is critical, obviously. So several teammates—I'm sure Cone was one of them—basically buried him in private and said, 'What the fuck are you doing? You go out and apologize.' So the next day Posada came out, went down to the umpires' room and apologized. It's the type of thing they do."

Thus, it surprised no one when Ramiro Mendoza made an uneventful, magnanimous slide into the bullpen to make room for El Duque. It was simply the right thing to do. In a way it seems like a small act, but it meant that a pitcher who was new to the major leagues, new to New York, new to America, new to capitalism, would be welcomed into the Yankee fold. The Yankees' principal virtue was selflessness. The collective attitude eliminated all distractions that might interfere with what had become a relentless assault on history.

EL DUQUE MADE his second start on June 9 at baseball's most desolate outpost: Olympic Stadium in Montreal. Even with the Yankees as a draw, the crowd looked like it was by invitation only. The upper deck was barren. In the lower deck, fans sat in clusters; it was a cult more than a crowd. The game held none of the drama of El Duque's first outing, yet in many ways it was just as extraordinary.

El Duque threw another improvisational puzzle, this time with Joe Girardi, who did not speak Spanish, behind the plate. Even from the press box, it is usually not difficult to make out the pitches: fastball, curveball, forkball, etc. But at times no one in the building except El Duque and Girardi had any idea what the pitcher was throwing.

The second hitter of the game was José Vidro, a left-handed batter. El Duque toed the rubber.

"He's got five pitches, that's what the scouts say," said Al Trautwig, calling the game with Singleton. The words were no sooner out of Trautwig's mouth than El Duque unleashed a pitch that traveled to the plate on a direct line, then dropped like a stone. Vidro flailed helplessly.

"There's one," said Singleton.

"What was it?" asked Trautwig.

"I don't *know*," said Singleton, chuckling.

He examined the replay. "It looked like a change-up. Let's call this a change-up. It starts knee-high and falls directly out of the zone."

That was pretty much the tenor of the evening. By the fourth, the Yankees were up 6–0 and El Duque, as they say, was in the rocking chair. By then, it seemed like he had been pitching in the majors for years. He was throwing nothing but strikes and near strikes, the pitches coming from all over Canada: over the top, three-quarters, sidearm and in between. It looked like he had nine different curveballs. For the Expos, Singleton noted, the mix had to be "very disconcerting."

With the Yankees in command, Trautwig and Singleton began to discuss the phenomenon they were now witnessing. Usually when a player is called up, the announcers try to spice things up with a little background information ("Orlando likes to hunt elk in the off-season"). But this, obviously, was off the charts. El Duque's bizarre career path was already stretching the boundaries of sports journalism. After his debut, the *Post* managed to squeeze Fidel Castro, El Duque's pitching line, the final score and the attendance into the same memorable paragraph:

> In seven innings, the former ace of the Cuban national team who escaped Fidel Castro's hell hole in a small raft with his wife and six others last December allowed five hits and one run and pitched the Yankees to a 7–1 win over the Devil Rays in front of 27,291 fans.

Now, as El Duque worked through the fourth inning against the Montreal Expos, Trautwig began to mix some political commentary into his play-by-play. The trigger was a billboard that the Yankees had passed on their way to the stadium. It was an advertisement inviting Canadians to vacation in Cuba— perfectly legal, of course, without a trade embargo.

"We've chronicled the story of El Duque having to leave Cuba on a small, uh, ship—some call it a raft—and surviving a rescue that wound up with him going to Costa Rica and finally signing a contract with the Yankees," Trautwig began. "And you know that relations between the United States and Cuba are such that you can't just go to JFK or LaGuardia and hop on a plane for Havana.

"But things are a little different up here in Canada. In fact, on the way to the ballpark here tonight imagine what El Duque thought as he was riding on the highway and saw an advertisement for people in Montreal to travel to Havana."

MSG flashed an image of the offending billboard, which bore the message: CUBA—AN UNFORGETTABLE WARMTH.

Vladimir Guerrero grounded out to short.

"Out at first base, big throw by Sojo," said Trautwig.

He continued.

"Seriously, can you imagine?" said Trautwig. "You've got a Communist country that prevents you from being with your family, forces you to escape to freedom and here's a travel poster? Yeah, that Fidel Castro, he runs a resort like Disney, you know what I mean?"

Guerrero broke up El Duque's shutout in the ninth, but by then everyone was plenty convinced that, as the *Post*'s Wallace Matthews wrote later in the season, "El Duque is no fluque." The next day, Olney made the rounds to get some reaction. One of his first stops was Mike Borzello, a Yankee assistant whose job was to chart pitches by type, speed and location. Borzello had been sitting behind the plate, but he confessed to Olney that he had often had no idea what El Duque was throwing. An American League scout sitting next to Borzello had been equally baffled. "My job is to find a pattern in what he does, eliminate possible pitches he'll throw in different situations," the scout said. "I couldn't eliminate anything. I don't think you can guess the pitches. The best thing to do might be to just look for something in one part of the strike zone. He's like a Rembrandt, or a Barbra Streisand. The guy is an artist. It was the best-pitched game I've seen this year."

Olney went into the Yankee clubhouse to talk to El Duque. The writer wondered exactly how high the pitcher could lift his leg. El Duque shrugged and twice whipped his right foot above an adjacent locker, holding it above Paul O'Neill's nameplate. The locker was six and a half feet tall.

Obviously, El Duque was here to stay. Before long, Olney had decided to start taking Spanish lessons in the off-season to better understand this fascinating new Yankee.

CHAPTER SIXTEEN

THE CIRCLE CHANGE

THE YANKEE FIRST-BASE COACH HAPPENED TO BE CUBAN: A FORMER major-league outfielder named José Cardenal. In the operation of a great and powerful baseball machine, Cardenal played a relatively minor role. Many fans had no idea who the Yankee first-base coach even was. But Cardenal became appreciably more important with El Duque's arrival. Among other things, he was the only Yankee who remotely understood the complexity of the pitcher's transition from pariah of the Cuban revolution to emerging star on the most famous team in American sports.

Cardenal had grown up in Matanzas, the province directly east of Havana. His father was a black carpenter who earned $5 a week. His mother was a white housekeeper. The family resided in a one-room apartment with a concrete floor and two beds: one for Cardenal, his father and two brothers, the other for his mother and two sisters. The apartment was part of a sweltering complex of brick and rock equipped with one communal outhouse for six families.

Cardenal's memory was still scarred by the embedded racism of prerevolutionary Cuba. More than four decades later, he could instantly recall the names of the pristine beaches and glittery private clubs he had been forbidden to enter. As a boy, one of his favorite pastimes was to hurl rocks through the windows of the Casino Español, a whites-only club whose uniformed attendants often kicked him off the sidewalk. "We'd break the windows and take off running," he said. "I was one of the leaders. There were six or seven of us. We hated the way they treated us, we just hated them."

From an early age Cardenal saw baseball as a way to transcend the poverty and racism that surrounded him. In 1954 his brother Pedro signed with the St. Louis Cardinals and started sending back $50 each month to help his family. On weekends Cardenal's father would take him by train into Havana to watch the Cuban professional league. After the games Cardenal would stand in the parking lot and watch the players drive away in their Cadillac convertibles. Among them was the national hero, Orestes "Minnie" Miñoso, who played for the Chicago White Sox during the summer. Cardenal couldn't help but notice that Miñoso was even blacker than he was. "He always drove a white Cadillac," Cardenal recalled. "And he always had three blondes in the backseat."

"I'm going to park my convertible right over there," Cardenal told his father.

Then, in the first hours of 1959, the triumphant caravan that carried Fidel Castro to power snaked through Matanzas on its way to Havana. Cardenal and his family stood in the blockaded streets, cheering as the charismatic thirty-two-year-old leader passed by. Fidel had fought for people like the Cardenals: the poor and the black and the marginalized. Their lives could only get better. Two years later, Cardenal signed with the San Francisco Giants for $250, joining his cousin Bert Campaneris, Tony Pérez, Tony Oliva and Luis Tiant as part of the last wave of Cuban ballplayers to migrate legally to the United States. Cardenal thought that, like his hero Miñoso, he would return home every winter. From his meager signing bonus, he gave $50 to his father and $50 to his mother. He used $100 to buy a new suit and a new glove. The other $50 he took with him to the States, where he played eighteen seasons in the major leagues. He didn't return to Cuba until his father's death in 1984.

Cardenal often said that he would never have taken the same risks as El Duque to play major-league baseball. "You have to ask yourself what's more important: freedom or death," he said. "For him it was freedom. For me it would be death." Cardenal was immensely proud of El Duque, as a Cuban and as a ballplayer. He was in awe of the pitcher's inner strength, his confidence and serenity on the mound. Most of all he could empathize with El Duque's poor upbringing; he liked to joke that they both had "smart asses" because they had grown up using the newspaper as toilet tissue. Cardenal sought to help ease El Duque into his new life and shield him from the distractions that came with being a professional athlete.

For the growing legions of Latin Americans in the major leagues, the transition to professional baseball was dramatic. Many players did not speak English. The economic pressures—to lift one's family out of life-threatening poverty—were enormous. The temptations were constant. As Marcos Bretón has written, cities like New York are littered with ex-ballplayers, their visas expired, their dreams and signing bonuses long gone. But El Duque carried with him a more unique burden of the Latin American experience: the legacy of communism. He had come from a place where friends, neighbors and even teammates informed on one another. "The big secret about repression in Cuba is that it's internal, it's psychological," said Jorge Morejón, a former journalist for Prensa Latina, the Cuban news agency. By the time El Duque arrived in the States, he had seen the capriciousness of success. In a New York minute his life had been torn apart over issues well beyond his control, issues of global politics and ideology. Inside Cuba it was widely assumed—although never proven— that his best friend, Germán Mesa, had helped precipitate his downfall. By nature, El Duque was private and suspicious, with a Cuban predilection to *discutir*, to argue, everything under the sun. He brought this baggage into the New York Yankee clubhouse and the world's largest media market.

"It was very hard for him in the beginning; the changes in his life were so drastic," said infielder Luis Sojo, who became one of his closest friends on the team. Within a year El Duque's combativeness would subside to the point where it was only occasionally an issue. In those first weeks, however, he seemed to fight constant battles. In a way, it was something of a paradox. El Duque's teammates, to a man, accorded him immense respect. The media, after months covering a powerful yet colorless team, feasted on his amazing story. The fans immediately adored him. Yet he seemed to see enemies lurking around every corner.

On one of his first days as a Yankee, El Duque announced to Cardenal that he was getting ready to pummel one of the team's relievers, Mike Stanton. The tension apparently surfaced over El Duque's unorthodox training style. On his own, the pitcher performed a number of don't-try-this-at-home exercises, most of which he had learned from his former Industriales teammate Euclides Rojas, a physical therapist. El Duque would stand on his head for several moments scissoring his legs, an exercise Rojas believed helped circulation. To increase his equilibrium he stuck his index fingers in his ears, flared his elbows, spun ten times, then planted his feet and focused. He did a series of lateral hopping exercises to strengthen his legs. After games, while his teammates went home, he sometimes ran wind sprints on the warning track then ate dinner in front of his locker.

"In essence he was training twice," said Cardenal. "He was doing his old routine and he was training with the team. Some of the pitchers, including Stanton, started bothering him about it. Stanton used to say that El Duque had his own program. He'd say that El Duque didn't want to work with anybody else. It was just a constant thing. So one day El Duque told me he was going to deck Stanton. He said, 'If he doesn't leave me alone I'm gonna hit him.' I told him, 'I don't want you to do that, but if he keeps fucking with you, go ahead, and I'll tell Joe why you hit him.' "

Cardenal was already suspicious of Stanton, whom he believed to be something of a hypocrite. The pitcher, along with other players, belonged to a team Bible study group. Cardenal, who was Catholic, thought the players sometimes failed to practice what they preached. "They always wanted you to pray with them and then when you turned around they were talking behind your back," said Cardenal. "Stanton was always getting into people's business. They'd talk about God for half an hour and then go into the dugout and start criticizing everybody. What kind of Christians are they?"

Cardenal went to Torre and Stottlemyre. "I told Joe and Mel, 'I don't want any problems here. El Duque works very hard and these guys keep fucking with him.' Mel said, 'No, he works harder than he has to.' And I said, 'Fine, then tell these guys to leave him alone.' "

The problems ended there. Torre told me that Stottlemyre informed the complainers that they, too, could work out on their own. "I remember Mel telling the other pitchers, 'If you want to do as much as he does, go ahead,' " said Torre. For his part, Stanton declined to comment except to acknowledge that there had been a problem. "It happened here in the clubhouse and it's going to stay here," he said. "If someone else wants to talk about it, that's fine, but I'm not talking about it."

To Luis Sojo the dispute stemmed not so much from Stanton and the other pitchers but from El Duque's early paranoia and stubbornness. "Stanton and [reliever] Jeff Nelson always had something to say; they fucked with everybody," said Sojo. "But when El Duque first came up, whenever he heard an American say his name he thought they were talking shit about him. He'd get enraged. He always wanted to fight. He'd say, 'That shit-eater is talking about me again. I'm going to break his neck.' I had to get in his face and explain, 'Look, they're not talking about you, okay?' "

Even Sojo nearly came to blows with El Duque. The explosive issue was the national anthem. A few weeks after El Duque's arrival, the Yankees were in Atlanta for a series with the Braves. "You know the way Americans are very strict about certain things," said Sojo, who is Venezuelan. "So one day El Duque didn't want to come out for the anthem. I said, 'Orlando, listen, I have a little more experience here than you. We have to be outside for the anthem. Let's go, Orlando, come on.' He got pissed. He was like, 'Don't fuck with me, *cojones!* I'm not going out there for any anthem.' I said, 'Look, shit-eater, I'm only doing my

job. I'm trying to help you!' We got into an argument right there in the clubhouse. I thought we were going to fight. He eventually made it out. We stopped
talking for a couple days but then we became friends."

Some of El Duque's most furious battles were with his new catcher, Jorge
Posada. Normally, rookie pitchers are more than content to let the catcher or
the bench call the pitches. El Duque shook off Posada in his very first game.
The tension was immediate. Posada was the son of a Cuban father, a ballplayer
who had fled the revolution, and a Puerto Rican mother. He was born and
raised in Puerto Rico. Generally speaking, the relationship between the two islands is a complicated one, fused with strong feelings about independence and
sovereignty. José Martí, Cuba's poet and independence hero, famously called
Cuba and Puerto Rico "two wings of the same bird." And yet after the Spanish-
American War, Cuba gained its independence from Spain while Puerto Rico
was handed over to the United States, of which it remains a commonwealth.

All of which is probably beside the point, but El Duque and Posada battled
each other like brothers. Similar in temperament, stubborn, both had something to prove. Posada would later become an all-star, but at this point he was
still trying to establish himself as the Yankees' everyday catcher. And here was
El Duque, a rookie—a thirty-two-year-old rookie, but still a rookie—challenging his pitch selection. In context, it was no small matter. The fundamental
issue was who controlled the game: the pitcher or the catcher.

Posada stormed out to the mound one afternoon during a game against
the Marlins. "I kept calling for a pitch and he kept shaking me off," said Posada.
"I don't remember what the pitch was, but I walked out there and I said, 'Look,
you have to throw this!' And he said, 'No, I'm not throwing it!' Right after that
they hit a shot off of him, and when we got back to the dugout we started cursing at each other. We used every curse you can possibly imagine."

Sojo was one of the few players who could fully understand the exchange,
not that it was difficult to decode. As he watched it unfold, the two players
stood toe-to-toe, arguing in the middle of the dugout.

"Posada was yelling, 'Look, you *comemierda* [shit-eater] you have to throw
what I *tell* you to throw!' And El Duque was in his face saying, 'No, I'm not
going to throw that shit!' "

"It was a growing experience for both of us," said Posada. "We both came
out of it closer friends. Over time it became easier for us to talk and disagree
without blowing up."

At times it seemed like El Duque had emerged not just from a different
country but from a different era entirely. In recent years, Cuban managers have

adopted American practices in handling pitchers, employing pitch counts, setup men and closers. But El Duque was accustomed to going the distance, throwing 150 or 160 pitches or more in an outing. The idea of exiting with a lead was unthinkable, no less than an assault on his manhood. In Cuba, if INDER statistics are to be believed, El Duque had completed 75 of 187 starts, more than 40 percent. Compare this with a hard-nosed American pitcher like David Cone, for example, who on entering the 2000 season had completed 56 out of 361 starts, or 16 percent.

It wasn't all that long ago that major-league pitchers had El Duque's mentality, but no longer. It was the age of specialization. Torre and Stottlemyre, who had come from a grittier time, loved El Duque's competitiveness and drive. They loved how he always wanted the ball. But it made for some uncomfortable scenes. The responsibility for notifying El Duque that he was out of the game often fell to his bilingual catcher.

The exchanges often went as follows:

El Duque: "No way, I'm not coming out."

Posada: "Look, that's it, you're done."

The catcher would then point out to the bullpen.

"Look, they're bringing in this guy. Here he comes."

El Duque would stand on the mound, glove on his hip, incredulous over the injustice of it all. "How can that be? I feel fine!"

"And then I'd have to explain it to him all over again," said Posada.

EL DUQUE SPENT his rookie season in a two-room suite at the Hotel Roger Smith at Forty-seventh Street and Lexington Avenue in Manhattan. Cardenal, who also lived there, had gotten him the room, bringing the pitcher out of his isolation at the Fort Lee Hilton. The Roger Smith, supposedly named after a mythical traveler, was small and unpretentious; it was located five blocks north of Grand Central Terminal, enabling Cardenal and El Duque to catch the number 4 subway and be at Yankee Stadium in twenty minutes.

El Duque traveled unnoticed at first, but before long his fellow commuters began to besiege him for autographs. The principal reason was that he continued to win. After his first two starts there had been some lingering skepticism, if only because the teams he had beaten, Tampa Bay and Montreal, were among the weakest in baseball. In his third start El Duque traveled to Cleveland to face the defending American League champions. There was no doubt that this would be a test. The Indians' pitching staff was young and erratic, but the batting order was loaded: Kenny Lofton, Omar Vizquel, David Justice, Manny Ramírez, Jim Thome, Travis Fryman. It went on and on. Cleveland's style was to bludgeon pitchers into submission.

It was June 18, a hot night in Cleveland, and El Duque took the mound at Jacobs Field in a turtleneck. He carried a shutout into the eighth inning. All night, he slithered in and out of desperate jams. El Duque has large hands, and at times as he threw he made the baseball seem like an egg in the hands of a magician. The third inning was typical: The Tribe put a runner on third with one out. El Duque then struck out Ramírez with a murderous slider and Thome with a change-up that had all the violent force of a Nerf ball. Thome, who would look just as comfortable hacking cordwood as he would a baseball, ripped straight through the pitch.

As the Indians' futility mounted, manager Mike Hargrove tried a novel tactic. Hargrove noticed that El Duque wiggled his fingers inside his glove when he went into the stretch. Twice he tried to argue that this behavior constituted a balk. Hargrove's tactics were pure gamesmanship, blatant attempts to unnerve an untested rookie.

As Hargrove argued, David Cone moved to the top step of the dugout.

"Hey, he came over on a boat! That's not going to scare him!" Cone yelled as the Yankee bench erupted in laughter.

The Yanks won 5–2. El Duque didn't get the win because the game was tied when he left, but no one cared. His ERA was 1.52. Now the praise was unrestrained. Cone called him "one of the most poised pitchers I've ever been around." Torre marveled: "He's just got such a calm about him." Tom Keegan, a veteran baseball writer for the *Post*, watched the performance with similar awe. Keegan was rarely given to oversentimentality. In 1999, when Mets manager Bobby Valentine volunteered that he should be fired if his team missed the playoffs, Keegan wrote a column beneath the headline: WHY WAIT? CAN THE PHONY NOW! But even Keegan was gushing over a pitcher with three major-league starts under his belt:

> Maybe it's the way his right knee nearly brushes his chin at the beginning of his delivery. It could be the swiftness with which he bounds off the mound and is at home plate in a flash when a runner is on third and a pitch is in the dirt. Or is it how he changes from a ground ball pitcher to a strikeout artist the moment a runner advances within 90 feet of scoring?
>
> So limber, so nimble, so clutch.

Whatever the cause, Orlando "El Duque" Hernandez is a pitcher who grips an audience and forces it to watch him. He's different, from his delivery to his high socks to his myriad arm angles to his quick feet.

El Duque had to lose eventually. And so it was that the Braves came to town and pounded him one evening at the stadium. El Duque was matched up against Tom Glavine, the great left-hander. He never really looked comfortable. He looked like the intensity of his long ordeal had finally caught up with him. Normally formal and well groomed, he looked somewhat disheveled on the mound. There were deep circles under his eyes, the shadow of a mustache on his upper lip. The fourth inning was interminable. It began with Javy López hitting a 450-foot foul ball. The Braves then fouled off pitch after pitch as they chipped away. El Duque, muttering, finally threw a belt-high fastball to Chipper Jones, as if he wanted him to hit it. Jones smacked a two-run single into center field, putting the Braves ahead 6–1. El Duque, done, jogged off the field. Cardenal whispered some encouragement into his ear. El Duque grabbed a cup of water and wrapped a towel around his neck, but he stayed in the dugout.

Sánchez and I went to see him after the game, expecting his mood to be dark. How, we wondered, would El Duque handle his first defeat? We found him philosophical.

"*Así es la pelota*," said El Duque. That's baseball.

AFTER THE ALL-STAR BREAK, Brook Larmer, *Newsweek*'s Latin America correspondent, followed El Duque out to Anaheim to watch him pitch against the Angels. Larmer had known El Duque in Cuba and had written several stories about his trials. Now he was preparing a feature on the pitcher's new life. He found El Duque surrounded by the trappings of wealth and success—tailored suits, Hugo Boss shirts, a cell phone that seemed surgically attached to his ear—yet painfully sad about his separation from his daughters. "On the surface, I try not to show anything," he told Larmer, "but underneath I'm suffering a lot."

Larmer told El Duque that he was traveling to Havana the following week. El Duque loaded him down with toys for the girls. He then went out and absorbed his worst defeat of the season, the Angels pounding him for 10 runs and 13 hits in 3⅓ innings. The game highlighted El Duque's principal weakness: his vulnerability against left-handed batters. The pitcher was less effective at concealing the ball from lefties, and if he failed to keep them honest by pitching in-side, they crowded the plate and pounced on his various curves. But that was an issue that could be worked out on the mound. El Duque's separation from his daughters was not so easily resolved.

Larmer arrived in Havana in early August. He first dropped in to see El Duque's mother, María Julia, still living across the street from the church in Wajay. María Julia said she no longer cried when someone asked about her son. But her calendar remained stuck on December 25, 1997—the First Christmas, the date that El Duque had left Havana, en route to the sea. Inside Cuba, there was an eerie déjà vu quality about the events unfolding in New York. The pre-vious summer, the island had pulsated with Liván's magical run to the World Series. Now, incredibly, El Duque appeared to be on the same path. On August 13—Fidel's seventy-second birthday—El Duque struck out 13 Texas Rangers in a 2–0 win. News of the performance, with all its uncanny symbolism, im-mediately reached Havana, where Larmer and María Julia toasted with a bottle of rum.

Larmer then went to deliver the toys to the girls. The powder-blue house, given to El Duque by a government that had since disowned him, still bore traces of his presence. On a rooftop water tank, his subversive name—EL DUKE—was scrawled in faded graffiti. Larmer arrived to a fairly surreal scene: The pitcher's ex-wife, Norma Manzo, was entertaining about thirty people in the shadow of the tank. In the backyard, her new boyfriend was shaving a re-cently deceased 300-pound pig with a disposable razor. It was a festive roast—financed, obviously, by George Steinbrenner and the man whose faded name appeared on the water tank.

Larmer gave the toys to the girls: dolls and some Disney paraphernalia. Eight-year-old Yahumara said she wanted her father "to keep on winning—and to get me all the Barbies he can." Larmer then pulled out another gift, a Mickey Mouse tote bag. Yahumara wheeled the suitcase down the walkway of her father's old house. "I'm going on a trip to New York!" she exclaimed.

For his part, El Duque was certainly enjoying his new life. He was able to buy a Miami Beach condo and a BMW—a vast improvement on Osmany's quarter-century-old Muscovy. But to anyone who spent time around him that summer, he often seemed preoccupied over his separation from his daughters and a litany of new concerns. He was smoking a pack a day of Marlboros, now readily available to him. He was facing tens of thousands of dollars in legal fees in Costa Rica, along with Juan Carlos Romero's lawsuit. He had an increasingly rancorous dispute with Tío over expenses from the escape and its aftermath. In Miami, Tom Cronin had resurfaced to sue Cubas for one-third of the commissions on El Duque's earnings, even though El Duque held Cronin partly responsible for his banishment in Cuba. El Duque ultimately would be deposed in the extremely bitter lawsuit.* At times he seemed most comfortable on the mound, where the rules were exactly the same as they had been in Cuba.

Very few of these issues were known around the Yankees. In many ways El Duque remained as mysterious as on the day he arrived. He kept a respectful distance from his teammates. After games he often retreated to a Cuban diner, Mambí, which he had stumbled upon one day after getting lost on his way to Yankee Stadium while still commuting in from Jersey. The restaurant was a hole-in-the-wall at Broadway and 177th Street in Washington Heights, but it had excellent Cuban cuisine and a down-to-earth clientele. It was there that El Duque relaxed, gorging himself on comfort food: pork ribs, beans and white rice. The owner, Billy Morales, had grown up in Remedio, the same town as El Duque's father, and he and the pitcher became friends. One night after a game Sánchez and I had dinner with El Duque at Mambí. Afterward, we all walked out onto Broadway. It was about two A.M., and in front of the restaurant on the sidewalk, two men were playing dominoes on top of a cardboard box. El Duque sat down on the curb and played for several minutes, slapping down the tiles as if he were back in Havana.

At times Sánchez and I wondered whether El Duque was entirely comfortable with his sudden wealth, his life among the privileged of capitalism. His life was certainly easier and he had more than enough toys. Instead of harassing him, the police now cut him slack as he drove like a maniac through Manhattan. He often relished the attention. But in Cuba, the distance between him and the average citizen had been not nearly as great, even during his salad days. He had had a house and certain privileges, but he had to scramble like everyone else. Roberto "Pelusa" Martínez, one of El Duque's best friends, once told me that El Duque had been "a revolutionary" in the same way that he was. They valued the revolution's achievements, the universal health care and the absence of extreme poverty and the commitment to education. They were fiercely proud of the country. "In that sense, yes, El Duque was a revolutionary," said Pelusa.

El Duque admitted that he never would have left Cuba had the government not essentially forced him out. One evening Sánchez and his girlfriend, Joyce Wong, went over to visit the pitcher at the Roger Smith. It was difficult to

---

*A Miami jury ruled in November 2000 that Cubas was not obligated to compensate Cronin for El Duque's contract. However, during the course of the trial Cubas reportedly disclosed that he had not filed tax returns since 1994, a confession that seemed to pique the interest of the Internal Revenue Service.

walk inside the small suite. The room was stuffed with the gratuitous perks of El Duque's new fame: designer sunglasses, compact-disc players, unwrapped sweaters, athletic shoes, cigars—boxes and boxes of free stuff.

"Look at all this," he said finally to Sánchez. "Look at how much I make, and I get all this shit for nothing. You make a fraction of what I make, and you can't afford it. There's something wrong there. There's something wrong with this system."

Sánchez asked him what he meant. El Duque backed off. "Ah, you're still better off here," he said.

OF ALL THE CHANGES in the pitcher's life, the constant presence of the media was perhaps the most profound. Inside Cuba, the Communist party press had been El Duque's invisible nemesis, an instrument used by the government to keep him down. Even when he had been a superstar he had little contact with reporters. By design the Cuban press tended to emphasize collective rather than individual achievements. Thus, there were no features on the players' private lives, no up-close-and-personal interviews, no sportswriters asking El Duque why he had thrown a curveball instead of a change-up. There were not even box scores. After El Duque was banned he frequently raged about the Communist media's refusal to print his version of events. He wanted to tell the country what had happened, but no one except foreigners and friends would listen to him.

New York was at the other end of the media spectrum. No fewer than eight newspapers and one radio station, WFAN, traveled with the Yankees full-time. At home, the coverage grew exponentially: fifteen papers, a dozen radio stations, two websites and the official team magazine, not to mention the visiting and national media. It was a small army that gathered in the clubhouse every afternoon to collect data on the comings and goings of the Yankee universe. The beat writers, particularly those from the tabloids, competed fiercely over the tiniest minutiae: injury updates, team meetings, trade rumors, adjustments in the pitching rotation, September call-ups. It was the ultimate in saturation coverage.

All of this made El Duque's situation more curious. Yankee Stadium was hardly the place to keep a secret. Yet even the most basic information about the pitcher—most notably his age and how he arrived—remained shrouded in mystery. El Duque was usually cordial with the writers; if he was occasionally testy, there was little of the coldness that had existed with Irabu (the *Post*'s George King referred to El Duque as "the anti-Irabu"). But he told them almost nothing about his pitching or his life, both of which of course inspired a million questions. I watched several times as El Duque spat out one-word answers to writers who rarely bothered to lift their pens. The language barrier actually made it easier for El Duque to conceal. The Yankees were not the United Nations; professional translators were not in great abundance. When the role fell to Cardenal, he often censored El Duque's answers for public consumption. "I wouldn't always translate everything he said," Cardenal told me. "I knew they were going to misinterpret it, so I wouldn't tell them everything."

No issue was more sensitive, of course, than the circumstances surrounding the great escape. From the moment El Duque arrived, he had been barraged with inevitable questions about his amazing journey, but the cover-up continued. El Duque didn't feel any moral misgivings; he believed that he was protecting the people who had returned to Cuba after delivering him to the Bahamas. But there was no way he could have imagined how wildly the story would spin out of control.

In the original version cooked up in the Bahamas, you may recall, the group supposedly had traveled on a twenty-foot sailboat that took on water after leaving Cuba. The fictitious boat ultimately sank, stranding everyone on Anguilla Cay. Had El Duque then failed, had he languished in the minor leagues or ended up like Alberto Hernández, repairing cars in a Costa Rica garage or even toiling in obscurity for the Pittsburgh Pirates, no one would have given it a second thought. But a funny thing happened: El Duque became a rising star with the 1998 New York Yankees, one of the greatest teams ever assembled. And so his story, in the absence of real details, began to take on a life of its own.

El Duque's posturing only contributed to the growing-fish story. When he arrived in Tampa, he told the media that the escape was still too painful to discuss. In Columbus, he repeated this explanation whenever writers broached the subject. Then, after he was called up, he again said the matter was too painful, his emotions too raw.

Over time even that story evolved. Cubas passed the word that a movie was in the works with Cuba Gooding, Jr., in the lead role and Antonio Banderas, more implausibly, playing the stumpy sports agent. There was also the prospect of a book.* El Duque used these impending deals as yet another excuse not to talk about the escape. The Yankee beat writers began to grow suspicious.

---

*In the interests of full disclosure, it should be noted that I was to be the coauthor of this as-told-to autobiography, which was floated to several publishing houses. As with the movie, the book—like the fictitious boat—apparently sank because of the rights fees demanded by Cubas, who told me at one point that he was seeking an advance comparable to what General Norman Schwarzkopf had received for his memoirs.

"When he wouldn't talk about it, that's when I started thinking that maybe it wasn't true," said George King. "The *Post* wanted it. God, you know, that's a great story. But he wouldn't talk about it, and the agent wouldn't talk about it. I started thinking maybe it wasn't what he had said it was."

"You know how press-box humor is: Guys would be talking about the yacht he came over on and stuff like that," said Jack O'Connell of *The Hartford Courant*. "But I think the story was so widely known by the time he got here that for our purposes it was like, 'Just tell us what this guy is like as a pitcher.' So we concentrated on that. I don't think there was much probing. To be honest, it never mattered to me. It was a good enough story that he got here in the first place. He certainly went through enough bullshit. The guy was an enemy of the state. He couldn't pitch anymore. And I think because he tried to be friendly with us, most of the writers cut him some slack. Who really gave a shit what size boat it was? Or whether it was a raft?"

As the season went on, the facts surrounding El Duque's liberation grew more fantastic with each telling. Never has the word *flotsam* appeared more frequently in the sports page. "I won't worry about him being afraid," Steinbrenner told the *Post* after El Duque was called up. "Not after he crossed that band of water in nothing more than a bathtub." The *Times* variously reported that El Duque had subsisted on "crabs" and "seaweed" while stranded on the island. The *Post* and several other publications commonly referred to the escape vessel as "a rickety raft," as if the pitcher were Huck Finn. There were reports of a severe storm and big waves, both of which happened to be true, but only after the group had been picked up by the Coast Guard. El Duque, again, was no help. With a nod and a wink he tacitly confirmed that the voyage had been worse than anyone could possibly imagine.

As far as I was concerned, the great lie was never that big of a deal. If not exactly honest, it was understandable. Later, it would be suggested that the embellishment was a marketing ploy by Cubas to peddle the movie, but that was never the case. Certainly, the story spun out of control. But at its core it was always a matter of loyalty to the people who had helped smuggle El Duque out of Cuba. Even Juan Carlos Romero, whose bitterness toward the pitcher was boundless, acknowledged that much. And the risks were real. Given El Duque's stature and the warnings issued by the Cuban government ("Stay out of Santa Clara!"), there was little question that the accomplices, had they been caught, would have been imprisoned.* For El Duque to declare publicly that the boat had gone back would have been tantamount to turning both of them in.

---

*Both eventually came to the United States but prefer to remain anonymous.

The story also took nothing away from what El Duque had accomplished. Most baseball players spend their off-season hunting and fishing. El Duque spent his fleeing an authoritarian government. In the span of ten months he had escaped Cuba on a fishing boat, survived four days on a deserted Bahamian island, spent another two days in a rat-infested refugee camp, pitched at a major-league tryout in San José, Costa Rica, signed a $6.6 million contract with the New York Yankees, then pitched his way onto one of the greatest teams in history.

El Duque finished the 1998 baseball season 12–4 with a 3.13 ERA in 21 starts.

Including the minor leagues he was 19–5.

A couple of weeks before the playoffs, the Yankees gathered for a rather obscure ritual of capitalist baseball: the postseason share meeting. The meeting is basically necessary because of the transience of baseball's labor force. Players come and go all season long. Playoff teams thus need to determine which players deserve a full cut of baseball's staggering postseason revenue and which deserve only partial shares. Financially speaking, it's no small matter. In 1998, each full share on the winning World Series team was worth $312,137.33, a figure that exceeded the salaries of Jorge Posada and Ramiro Mendoza that year.

Veterans David Cone and Joe Girardi chaired the meeting. Obviously, it is no easy task. Underlying the vote is the knowledge that any partial shares given out—to clubhouse attendants, video technicians, players who pass through for just a few games—will dilute the value of a full share. Since there are 182 days in a season, disputes are often settled by calculating the number of days a player has spent with the team.

But El Duque was a unique case. Although he did not pitch his first game until June 3, missing one-quarter of the season, he had contributed twelve wins and 141 innings. To most Yankees, the issue was clear-cut: El Duque had been a major contributor and he was likely to contribute more in the postseason. Unspoken but also hanging in the air was the knowledge that his previous salary had been $8.75 a month and that he had taken a fairly circuitous route to reach the majors. Most players felt he deserved a full share. But to the shock and disgust of some people present, there was some dissent. It was led by a serviceable outfielder, Chad Curtis, who had batted .243 with ten homers and fifty-six RBIs. Curtis's modest statistics suggested it was he who had been around for just part of the season, but now he made the case against El Duque.

"Curtis always had to have the last word," said Luis Sojo. "He was saying this guy deserves this much and this guy gets that much. He said that El Duque didn't deserve a full share because he hadn't played a full season. As soon as he finished speaking, most of us looked at him like he was crazy. We were opposed, obviously. We said no. Then Coney said, 'Okay, if you think El Duque should get a full share raise your hand, if not keep your hand down.' We all raised our hands except for Curtis. He kept his mouth shut after that. What could he say?"

"It was envy, it was greed," said José Cardenal, who did not attend the meeting but got an earful afterward. "If not for El Duque we're home watching the World Series on television." On that point, there would soon be little doubt.

THE YANKEES FINISHED 114–48, winning the American League East by twenty-two games. It was the most regular-season victories in American League history. The postseason loomed more as a coronation than as a test of the team's greatness; few people believed the Yankees could lose.

The wild-card round did nothing to dispel that idea. The Bombers put away Texas in three straight games. El Duque, as the fourth starter in the rotation, did not pitch. But he assumed that since his turn was up he would start the opener of the American League Championship Series against Cleveland. Cardenal had to break the news to him that the rotation would stay the same. El Duque was slated to pitch Game 4, which, for all anyone knew, would probably be the clincher.

The Yankees won Game 1 on a brisk fall evening at Yankee Stadium. It was another bloodless walkover. New York scored five runs in the first inning against the Indians' top pitcher, Jaret Wright, and cruised, 7–2. David Wells, who won eighteen games during the regular season, including a perfect game, was dominant. Afterward, Yankee second baseman Chuck Knoblauch described the Yankees as "a steamroller building up steam."

Knoblauch had every reason to be confident. It was his first postseason since 1991, when he broke in with the Minnesota Twins as American League Rookie of the Year. That season had been a charmed one for Knoblauch, down to its riveting final moments. In Game 7 of the World Series against the Atlanta Braves, he had made a heads-up play for the ages. With the score 0–0 in the eighth inning, he bent over to field a ground ball, apparently starting a double play. In fact, it was all a ruse: Atlanta's Terry Pendleton had hit the ball into the left-center-field gap for a sure double. But Knoblauch's elaborate pantomime fooled its intended victim, Lonnie Smith, who was running from first on the pitch. Instead of scoring, Smith stopped in the base path, looking like a bewildered child who had wandered into traffic. He made it only to third. Jack Morris held off the Braves until the tenth, when the Twins finally won, 1–0, closing out one of the greatest World Series in history.

Seven years later Knoblauch was quite a bit richer—he earned $6 million that season—but he was not the player he had been in Minnesota. He seemed cowed by the immensity of the New York stage. Now, in Game 2 of the ALCS, he was about to get the Lonnie Smith treatment. He committed a mental error that, in its own way, was just as unusual and potentially as devastating. As many writers pointed out, the blunder was Buckneresque in magnitude. The game was 1–1 in the twelfth when Cleveland's Travis Fryman dropped a sacrifice bunt up the first-base line. Charging from first, Tino Martinez fielded the ball and turned to throw to Knoblauch, who had moved to cover the base. With Fryman bearing down—he had been running well inside the baseline— Knoblauch stepped aside and the ball hit Fryman square in the back.

Knoblauch turned to argue for an interference call. As he pleaded, pinch runner Enrique Wilson circled the bases with the tie-breaking run. It was a surreal moment: The Yankee bench, a crowd of 57,128 and all of Gotham were screaming at Knoblauch to pick up the baseball, which lay in the dirt like a live grenade. He stood there, oblivious, pointing and arguing as if he were locked in a soundproof booth. The Yankees went down, 4–1.

The appalling mistake seemed to sheer the invincibility off the Yankees. Two nights later in Cleveland, the Indians pounded Andy Pettitte for four home runs, winning 6–1. Quite suddenly, the Yanks were down 2–1, with two more games to play at Jacobs Field. For the first time all season, New York was facing a must-win situation. Historically, the odds of coming back from a 3–1 deficit are astronomical. The Yanks had to win Game 4. At stake was not only the series but also the team's claim on greatness. As Pettitte said, no one gave you credit for just being there.

And so it came to pass that the Bombers turned their eyes to Orlando "El Duque" Hernández, late of Havana, Cuba, and the Florida Straits. As Buster Olney pointed out, the club had spent years in the careful construction of a dynasty, only to see the biggest game of the season come down to a pitcher who had washed ashore in the Bahamas ten months earlier.

No one had a clue what to expect. El Duque had been remarkable, but there was still a vague sense that he had stepped out of a closet into the Yankee rotation. Moreover, he had not pitched in fifteen days, his last appearance a five-inning stint against Tampa Bay. Although he had beaten the Indians once, the Tribe had pounded him later in the summer. Even more ominous was the weather; the temperature was expected to be in the low fifties. El Duque, who had grown up on a tropical island, told Cardenal that he would be pitching in the coldest weather of his life.

During the postseason, the league always holds a press conference for the next day's starting pitchers. When El Duque strolled before the national media, he did not give the impression of a man under duress. All questions about the escape, of course, were off-limits ("I cannot respond to that question") but he did answer other queries, most of which were variations on the same themes: the weather and the backbreaking pressure.

El Duque dismissed the cold as a factor—he noted that he had once pitched in Ireland. Then someone asked him what exactly was the biggest game he had pitched. "The biggest game that I've pitched to this date is jumping on the boat and leaving Cuba," he responded.

The following day, Bob Klapisch, a baseball writer for the Bergen County, New Jersey, *Record*, walked into the coffee shop of the Cleveland Marriott, where the Yankees were staying, and spotted El Duque, who was sitting down with Noris for his traditional pregame meal. Klapisch had covered New York baseball since 1983, had himself pitched at Columbia University, and knew better than to violate the sanctity of a starting pitcher's solitude, particularly before the biggest game of the season. But to the writer's astonishment, El Duque invited him over to have lunch with him and his girlfriend.

Klapisch spoke fluent Portuguese—his mother was Brazilian—and knew enough Spanish to carry on a conversation. El Duque, who at that point could barely read a menu in English, enlisted the writer to help him order. El Duque may be the most finicky eater ever to pick up a fork—he has been known to send back french fries if they've been peppered—and he carefully talked Klapisch through his traditional pregame selection. "He wanted spaghetti, naked spaghetti, no sauce, with just a little butter, not too soft," said Klapisch. As they waited for the food, Klapisch noted how relaxed El Duque seemed. From his outward appearance, you would never know that he was pitching that night. El Duque told Klapisch he planned to go back to his room and take a nap before heading over to the ballpark.

The wait for the food was endless, and El Duque tried unsuccessfully to flag down a waiter. "Then finally he said to hell with this," Klapisch recalled. "He got up and walked back into the kitchen. I thought he was going to get the waiter, but when he came back five minutes later he was carrying trays with plates full of food. He brought our food. He brought food for the next table. He basically took over the restaurant! He turned himself into an impromptu waiter. The staff of the restaurant came out to watch him. They all loved it. Nobody could believe it."

Joe Torre happened to be sitting on the other side of the restaurant. The Yankee skipper looked up from his own meal to see that night's starting pitcher moonlighting as a waiter at the Cleveland Marriott. "He was helping serve food to members of his party," Torre recalled, smiling. "He was up getting some dishes and silverware, then sitting back down. I remember seeing George Steinbrenner later that morning and I said to him, 'I don't know if El Duque's gonna win, but I know one thing: He's not afraid.'"

El Duque spent the rest of the day in his room, listening to music, relaxing. By then, wherever he traveled, the pitcher brought a makeshift shrine to Changó, the all-powerful Santería deity. The small shrine sat in a corner with the usual offerings: the half-smoked cigar, the mini Statue of Liberty, a cup of red wine. In due course he made his way over to the ballpark.

The weather, as expected, was frigid, even for the fall. Just before he took the field, El Duque had a liniment rubdown so that he would be relatively warm in the first inning. He wore an undershirt and a navy turtleneck, over which he buttoned the familiar Yankee grays, the words NEW YORK stitched across his chest in block letters.

The game was broadcast nationally by NBC, with Bob Costas handling the play-by-play. At this point, El Duque had become something of a cult figure around New York, but this would be his coming-out for the rest of America. It was also the moment when the evolution of the great escape reached its absurd apex. The story had had nearly a year to percolate, churning and churning in the media until it was now barely recognizable—not only from reality but also from the lie that El Duque had concocted around the campfire on Anguilla Cay.

As El Duque warmed up in the bullpen, Costas commented on what a long, strange trip it had been for tonight's Yankee starter. "Somebody asked Hernández whether or not he was frightened about starting in this game with all the responsibility attached to it," said Costas. "He said, 'Hey, if the sharks didn't frighten me while I was floating around in the Caribbean trying to defect, the Indians aren't going to frighten me!'"

IN A TIDY BIT OF SYMMETRY, the opposing pitcher was Dwight Gooden. The good doctor was not nearly the pitcher who had once inspired El Duque's massive leg kick. In fact, the pitchers were nearly the same age—Gooden was thirty-three; El Duque would turn thirty-three the following day—but Gooden seemed quite a bit older, his body weakened by impurities and neglect. For all his greatness Gooden had never won in the postseason and he got off to another rough start. In addition to the cold, the wind was blowing out to right field. Gooden threw a low curve to Paul O'Neill, who pulled it into the jet stream. The ball wasn't hit that hard, but it carried well into the right-field seats, giving New York a 1–0 lead.

As El Duque took the mound, NBC panned the Yankee dugout. It was like a midwinter Packers game; the players sat in heavy blue coats huddled against the cold. I watched the game from our living room couch in Manhattan. As El Duque stood there, blowing warm air into his fist, I flashed back to the previous year. It was a hot September afternoon in Havana, and El Duque had just played in one of his unauthorized weekend games at Lenin Park. Afterward, El Duque, Osmany, Noris and I hopped into the trusty Muscovy to go swimming. El Duque, as usual, was driving—he would never let anyone else drive—and the car stalled perhaps ten or twenty times before we reached our destination, a pool open to those fortunate enough to have dollars. There we spent the afternoon, drinking beer, passing the time. El Duque, of course, had nothing but time. A few people came by for his autograph and a few words of encouragement. At one point, we all took a dip. We were talking in the shallow end of the pool when suddenly the sky opened up and the rain came down in relentless solid sheets.

Several hours later, I went back to my hotel and flipped on the television. In Cuba, cable is illegal to everyone except the tourists and Fidel, so many hotels get CNN. The major-league baseball highlights happened to be on, and, after spending a hot, beer-drenched afternoon with El Duque, I was now standing in front of the TV in my Havana hotel room, watching highlights of Liván Hernández pitching at Dodger Stadium.

And now here we were a year later. The first inning was critical. El Duque was not yet loose and would be at his most vulnerable. With two out, he walked Manny Ramírez, putting runners on first and second. The next batter was the Indians first baseman, Jim Thome. Thome was six-foot-four and 225 pounds and he had been torturing the Yankees all week. The night before, he had clubbed two homers off Pettitte. He would hit four in the series, an ALCS record. With El Duque's problems against left-handed batters now well established, Thome, with his punishing swing, was the last person the Yankees wanted to see in this early, critical moment.

El Duque fell behind 3–1 and the stadium began to rock. For time eternal, a solitary lunatic has sat in the bleachers at Indians games, beating a drum like a tom-tom during rallies. Now, the sound pounded through the stadium— *Boom! Boom! Boom! Boom!*—audible even above the roaring crowd of 44,981.

El Duque unleashed a high fastball and Thome took a cut big enough to change the weather. "He loosened a couple buttons on his shirt on that swing," noted Costas. Now the count was full.

The next pitch was a high strike and this time Thome killed it. Everyone in the stadium knew immediately that it was gone. Costas went into his home-run call: "A long drive to right . . . !" El Duque's head snapped back as he followed the flight of the ball. The crowd exploded. The Indians moved to the top step of the dugout as the ball was going, going . . .

And then, in midair, it stopped, as if it had struck an invisible wall, as if the hand of the mighty Changó had reached out and slapped the ball back to earth. Incredibly, imperceptibly, the wind had shifted between innings. Instead of blowing out, it was now blowing in. "Oh, yeah," said Thome when I asked him later if he thought the ball was gone. "Off the bat, I thought for sure, man, we were going up. But it was one of those things where Mother Nature kind of controlled things." Paul O'Neill caught the ball in front of the right-field wall. Thome, halfway down the line, pulled up in stunned disbelief. He flipped away his helmet. The inning was over. "As the game progressed, I remember looking back saying, 'Man, that would have been huge to get that 3–1 lead,'" said Thome.

After that, El Duque fell into a trance. "He could have pitched with his eyes closed," said Posada, who was catching. Normally, El Duque's ratio of fastballs-to-off-speed pitches was relatively low, but as the game progressed he began to throw more and more hard stuff. He threw many of the pitches sidearm and the effect was hypnotic. El Duque would go into his windup, slow and beautiful, folding himself, unfolding, then catapult a 92-mile-per-hour fastball on the corner. He struck out Roberto Alomar in the second with a sidearm fastball. He struck out Manny Ramírez in the fourth with a sidearm fastball. He struck out Thome in the same inning with three straight fastballs. "He's just bringing it now," said Joe Morgan, who was calling the game with Costas. "He's reaching back saying, 'Well, let's see if you can hit my fastball.'"

El Duque carried a 3–0 lead into the sixth. His expression was different now, even more intense, a kind of dead-eyed remorselessness. Torre had played with Bob Gibson, one of the most competitive players in the history of the game. In El Duque, he would later say, he recognized the same rare quality. "I'm not sure if it's the desire to win or hating to lose; I'm not sure which is overriding," said Torre. "But it's very recognizable. It's a presence on the mound." El Duque had given up just two hits, both to Omar Vizquel. With one out in the sixth, Vizquel came up again and slapped a single to left center. El Duque then tried to come inside with a fastball to David Justice and hit him in the right elbow.

Suddenly, El Duque was in trouble. He was now facing Manny Ramírez and Thome with nowhere to put them. Ramírez, a right-handed hitter, was particularly dangerous, an RBI machine. That season, he had 145 RBIs in 150 games, nearly one a game. El Duque quickly fell behind 2–0, but with runners on first and second he had no choice but to pitch aggressively. He threw a sidearm fastball and Ramírez fouled it off. The tom-tom again was pounding: *Boom! Boom! Boom!* The crowd was screaming. Another sidearm fastball: Ramírez swung and missed. The count was 2–2. Ramírez stepped in and out of the box. When he finally settled in, El Duque threw yet another sidearm fastball. Ramírez swung and missed for strike three. The camera panned to the Indians' bench. Ramírez was *laughing,* incredulous. "He was unbelievable," Ramírez said later. "He had everything going. Man, he was tough."

Up came Thome, lugging his menacing black bat, a 35-inch, 32-ounce flame-treated Rawlings cut from select northern ash. On this freezing night in the Midwest, with the wind roaring off Lake Erie, Thome was wearing a V-neck T-shirt beneath his white Indians jersey, a sprig of brown chest hairs visible at the base of his throat. His batting helmet was smeared with a season's worth of pine tar. On his broad left forearm Thome wore a red sweatband and, on his right ankle, a shin guard to protect against pile-driving foul balls. He wore his stirrups like El Duque: a block of solid red. Shorn of the earrings and the gold necklaces common among modern ballplayers, Thome looked like he could easily have stepped into the lineup with Rocky Colavito. In fact, he was something of a throwback, an exceedingly gracious man who cherished every moment in the major leagues.

Thome called himself "your normal typical midwestern kid. Everything I've had, I've done it through hard work because I never had the great talent just to get by, just to show up and be good." Thome grew up in Peoria, Illinois, the corporate headquarters for Caterpillar, the construction-equipment manufacturer. His father, Chuck, was a foreman in Caterpillar's transportation department for thirty years. Thome was the youngest of five children: three strapping boys and two girls. One brother, Randy, worked as an engineer at a Peoria electricity plant. The other, Chuck, was a construction worker. His sister Jenny was a bank teller; his other sister Lori worked in Caterpillar's industry department.

Thome had worked at United Parcel Service while playing baseball and basketball at Illinois Central College in Peoria. "I would get up at four o'clock and unload boxes for UPS and then I would go practice baseball at six," he recalled. "I would be in the gym working on baseball or basketball, whatever season it was, and then go to class. Then I'd go back to practice in the afternoon." Thome had hoped to play professional basketball, but he peaked in that sport and ended up signing with the Indians as the club's thirteenth-round draft choice in 1989. He received a $20,000 bonus, which he deposited in a savings account.

"Even though I never had all the talent in the world, I had that desire to keep getting better," said Thome. "I would peak a little bit and then fall off, peak and fall off. When I came to the big leagues, I'd heard stories that it's easy to get there—which it's not; it's not easy to get to the big leagues—but once you get there it's even tougher to stay. And my goal was always to play ten years, to be one of those guys who has longevity and has stuck around a long time."

The 1998 season was Thome's sixth in the majors. He had been on his way to his best season when a pitch broke his right hand in early August. He still hit 34 home runs. Thome was now making money beyond his wildest dreams—$4.8 million that year. He owned a black Humvee ("a man's car"), which he drove to the ballpark. When the postseason ended, Thome retreated to a spacious log home he had built in Ellisville, Illinois, a small burg in the southern part of the state, where he worked out in the off-season and hunted turkeys and deer and went bass fishing.

Above all, baseball has remained America's pastime because its players reflect the broad composition of America. The game is slow to change, but it eventually incorporates every segment of the culture, every immigrant group ever exposed to the sport, in their own country or in their adopted one. Only in baseball will you see the season come down to a confrontation between an overachieving, hardworking defector from Havana, Cuba, and an overachieving, hardworking son of a Caterpillar foreman from Peoria, Illinois. The matchup was timeless.

Thome dug in. El Duque threw a ball, and then a strike, which Thome fouled back, then another strike, making the count 1–2. El Duque was so focused he essentially forgot about the runners, allowing Vizquel to steal third uncontested. El Duque then tried a fastball down and away. Thome took it for ball two. He threw a fastball inside. Thome checked his swing for ball three. Between the drums and the screaming, the noise was deafening. El Duque looked in for the sign from Posada then stepped off the rubber. The crowd booed. On his one hundredth pitch of the night, El Duque threw yet another fastball. Thome took a huge rip and fouled it back.

Now, with the count still full, two out, runners on first and third and the 1998 baseball season on the line, what would El Duque throw next? All night, he had been beating the Indians with his fastball. His best pitch, however, was his curve, which he could throw from any angle, at any speed. When El Duque arrived in the States, his weakest pitch was his change-up—so weak, in fact, that he didn't have one. Gordon Blakeley and Lin Garrett had picked up on this deficiency in Costa Rica, noting in their scouting report that El Duque would have to learn a new pitch to make it in the major leagues. The Yankees worked on the pitch soon after his arrival in Tampa. Billy Connors, the organization's pitching specialist, taught El Duque the most common pitch of the genre, the "circle change," so named because it is gripped with the thumb and forefinger forming a circle on the side of the ball.

The key to a good change-up is to make the pitch look like a fastball when it leaves the pitcher's hand. "Arm action is the whole secret," said Connors. The Yankees knew that El Duque needed the pitch to keep hitters—particularly left-handed hitters like Jim Thome—off balance. After spring training, Connors traveled to Columbus for more instruction. It was a season-long process. El Duque's enthusiasm for the pitch came and went. "He didn't throw it a whole lot but he tried it," said Connors. "It's back and forth with him. It's confidence more than anything else." In fact, El Duque had abandoned the pitch entirely late in the season, only to pick it up again to beat the Boston Red Sox in September to seal a spot in the postseason rotation.

Logic would dictate that El Duque was not likely to throw a change-up with a full count in the biggest at-bat of the biggest game of the season. But that is exactly what he did. When I asked him about it later, he shrugged. "These are things that happen in the moment," he said. "That's the way it always must be. You only have two or three seconds to think. You have to go with what you feel." Before each pitch, Thome steadied himself by pointing his long black bat at the mound. Only when the pitcher went into his windup would he pull the bat back and cock. Thome was clearly looking for a fastball, the pitch El Duque had been throwing all night. When the change-up hurtled limply toward the plate, Thome swung through it, weakly, awkwardly. El Duque leaped off the mound and jogged back to the dugout, pumping his fist as he went.

That was the game, basically. In the eighth, Torre brought in Stanton, then Mariano Rivera. The Yankees won, 4–0. El Duque had given up three hits, all to Vizquel. Steinbrenner called it the finest performance he had seen since Ron Guidry beat the Red Sox on three days' rest in the 1978 playoff. The Yankees won Game 5 behind Wells. The series then returned to New York, where the

Tribe came unglued, allowing 5 unearned runs in Game 6 and bowing out, 9–5.

Later, when Thome reminisced about the game, he had nothing but admiration for El Duque. He compared him to Pedro Martínez, the Red Sox ace from the Dominican Republic. "What really impressed me about him is that not only did he have this good heater, he had a good curveball and he had a good change-up," said Thome. "Just like Pedro. Pedro has got three pitches he can throw at any time. That's how El Duque is. He can drop a hook on you and a 3–2 change-up like he did to me, you know? That's really impressive."

Baseball is a funny game. The Cleveland Indians' history of futility is long and woeful. For decades, the team played before a smattering of loyalists in a hulking mausoleum known as Cleveland Stadium. Then came a shiny new downtown ballpark, the resurrections of the team and the city, and suddenly the Indians were legitimate contenders again. In consecutive seasons, the Tribe had golden opportunities to win their first World Series in fifty years, only to be thwarted by Cuban defectors, brothers, in fact, one of whom came to the major leagues via a northern Mexican industrial park, the other via a deserted Bahamian island.

Allen Bandrowsky happened to watch Game 4 from the Dominican Republic. Bandrowsky was a boarding officer in the United States Coast Guard. He hailed from Cleveland, and after his boat came in to port he settled down to see if the Indians might fare better against the Yankees than they had against the Marlins in the World Series. Bandrowsky looked up at the television, only to see the man he had rescued ten months earlier in the Florida Straits now throttling the Tribe like his brother had the year before.

"It was unbelievable," Bandrowsky told me. "It was like not even a year ago we pick this guy out of the water and now he's making ten million dollars a year and beating my team."

CHAPTER SEVENTEEN

DIVINE INTERVENTION

Osmany, Joel and Tío flew up from Miami for the World Series. The lesser-known members of the Anguilla Cay crew decamped at the Roger Smith for the week. For the Series, Torre had shuffled the pitching rotation; El Duque was now scheduled to start Game 2. Osmany, Joel and Tío planned to attend the first two games, then hang out in New York until El Duque returned to pitch Game 6, or, more likely, to participate in the victory parade.

The Series itself was unmemorable. The San Diego Padres, playing beyond their small-market means (nearly every year, some underfunded team rose up to refute the owners' grand economic theories) had stunned the Braves in the NLCS. For the Yankees, however, El Duque's victory in Game 4 had been a watershed. It would carry over not only into the World Series but also into the following season and postseason. It was perhaps the biggest victory of what would become a new Yankee dynasty under Torre. By Game 1, all was right again in the Yankee universe. Even Knoblauch, rescued from eternal goathood, hit a three-run homer in the 9–6 win.

Before Game 2, I picked up a Cuban flag at the South Street Seaport for Osmany, who wanted to wave it during the game. The $30 flag was as big as a bedspread, but I was able to cart it up to the Roger Smith on the subway. I figured El Duque would be hidden away somewhere, meditating, but in fact his room was not so different from Grand Central, where I had just disembarked. The phone was ringing off the hook. People were coming in and out. El Duque, fastidious about his appearance in good times and bad, was ironing his shirts and packing for the trip to San Diego after the game. There wasn't a hint of tension in the air.

Soon it was time for him to leave for Yankee Stadium. Osmany, Joel and I walked him down to the garage. With his growing stardom, the subway had become unmanageable. He had taken to commuting in a red Mercury Mountaineer that a New Jersey dealer allowed him to drive gratis. An attendant pulled the car around. As El Duque climbed in, we all shook his hand and wished him luck through the driver's side window. If he was nervous, I couldn't tell. He moved with the distracted hurriedness of a man running late for work. The car turned onto Forty-seventh Street and disappeared. "There goes El Duque," I said to no one in particular, "on his way to pitch in the World Series."

Fox was broadcasting the game. Not surprisingly, the network that later brought the world *Who Wants to Marry a Multi-Millionaire* played up the intrigue, billing El Duque as "the Fearless Man of Mystery." With Sarah McLachlan ("Hold on to yourself, for this is gonna hurt like hell . . .") setting the somber mood, Fox showed footage of desperate Cubans plunging into the surf on, what else, a rickety raft. "Instead of surviving rough innings," an announcer intoned, "El Duque had to survive rough seas, hunger, and shark-infested waters."

True enough. As El Duque warmed up, Skip Caray and Tim McCarver took up the age issue again: "The right-hander, anywhere from twenty-five to thirty-five years old . . ." McCarver began.

Caray agreed it was murky: "He's in some demographic."

The game, like the Series, was a snoozer. Sánchez and I had seats on the third-base side. As El Duque took the mound, we sat there marveling at how it had all come to this. The most dramatic moment came and went in the first inning. With two on and two out, Wally Joyner lifted a fly ball to deep right field. For a moment, the ball looked like it might be gone. Instead, it was merely a repeat of Jim Thome's blast in the first inning of Game 4. O'Neill climbed the wall and made the catch in front of an advertisement for The Wiz, a New York electronics chain.

The Yanks won, 9–3. El Duque gave up a run on six hits in seven uneventful innings. The weather had been unseasonably warm that night and by the time Sinatra was crooning it felt like any midsummer trouncing. Including the minor leagues, El Duque was 21–5 on the year. At that point, everyone knew the Series was over. There would be no more letdowns for the Bronx Bombers.

Two nights later, Sánchez had Osmany, Joel and me over to watch Game 3. The defectors supposedly had been in hiding. The *Post* reported that El

Duque's "boatmates" were somewhere in New York, but the pitcher was guarding their whereabouts "like his two-seamer." Dave Anderson, the Pulitzer Prize–winning *Times* columnist, wrote that El Duque was cagey when asked about the reported sightings of Osmany and Joel.

"Did they come?" the pitcher said, responding to a question with a question.

"I was told they came," said his interrogator.

"Who told you that?" said El Duque.

"One of the broadcasters from Miami."

"Yes, they are here. Now that you told me who told you, we're even."

The mysterious boatmates agreed to come out for beer and pizza. The four of us gathered in the late afternoon at Sánchez's one-bedroom apartment at Eighty-ninth Street and West End Avenue (Osmany immediately pronounced the apartment "a matchbox," proving that even Cuban defectors find New York living degrading). Osmany and Joel were drawn immediately to a photo of Fidel and Hemingway that Sánchez had hanging in a corner. The Cubans began to heckle the host. "I always knew you were a *Fidelista*," Osmany said to Sánchez. He and Joel then lined up to have their picture taken with the Maximum Leader. "Here we are with Fifo," said Osmany as he pretended to hold up the picture. When the photo session ended we sat down to watch the Yankees rack up another win. Third baseman Scott Brosius was the hero this time, belting a three-run bomb off Padres closer Trevor Hoffman in the eighth inning. Brosius would later be named Series MVP, which was perfect. Earlier Yankee championships ended with thunderous curtain calls for one-named legends: "Reg-gie! Reg-gie! Reg-gie!" This one would end with the anonymous Yankees chanting for their teammate: "Scot-ty Bro-sius! Scot-ty Bro-sius! Scot-ty Bro-sius!"

UNBEKNOWNST TO ALL OF US, the real drama of the World Series was taking place behind the scenes. There was a diplomatic movement afoot to get El Duque's daughters out of Cuba. The negotiations were taking place at the highest levels of the United States and Cuban governments—the *very* highest levels.

René Guim, Cubas's press agent, had initiated the effort. All season long, he had listened to El Duque lament his separation from his daughters. Guim was particularly sympathetic on the issue. He spent much of his own time with his three-year-old son René Jr., who suffered from Angelman syndrome, a rare genetic disorder. The syndrome causes frequent seizures and severely impairs development; Angelman children are often unable to walk before age ten and learn but three or four words in their lifetimes.

"I was lying there on the couch one night in late September watching Mark McGwire chase the home-run record and high-fiving his little boy at home plate," Guim told me. "I was holding little René in my arms and thinking that regardless of his disabilities, I'm really very fortunate to have him with me every day. I had talked on the phone with El Duque a few days earlier and he had mentioned how depressed he was because he had not seen his two little girls in over a year, and that he feared he would never see them again as long as Castro was in power. So that's what started the idea." Guim recalled the hoopla when Liván's mother came to Miami to see her son during the 1997 World Series. He began making phone calls to see if he could do the same for El Duque's daughters.

At the same time, a woman named Pamela S. Falk had also become interested in the El Duque saga. Falk was a professor of international relations at the City University of New York, but that was perhaps the least-interesting item on her résumé. Pam Falk was a professor of international relations in the same way that Indiana Jones was a professor of archaeology. She was once shot at going to visit future Guatemalan president Vinicio Cerezo outside Guatemala City. During the civil war in El Salvador she participated in secret peace talks in Panama between the Salvadoran government and guerrilla leader Ruben Zamora. In recent years, Falk spent much of her time navigating the murky back channels of Cuban-American relations. She was a master of the delicate interplay between Havana, Miami and Washington. Falk seemed to know everyone and offend no one. She used these skills to wrestle emergency visas out of the Cuban government, organize exploratory visits to Havana by American business executives and funnel occasional humanitarian grain shipments through Venezuela. Pretty, with an aura of competence, Falk also possessed an extraordinary physiology: seemingly she never slept. She liked nothing better than to leave phone messages and write up applications for Treasury Department licenses at four A.M.

Falk's biggest coup to date had been to secure visas for the parents of the ex–fighter pilot Orestes Lorenzo. In Miami, Lorenzo was a legend, having defected to the United States in 1991 in a stolen MiG. After his escape, Lorenzo petitioned the Cuban government to release his wife and two sons, to which Raúl Castro, Fidel's brother and the Cuban defense minister, replied that Lorenzo would have to come back and pick them up himself. Lorenzo thus returned to Cuba in a borrowed Cessna, landed the plane on a Matanzas highway and made off with his family. He and his wife later had another son, John Paul, whom they named after the pope. Against all odds, Falk had managed to obtain visas for Lorenzo's parents to visit their new grandson in Miami.

In the fall of 1998, Falk was working on a book about divided Cuban families. "That to me is the core of the whole Cuba story," she said. "I'm very empathetic to both sides." Orestes Lorenzo, forever indebted, called her up one day to ask if there was anything he could do for her. Falk had begun to follow El Duque in the New York media and thought his story might make good material for her book. She asked Lorenzo if he had a contact who could set up an interview with the pitcher. He didn't, but he said he would get back to her.

"Five minutes later I get a call from René Guim," said Falk. "He says, 'General Lorenzo gave me your number and said to call.' I said, 'Oh my god, thank you. I don't need this interview right away. This isn't something that's going to come out right away.' And René said, 'What are you talking about?' I said, 'The interview.' He said, 'What interview? General Lorenzo told me that you were the most powerful woman in Washington and that you could help get El Duque's children out of Cuba.'

"I just started laughing," said Falk. "I howled. I said, 'No, no, no. I was calling about an interview.' And he said, 'Well, can you help with this?' And then he starts telling me this story that tears at my heartstrings: how he came in and went from rags to riches, to a $6 million contract, and all he does is think about his girls. My blood is flowing and my little hormonal thing, you know, my heart is pounding, and then as a mother I say, 'So how old are the kids?' 'Three and eight.' I said, 'Oh my god.' Right then I was hooked."

Falk was under no illusions about the difficulty of the task. At that moment, there was perhaps no symbol of Cuban resistance more prominent than El Duque Hernández. Although the pitcher had toned down his rhetoric, he had emerged from Cuba hurling darts at Fidel, frequently referring to the Maximum Leader as "the Devil." And yet Falk knew that the only man in Cuba with the power to release El Duque's daughters was Fidel himself. She knew that she would need to find an intermediary who could persuade Castro that it was in his best interests to make a grand humanitarian gesture in the middle of the World Series, an event certain to give it widespread visibility.

Falk considered the range of international figures known to be friendly with Castro: Muhammad Ali, Gabriel García Márquez, the Reverend Jesse Jackson. She decided to approach Jackson, who in the 1980s had negotiated a prisoner exchange between the United States and Cuba. Jackson declined. Falk continued her search. In the past, she had worked with the New York archdiocese on Cuba issues. She turned there as her next option. In retrospect, it seems like a logical choice, but at the time the idea that the Roman Catholic church could perform the role of interlocutor was something very new. To a large degree it was made possible by Pope John Paul II's historic visit to Cuba in January that year. In the United States, the visit had been overshadowed by the Monica Lewinsky scandal, which sent the network news anchors retreating back to Washington and diminished the pope's coverage considerably. But the papal visit had shaken Cuba to its core. It ended with John Paul saying mass before 500,000 people, including Fidel, on the most sacred ground of Cuban socialism, the Plaza of the Revolution. To anyone standing in the crowd that day, the feeling of change was overpowering. Solitary cries of "Freedom!" and "Justice!" rang out as the pope delivered his homily before a twenty-story image of the atheist martyr Che Guevara. "The attainment of freedom," the pope said, "is a duty which no one can shirk." Cubans of all stripes laughed and cried, shook their heads in disbelief. "For the first time in the entire history of the revolution, another voice has been heard," Lourdes María Alonzo, a thirty-four-year-old psychologist, told me after the mass. Of the thousands of words spoken by the pope during the visit, none reverberated more than these: "Cuba needs to open herself up to the world and the world needs to draw close to Cuba."

Falk contacted the New York archdiocese to see if the pope could petition on El Duque's behalf. The church sent back word that the pontiff could not intervene but that John Cardinal O'Connor, the archbishop of New York, had decided to take on the case. Falk was thrilled: O'Connor was perfect. He was the most powerful Catholic in America. He was a frequent critic of the U.S. trade embargo against Cuba. He had attended the papal visit in Havana and, even better, he had a longtime relationship with Fidel. O'Connor had first visited Cuba in 1987 with his liaison to the Hispanic community, Mario Paredes. The trip had nearly been a disaster. As O'Connor and Paredes made their way to Havana to meet with Fidel, the cardinal received word on the plane that the Cuban news agency Prensa Latina, had issued a cable alleging that two agents of the CIA—O'Connor and Paredes—were visiting Cuba.

"When we landed in Havana, I asked the cardinal to stay on the plane, and I went down to meet with the official responsible for religious affairs in the Communist party," said Paredes. "I said to him, 'This cable that your government released, is this hello or good-bye?' " Paredes demanded a public apology. The official relented, but the atmosphere was still tense as O'Connor exited the plane.

That night, the church held a celebratory mass at the cathedral in Old Havana. As O'Connor walked down the aisle, worshipers pelted him with rolled up pieces of paper, desperate petitions to intervene in their lives: "There were thousands of these things," said Paredes. "They said: 'Take us out of the country. Take my father. Take my uncle. Send me medicine. Send me money.' It took us literally twenty-five minutes to get to the altar. People were grabbing the cardinal to give him messages as he walked. And I was grabbing all these messages as I walked behind him.

"Because of the crowd, the cardinal was terribly late to meet Fidel. Fidel had scheduled the meeting for eleven [P.M.], and when we showed up it was now close to two." Castro, whose tardiness is legendary, began to chastise O'Connor. "He lectured the cardinal for forty-five minutes," said Paredes. "And finally the cardinal lost patience with him. He told him, 'Mr. President, you invited me to speak to you, and I want to know what you have to say to me. Otherwise, I will leave this meeting.'

"So Fidel changed the tone. Now he went back to criticizing the United States, not the cardinal for not being on time. He criticized everything: the embargo, the abuses, the killing, you name it. The cardinal interrupted him again: 'Mr. President, I am a North American citizen. I fly the flag of the United States. You are insulting my country, right in front of me. Do you have any respect for me? I am the cardinal of New York. But never forget: I am a citizen of the United States.' " Paredes translated as O'Connor, a former military chaplain, informed Fidel: "I served proudly in the United States Navy, for over thirty years."

From that point on, according to Paredes, the conversation between O'Connor and Fidel shifted to one of dialogue. It lasted until dawn. It was a dialogue that essentially continued until O'Connor's death on May 3, 2000. "I think it's about the virility of the man. That captured Fidel," said Paredes. "I think Fidel was taken by the fact that O'Connor was direct with him." Two months later, Paredes was visiting Havana and Castro summoned him back to the palace. "He said, 'I just wanted to make sure that you convey my greetings to the cardinal and let him know that I enjoyed meeting him immensely.' And Fidel, to my amazement, maintained all the courtesies in the world with the cardinal from then on. For Christmas, for his birthday, you name it, he would send cards, cigars, gifts. He seemed fascinated with him."

Paredes also knew that the relationship was useful politically. "Fidel knew that O'Connor carried a prestige that few people in the church carried, and that he would have access to the White House," he said. "Fidel wanted to have an open door, just in case. He used O'Connor in the best sense of the word, to convey or communicate matters that were important to the administration, whether it was Reagan or Bush or whoever."

Now, in October 1998, Cardinal O'Connor was seeking a favor from Fidel. Coincidentally, Paredes had a prescheduled meeting with Castro that week in Havana to discuss church affairs. "There's a lot of serendipity in this story," said Pam Falk. "Would Fidel have scheduled a meeting just for El Duque's daughters? I don't think so." Time was now of the essence. Guim and Falk had begun the process hoping to have El Duque's daughters in New York in time for the World Series. But the Yankees were blowing through the Padres so fast that it soon might all be over. The chances that El Duque would pitch Game 6 had grown extremely slim. The goal was now to get the girls to New York in time for the Yankee victory parade.

Mario Paredes and another church emissary, New York physician Ramón Tallaj Fermín, arrived in Havana on October 20 carrying a letter from O'Connor to Fidel. The letter was written on stationery from the New York archdiocese:

Your Excellency Mr. President:

It has come to my attention that Mr. Orlando "El Duque" Hernández, pitcher of the New York Yankees, wishes to be reunited with his beloved mother, his two daughters and the mother of his children, during the final game of the World Series of the Major Leagues in the United States. I am very moved by this petition and I write you with the hope that you will permit the family of Mr. Hernández to travel to this country as soon as possible.

As you know, the World Series is in a very advanced stage at this time and if you are going to permit them to travel, they should leave Cuba immediately.

In my opinion, a gesture this generous would be very well received in New York City and all of the United States.

With a promise of prayer, yours truly;

Faithfully,
John Cardinal O'Connor
Archbishop of New York

The following evening, Paredes carried the letter over to the Palace of the Revolution. The emissary was led up the steps of the monolithic structure, as dense and unchanging as the ideas it represented. He was led through the corridors of one of the last standing monuments to communism to see a seventy-two-year-old leader whose powers were so vast that only he and he alone could decide whether to allow two little girls to visit their father, a famous ballplayer, in the United States. As he grew old, Fidel Castro's legacy was not as a revolutionary but as a politician, one of the greatest of the twentieth century. As a guerrilla, as a military man, his credentials of course were impressive. To begin with a twenty-man army and bring down a government three years later was a feat that spoke for itself. But the government that Fidel defeated in 1959 had been less a government than a crime syndicate. Run by inhuman thugs, financed by Meyer Lansky, the Batista dictatorship was in a state of moral and physical decay by the time Fidel began to move on Havana.

Fidel's genius was as a politician, as a survivor. In the tumult of recent Latin American history, he could easily have ended up like Arbenz or Allende, another tragic leftist taken down by the imperialists and their CIA henchmen. But he did not. As Paredes made his way through the palace that evening, Fidel had survived Eisenhower and Kennedy and Johnson and Nixon, Ford and Carter and Reagan and Bush. He was now surviving Bill Clinton, a man regarded as a master politician who, next to Fidel, seemed dwarfed. Fidel had survived Moncada and prison and the Granma expedition. He had survived the Bay of Pigs and the Missile Crisis and the collapse of the Soviet Union. He had survived because of his skills as a politician, his extraordinary ability to shape any event to his political advantage. Paredes recalled something Fidel had said during his first meeting with O'Connor: "Your Eminence, I want to let you know that in my government *everything* is negotiable, except honor." It was a simple statement, Paredes noted, yet complicated. "It meant that he is willing to sit down and negotiate everything," Paredes said, "but honor meant the revolution." To protect his revolution, Fidel had become the Midas of politicians: Everything he touched turned to politics. Religion as politics. Business as politics. Baseball as politics. The bond between a man and his daughters as politics.

As Paredes entered the room, Fidel was sitting alone in his military fatigues. He was staring at a large color television. Paredes was a soccer fan; he knew nothing about baseball, "where it starts or where it ends," but he knew enough to recognize that Fidel was watching Game 4 of the 1998 World Series between the New York Yankees and the San Diego Padres. The game was being piped into the Palace of the Revolution via satellite. As Paredes sat down, the game was a scoreless pitcher's duel between Andy Pettitte and Kevin Brown, a pitcher who the following year would sign a $105 million contract with the Los Angeles Dodgers. Paredes handed Fidel the letter from O'Connor. In return, he expected to hear Fidel rant about how El Duque had betrayed the Cuban revolution. Instead he heard nothing but praise. "Fidel likes this fellow," Paredes would say later. "He respects the quality of this young man. He was proud of him. He enjoyed watching him. He knew that this young man was a natural sports star and he was rejoicing in the fact that this man was so successful with the most important team in the world."

Only two people know exactly what was said that night. I haven't had the opportunity to ask Fidel. Paredes said he made an agreement with Castro not to disclose the specifics of their conversation. He refused even to divulge who Castro was rooting for, except to say: "He likes New York; remember, he spent his honeymoon in New York for six weeks.

"We have too many things at stake here," Paredes said apologetically. "What things are going to happen between Cuba and this country? And [the church] will have to play a role. You know how Fidel is. If Fidel would drop dead or he resigned or something it would be a different story. But it's too serious right now, too delicate. . . . There are basic principles in life. If you don't want something to be known, don't say it."

Regardless of what led up to the decision, the answer was yes. "Fidel is a very bright, very astute man," said Paredes. "He knew since day one when he was confronted with this issue that he had only one choice: to allow El Duque to be with his family because it was something that was good to do. It was something positive." Paredes, knowing that he had very little time, thanked Fidel and raced back to the hotel. He and Tallaj were staying at the Melia Cohiba, a glass tower overlooking the Malecón, not far from the U.S. Interests Section. The two men went straight for the phone.

FROM HIS HOTEL ROOM in Havana, Paredes placed a call to Qualcomm Stadium in San Diego (named originally for a beloved local sportswriter, now for a high-tech company that had purchased the rights). Game 4 of the World Series was still in progress. Paredes told the stadium operator that he had a family emergency. He needed to be patched through immediately to the New York Yankee pitcher Orlando "El Duque" Hernández.

David Szen, the Yankees traveling secretary, burst into the visitors dugout. The Padres were batting. Szen approached José Cardenal. "He says, 'José, I have some people calling from Cuba. It's about El Duque's family,' " Cardenal recalled. "I ran back to the phone in the clubhouse. I said, 'This is José Cardenal.

I'm a coach here. How can I help you?' They said they were calling from Cuba and that El Duque's family had permission to leave Cuba tomorrow. So I ran back to the dugout and told El Duque. He ran into the clubhouse. I had to go back to coach first base because now the inning was over."

Paredes delivered the news to El Duque. "It was a very pleasant conversation," he recalled. "We just told him, 'We need your mother's telephone number.'"

Joe Cubas had been watching the game with Noris in the Yankees family section. Two days earlier, he had told El Duque that something was in the works, but no one knew what to expect. Cubas had gone to the concession stand with Noris and the wives of pitchers Ramiro Mendoza and Mariano Rivera. "As I'm coming back to our section there was a commotion of people running with walkie-talkies," Cubas said. "It was the head of security for the Yankees. They were all looking for me. He says, 'You need to get down to the clubhouse right now to take a call from Cuba.' As soon as he said it I thought my legs were turning to Jell-O.

"I get goose bumps just telling this story," Cubas continued. "They escorted me out the way they escort somebody out of the stadium after a fight. They walked me through a corridor and down to the clubhouse level. I'm walking down this long corridor and I could see El Duque in his Yankee uniform, no hat. He has his head up against the wall. He's pounding on the wall of the clubhouse.

"All of a sudden he charges me and he's kissing me and he's hugging me. 'We did it! We did it!' We just broke down. We lost it completely. The Yankees head of security—he breaks down. He's crying. We're all crying and hugging and the game is still going on."

IN NEW YORK, Pam Falk was equally elated. Within minutes, the Cuban mission at the United Nations had dispatched a letter to O'Connor, whose office in turn faxed the letter to her, confirming Castro's decision:

New York, October 21, 1998

Your Eminence,

In regard to your letter to President Fidel Castro, dated yesterday, October 20th, in which you request that Mr. Orlando "El Duque"

Hernández's mother, two daughters and the mother of his daughters be allowed to travel to this country as soon as possible, I have the honor to forward the following reply:

"The Government of the Republic of Cuba is willing to allow them to go and, if they wish to do so, return."

With the assurances of my highest consideration,

Bruno Rodríguez Parrilla
Ambassador
Permanent Representative

But even though Castro had given the okay, El Duque's family still needed clearance from the U.S. government to enter the country. Falk didn't have it. From the beginning, the State Department had flatly rejected her request. Falk was shocked. "It was the one side I thought I could deal with," she said. She later learned that many U.S. officials were still angry over El Duque's decision to toss aside the humanitarian visa that had been extended to him while he was detained in the Bahamas. The anger was also directed at Cubas, who had persuaded El Duque to establish residency in Costa Rica so the pitcher could declare free agency.

Falk begged, but the State Department refused to budge. Lula Rodríguez, the official who was instrumental in obtaining the earlier visa, was particularly adamant. Rodríguez told me later that her decision had nothing to do with the pitcher's visa shuffling in the Bahamas. She said she understood El Duque's desire to seek free agency. "It would be almost un-American not to accept $6 million over $1 million," she said. Referring to the parade, she said she believed it was simply wrong to issue emergency visas "because some people wanted to go to a party."

But Rodríguez's bitterness over the New Year's Eve episode was widely known inside and outside the government. "Listen, he's no saint," she told Falk at one point. "We spent New Year's Eve trying to get him into the country and the guy not only doesn't take U.S. citizenship but he never even thanked us."

It was now two A.M. and Pam Falk was desperate. She tried another source, María Echeveste, the deputy chief of staff at the White House. She reached Echeveste at home in New York.

"Look, I've gotten nothing but no's so far," Falk pleaded. "I've gotten them out of Cuba but now I can't get them into the United States."

Falk found Echeveste unsympathetic. She was concerned less with El

Duque's family than with how the Clinton administration would be portrayed in the press. "She says to me, 'You know *The New York Times* hates us,'" said Falk. "She says, 'They're going to write how Mr. Six Million Dollars can get his kids into the United States and José in Miami can't.' And I said, 'No, no, this is going to be written as a sports story. This is a good news story. This is a happy reunion.' She said, 'Okay, go ahead and write *The New York Times* editorial for me.' I said, 'I'll write it for you as it would be written right now: "Castro says yes, Clinton says no."'"

"She says to me, 'You're threatening me!' Then she hung up the phone."

"That's the only point where I almost cried," said Falk. "I had these visions of these little kids with their suitcases packed and going to the airport and having no place to go."

Falk was faced with an unbelievable scenario. She had demanded that Cubas keep the sensitive negotiations from the politicians and the press. She was worried that if the latest development leaked out there would be pandemonium. "I thought it might be like the situation later with Elián," she said, referring to protests over the administration's efforts to repatriate six-year-old Elián González. "I was worried there would be people marching on Yankee Stadium." Then, in an astonishing reversal, María Echeveste called back to say that the White House was reluctantly on board. She had spoken with her boss, John Podesta, the White House chief of staff, who had agreed with Falk's assessment. But she said nothing could be done without the approval of Attorney General Janet Reno. El Duque's daughters could be admitted under the terms of the pitcher's work visa. But his mother and ex-wife could only be "paroled" into the country under an emergency provision of the Immigration and Nationality Act.

Falk, desperate, went back to O'Connor one more time. She spoke with the cardinal's personal assistant, Eileen White, and explained her situation. White told Falk she would see what she could do. A few minutes later, Falk received a copy of a letter that White had faxed to Reno on the cardinal's behalf. In his last dramatic act to secure El Duque's family's release, O'Connor had basically given the attorney general of the United States a subtle nudge. "His Eminence is keenly interested in trying to assist Mr. Hernandez and is grateful for any consideration that might be given by you and your associates," White wrote. Falk noticed that on the fax cover sheet White remarked that she also had been in contact with FBI director Louis Freeh, who, it turned out, was Catholic and a longtime friend of the cardinal's.

In the end, it was an avalanche of political pressure that would bring El

Duque's family to New York. The pressure overcame the intransigence of the U.S. State Department, the residual anger over the Bahamas episode, the crushing deadlines, the incomprehensible immigration laws. Even Lula Rodríguez, without acknowledging the anger, acknowledged the enormous pressure brought to bear by the cardinal.

"They found another route," she told me.

IT WAS NOW a matter of logistics: how to get El Duque's family from Havana to New York. As Game 4 progressed, it became clear that the Yanks were about to sweep. Andy Pettitte had been masterful. New York scored two more runs in the eighth inning to go ahead, 3–0. If El Duque's family was going to make it to New York in time for the victory parade, a private jet was going to be necessary. It was again time for a man of action. "I decided, 'I'm going to talk to George,' " said Cubas.

With some trepidation, the agent made his way over to George Steinbrenner's private box at Qualcomm Stadium. He tapped on the door. "The first guy I see in George's box is Charlie Sheen," said Cubas. "He's in there eating and drinking and he's got a lot of people there. There was George's son, Hal, and Steve, his son-in-law. George was standing off to the side watching the game. Then Charlie Sheen looks at me and George looks at me and I said, 'George, how are you? I need to talk to you.' He snaps at me: 'Not now! Not now! We're in the middle of the game! We talk after the game!' I looked at him and I said, 'George, I'm not sure there is time.' He said, 'Not now. We're not going to talk now. It's the last game of the World Series. We talk after the game.'

"I said, 'George, I don't have that luxury.' And then I remember I said these exact words: 'I can't wait until after the game. I've got lives in my hands right now and I need help.' I turned around and I started walking toward the door. Then George says, 'What is it? What's so important?' I said, 'I need your help. I need to be able to bring El Duque's family to New York and hopefully be a part of the parade.' He said, 'What do you need from me?' I said, 'I was going to ask you to volunteer your plane.' He says, 'No problem.' He yells out, 'Where's a phone?' Three people rush up to him with cell phones. He makes a call and tells them he needs a plane in Miami tomorrow. In two minutes he resolved it right there.

"I'm getting ready to walk out the door, and then he says exactly these words: 'Shit, don't I get a hug out of this?' I turned around and I hugged him. I thanked him. I said, 'You don't know how much this means to El Duque's family.' George is a great guy, man. He's got a great heart. He said, 'Whatever you need from me let me know.' "

As it turned out, Steinbrenner's plane could not enter Cuba without clearance from the Treasury Department, a process that takes months. So at a cost of $6,000 Falk contracted a preauthorized plane to fly from Fort Lauderdale into Havana. El Duque's family would be flown from Havana to Miami, where Steinbrenner's Learjet would transport them the rest of the way.

The visas were for El Duque's mother, María Julia Pedroso, his two daughters and his ex-wife, Norma Manzo. That night, Cuban security agents appeared at Norma's and María Julia's homes to tell them that they would be leaving for the United States the following day. Norma was devastated. She had begun a new relationship. She knew no one in the United States. Her relationship with El Duque's family had deteriorated to the point where she and María Julia rarely spoke. "I didn't want to come," she told Sánchez and me. "All my family is back in Cuba. I don't know anybody here." But it seemed that she had little choice.

María Julia had spent her entire life, fifty-two years, in Cuba. Now she had been given a few hours' notice that she would be leaving, possibly never to return. "I had never even thought about leaving Cuba," she said. "There was no time, no time at all." The next morning, Paredes took her, Norma and the girls to the Cuban immigration office to pick up their visas. "I had never seen those offices," María Julia said. "I was so nervous. Everyone started calling me Doña and Señora; I was no longer Comrade María Julia." The group then went to the U.S. Interests Section to pick up the American visas. "Norma and I got there and sat down," she said. "No one asked us anything. A blond woman came in and took our papers. She carried a yellow envelope and a white piece of paper. She handed back our passports. There were people lined up outside—long, long lines of people waiting for visas to leave Cuba. People started shouting when we came out, applauding and congratulating us. They were yelling, '¡Felicidades! [Congratulations!] ¡Felicidades!' "

There was almost no time to pack. María Julia filled a small bag with clothes and an old baseball jersey that had once belonged to Arnaldo, her late son. Like El Duque, María Julia practiced Santería and she packed the accoutrements of her religion: necklaces, a ladle, a small ceramic bowl. Inside the bowl she placed an old photo of El Duque and Arnaldo as boys, both in their baseball uniforms. A few months earlier, María Julia had gone back to Arnaldo's grave. It was the same as she had last seen it, the gray concrete headstone reading ¡TODO BIEN! María Julia asked the caretaker to remove the concrete lid of Arnaldo's casket. In a Santería ritual, she then exhumed her firstborn son.

"Some family members and friends went with me," she said. "When I saw his skull, I cried. But after that I picked him up and cleaned him, bone by bone." For hours, María Julia kneeled in the dry grass, cleaning Arnaldo's remains with talcum powder and perfume and toothbrushes. "Then I wrapped him in a tourniquet and took him to his new grave," she said. "We threw cement over it and put a number on it. It's a nameless grave. Only the caretaker and I know where it is."

Now, before she set off to see her oldest surviving son, María Julia stopped by the Wajay cemetery one more time to say good-bye to Arnaldo. "I couldn't stop crying," she said. "We came to the United States for Orlando and the girls, but we left so much behind, an entire life."

By late in the afternoon a crowd had gathered at El Duque's old house across from the airport. There were neighbors and friends and El Duque's relatives, many wearing New York Yankee T-shirts, along with a growing contingent of international media. Reporters from CNN and Reuters were there, as well as some freelancers. Pam Esteroson, an American filmmaker, happened to be in Havana working on a documentary on Cuban baseball for the BBC. She began to film the extraordinary scene. Inside the house, amid a riot of Mickey Mouse toys and Barbie dolls, Norma was scrambling to prepare the girls, combing their hair, pulling it back with barrettes, helping them dress. "It was really, really heavy," said Esteroson. "They knew they were going, and they knew they weren't coming back. It seemed so stupid: You're only going ninety miles, and you may or may not be seeing any of these people again."

Before long it was time to go. It was dark now and Norma took the girls by the hand and then everyone walked through the back door of El Duque's old house, the same house that the government had once awarded him for his patriotic service to the Cuban revolution. The terminal was just a few hundred yards away. The crowd had grown to perhaps fifty people. Illuminated by the lights of the CNN cameras, which filmed the ensuing pilgrimage, the crowd followed Norma and her two children across the airport parking lot. The entire group then walked through the terminal and straight to the gate. No one bothered to stop them. In the end, the thicket of bureaucracy that ruled everyone's lives simply melted away. And then María Julia and Norma and the girls waved good-bye and stepped out onto the tarmac and waved again and flew away from Cuba, perhaps forever.

René Guim called Sánchez and me in New York to let us know what was going on. At first, I was reluctant to leave the apartment. Erin was pregnant, due any day. El Duque's family was scheduled to land after midnight at a tiny private airport out in Teterboro, New Jersey. By then, I had written so many stories about El Duque Hernández that I couldn't believe my newspaper would be interested in another. But I had to see it. After three years, it was the culmination of everything, the happy ending. I grabbed a cell phone and headed out into the cold night. I met up with Sánchez at his apartment and we made our way in a cab down to the Roger Smith to catch up with El Duque and the others.

Unlike the atmosphere before his World Series appearance, the tension inside El Duque's room was thick and palpable. When we arrived El Duque was putting on a tailored olive suit. He was as nervous as Sánchez and I had ever seen him. Everyone was speaking in muffled tones. Sánchez and I felt out of place and we went back downstairs. At the curb in front of the hotel was a black limousine that Falk had hired to ferry everyone to the airport. At around eleven P.M., Falk, El Duque, Noris, Joel and Osmany piled in. Sánchez and I, more outsiders than insiders on this solemn occasion, caught a cab and followed the limo out to New Jersey.

The terminal contained a ticket counter, a waiting area and little else. A small media contingent—a few television cameras and some print reporters—was already there when we pulled up. The plane was running late, so for the next few hours everyone camped out. El Duque made a statement and answered a few questions, and then he, Osmany and Noris retreated to the small lounge. Sánchez and I conducted a brief interview with El Duque because we knew that when the plane arrived there would be no time to talk. "With every day that passed, with every win, my past in Havana would flash back in mind," he told us. "It has all been so incredible. That is why I say all of this can only be the wonderful work of God." Without notes, he then proceeded to thank "the pope, Cardinal O'Connor, Mario Paredes, the Vatican, the president of the United States, the vice president, Attorney General Janet Reno, Secretary of State Madeleine Albright and everyone else who helped bring me this happiness."

I started to ask about Fidel. "After everything that you've been through, everything that's happened, the fact that he would make this gesture . . ." El Duque cut me off before I could finish the question.

"I'm not going to talk about politics," he said.

At 2:30 A.M., Steinbrenner's Learjet touched down. We all followed El Duque through the doors out to the tarmac. There was nothing to shield us from the wind and the bone-chilling cold. For some reason, the days after the World Series almost always seem especially cold. El Duque didn't have a coat and he shivered as the plane taxied along the runway. As it grew closer the jet seemed amazingly small to me. It pulled up within just a few feet of us and stopped. El Duque walked right up to the door, as if he were approaching a large car that also happened to fly. Then the door flew open, a stairway appeared and out stepped María Julia, Norma, the two girls, Mario Paredes, Ramón Tallaj, Cubas and his wife, María.

El Duque and his mother fell into each other's arms.

"God is great," said El Duque, sobbing.

"Sí, señor," replied his mother, who was crying as well.

Yahumara and Steffi were, understandably, bleary-eyed and somewhat confused. The girls were wearing Yankee shirts and caps and carrying plastic dolls. El Duque gathered them in his arms and cried some more. Before she had left her Manhattan apartment, Pam Falk had grabbed coats belonging to her two sons, eight-year-old Richard and six-year-old Willie (a week later, Richard would dress up as El Duque for Halloween). El Duque wrapped the girls in the coats. Off to the side stood his ex-wife, Norma, crying for entirely different reasons.

Cubas opened a bottle of champagne and handed out glasses. El Duque made a toast next to the plane.

"We drink to God, to the reunification of our family and to love," he said.

Two black limousines pulled up on the tarmac. This time Sánchez and I squeezed in with Paredes, Falk, Ramón Tallaj and the Cubases. The limo was, above all, warm. The interior had the quiet ambience of an elegant hotel lounge. There were black leather seats and soft lighting that emitted from the base of the doors and the ceiling. Paredes talked about his adventures with Fidel as we cruised back into the city. We crossed over the George Washington Bridge into Manhattan. To the south loomed the spectacular New York skyline. We made our way down the FDR, flanked to our left by the inky East River, then crossed finally into Midtown.

It was about four A.M. when we finally pulled up in front of the Roger Smith. The girls had already been taken upstairs. In a few hours the 1998 Yankees would parade up the Canyon of Heroes amid a blizzard of ticker tape. Cubas was checking in to the hotel, paying for his room with a thick wad of cold cash. El Duque was standing in the lobby, wired and happy. Sánchez and I went to congratulate him and say our good-byes. He walked us outside, through the revolving glass doors, and we embraced on the sidewalk in the cold. Despite the hour, battalions of yellow taxis were racing down Lexington Avenue in the city that never sleeps. As Sánchez and I went to hail one of these many cabs, Norma suddenly appeared beside us. She told El Duque that Yahumara and Steffi were thirsty and needed some milk. "Okay," said El Duque eagerly. "Okay."

New York, of course, is the epicenter of capitalism. It is the kind of city where a dozen umbrella salesmen appear the moment a raindrop hits the pavement. In New York, New York, it is the easiest thing in the world to purchase a quart of milk, or a cheesecake, or a ball-peen hammer at four A.M. And so it was not unusual at all that El Duque Hernández, dressed in his nice olive suit, ambled down Lexington Avenue in the predawn, shopping for his two little girls, the newest immigrants in the city.

THE VIEW FROM THE POOL

A FEW WEEKS AFTER THE WORLD SERIES, GERMÁN MESA WAS reinstated into Cuban baseball for the start of the 1998–99 season. The INDER regime that had banned El Duque, Mesa and Alberto Hernández had been purged. There was no official explanation for the housecleaning, but it was believed to have stemmed from a disastrous loss to Japan in the 1997 Intercontinental Cup, a murky corruption scandal and, not least, the INDER's ham-handed efforts to manage the defections. The banishments had done nothing to kill the major-league dreams in quiet gestation all over the island. On the contrary, El Duque's success with the Yankees would only stoke them further.

Forty thousand fans turned out at El Latino to welcome Mesa back into the fold. The fans gave Mesa a ten-minute standing ovation, chanting, "¡Germán! ¡Ger-mán! ¡Ger-mán!" as he assumed his usual position at shortstop. Mesa, in tears, fell to his knees and kissed the infield dirt. He then motioned to Antonio Scull, the Industriales first baseman, to toss him a grounder. Scull instead walked across the diamond, handed the ball to Mesa and threw his arms around him. Mesa's teammates followed, each lining up to embrace the legendary shortstop, and then his opponents from Pinar del Río, and then finally the umps. "It was like a Christmas gift," Mesa later told Milton Jamail. To lose the game of baseball, he said, "was as if someone took away your dream."

To El Duque's family and friends Germán Mesa remained a figure of considerable scorn. It had become accepted wisdom that the shortstop, to save his skin, had ratted out Juan Ignacio Hernández, the imprisoned courier, dragging down El Duque and Alberto as well. Mesa, it was said, was a *trompeta,* a trumpet, a snitch. Beyond the fact that Mesa had chosen to remain in Cuba while El Duque and Alberto had fled, there is scant evidence to support this scurrilous charge and I have never believed it. After the sanctions, the Cuban government's attitude toward the banned players was not unlike Major League Baseball's shabby treatment of Pete Rose, who to gain reinstatement was expected to humiliate himself before the nation. The alleged crimes, of course, were vastly different, but El Duque, like Rose, refused to perform this act of self-flagellation. Mesa complied.

One warm evening Sánchez and I sat with El Duque on his patio in Coral Gables, Florida. The pitcher was wearing powder blue terry-cloth shorts and smoking a fat Romeo y Julieta. The pool lights were on and the clean blue water shimmered in a slight breeze. Every fifteen minutes or so, Noris would appear to freshen up El Duque's drink, Havana Club on the rocks, which he sipped from a thick tumbler. El Duque was in a good mood. He had just bought the rambling house, and every night it was filled with family and friends: his mother and the girls, Osmany Lorenzo, old friends from Wajay who now lived in Miami.

As we sat on the patio I asked El Duque if he thought his former best friend, Germán Mesa, was a snitch for the Castro government. He became very quiet. Then he said softly: "If he was an informant, God will judge him accordingly. If he was an informant—fuck, it would hurt me very deeply. [But] if for some reason he became an informant, I believe he did it to protect his family. Things look very easy from here. You have to look at them from over there, how his family suffered. His mother was very sick and his father, well, [Germán] was the pride of the family. Not everyone can take it. Not everyone has the resistance. If he did something bad against me, I have no problem with that. I wish his family good health. I love his family like I love my own family. He should know that he always has a brother here. When he needs me, I will be there."

The night was nearly over. El Duque shook his head. He was no doubt thinking about Germán Mesa the legend, bare-handing slow rollers, turning clandestine back flips, stretching out his lithe torso to steal another base hit. And his hands: No one, but no one, got rid of the ball faster than Germán Mesa. At times the ball seemed to pass through his glove without actually touching it. "Oh, *chico,*" El Duque sighed. "Germán Mesa, oh, fuck. He doesn't know what he's missing. He's never going to know what he's missing, him and so many others."

In the summer of 1999 the Cuban government allowed Mesa to travel for the first time since his reinstatement. His first appearance outside the country would be at the Pan American Games in Winnipeg. There was considerable speculation that Mesa, who had come back better than ever, would use the opportunity to defect. I flew up to Winnipeg to see what might happen. By the time I arrived it was already Defection Central. The Cubans had lost a pistol shooter, a trainer, even a sportswriter from *Granma*. I'VE GOT CUBANS UP THE WAZOO! read the headline over one local column. None of the baseball players had bolted as yet, but Winnipeg was crawling with agents and scouts. Cubas and his rival, Gus Domínguez, were in town. So was Tom Cronin, the Cape Cod real-estate agent who had once wooed El Duque and Mesa on Cubas's behalf. Rudy Santín, the inventor of the Cuban market, was also around.

That first afternoon, the phone rang in my room at the Sheraton. It was Domínguez and Ramón Batista, another former Cubas operative. Batista had split with Cubas—over money, of course—and was now working for his rival. "We're in the lobby," said Domínguez. "Come on down. No, wait, we'll come up there. We've got something serious to discuss."

Moments later Domínguez and Batista breezed into the room. We exchanged pleasantries and Domínguez got down to business. He wanted me to contact a prominent Cuban outfielder. He wanted me to approach the player as he left practice, as if I were seeking an interview. "Then give him this card," said Domínguez. It was one of the agent's business cards. On the back it said, basically, "If you want to defect, call this number."

The next question seemed obvious to me.

"Are you guys crazy?"

Batista got up and walked toward the bathroom.

"Let me get you some toilet paper," he said. "It seems like you're shitting your pants."

I explained that I'd prefer to keep my job, thank you, rather than help them persuade a ballplayer to defect. Domínguez responded that there was no risk whatsoever. And, as an added bonus, he told me, I'd be helping someone gain his freedom. Thanks, but no thanks, I replied. There were no hard feelings, though, and Domínguez then suggested that we all go out to baseball practice to check out the scene. I didn't see any harm in that. By the time we were ready to leave, Tom Cronin had also hooked up with Domínguez and he tagged along as well.

Domínguez was driving a rented van, spacious enough to carry several defectors, if necessary. But when we got to the practice field it was deserted. The Cubans had apparently changed venues without telling anyone. We drove over to an air force base where Team Cuba was holed up. Again no luck. Domínguez then suggested that we head over to the mall, the idea being that the players might be using their spare time to shop for household items unavailable in Cuba.

Unlike Cubas, who lived for these strange cat-and-mouse games, Domínguez didn't seem like he was having much fun. It wasn't hard to see why. Up close, the hunt for Cuban defectors was more Peter Sellers than Sean Connery. On this occasion, for example, the hunt had led us to a Winnipeg mall, where we spent a large chunk of the afternoon shopping for Cuban ballplayers. We shopped at the food court, at the sunglasses hut, at The Gap, at Hallmark, before turning around to make another pass. "I hate this shit," Domínguez said finally as we took an escalator back to the ground floor.

We were making our way back across the parking lot when who should we suddenly bump into but Joe Cubas. It was Batista who spotted his former employer. The agent stood about fifty yards behind us, flanked by two new operatives, neither of whom I recognized. He had apparently decided to do a little trolling himself. He wore dark glasses, a broad straw hat and an untucked polo shirt over his jeans. What followed was a kind of "Showdown at the Winnipeg Mall." Cubas and his men glared across the parking lot. Domínguez, Batista and Cronin glared back. My allegiance was to neither side, and I began to walk over to speak to Cubas. As I crossed the parking lot, his operatives began to walk toward me, as if they feared I might attack. We walked straight at each other, coming closer and closer in a bizarre game of chicken until suddenly the men parted and I walked between them as if they were goalposts.

"I want a piece of your partner over there," one of them growled. He was pointing at Tom Cronin.

Behind me, Cronin was desperately trying to open the door to the van. Unfortunately, it was the wrong van.

I walked up to Cubas.

"*No te manches,*" he said to me in Spanish. "Don't stain yourself." Then in English: "You're hanging out with the wrong crowd."

"I'm working," I told him.

"*No te manches,*" he kept repeating. "*No te manches.*"

The conversation never rose above that level. I asked Cubas if I could interview him later and he angrily refused. He accused me of picking sides (Cubas later relented and agreed to a lengthy interview for this book). I soon got back in Domínguez's van and we drove away without further incident.

Two days later Team Cuba held another practice, this one open to the public. The crowd consisted mostly of major-league scouts and agents. Cubas sat in a van parked beyond the center-field fence. Domínguez and Batista sat in a van parked on a hill above right field. The message couldn't have been clearer: Any player who wanted to defect needed only to hop the outfield fence and escape with one of two franchises standing by in getaway cars. No one took the offer, though, and when practice ended, the players slowly filed toward their bus. That's when Tom Cronin made his move. Cronin had come to Winnipeg to make one last run at Germán Mesa. The rehabilitated shortstop was walking off the field with the rest of the team. Cronin followed him up the third-base line. Then, just as Mesa was about to board the team bus Cronin extended his hand, which concealed a folded piece of paper, on which was written the following note:

> I have come to Winnipeg for you. I have everything arranged. Don't worry. It will be safe. You can reach me on my cell phone number, any time, 24 hours.

Mesa tried to wave Cronin off, saying, "No, no, no." But Cronin reached out, grabbed the shortstop by the arm and shook his hand, surreptitiously slipping him the note. Mesa of course never called. The following day in Havana, *Granma* reported the craven effort to steal the patriotic shortstop. Mesa apparently had handed the note to one of his coaches, who in turn informed the Communist party press. That day happened to be July 26—the forty-sixth anniversary of Moncada. In Cuba, Fidel Castro gave his annual speech commemorating the attack that launched the Cuban revolution. The Maximum Leader used the speech to rage against the polluted atmosphere in Winnipeg.

"The perennial criminals and the frustrated enemies of the Revolution and the sports merchants have been tolerated and allowed to create all the conditions and possibilities to harass our delegation and urge defections by offering up *The Arabian Nights*!" said Fidel. "The place is full of scouts seeking athletes, advertising in the press—either subtly or openly, directly or indirectly, on television and other media—exhorting people to defect. . . . It is in that spirit that our athletes have been competing, in the face of hostility, seduction and traps, on a field that has been turned into enemy territory."

Like Cronin, Domínguez and Batista left Winnipeg empty-handed. Then, on the day of the gold-medal baseball game, an unknown pitcher named Danys Baez slipped out of a Canadian air force base where Team Cuba was staying. He ambled down a frontage road until Cubas and his men swooped in with their rented van, pushed Baez to the floor and sped away.

A few months later, Danys Baez signed a $14.5 million contract with the

Cleveland Indians. The Indians immediately dispatched him to the minors, hopeful he might be their own answer to the Cuban brothers who had knocked them out the last two years.

LATER, IN MIAMI, I bumped into José Basulto, the founder of Brothers to the Rescue. We were both standing behind a police barricade in front of the house where Elián González, the famous rafter boy, was living with his relatives. Basulto was part of a sizable crowd protesting U.S. government efforts to send Elián back to Cuba. I was covering the scene for the *Globe*.

Basulto mentioned that Brothers to the Rescue was still flying missions every Saturday out of Opa-Locka Airport. The missions were mostly symbolic, he said, because so few people were fleeing Cuba by boat these days. But the Brothers still liked to make their presence known. Basulto invited me to fly one Saturday morning. I eagerly accepted. Among other things, I knew that it would be an opportunity to get a look at Anguilla Cay, where El Duque had been stranded.

I showed up at Opa-Locka around seven A.M. I wasn't the only guest, it turned out. Basulto had also invited Donato Dalrymple, the fisherman who had plucked Elián from the water on Thanksgiving Day. In South Florida, Dalrymple had come to be known as the Kato Kaelin of the Elián saga; he seemed to turn up everywhere, not unlike O. J. Simpson's famous houseboy. (Dalrymple later appeared in the classic photo at the end of the drama, holding the terrified boy in a closet as a helmeted government agent held an automatic rifle.) Dalrymple explained to me that he was not a professional fisherman, as he was often depicted; rather, he was a transplanted housecleaner from Poughkeepsie, New York, now living in Fort Lauderdale.

As we waited to take off, Dalrymple tried to impress upon us that someone *had* to make a movie out of the Elián story. Indeed, it sounded pretty dramatic. On the fateful morning, Dalrymple had gone fishing with his cousin, a roofer, when they spotted an inner tube floating off the Lauderdale coast. Neither thought much of it, but as they drew closer Dalrymple commented to his cousin: "You know, it looks like there's something inside that inner tube." Upon closer examination, he saw that it looked very much like a human being. Dalrymple guessed it was a dead body. His cousin thought it was probably a mannequin.

"And then I saw a little hand move," said Dalrymple.

Dalrymple scrambled to pull Elián from the water. The boy was wearing bright orange pants and a T-shirt and seemed to be in shock. On his ankles were dozens of red markings that appeared to be fish bites. It turned out that the five-year-old boy had been floating in the Atlantic for three days after his boat—a seventeen-foot aluminum skiff crammed with thirteen others, including his mother—began to take on water after the motor conked out in a storm.

"I said, 'Do you speak English? Do you speak English?'" Dalrymple recalled. "There was no answer. And then I said, '¿Tu hablas español?' And he said real quietly, 'Sí.'" The cousins used a cell phone to notify the Coast Guard. The rest, of course, is history.

Dalrymple was telling this incredible story as we all sat around the terminal sipping coffee. Guillermo Lares, the chief pilot for Brothers to the Rescue, was standing near a house phone when suddenly he held up the receiver and shouted: "Hey, Donato, they're calling from Hollywood! They want to make a movie!"

Dalrymple, with amazing gullibility, shot out of his seat: "You're kidding!"

"Ah, I was just pulling your leg, man," said Lares. "I was just getting Hispanic on you."

A few minutes later we made our way to the planes, Cessnas like the ones the Cuban air force had blown out of the sky. To see the planes up close was to realize what a mismatch the airborne confrontation had been. The planes were smaller than some trucks, and certainly lighter. They had been taken out by MiG fighters. Before we took off, the Brothers to the Rescue pilots joined hands in a prayer circle as Basulto led the roll call for the pilots who had been killed:

"Carlos Costa," said Basulto.

"*Presente,*" shouted the pilots.

"Pablo Morales."

"*Presente.*"

"Mario de la Peña."

"*Presente.*"

"Armando Alejandre."

"*Presente.*"

I flew with Bill Schuss and Raúl Martínez, two friendly Bay of Pigs veterans. We took off and immediately banked south over downtown Miami, then the hotels of Miami Beach, until we were cruising over the open water of the Florida Straits. What was most striking was the vastness of it all, the miles and miles of vacant sea. It was a cold day, windy, and there were only a few boats on the water. Occasionally, we would fly over a sailboat or a fishing boat—boats as big or bigger than the one that had carried El Duque. The boats looked like specks. At times it was hard to tell whether I was looking at a boat or merely a whitecap.

After about forty-five minutes of this blue sameness we flew over the Cay Sal Bank, the island chain that includes Anguilla Cay. We passed first over Dogs Rocks—appropriately named, for the islands in fact are godforsaken slabs in the middle of the sea. Like Anguilla, Dogs Rocks was a common transit point for rafters. In 1997, the same year of El Duque's escape, a group of Cubans became stranded on Dogs Rocks for nearly two weeks. By the time the refugees were found, three had died: a twenty-six-year-old man, an eleven-year-old girl and a four-year-old girl. "There's no sand there," said Mario Miranda, head of security for the Cuban American National Foundation, who was involved in the rescue. "It's just rock. They couldn't dig a hole and they couldn't get sand to cover the bodies. So they were just left exposed."

We moved on and, finally, there it was: Anguilla Cay. Compared to Dogs Rocks it was paradise, but still it was nothing much, a cluster of small, unimpressive islands. The main island was eight miles in length, a long, narrow sliver surrounded by miles of transparent blue sea. The island was covered with dry brush and palmettos, thousands of stumpy palm trees spread across the flat terrain. The only sign that Anguilla Cay had ever been inhabited was the gnarled wreckage of a long-abandoned plane, rusting in the middle of a swamp. Along the island's fringes were brown rocks and patches of white sand. It was on one of these patches that El Duque Hernández and his seven companions had disembarked and resided for four days.

After two passes over the island, we flew off. I came away from the brief visit more impressed than ever at what El Duque had accomplished. Over time, the doubts about his escape had caused it to become something of a joke, which was sad. It diminished some of the harsh realities of his ordeal, namely his banishment from the game, his persecution by the Castro government and his clandestine journey across a huge expanse of dangerous open sea. *Sports Illustrated*, in a particularly cynical assessment, punched a few holes in the escape story and called El Duque "a savvy opportunist," implying that the embellishments were part of an effort to exploit his ordeal for profit. If that was the case, I never saw it. Did the escape really need to be embellished?

To me, Anguilla Cay, in its stark desolation, was proof enough of the pitcher's unusual path to the majors. The island was a dot on the planet Earth. In fact, El Duque had taken a highly unusual path for a professional baseball player but not for a Cuban refugee. In Miami and Jersey City, there were tens of thousands of people who had come to America in the same harrowing manner.

Thousands of others had perished trying. Fortunately, El Duque and his companions were discovered after four days and not two weeks, like the group that had ended up on nearby Dogs Rocks. Fortunately, his boat had delivered him to his destination, unlike the one that sank in the middle of the ocean, killing Elián González's mother and ten other people and turning a little boy into a political football. "It's amazing that more people aren't killed out there," said Allen Bandrowsky, a Coast Guard officer who estimated that he has rescued twenty thousand refugees in the Florida Straits, including El Duque. "To risk your whole life crossing that body of water, those people go through a lot. It's only ninety miles, but it's some of the hardest ninety miles in the world."

ONE FINE SPRING afternoon, Osmany Lorenzo dropped by the Ritz Plaza Hotel in Miami Beach to catch some rays with Sánchez and me. He brought along El Duque's cousin Joel Pedroso and another friend from Havana, Victor Ortega. It was a typical Saturday in Miami. The weather was perfect. Around the pool of our art deco hotel lay a collection of models and aspiring models, their perfect bodies—natural and surgically enhanced—glistening in the afternoon sun.

The news of the day was the just announced sacking of Fidel Castro's right-hand man: Foreign Minister Roberto Robaina. Outside Miami, of course, no one cared, but the news had rippled quickly through the exile community. Robaina, a smooth-talking apparatchik who favored shiny suits, had been pegged as a possible successor to Fidel. Now, without warning, he was out, giving everyone another excuse to ponder the eternal Cuban question: What happens when Fidel dies?

For the three Cubans, the afternoon was a break from the hard immigrant's life that they had settled into. Osmany was delivering pizzas in a white Ford Explorer that El Duque had bought him with his Yankee signing bonus. The restaurant where he worked was called—no small irony—La Dolce Vita, the sweet life. He lived in a cramped one-bedroom apartment behind a cemetery in Little Havana. Joel was moving furniture and studying English. Victor, whose brother William was an outfielder in the Cardinals' minor-league system, was working in construction.

After our spirited round-table discussion of the ouster of Roberto Robaina, the conversation turned to broader matters. Victor, an articulate man, had given everyone the impression that he felt life in Miami was not everything it was cracked up to be. Osmany, somewhat annoyed, began to press him on this point. Osmany was an interesting case. Despite his hardships, you just knew he was going to make it. In Cuba, after all, he had already been a successful capitalist. It was obvious that he would soon rebuild his life in the same way that he had put together his best friend El Duque's escape from Cuba.

"Let me ask you a question," Osmany said to Victor: "Where do you live better, here or in Cuba?"

"I'll answer that if you allow me two conditions," responded Victor.

"What conditions?"

"With food and dollars, I'll stay in Cuba."

"In Cuba, the government tells you no one is hungry. So why do you say you would only stay in Cuba if you had food?"

"Cuba is a reality in which sometimes even we deceive ourselves," said Victor. "There isn't as much hunger in Cuba as the hunger that we ourselves create. In Cuba, none of us had to work hard. We just didn't."

Victor pointed at Osmany: "This guy is shameless. He had a Muscovy for himself." Then he pointed at Joel: "This other one lived like a king. He used to ride around on his motorcycle with all his women." Joel said nothing.

"So you're saying you were better off in Cuba?" said Osmany.

"Of course we were better off."

"That is a lie!" Osmany said, turning to us to make his point. "It's a lie. He can live here wherever he wants and drive whatever he wants."

"Yeah," said Victor. "You have the home you want, the car you want and you spend the whole week alone. Alone."

"I have a car because Orlando gave it to me," Osmany pointed out.

"In Cuba, Osmany had his house and he didn't live in fear," said Victor. "His Muscovy was parked outside and his friends came and went. They gave him gasoline when he needed it. They got him a woman to fuck whether she was fine or not. In Havana, Osmany could show up at the Hotel Riviera with five dollars in his pocket and walk away with the finest woman at the pool. Here he could have a hundred dollars in his pocket and he can't pick up the same woman."

"That is true," Osmany allowed. "I agree."

"I'm not talking about this anymore," said Victor dismissively. "I won't go any further."

But he did. He raged about the bizarre school shootings that were sweeping the United States, the Haitian immigrant who had been sodomized with a plunger handle in the bathroom of a New York police station, the general rigidity of the American system. He seemed to prefer Cuban-style capitalism: off the books, out of sight, no rules.

Osmany began to mimic an announcer's voice, as if he were speaking directly to Fidel: "Listen, Fifo, we have here the next Roberto Robaina. . . ."

We all laughed.

"You should start a cruise line to Cuba," Osmany told Victor.

"The problem is that I'm not even older than these guys," said Victor.

"How old are you?" asked Sánchez.

"I'm twenty-eight, but the problem is—"

Sánchez cut him off: "Is that in real years or Cuban baseball years?"

We laughed again.

"In real years I'm thirty-three," admitted Victor.

"We are here with Robertico Robaina . . ." said Osmany, holding up his beer like a microphone.

"Your problem is not Cuba," Victor snapped, "it's communism."

"Yeah, there's a saying in Cuba," said Osmany: " 'If you're not a Communist by the age of thirty you're heartless. If you're a Communist after the age of thirty you're brainless.' "

So why are you here, someone asked Victor.

"In reality, I came here because once I dreamed of coming to Miami," he said. "But I knew it wasn't going to be like they painted it. Sometimes you hear a story and it stays in your head and from that you create an illusion and live off of it. Then you get there and the reality is something else."

"It's a different country," said Osmany. "That's what I'm telling you. The cultures are different. Over there you have your people, the people you were born with and see every day. The truth is that this is a foreign country to us."

The debate thus turned to El Duque.

"If Orlando left Cuba it wasn't because he didn't like Cuba," asserted Victor. "He just didn't like the way the system was applied."

On this point Osmany grew disgusted: "Of course, my homeland is the best," he said sarcastically. "My country is the best. Forget about it."

"Orlando feels more secure in Cuba than in this country," said Victor. "Secure about life, secure about his health, his family, spiritual security. He felt better in Cuba. When Orlando was Orlando in Cuba, he lived the way he wanted. He had it all."

"Not like here," said Osmany. "He used to ride buses to the games. Here he flies. He used to have a bike in Cuba and here he gets a free car. He didn't even have a phone in Cuba."

"But he was more secure in Cuba."

"Secure? Who's going to kill Orlando here? How many big-league players are killed each year?"

"I'm not talking about getting killed," said Victor.

"Maybe he felt better in Cuba, more comfortable," Osmany allowed. "But here you can be a millionaire."

"But it's not your country!"

"So what, you have millions."

"Give me all the money you want, I'll go to Cuba."

"Then why don't you go back to Cuba, without money?"

"I can go back to Cuba right now, without money, and still live better than you do here."

"No way, not better. Maybe you have to work less than I do here. But you won't live better, even if I stayed in that miserable little room where I live now. Out of ninety people in Cuba, maybe ten sleep with air-conditioning."

"Air-conditioning was a scientific invention that fucks up your lungs, just like cigarettes. Over there you lived with a fan and fresh air and you were fine with it. You're an American now."

"Without this country Orlando would not be as famous as he is today," said Osmany.

We all fell silent for a few moments. I got up to take a dip in the pool, then climbed out and sat down again. The table was covered with five-dollar beers and curdling plates of nachos. Victor was saying, "And while we're on the subject, let's go see who's the finest woman on the beach." As we got up to do just that, Victor shook his head, smiled and sighed.

"Politics, politics," he said.

ACKNOWLEDGMENTS

To write a first book is to immediately understand why the acknowledgments section was invented. We have been humbled by the generosity extended to us by the many people who came in contact with this project. Most of all, we would like to thank Orlando Hernández. For the past five years, El Duque allowed us to accompany him to the lowest valleys and the highest peaks of his amazing journey. Our reward has been to witness up close a staggering achievement of human will. We are also grateful to El Duque's extraordinary family—in Cuba and in the United States—for allowing us into their lives and sharing their personal memories so openly and eloquently.

We would also like to thank the New York Yankees for their repeated and gracious assistance. Director of media relations Rick Cerrone and his assistant, Jason Zillo, extended us credentials, granted our interview requests, and patiently answered our numerous questions, all on top of their crushing daily workload. We are also grateful to the intrepid Yankee press corps, which sets the standard for hospitality and professionalism amid the fiercest competition in sports journalism. We would especially like to thank Buster Olney and Jack Curry of *The New York Times*; George King, Ursula Reel and Tom Keegan of the *New York Post*; Jack O'Connell of *The Hartford Courant*; Bob Klapisch of the *Bergen Record*; Larry Rocca and Dave Lennon of *Newsday*; Suzyn Waldman of WFAN; and Yankee broadcaster Michael Kay.

Jim Scott, Dina Panto, and Mike LaManna of Major League Baseball Productions afforded us the time, space, and equipment to review the 1998 season at MLBP's Chelsea studios, an act of generosity that proved invaluable.

At Villard/Random House, Bruce Tracy ushered the book to completion with immeasurable patience and support, even as we repeatedly pushed the envelope on deadlines. We would also like to thank production editor Benjamin Dreyer, designer Barbara Bachman, production manager Erich Schoeneweiss, legal counsel Diana Frost, copy editor Christine Tanigawa, proofreaders Michael Burke and Maria Massey, publicist Brian McLendon, and, not least, Katie Zug, who cheerfully handled all the loose ends. We are also grateful to David Butler of *The Boston Globe*, who created the maps that appear at the front of the book.

For the self-imposed isolation of writing a book, it would be difficult to find a more inspiring venue than the New York Public Library. We would like to thank Denise Hibay, assistant chief librarian for collections, and Fernando Acosta-Rodriguez for helping us get started, and the many helpful people who made working there such a pleasure.

We are especially grateful to our agent, Simon Lipskar, and his associates at Writers House. In the first few seconds of a cold call, Simon "got" the book, then did everything he could over the next two years to turn it into reality.

Claudia Kalb, Brook Larmer, Mark Fainaru-Wada, and Jack Curry all read portions of the manuscript and made suggestions that improved it. We owe special debts of gratitude to Jack, who carved out time even as the Yankees and Mets were closing in on the Subway Series, and to Brook, who during one long reporting stretch allowed us to take over his house in Miami, a real leap of faith.

We would also like to thank Enríque Lopez Oliva and his wife, Mimi, for their boundless generosity and insight.

This is also the space where we would like to list the many people who assisted us in Cuba. Unfortunately, the Cuban government has made that difficult. From the beginning, the government refused to cooperate with the book, at one point citing Fainaru's relationship with "a certain ballplayer who will have to remain nameless." The government's embarrassment over El Duque is understandable and, of course, revealing. But it also prevents us from thanking many people who housed us, drove us, and, most important, steered us to critical information. At one point Fainaru asked one such person how we could acknowledge our tremendous debt to him. He said: "Just write 'Thank you to our friends in Cuba.' I'll know who you mean."

So there you have it: Thank you to our friends in Cuba. We are forever grateful.

STEVE FAINARU

I would like to thank the editors of *The Boston Globe,* where I was privileged to work for eleven years. The *Globe* allowed me to chase the El Duque saga all over the hemisphere. I am especially grateful to my old boss, Ben Bradlee, Jr., and longtime colleagues Matt Storin, Dave Beard, David Filipov, Joe Sullivan, Sean Mullin, Gordon Edes, Nick Cafardo, Kathleen Hennrikus, Margaret Murray, Linda Hunt, and the crack library staff. I am forever indebted to my friend Don Skwar, the hardest-working editor in the business, and to John Yemma, who gave me the opportunity to cover Latin America.

I am also thankful to Bruce Jenkins, Scott Price, Sean Horgan, Jackie MacMullan, and Ian Thomsen. All are among the most gifted sportswriters working (or, in Jackie's case, resting) and constant sources of inspiration and support. I am also grateful to Phil Bennett for his uncommon wisdom and guidance regarding Latin America. Years ago, Dan Shaughnessy and John Lowe taught me how to cover baseball; I still can't believe how lucky I was to fall under their expert tutelage. Thanks as well to Sheldon Ocker for a big, late assist on Jim Thome.

I am grateful to my friend Todd Lee Coralli, who inspired the title during one of many nights watching the Yanks, and his wife, Pauline, for their support and inspiration during the long, isolated summer of 2000.

This book would never have been written without the support and generosity of my amazing grandmother, Rose Gilbert. For their unflagging encouragement, I would like to thank my mother, Ellen Gilbert, and my sister-in-law, Nicole Fainaru-Wada. I am also grateful to Colleen Brooks for her tender loving care of little Will during the final edits, and Monica Aramburo, who kept our family together during the long hours away. My beautiful wife, Erin Callahan, read the chapters as fast as I could write them and even made one trip to Cuba that ended with an unplanned journey through the vaunted Cuban health-care system.

Finally, I am blessed with a brother, Mark Fainaru-Wada, who is not only my best friend but also a brilliant sportswriter. There is not enough space to list the ways he helped see this book through. His presence is in every line.

RAY SÁNCHEZ

I would like to thank the editors and reporters of *Newsday* for the extraordinary tolerance extended to me during the more than two years it took to make this book. I would like to thank Tony Marro, Les Payne, Lonnie Isabel, Charlotte Hall, Paul Moses, Calvin Lawrence, and Tony DeStefano for their support. I also owe much to many others at *Newsday*, including Tim Phelps, Mike Muskal, Jimmy Breslin, Ellis Henican, Mohamed Bazzi, Yvette Rodríguez, Sophie Williams, Chris Hatch, Moises Saman, Audrey Tiernan, and the rest of the photo staff.

On both sides of the Florida Straits, I am immensely grateful to the many people who generously shared their knowledge of Cuba before and after Fidel Castro, their photographs and countless memories and anecdotes. I also want to thank the late Rodolfo Fernández and his wife, Matilde, for their patience and a treasure trove of memories. For their remarkable generosity, I would like to acknowledge my longtime friends Elvin Molina and Dr. Robert Whittington. For encouraging me, and supporting me and surrounding me with affection, I would like to thank my loving parents, Ramón and Rosa Sánchez, my sister, Nancy, and my wonderful nephew Stephen.

Most of all, my deepest gratitude goes to Joyce Wong for surrounding me with nothing but love and support and encouragement from the very beginning. I would like to thank her for her all-enabling love and strength. I couldn't have done it without her.

BEN CRAMER, A FREELANCE journalist based in New York City, played a critical role in the completion of this book. His diligent research, thorough proofreading, and keen insight found their way into all corners of the manuscript. His commitment was unwavering. He is a tireless, dedicated journalist and we are immensely grateful for his contributions. This is his book too.

INTERVIEWS/SOURCES

THE FOUNDATION OF THIS BOOK WAS CONSTRUCTED PRIMARILY from interviews conducted from February 1999 through October 2000 in Cuba, Costa Rica, Venezuela, Florida, Arizona, New York, Chicago, Boston, Los Angeles, and Winnipeg. With few exceptions, the interviews were tape-recorded. Of the 118 interviews listed below, 65 were conducted in Spanish by one or both authors. Those interviews were then translated into English. In rare instances when the translation of a quotation was unclear, the authors returned to the source to try to clarify the exact meaning of what was said. We also relied heavily on our own notes and observations from a combined fifteen reporting trips to Cuba from 1995 through 2000. In many instances throughout the book, we culled liberally from dozens of our own articles written for *The Boston Globe* and *Newsday*. For the Yankee chapters, we relied on interviews, videotapes, newspaper articles, and our personal memories and observations from the 1998 baseball season.

In addition to the interviews, a number of books were of particular assistance. One was the bible of Cuban baseball, *The Pride of Havana*, Roberto González Echevarría's remarkable tome on the evolution of the sport on the island. It should be noted that, among other things, we unabashedly stole González Echevarría's perfect description of Manuel "Cocaína" García's ability to "anesthetize" hitters. Also helpful was *Full Count: Inside Cuban Baseball*, a more contemporary view by Milton H. Jamail. Of particular use was Jamail's dramatic account of Germán Mesa's return to Cuban baseball in the fall of 1998. *Pitching Around Fidel: A Journey into The Heart of Cuban Sports* is an intimate, lyrical survey of the Cuban sports machine by S. L. Price. It contains, among other nuggets, revealing passages on Lázaro Valle, El Duque's hard-throwing former teammate, and mind-numbing lectures by INDER chief Humberto Rodríguez and Cuban baseball commissioner Carlos Rodríguez, who blithely trots out the El Duque–as–choker theory. We also relied on *Sport in Cuba: The Diamond in the Rough*, a thorough study by Paula J. Pettavino and

Geralyn Pye, for descriptions of the Cuban sports system and its academies. Also helpful were *Summer of '98: When Homers Flew, Records Fell, and Baseball Reclaimed America*, by Mike Lupica; *Away Games: The Life and Times of a Latin Ballplayer*, by Marcos Bretón and José Luis Villegas; *Béisbol: Latin Americans and the Grand Old Game*, by Michael M. Oleksak and Mary Adams Oleksak; *The Curse of the Bambino*, by Dan Shaughnessy; *Che Guevara: A Revolutionary Life*, by Jon Lee Anderson; *Fidel: A Critical Portrait*, by Tad Szulc; *Fidel & Religion*, a series of conversations between Castro and Brazilian priest Frei Betto; *Fair Ball: A Fan's Case for Baseball*, by Bob Costas; *Palo Mayombe: The Dark Side of Santería*, by Carlos Galdiano Montenegro; *Miami*, by Joan Dideon; *Our Man in Havana*, by Graham Greene; *Joe Torre's Ground Rules for Winners*, by Joe Torre (with Henry Dreher); *Eight Men Out*, by Eliot Asinof; the *Guía Oficial de Béisbol*, published by the INDER; and the always indispensable *Baseball Encyclopedia*.

The following list of interviews is incomplete and somewhat misleading. A number of people who were interviewed are not listed; they requested anonymity out of fear of reprisal by the Castro government. The interviews also varied in length. Orlando Hernández, for example, was interviewed formally seven times in New York, Boston, Chicago, and Miami and on numerous occasions in Cuba, Costa Rica, and the United States. The sports agent Joe Cubas was interviewed for nine hours over a two-day period in Sarasota, Florida, during spring training 2000, and formally and informally on numerous other occasions in Costa Rica and the United States. Yankee manager Joe Torre, on the other hand, was interviewed for about fifteen minutes in the home dugout at Yankee Stadium one October afternoon in the Bronx. The interviews, of course, also varied in quality. Many people were overwhelmingly forthcoming; others were more reticent. Excluded from the list are interviews that may appear in the text but were not conducted specifically for this book. Thus, the interview with President Fidel Castro, described in Chapter 9, does not appear below, nor does the interview with Cuban slugger Omar Linares, which is described in Chapter 4.

Interviews for THE DUKE OF HAVANA

Regla Albarrán Miller, Sandy Alderson, Juan Angulo, René Arocha, Rolando Arrojo, Al Avila, Ralph Avila, Danys Baez, Allen Bandrowsky, Geidy Barreto, José Basulto, Ramón Batista, Gordon Blakeley, Miguel Borroto, Noris Bosch, Mike Brito, Juan Carlos Bruzon, Geraldo Capó, José Cardenal, Brian Cashman,

Pedro Chávez, Omar Claro, Mario Cobo (Cebolla), Roberto Colina, Billy Connors, Michel Contreras, Jimmy Cronin, Tom Cronin, Antolina Cruz Sánchez (Antola), Gonzalo Cruz Sánchez, Ocilio Cruz Sánchez, Joe Cubas, Donato Dalrymple, Jorge Díaz, Juan Carlos Díaz, Gus Domínguez, Timothy Dwyer, Louie Eljaua, Pam Esteroson, Pamela Falk, Osmani Fernández (Capuro), Osvaldo Fernández, Rodolfo Fernández, Andrés Fleitas, Joe Girardi, Guillermo Alvarez Guedes, René Guim, Adrián Hernández (El Duquecito), Alberto Hernández (Albertico), Alberto Hernández (Lingote), Alexis Hernández, Arnaldo Hernández Montero (the original El Duque), Liván Hernández, Michel Hernández, Orlando Hernández Pedroso (El Duque), Juan Iglesias, Maikel Jova, Michael Kay, Joe Kehoskie, George King, Bob Klapisch, Chuck LaMar, Brook Larmer, Ricky Ledee, Doug Logan, Al López, Enrique López Oliva, Osmany Lorenzo, Roberto Martínez (Pelusa), Agapito Mayor, Gloria Mayor, Tom Miller, Mario Miranda, Lázaro Montero, Beverly Morales, Billy Morales, Jorge Morejon, Bobby Muñoz, Marta Nodar, Rolando Núñez (Chavito), Jack O'Connell, Buster Olney, Edilberto Oropesa, Gene Orza, Mario Paredes, Juan Antonio Pedroso Cruz (Miñosito), María Julia Pedroso, Bryan Peña, Josue Pérez, Miguel Pérez, Ninoska Pérez, Arturo Polo, Jorge Posada, Ariel Prieto, Irving Puig, Nataniel Reyñoso, Nuvia Rifa, Lenin Rivero, Lula Rodríguez, Cookie Rojas, Euclides Rojas, Juan Carlos Romero, Arelis Ruiz, Alex Sánchez, Osmany Santana, Francisco Santiesteban, Rudy Santín, Luis Sojo, Jim Thome, Luis Tiant, Joe Torre, Carlos Tosca, René Valle, Lázaro Vichot (Lache), Eduardo Vilchez Hurtado, Julio Cesar Villalon, Sue Walitsky, Don Zimmer.

ORLANDO HERNÁNDEZ PEDROSO

(EL DUQUE, EL DUKE, SEÑOR OCTUBRE)

6' 2", 210 pounds   Bats: Right   Throws: Right
Born: October 11, 1965, in Havana, Cuba

CAREER PLAYING RECORD*

Year	Club	W–L	ERA	G	GS	CG	SHO	SV	IP	H	R	ER	BB	SO
86–87	Industriales	2–1	2.78	8	3	1	1	0	27.2	25	14	13	10	19
87–88	Industriales	6–2	4.34	11	7	1	0	0	64.1	74	39	31	25	63
88–89	Industriales	7–0	3.74	9	8	1	0	0	55.1	67	26	23	15	31
89–90	Industriales	7–3	2.98	11	10	6	2	0	81.2	57	30	27	22	73
90–91	Industriales	6–5	2.96	15	11	4	0	1	85.0	64	34	28	26	68
91–92	Industriales	3–1	3.18	8	8	1	1	0	51.0	44	24	18	20	32
92–93	Industriales	12–3	2.20	16	16	8	2	0	127.0	95	34	31	22	104
93–94	Industriales	11–2	1.74	14	14	5	1	0	108.1	81	21	21	33	109
94–95	Industriales	11–1	2.16	13	13	8	3	0	96.0	66	25	23	22	96
95–96	Industriales	7–2	3.49	11	11	6	1	0	80.0	77	38	31	19	92
96–97	DID NOT PLAY—BANNED FROM BASEBALL													
1998	Tampa	1–1	1.00	2	2	0	0	0	9.0	3	2	1	3	15
	Columbus	6–0	3.83	7	7	0	0	0	42.1	41	19	18	17	59
	YANKEES	12–4	3.13	21	21	3	1	0	141.0	113	53	49	52	131
1999	YANKEES	17–9	4.12	33	33	2	1	0	214.1	187	108	98	87	157
2000	YANKEES	12–13	4.51	29	29	3	0	0	195.2	186	104	98	51	141
Cuba totals		129–47	3.05	246	187	75	NA	9	1514.1	1339	581	513	455	1211
Major League totals		41–26	4.00	83	83	8	2	0	551.0	486	265	245	190	429
Overall totals		170–73	3.30	329	270	83	NA	9	2065.1	1825	846	758	645	1640

DIVISION SERIES RECORD

Year	Club/Opp	W–L	ERA	G	GS	CG	SHO	SV	IP	H	R	ER	BB	SO
1998	NYY vs. Texas			DID NOT PLAY										
1999	NYY vs. Texas	1–0	1.80	1	1	0	0	0	8.0	2	0	0	6	4
2000	NYY vs. Oak.	1–0	2.45	2	1	0	0	0	7.1	5	2	2	5	5

* Year-by-year Cuba statistics do not includes games from the now-defunct Selectiva, a lengthy postseason all-star tournament, or international play. However, Selectiva statistics are reflected in aggregate Cuba totals.

LEAGUE CHAMPIONSHIP SERIES RECORD

Year	Club/Opp	W-L	ERA	G	GS	CG	SHO	SV	IP	H	R	ER	BB	SO
1998	NYY vs. Clev.	1–0	0.00	1	1	0	0	0	7.0	3	0	0	2	6
1999	NYY vs. Bos.	1–0	1.80	2	2	0	0	0	15.0	12	4	3	6	13
2000	NYY vs. Sea.	2–0	4.20	2	2	0	0	0	15.0	13	7	7	8	14

WORLD SERIES RECORD

Year	Club/Opp	W-L	ERA	G	GS	CG	SHO	SV	IP	H	R	ER	BB	SO
1998	NYY vs. SD	1–0	1.29	1	1	0	0	0	7.0	3	1	1	3	7
1999	NYY vs. Atl.	1–0	1.29	1	1	0	0	0	7.0	1	1	1	2	10
2000	NYY vs. Mets	0–1	4.91	1	1	0	0	0	7.1	9	4	4	3	12

INDEX

ABOUT THE AUTHORS

STEVE FAINARU is an investigative sportswriter for *The Washington Post*. He was a reporter for *The Boston Globe* for eleven years, covering major-league baseball, Wall Street, and Latin America. He lives in Washington, D.C.

RAY SÁNCHEZ writes a column for *Newsday*, where he served four years as Latin America correspondent. He lives in New York City.

Printed in the United States
by Baker & Taylor Publisher Services